Tatsuki Fujimoto

I love the *Kowasugi!*
(*Too Scary!*) series!

Tatsuki Fujimoto won Honorable Mention in the
November 2013 Shueisha Crown Newcomers' Awards for
his debut one-shot story *Love Is Blind*. His first series,
Fire Punch, ran for eight volumes. *Chainsaw Man* began
serialization in 2018 in *Weekly Shonen Jump*.

CHAINSAW MAN

11

SHONEN JUMP Edition

Story & Art TATSUKI FUJIMOTO

Translation/AMANDA HALEY
Touch-Up Art & Lettering/SABRINA HEEP
Design/JULIAN [JR] ROBINSON
Editor/ALEXIS KIRSCH

CHAINSAW MAN © 2018 by Tatsuki Fujimoto
All rights reserved.
First published in Japan in 2018 by SHUEISHA Inc., Tokyo.
English translation rights arranged by SHUEISHA Inc.

The stories, characters, and incidents mentioned in this publication are
entirely fictional.

No portion of this book may be reproduced or transmitted in any form or
by any means without written permission from the copyright holders.

Printed in Italy

Published by VIZ Media, LLC
P.O. Box 77010
San Francisco, CA 94107

10 9 8 7 6 5
First printing, June 2022
Fifth printing, January 2023

PARENTAL ADVISORY
CHAINSAW MAN is rated T+ for Older Teen
and is recommended for ages 16 and up.
This volume contains violence and gore.

CHAINSAW MAN

11

Go Get 'Em, Chainsaw Man

Tatsuki Fujimoto

CHARACTERS

Denji

A young man-slash-Chainsaw Devil who carries his partner Pochita inside him. He's always true to his desires. Likes Makima, the first person to ever treat him like a human being.

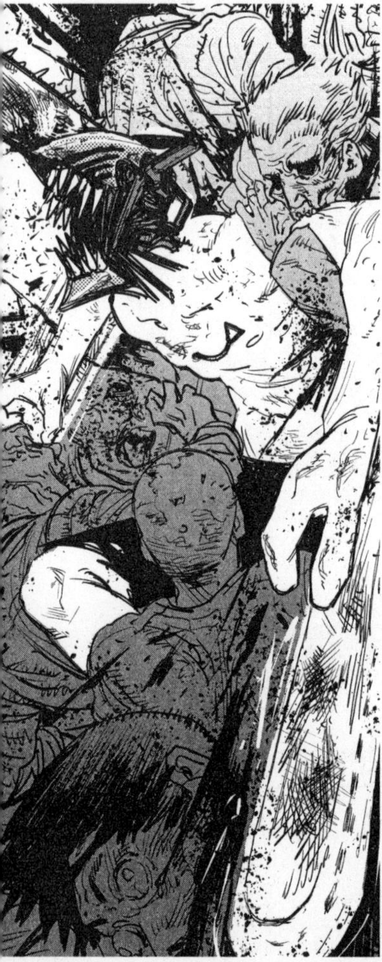

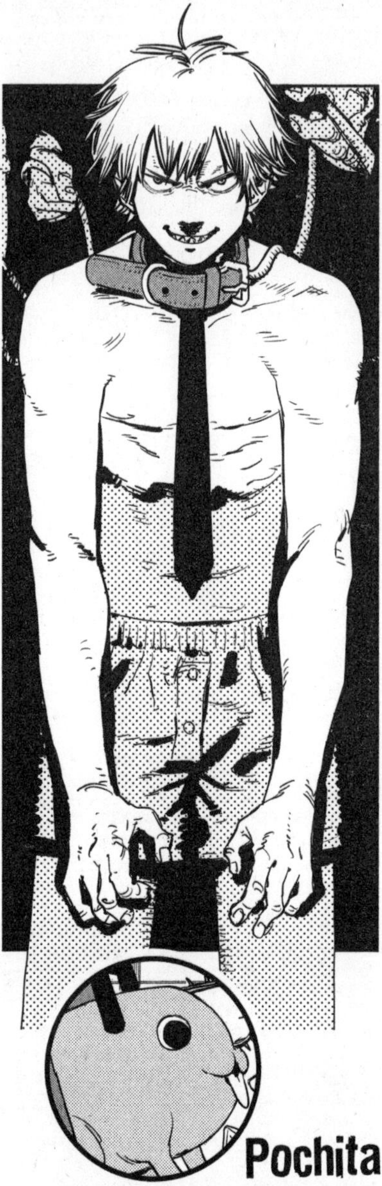

Pochita

Chainsaw Devil. Gave up his heart to Denji, becoming part of his body.

Makima

The mysterious woman in charge of Public Safety Devil Extermination Special Division 4. Her true identity is the Control Devil.

Power

Blood Devil Fiend. Egotistical and prone to going out of control. Her cat Meowy is her only friend.

Kishibe

A man with extraordinary fighting ability who belongs to the Special Division. The strongest devil hunter. Wary of Makima?

Kobeni Higashiyama

Former Public Safety Devil Extermination Special Division 4 devil hunter, current hamburger shop employee.

STORY

Denji is a young man who hunts devils with his pet devil-dog Pochita. To pay off his debts, Denji is forced to live in extreme poverty and worked like a dog, only to be betrayed and killed on the job without ever getting to live a decent life. But Pochita, at the cost of the pooch's own life, brings Denji back—as Chainsaw Man! After Denji buzzes through all their attackers, he's taken in by the mysterious Makima, and begins a new life as a Public Safety Devil Hunter.

Stricken with guilt over killing Aki and with his brain turned to mush, Denji tells Makima he wants to be her dog, just in time for her to murder Power right in front of him. All along, Makima's plan was to open the door to Denji's memories by giving him happiness and then taking it all away. With Denji's mind and heart now broken, he awakens as Chainsaw Man, Hero of Hell. Makima's true objective is to use Chainsaw Man's ability to erase the names of the devils he eats from existence to create a "better world."

Determined to stop her machinations, Kishibe tries to take out Makima, but this too fails. With seven special devils under her command, the next step in Makima's plan is to defeat Chainsaw Man and take control of him. It's devil versus devil in this bloody battle royale, but who will emerge top dog?

CONTENTS

[89] Go Get 'Em, Chainsaw Man *007*

[90] Super Power *027*

[91] Power, Power, Power *049*

[92] Vanilla Sky *068*

[93] You & Crappy Movies *091*

[94] Chainsaw Man vs.
the Weapon Humans *111*

[95] Chainsaw Man vs.
Control Devil *131*

[96] This Kind of Taste *151*

[97] I, Love, Chainsaw *170*

Chapter 89: Go Get 'Em, Chainsaw Man

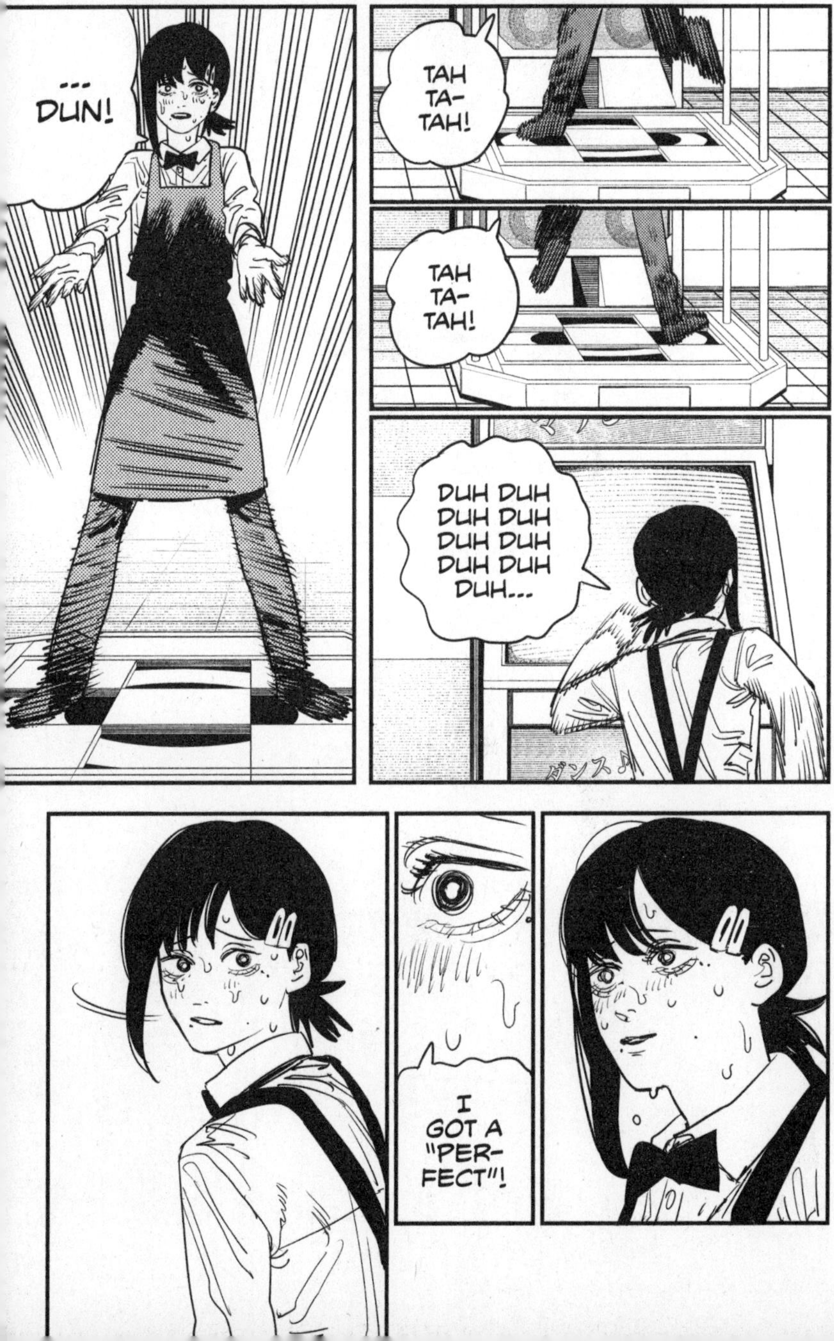
TAH TA-TAH!
TAH TA-TAH!
DUH DUH DUH DUH DUH DUH DUH DUH DUH...
ダンス♪
... DUN!
I GOT A "PER-FECT"!

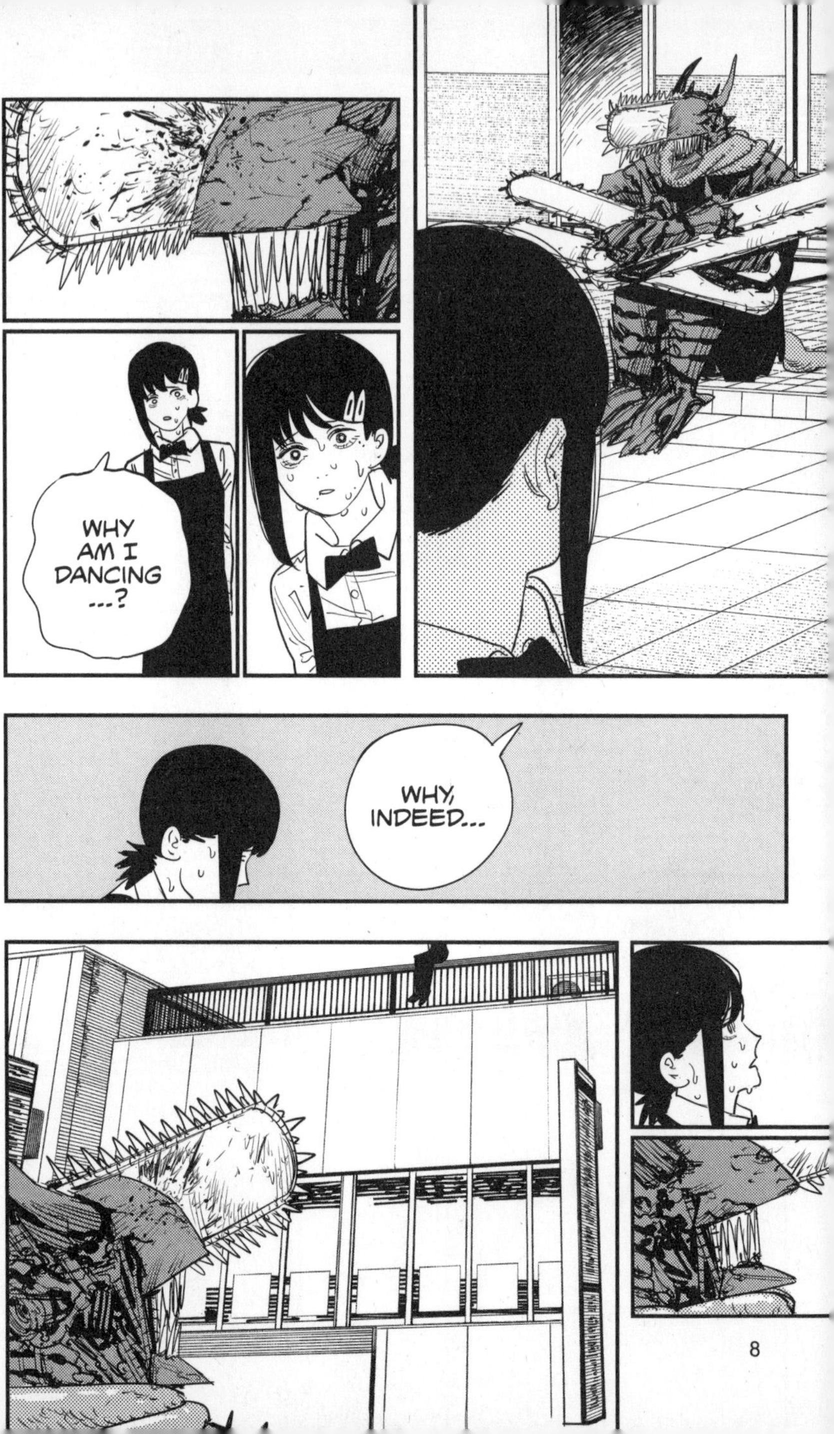
WHY AM I DANCING ...?
WHY, INDEED...

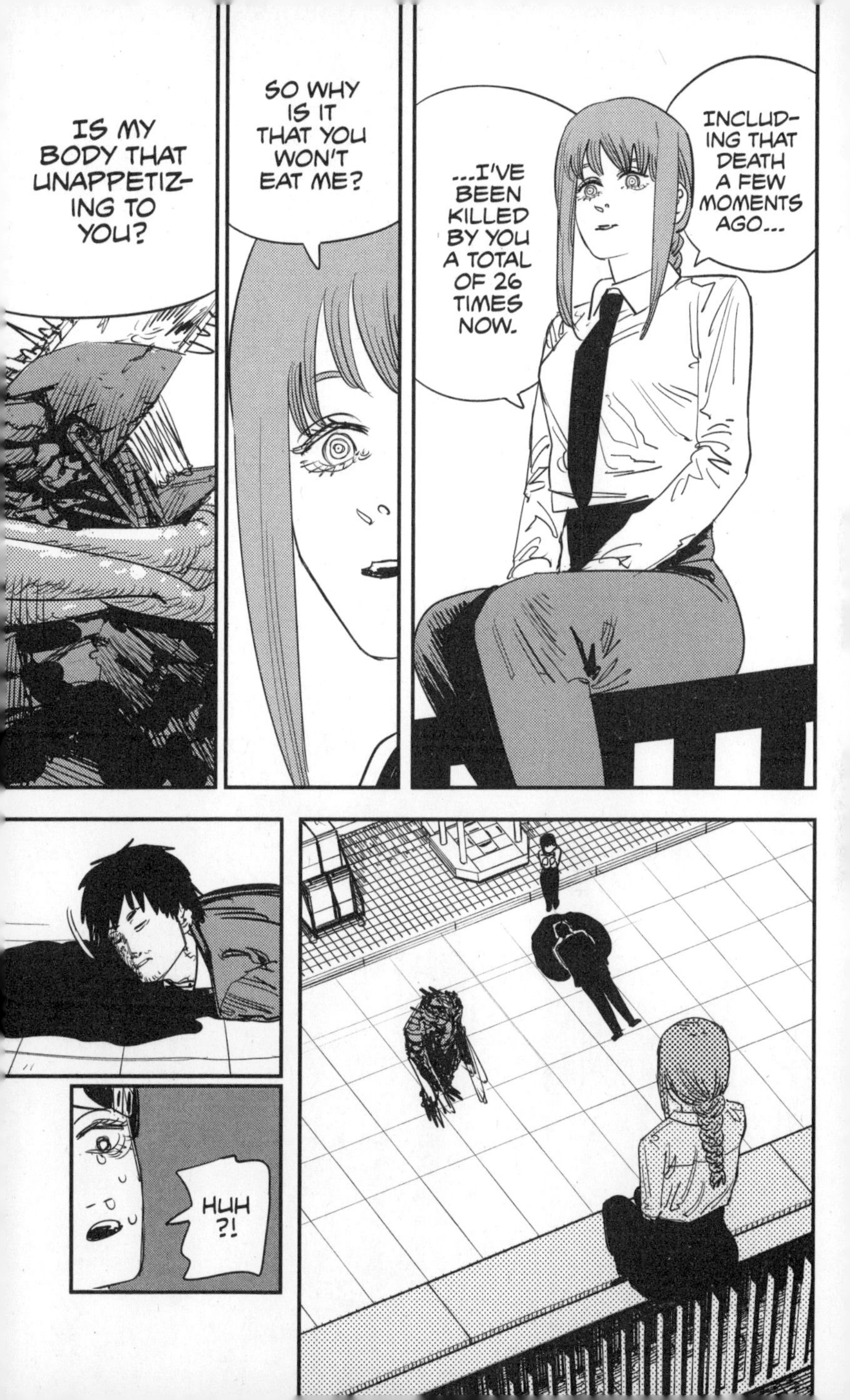
INCLUDING THAT DEATH A FEW MOMENTS AGO...
...I'VE BEEN KILLED BY YOU A TOTAL OF 26 TIMES NOW.
SO WHY IS IT THAT YOU WON'T EAT ME?
IS MY BODY THAT UNAPPETIZING TO YOU?
HUH?!

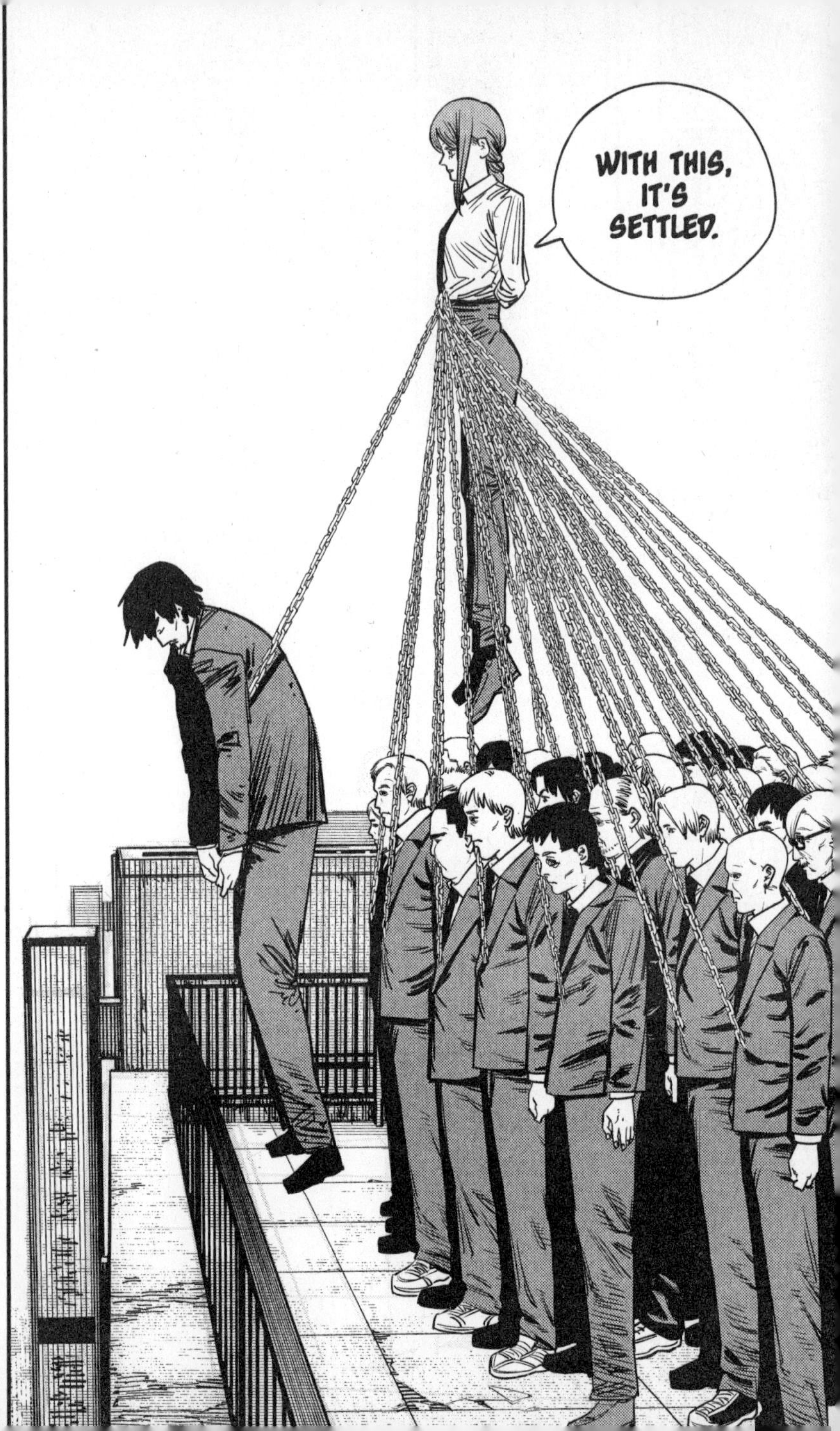
WITH THIS, IT'S SETTLED.

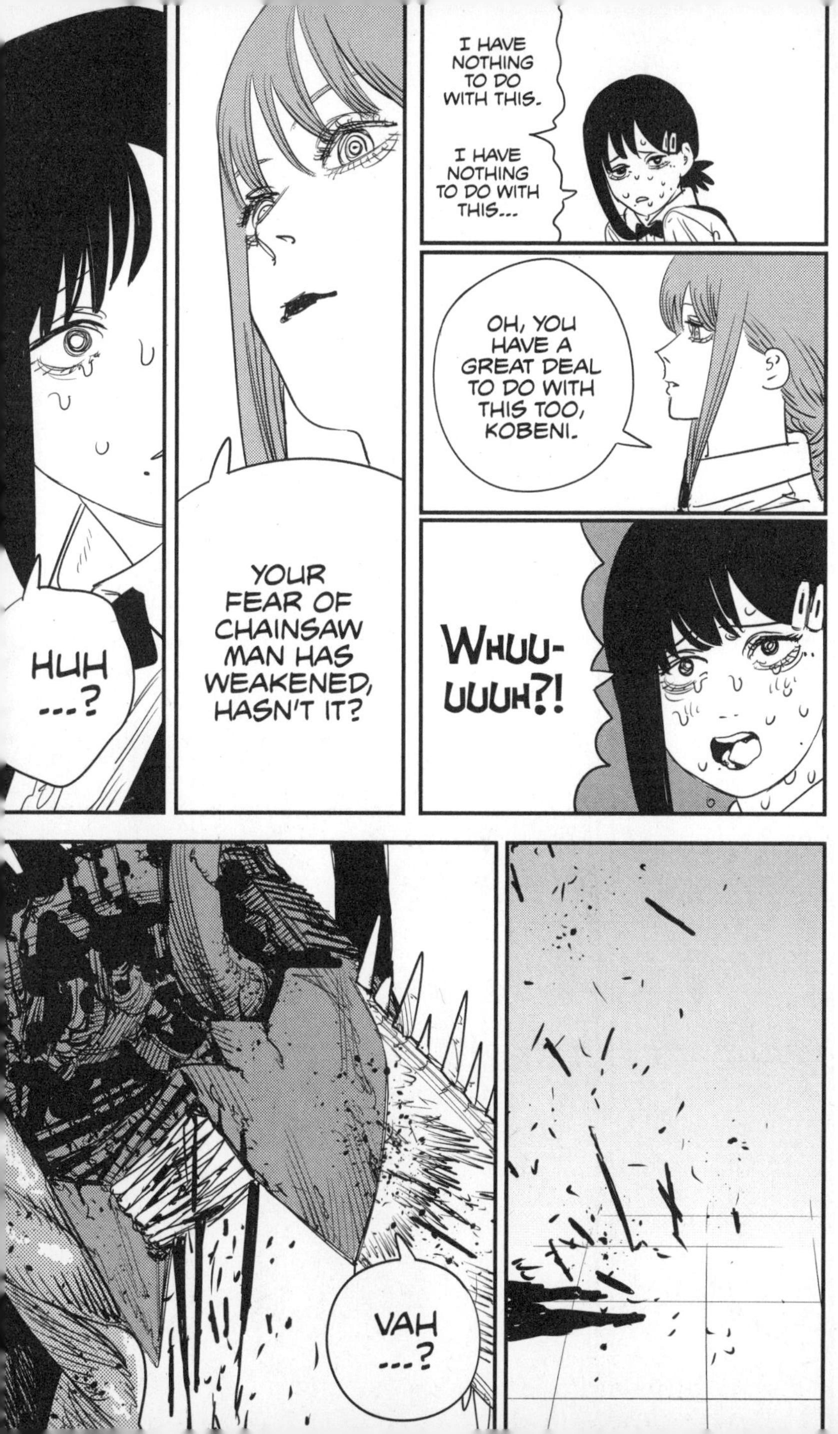
I HAVE NOTHING TO DO WITH THIS.
I HAVE NOTHING TO DO WITH THIS...
OH, YOU HAVE A GREAT DEAL TO DO WITH THIS TOO, KOBENI.
WHUU-UUUH?!
YOUR FEAR OF CHAINSAW MAN HAS WEAKENED, HASN'T IT?
HUH ...?
VAH ...?

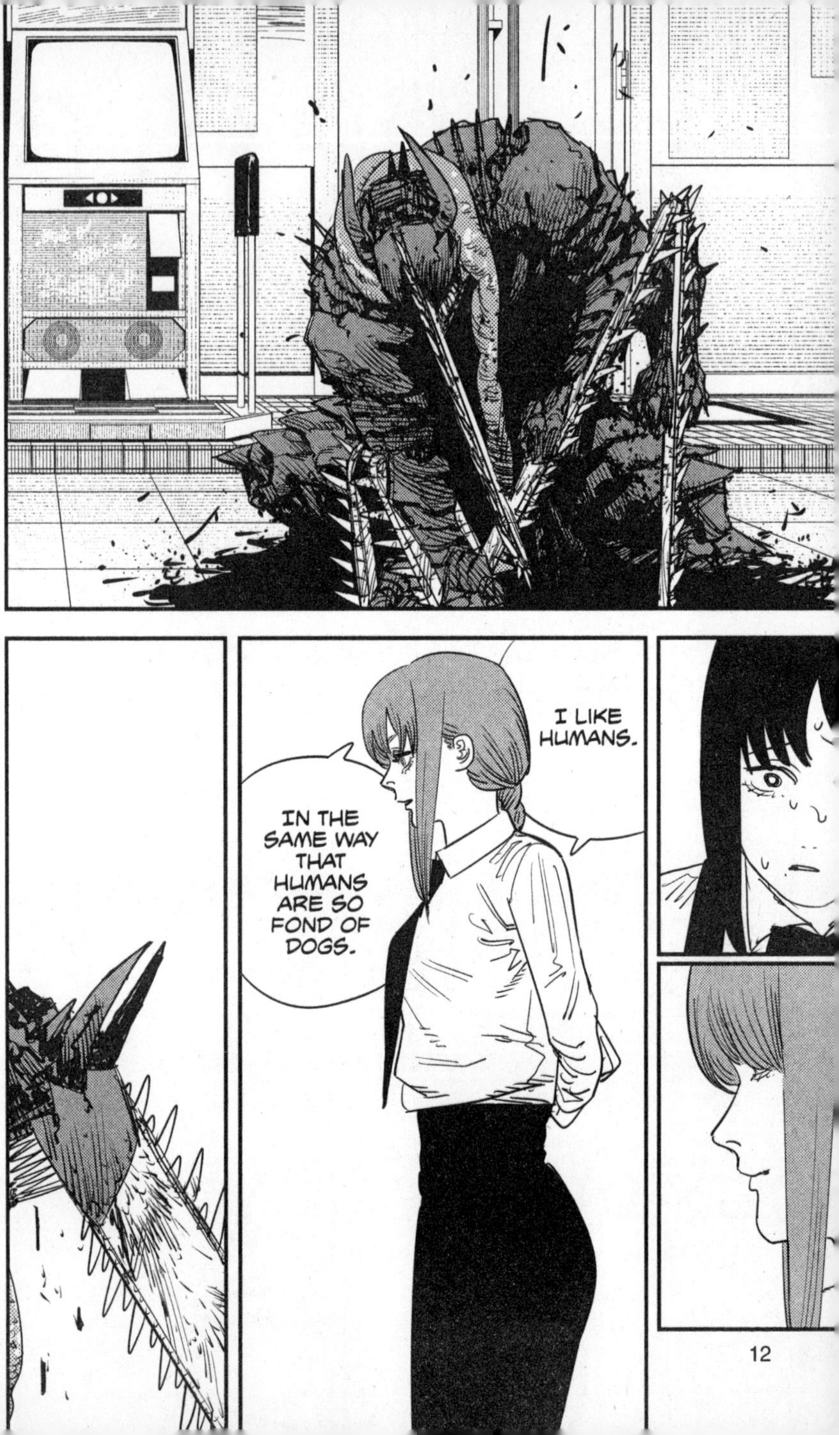
I LIKE HUMANS.
IN THE SAME WAY THAT HUMANS ARE SO FOND OF DOGS.

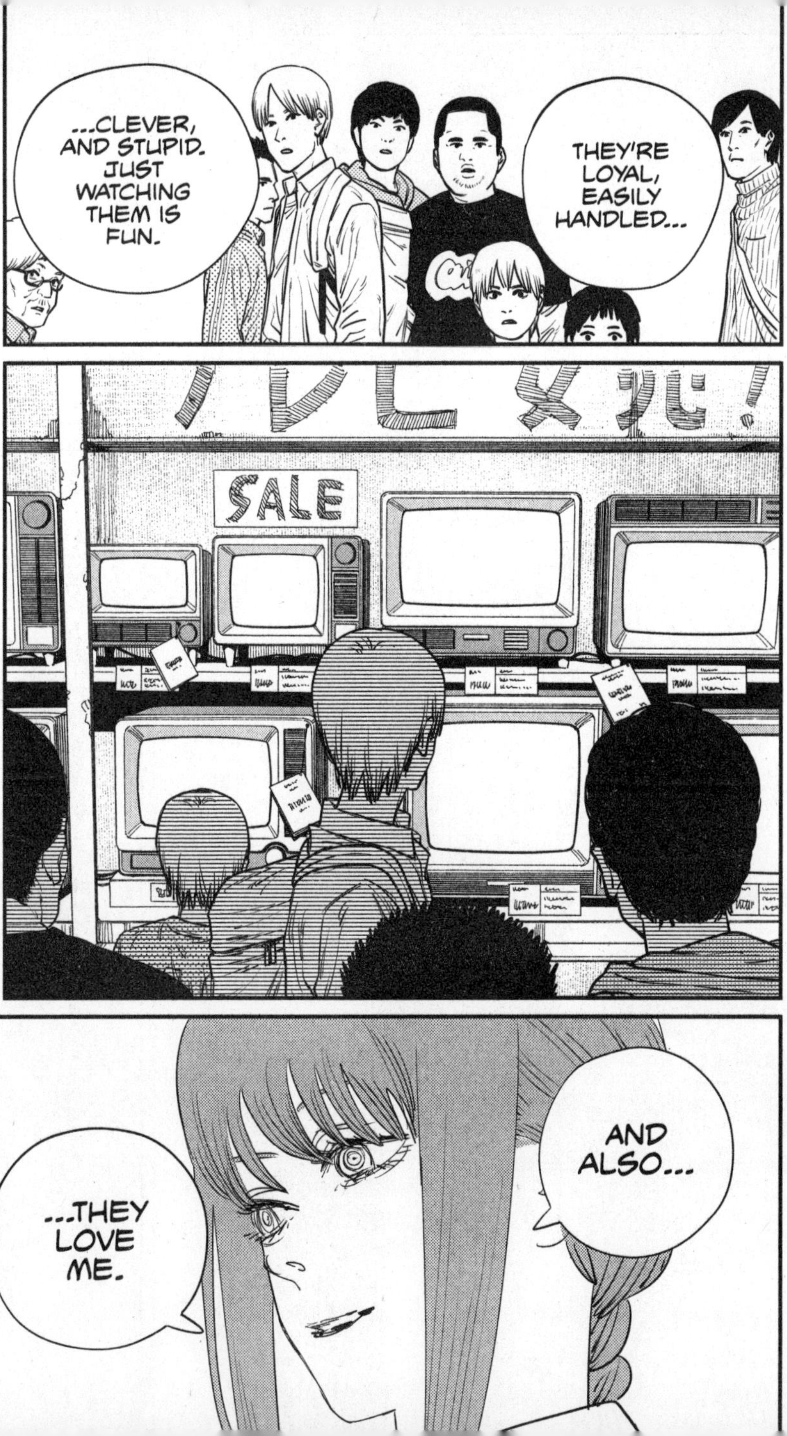
THEY'RE LOYAL, EASILY HANDLED...
...CLEVER, AND STUPID. JUST WATCHING THEM IS FUN.
SALE
AND ALSO...
...THEY LOVE ME.

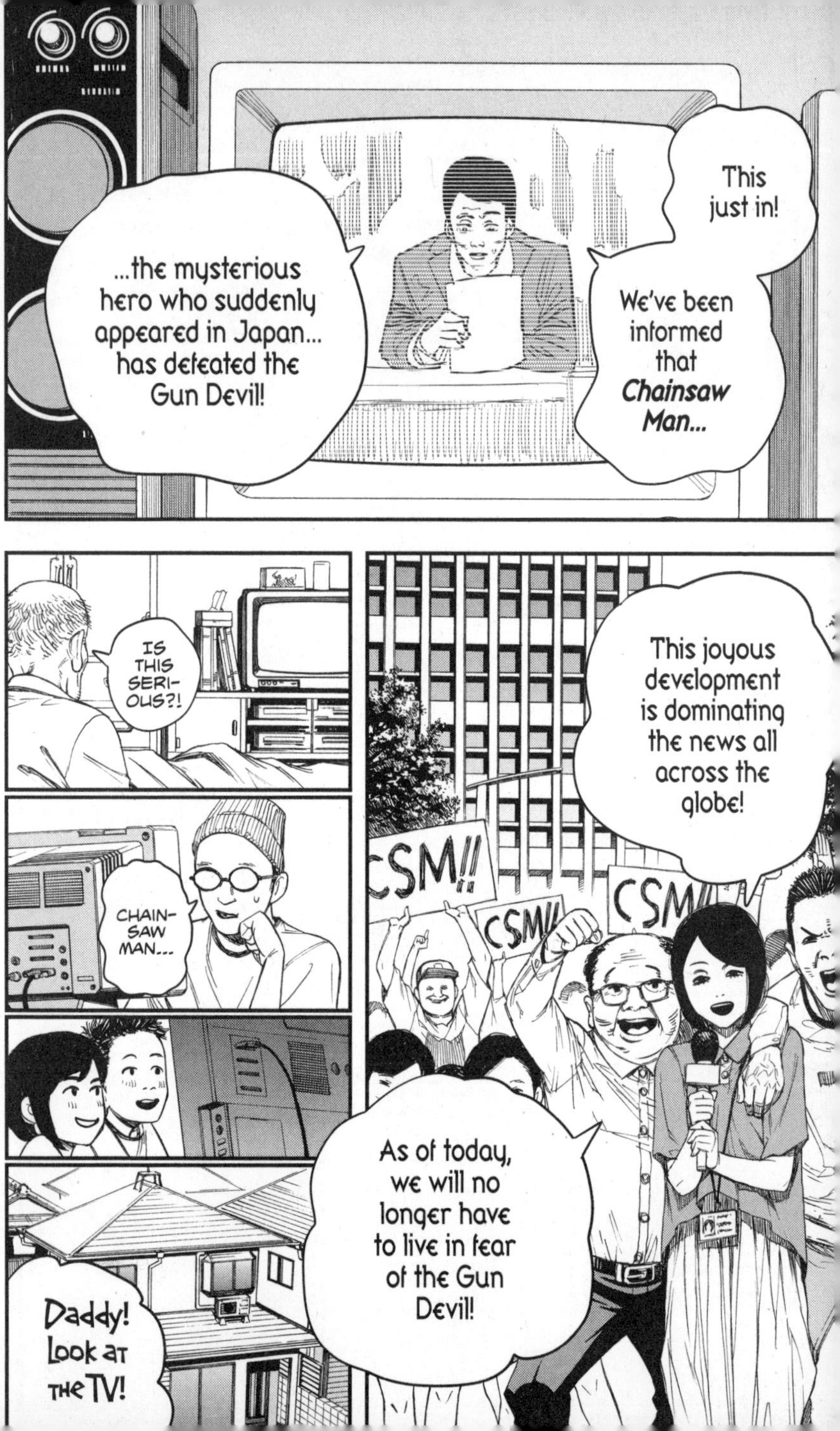
This just in!
We've been informed that *Chainsaw Man...*
...the mysterious hero who suddenly appeared in Japan... has defeated the Gun Devil!
This joyous development is dominating the news all across the globe!
CSM!!
As of today, we will no longer have to live in fear of the Gun Devil!
IS THIS SERIOUS?!
CHAINSAW MAN...
Daddy! Look at the TV!

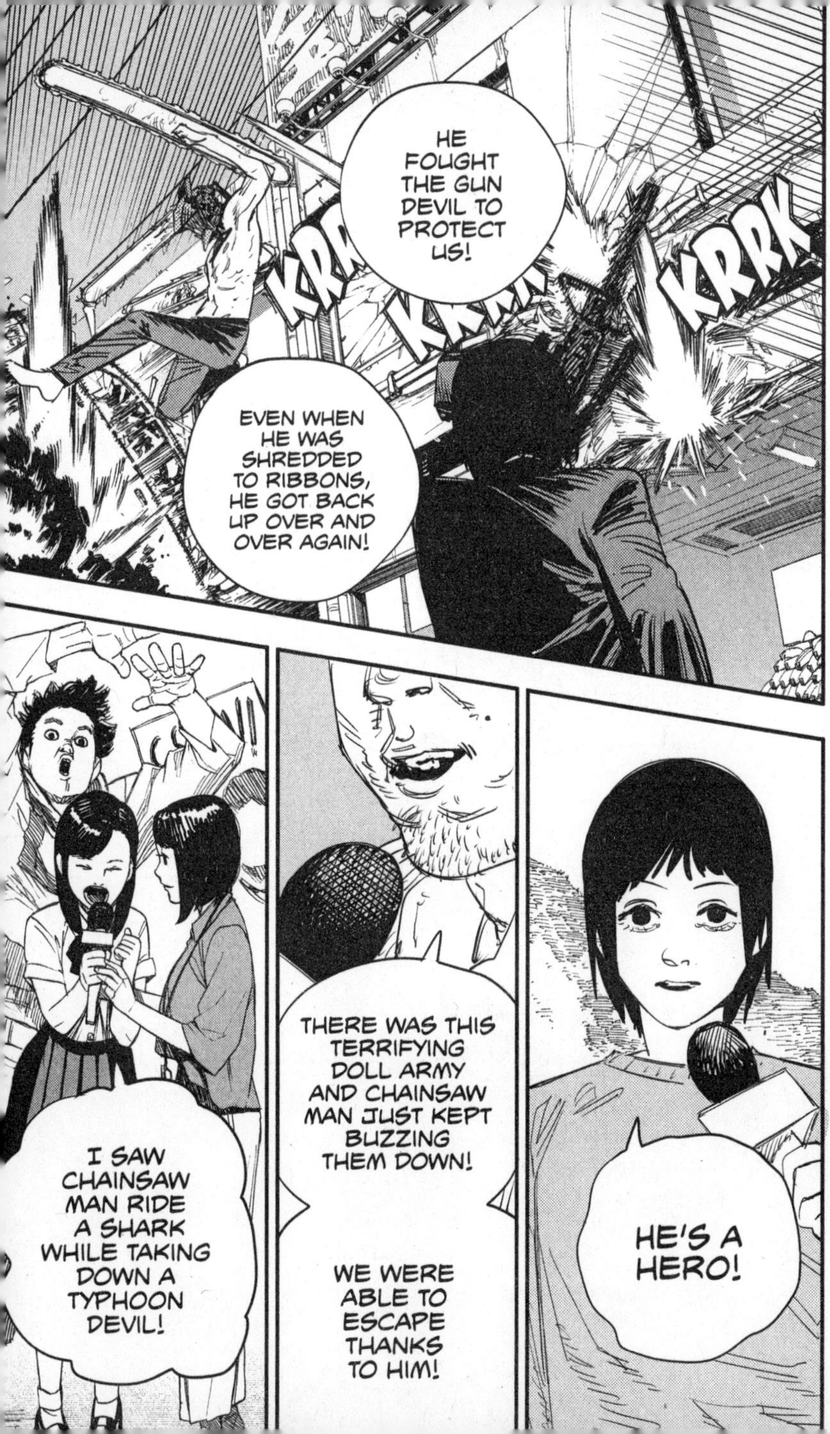
HE FOUGHT THE GUN DEVIL TO PROTECT US!
KRRK
EVEN WHEN HE WAS SHREDDED TO RIBBONS, HE GOT BACK UP OVER AND OVER AGAIN!
HE'S A HERO!
THERE WAS THIS TERRIFYING DOLL ARMY AND CHAINSAW MAN JUST KEPT BUZZING THEM DOWN!
WE WERE ABLE TO ESCAPE THANKS TO HIM!
I SAW CHAINSAW MAN RIDE A SHARK WHILE TAKING DOWN A TYPHOON DEVIL!

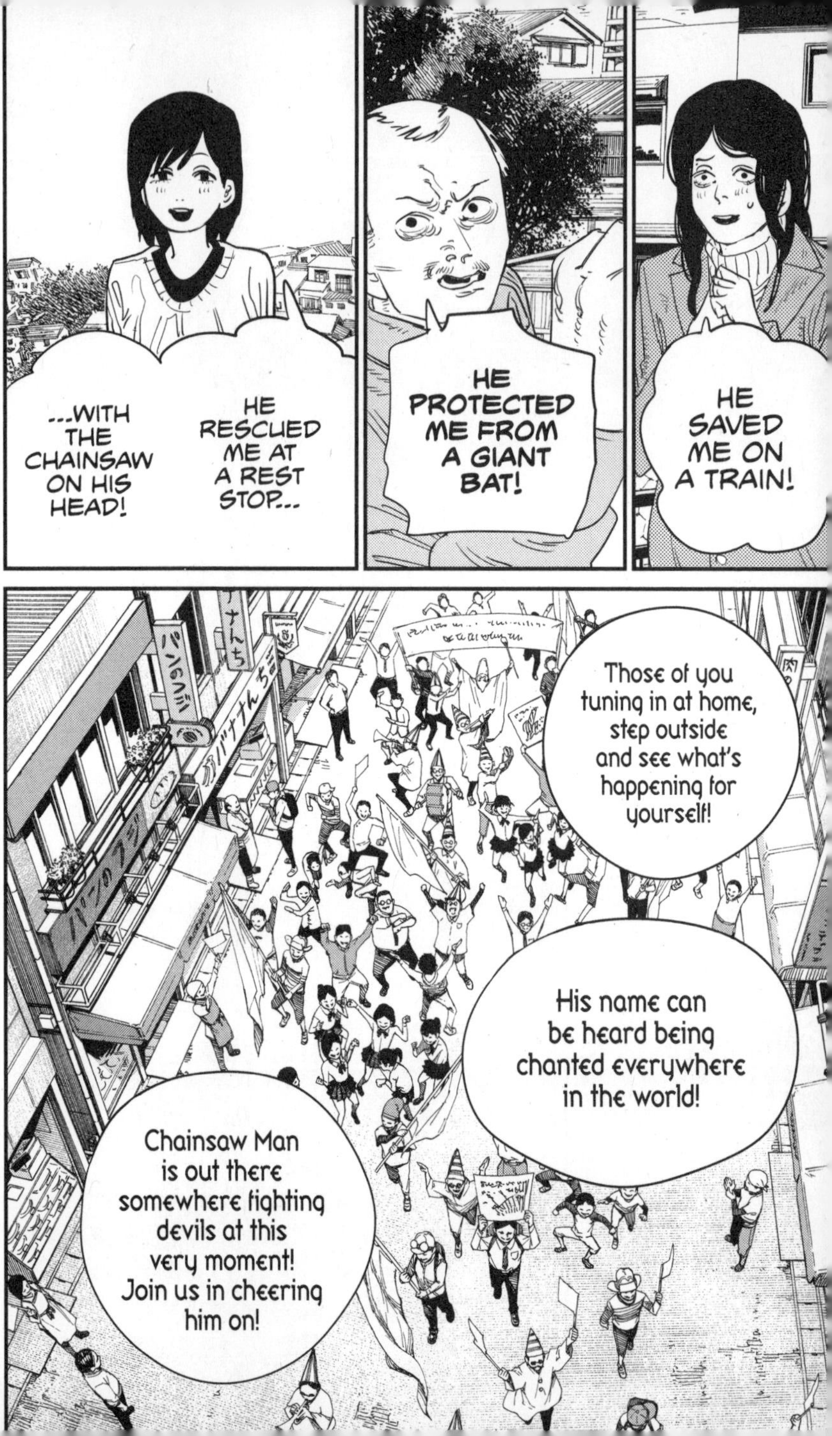
HE SAVED ME ON A TRAIN!
HE PROTECTED ME FROM A GIANT BAT!
HE RESCUED ME AT A REST STOP...
...WITH THE CHAINSAW ON HIS HEAD!
Those of you tuning in at home, step outside and see what's happening for yourself!
His name can be heard being chanted everywhere in the world!
Chainsaw Man is out there somewhere fighting devils at this very moment! Join us in cheering him on!

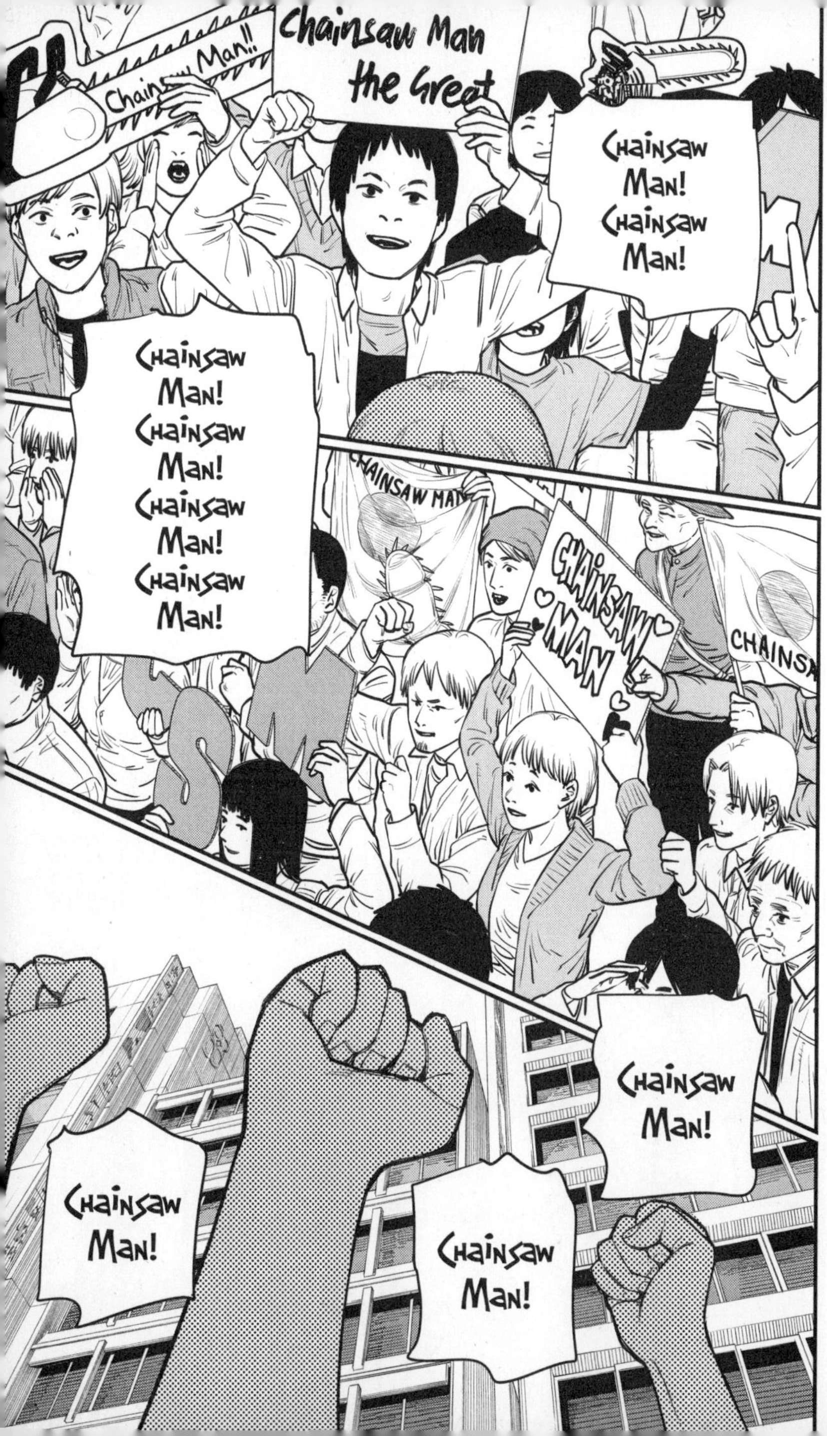
Chainsaw Man! Chainsaw Man!
Chainsaw Man the Great
Man!!
Chainsaw Man! Chainsaw Man! Chainsaw Man! Chainsaw Man!
CHAINSA
CHAINSAW MAN
CHAINSAW MA
Chainsaw Man!
Chainsaw Man!
Chainsaw Man!

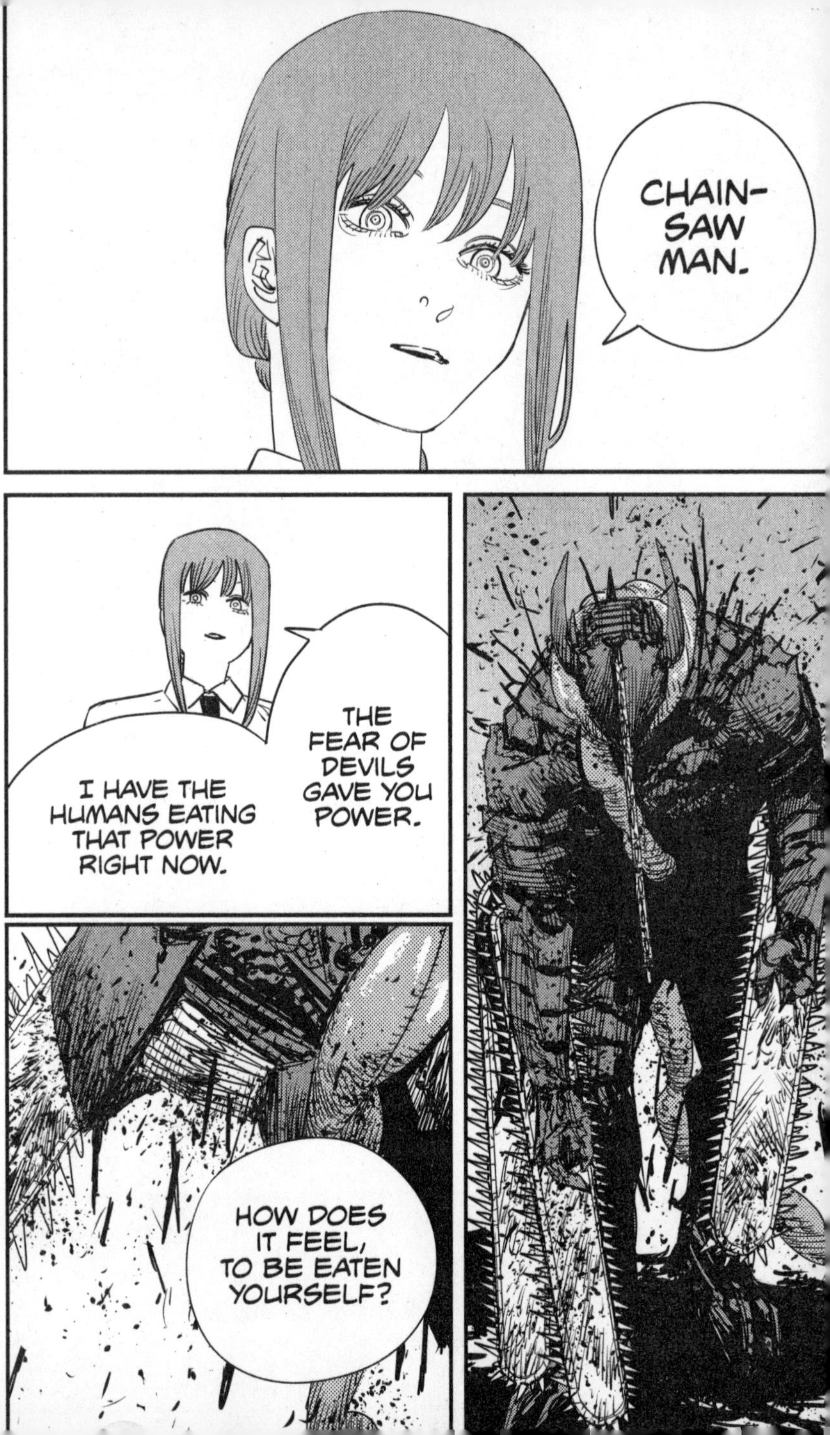
CHAIN-SAW MAN.
THE FEAR OF DEVILS GAVE YOU POWER.
I HAVE THE HUMANS EATING THAT POWER RIGHT NOW.
HOW DOES IT FEEL, TO BE EATEN YOURSELF?

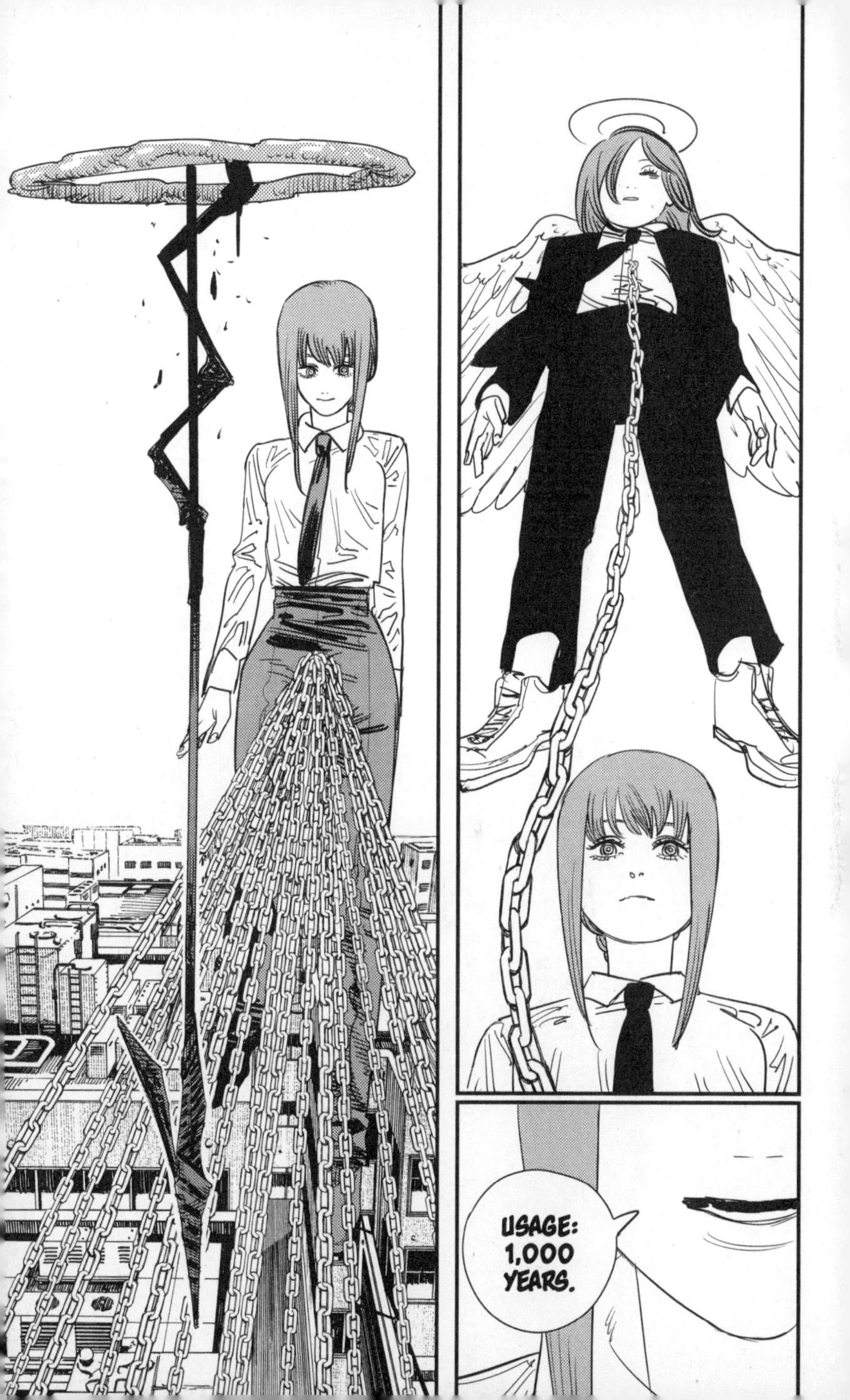
USAGE: 1,000 YEARS.

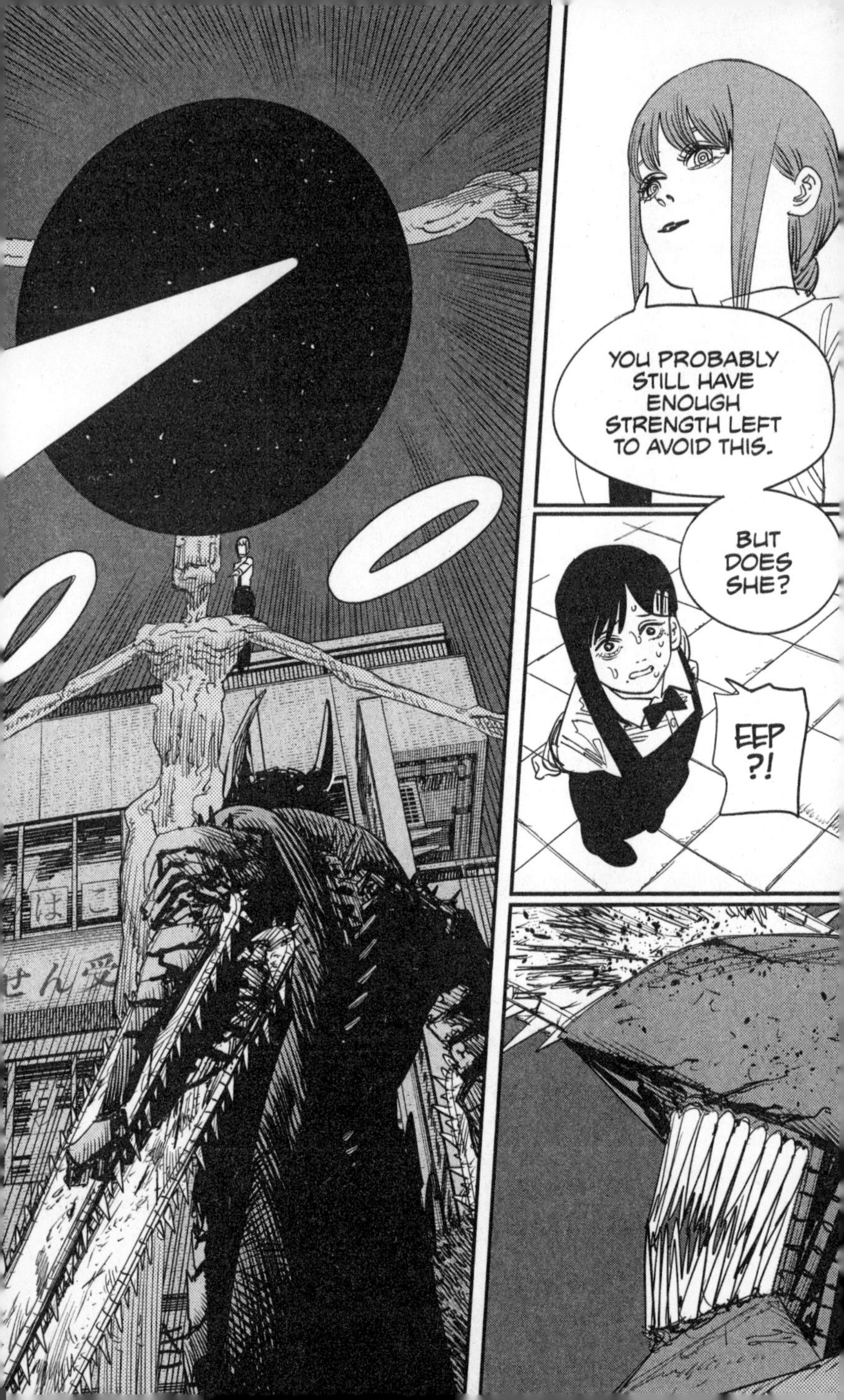
YOU PROBABLY STILL HAVE ENOUGH STRENGTH LEFT TO AVOID THIS.
BUT DOES SHE?
EEP?!

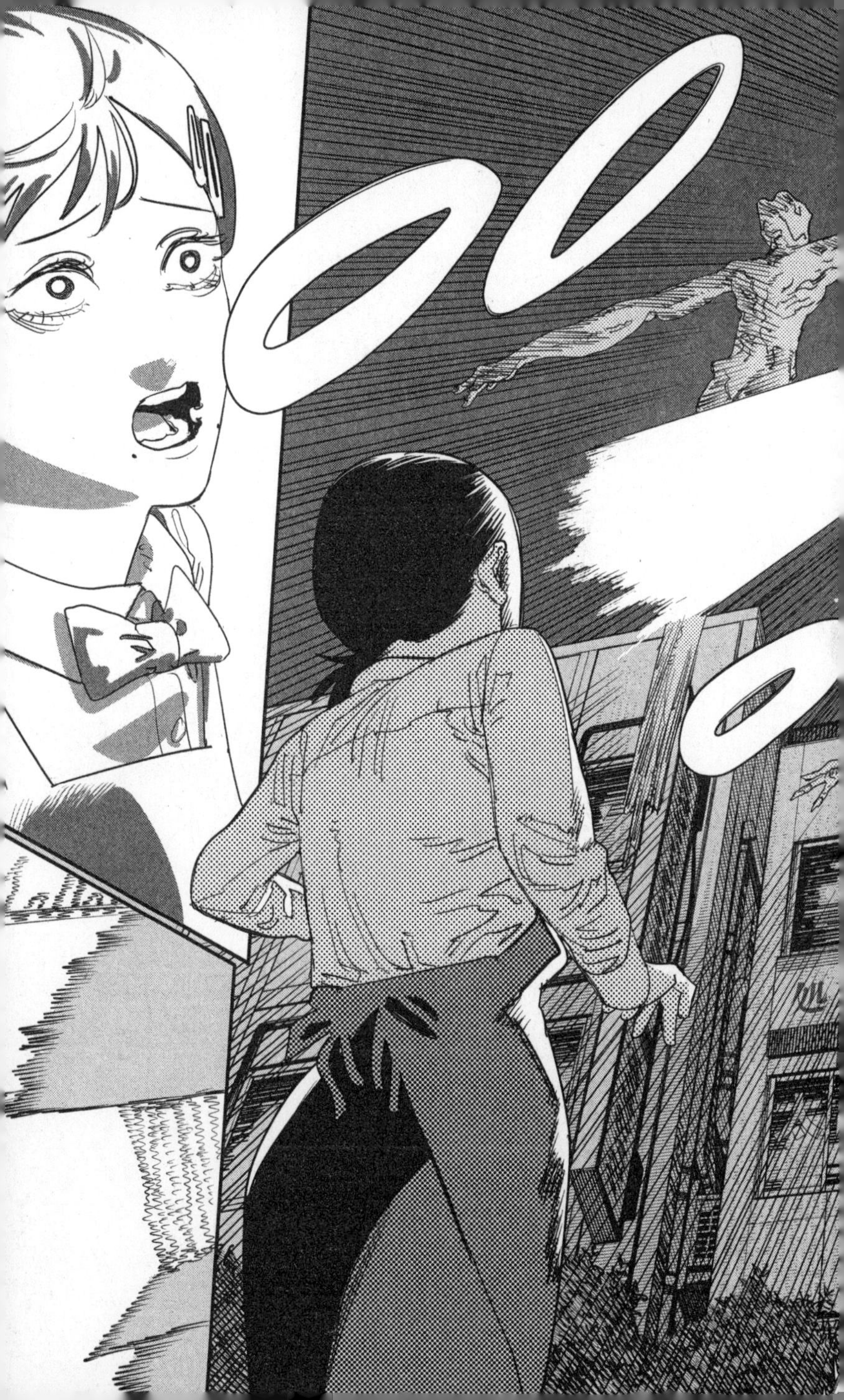

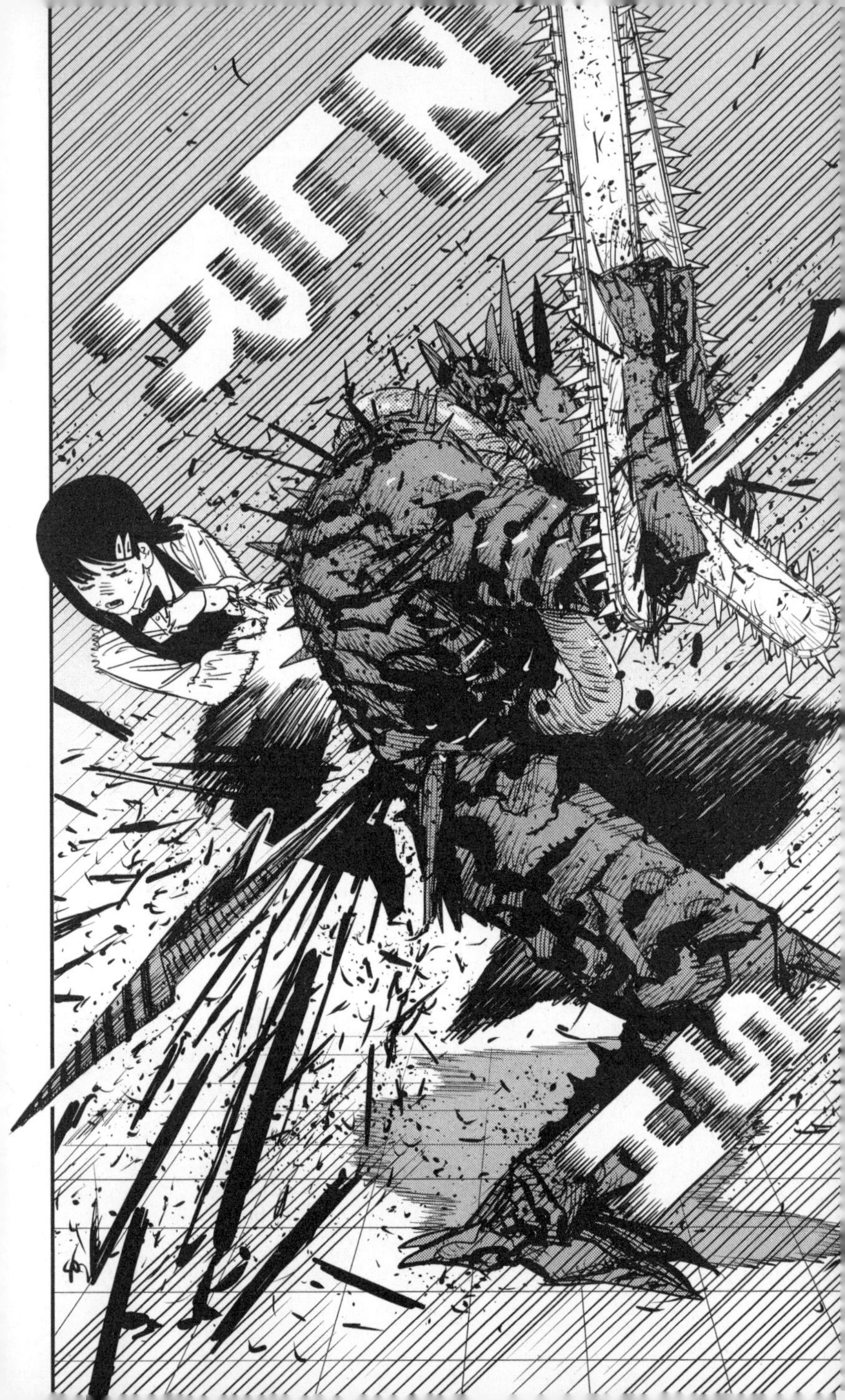

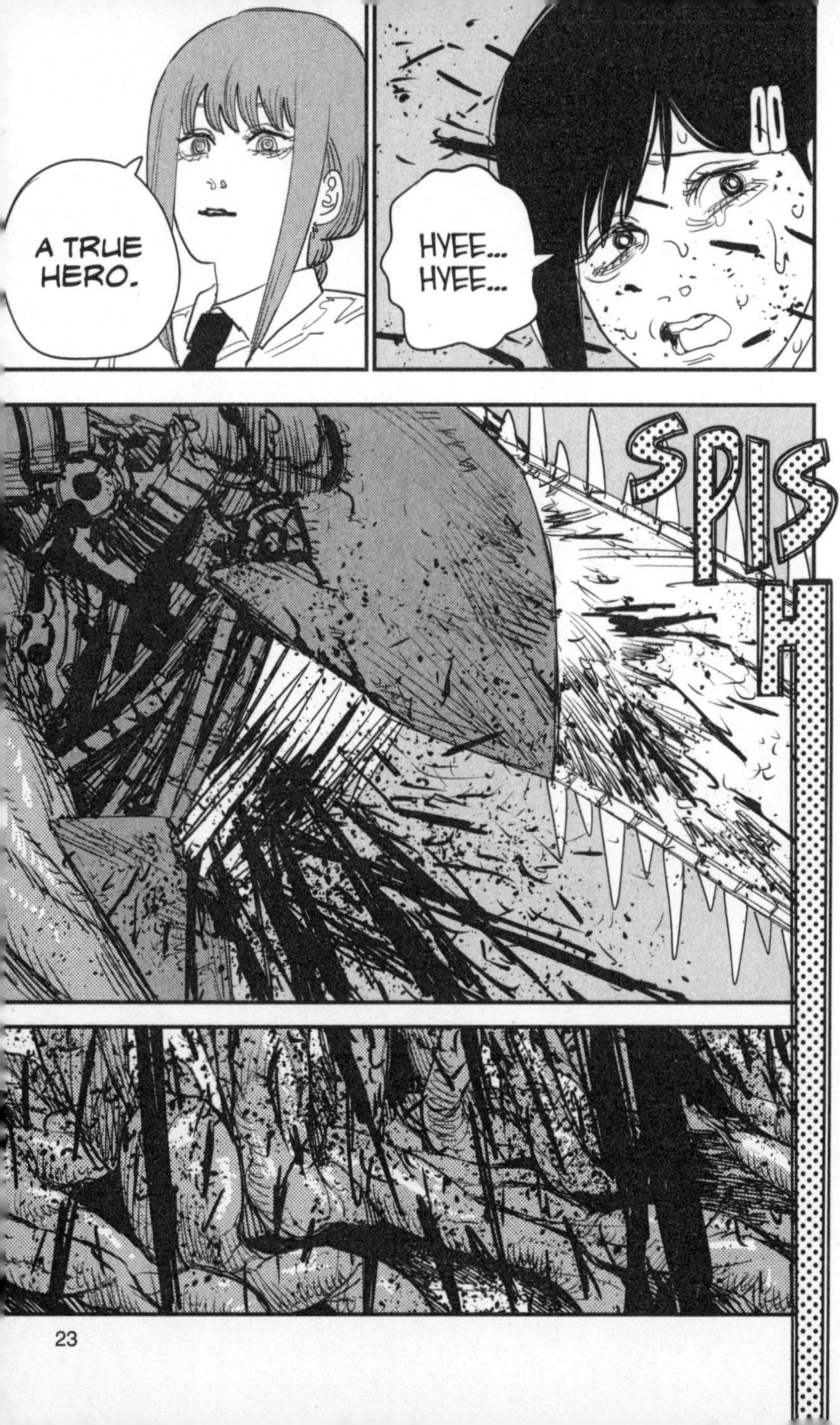
HYEE... HYEE...
A TRUE HERO.
SPISH

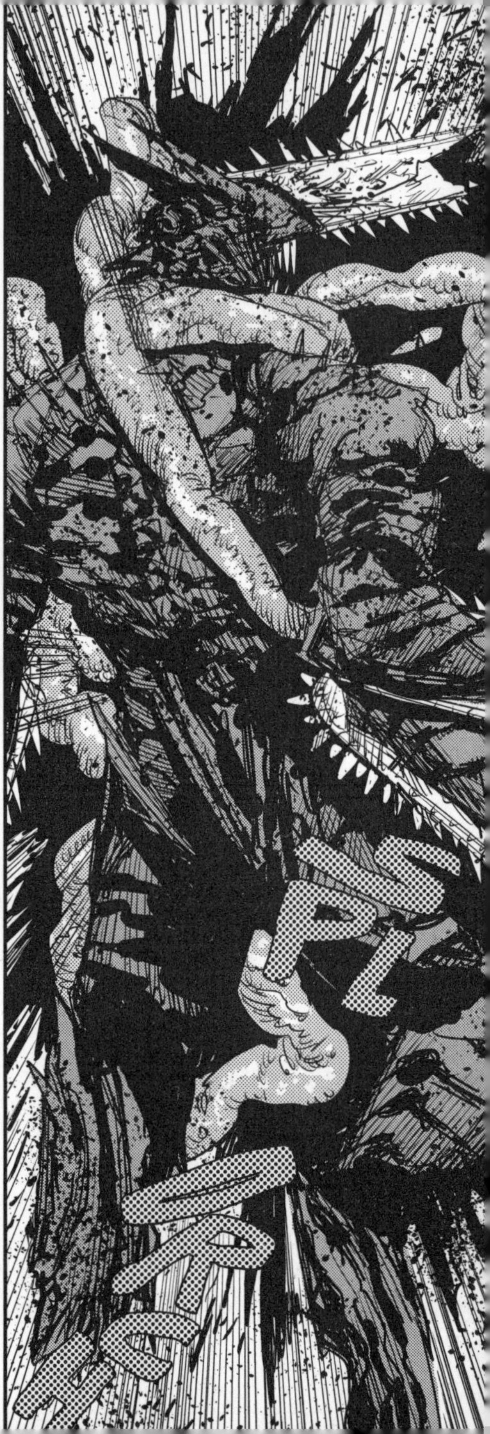
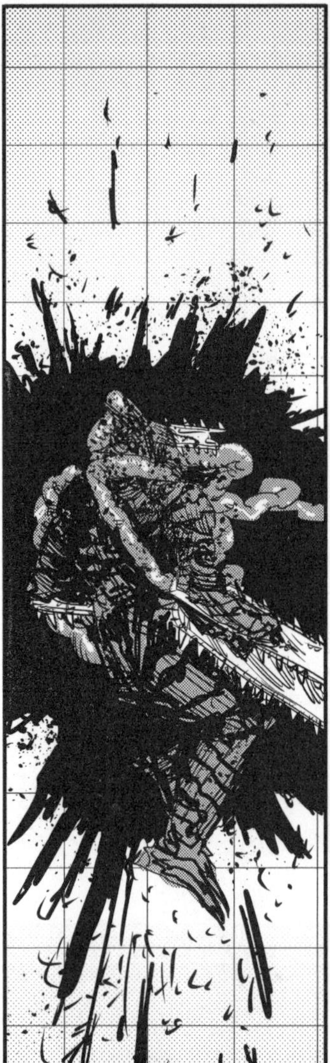

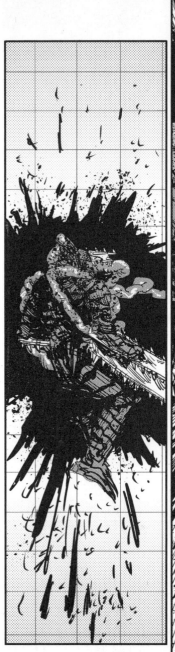

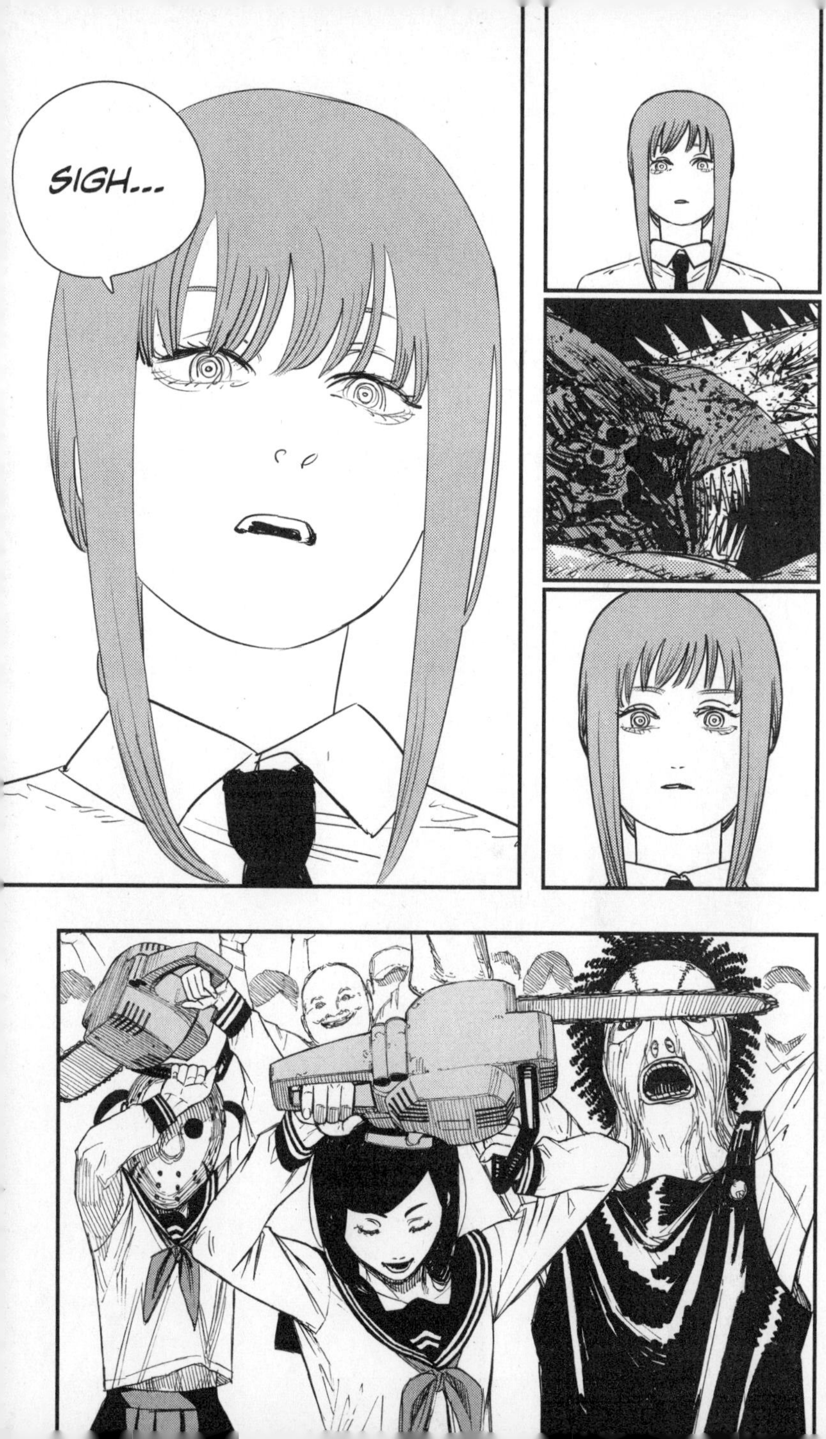
SIGH...

CHAINSAW MAN

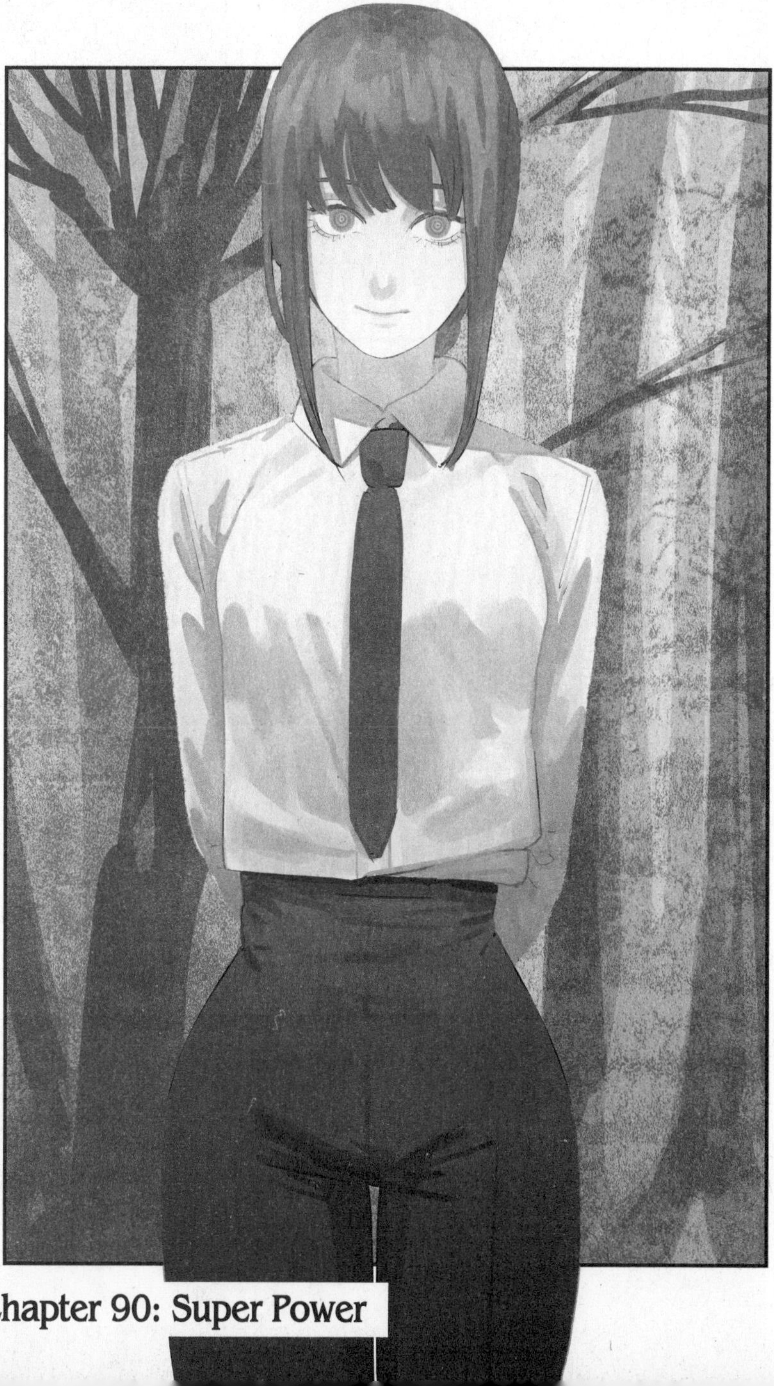

Chapter 90: Super Power

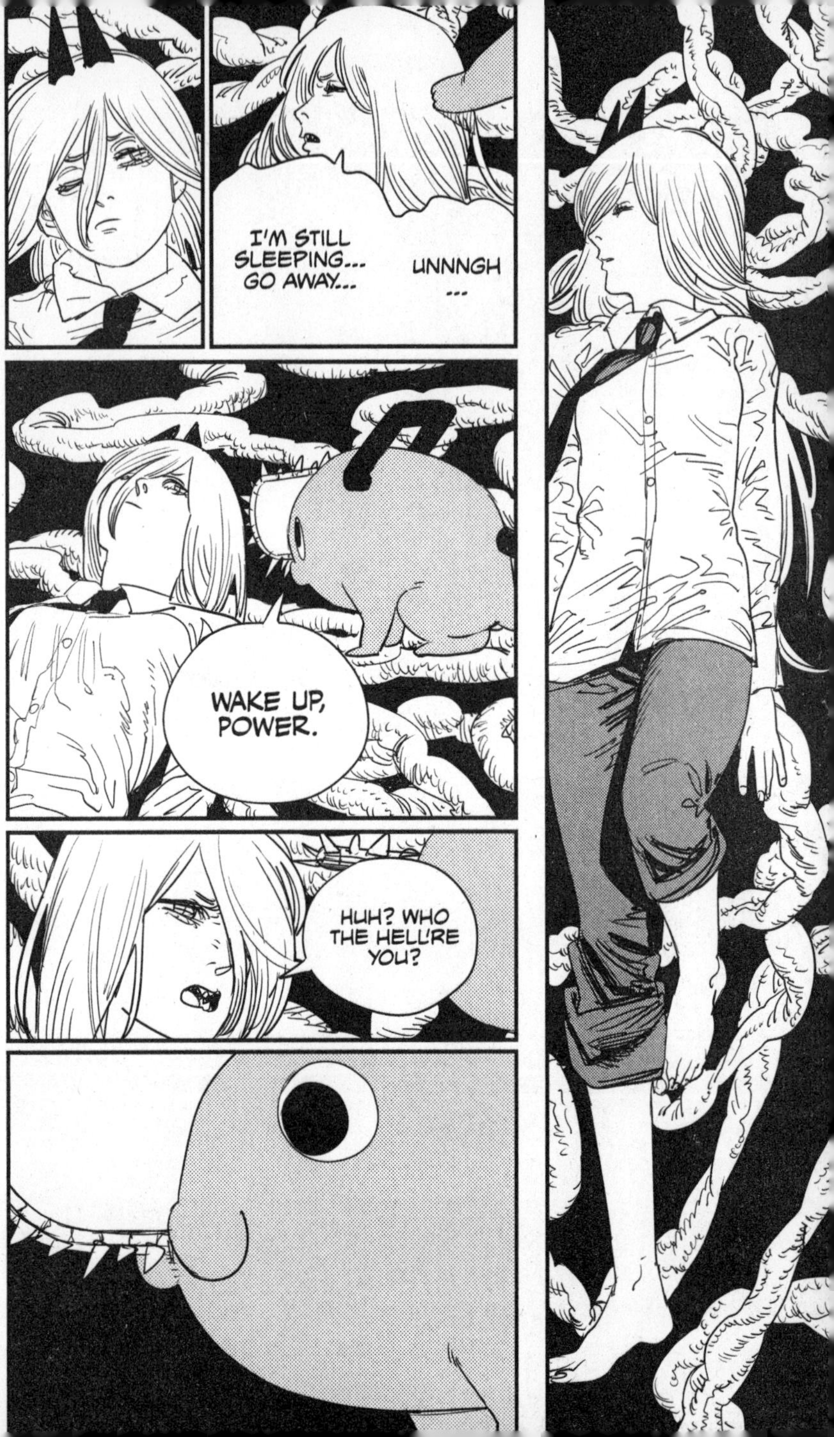
UNNNGH ...
I'M STILL SLEEPING... GO AWAY...
WAKE UP, POWER.
HUH? WHO THE HELL'RE YOU?

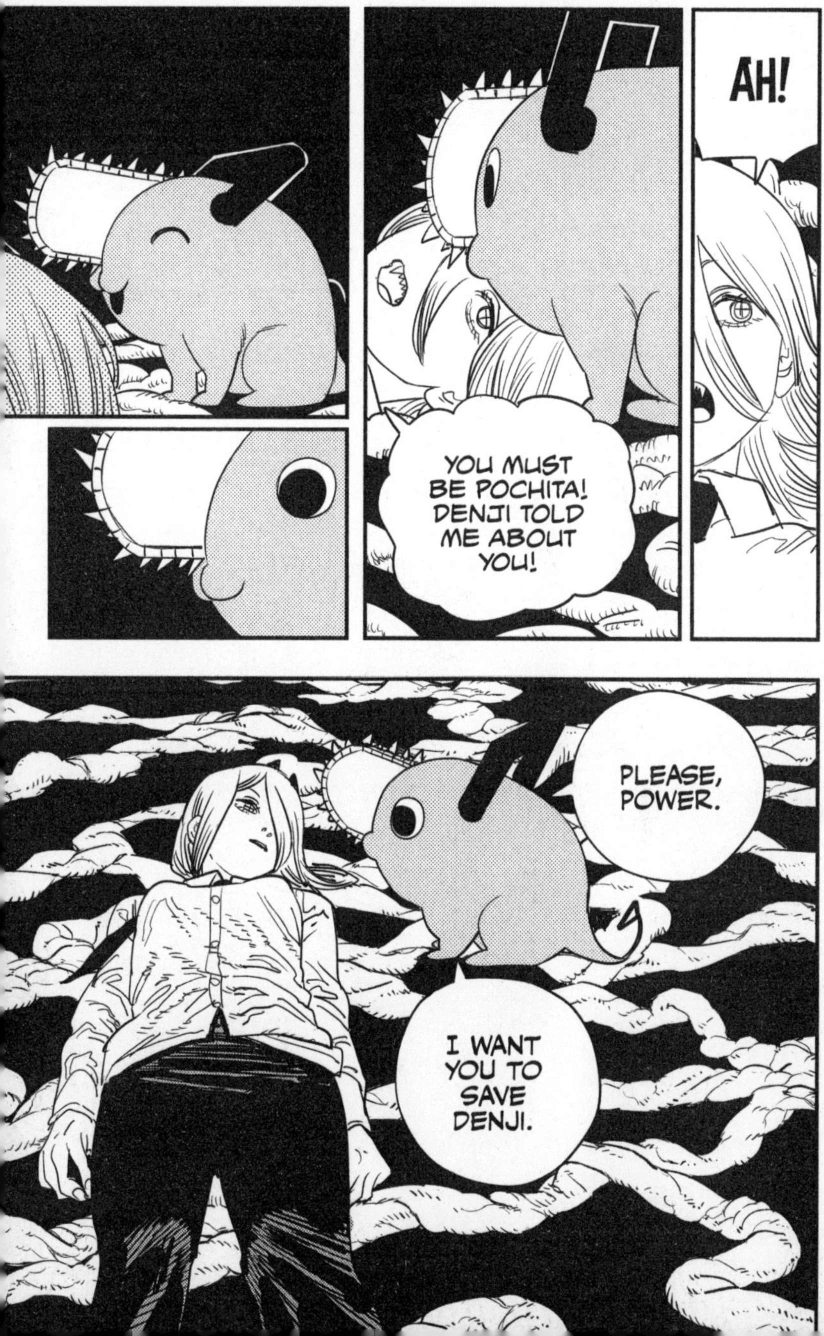
ĀH!
YOU MUST BE POCHITA! DENJI TOLD ME ABOUT YOU!
PLEASE, POWER.
I WANT YOU TO SAVE DENJI.

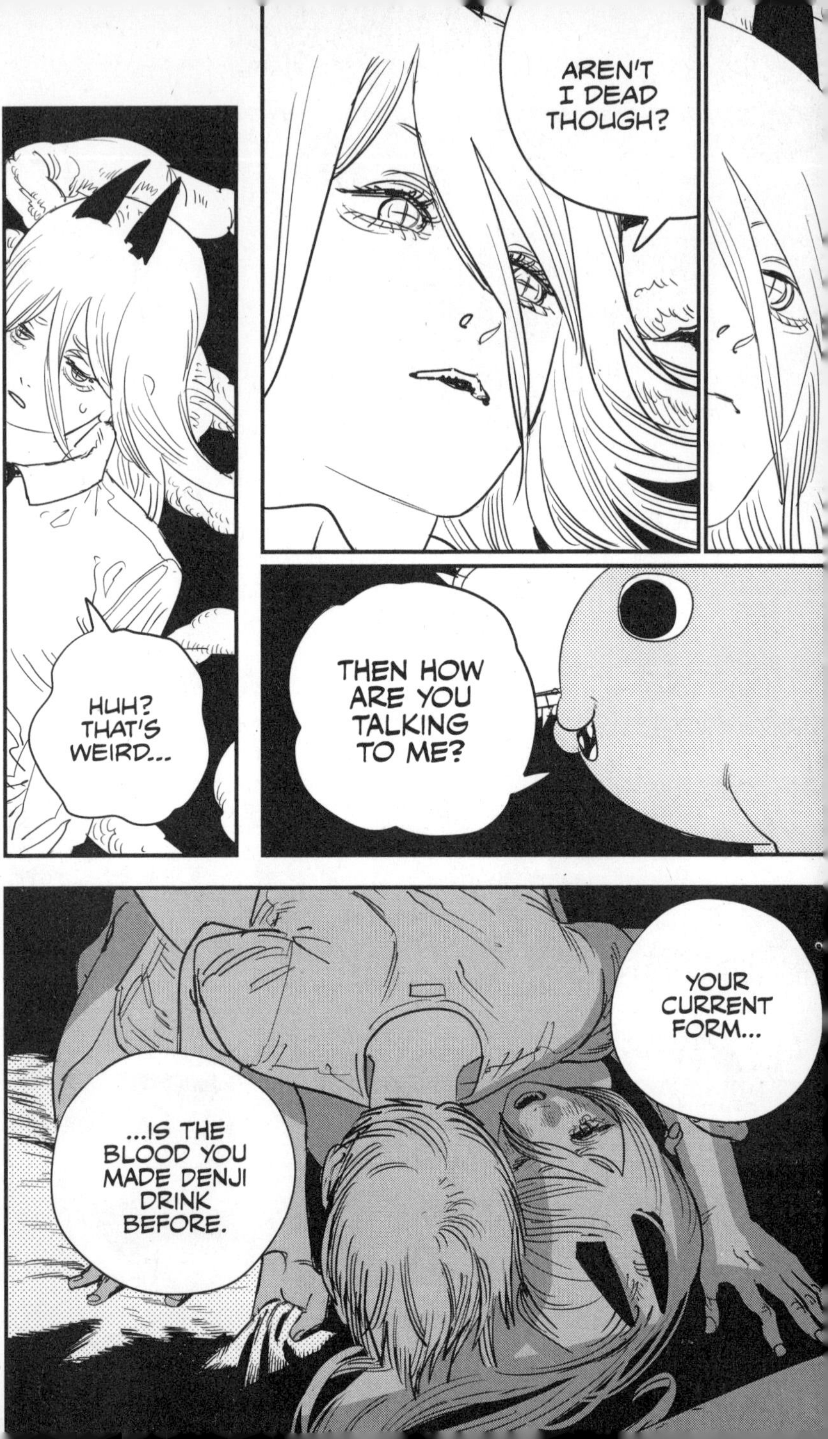
AREN'T I DEAD THOUGH?
THEN HOW ARE YOU TALKING TO ME?
HUH? THAT'S WEIRD...
YOUR CURRENT FORM...
...IS THE BLOOD YOU MADE DENJI DRINK BEFORE.

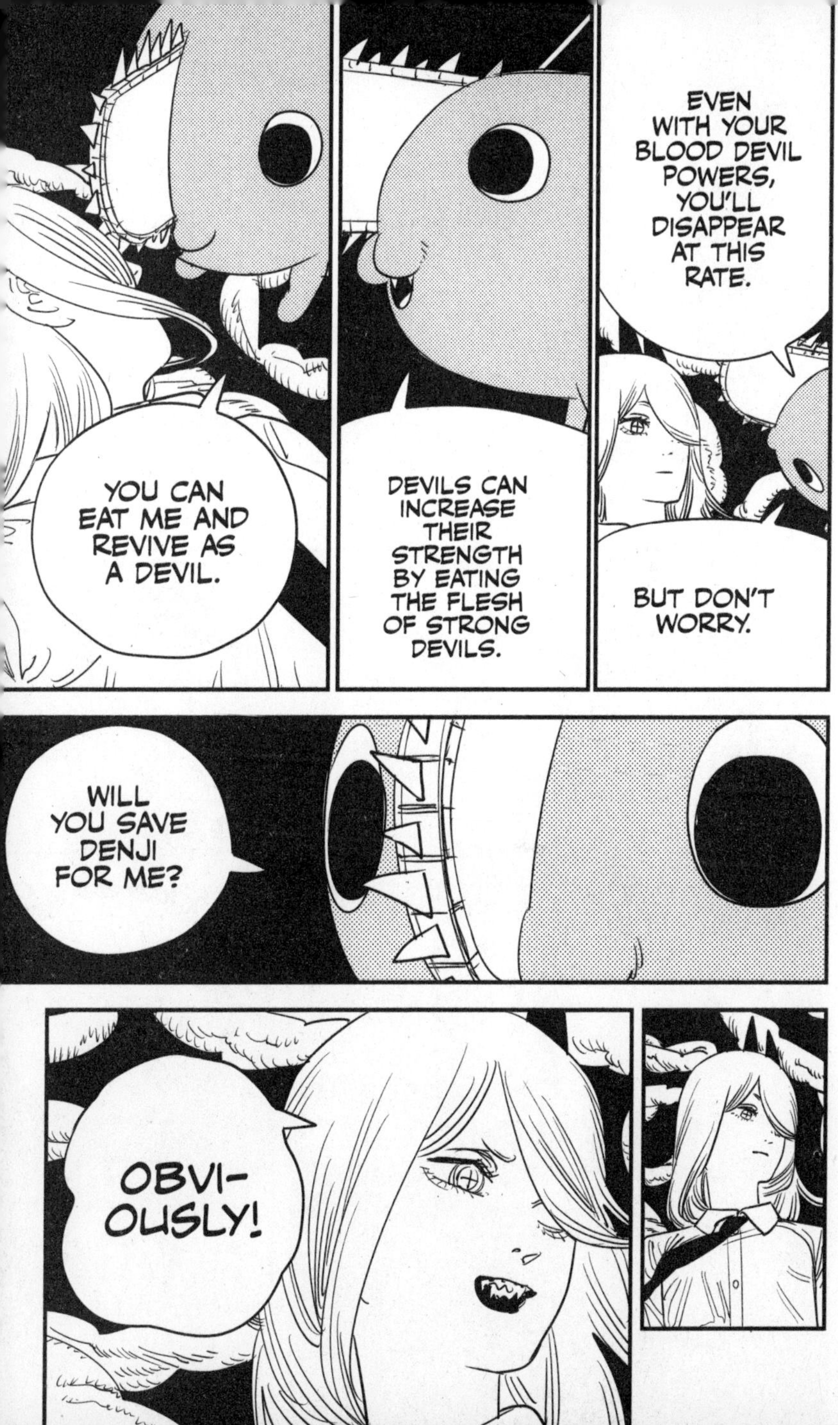
EVEN WITH YOUR BLOOD DEVIL POWERS, YOU'LL DISAPPEAR AT THIS RATE.
BUT DON'T WORRY.
DEVILS CAN INCREASE THEIR STRENGTH BY EATING THE FLESH OF STRONG DEVILS.
YOU CAN EAT ME AND REVIVE AS A DEVIL.
WILL YOU SAVE DENJI FOR ME?
OBVI-OUSLY!

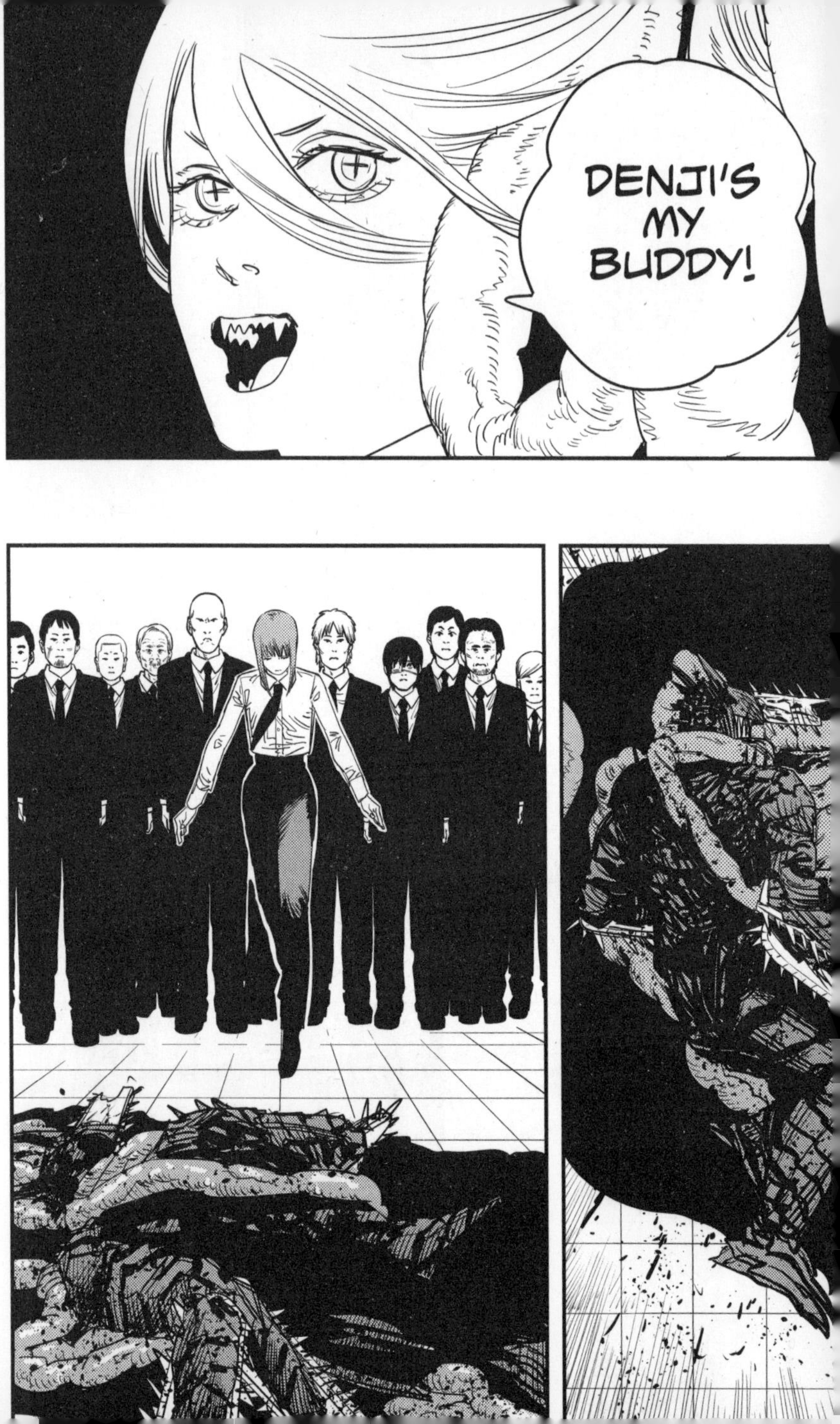
DENJI'S MY BUDDY!

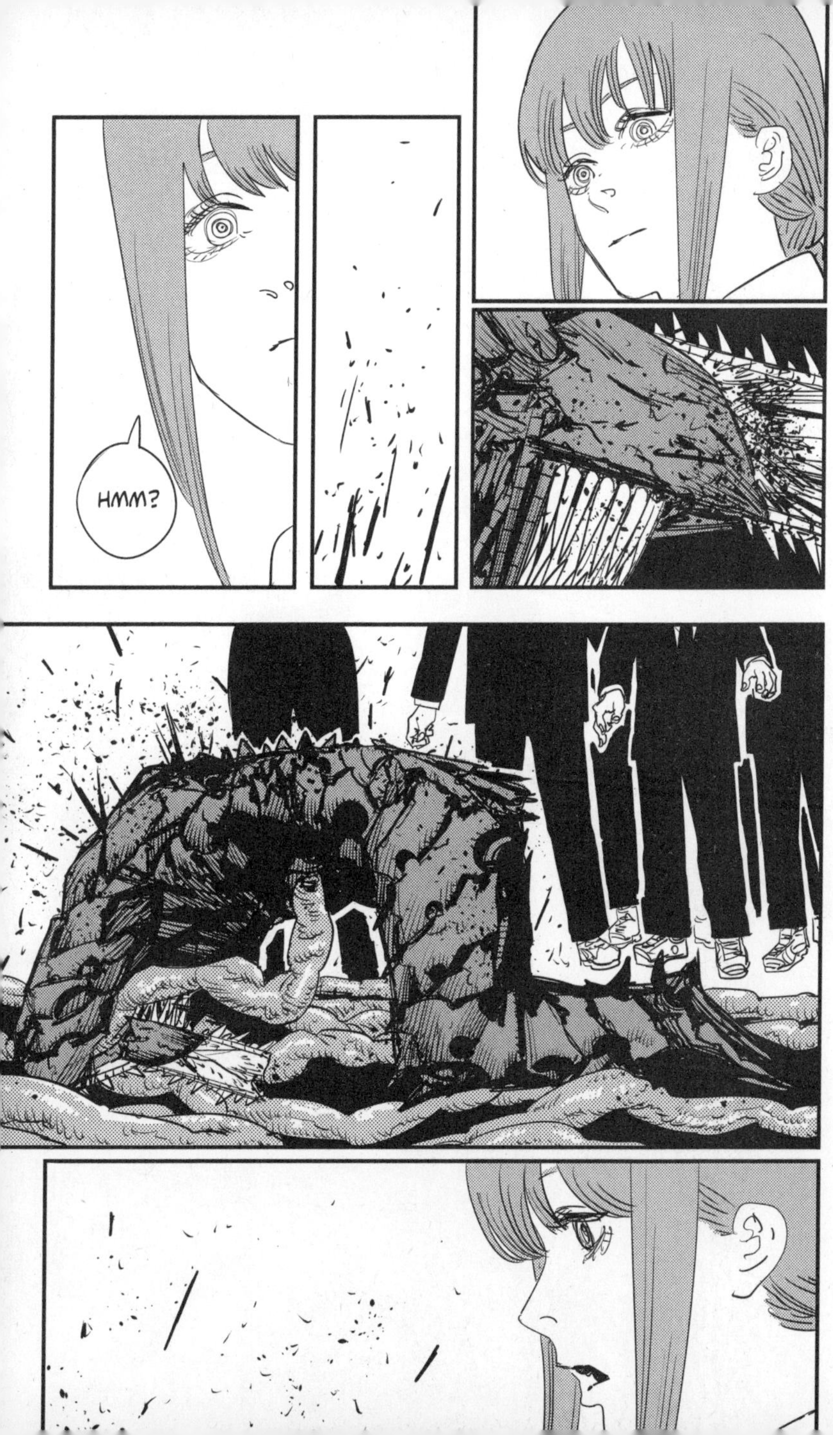
HMM?

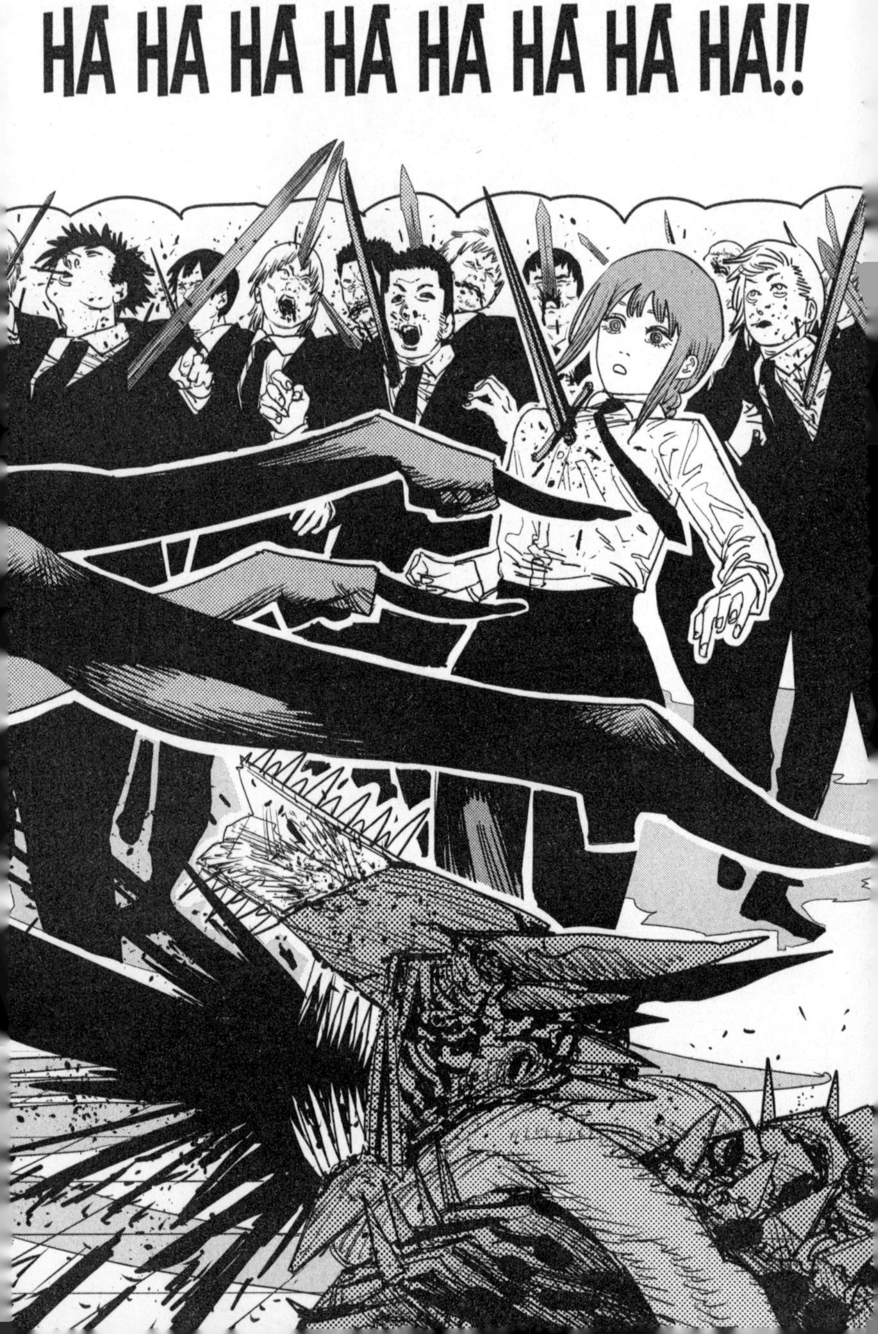
HA HA HA HA HA HA HA HA HA!!

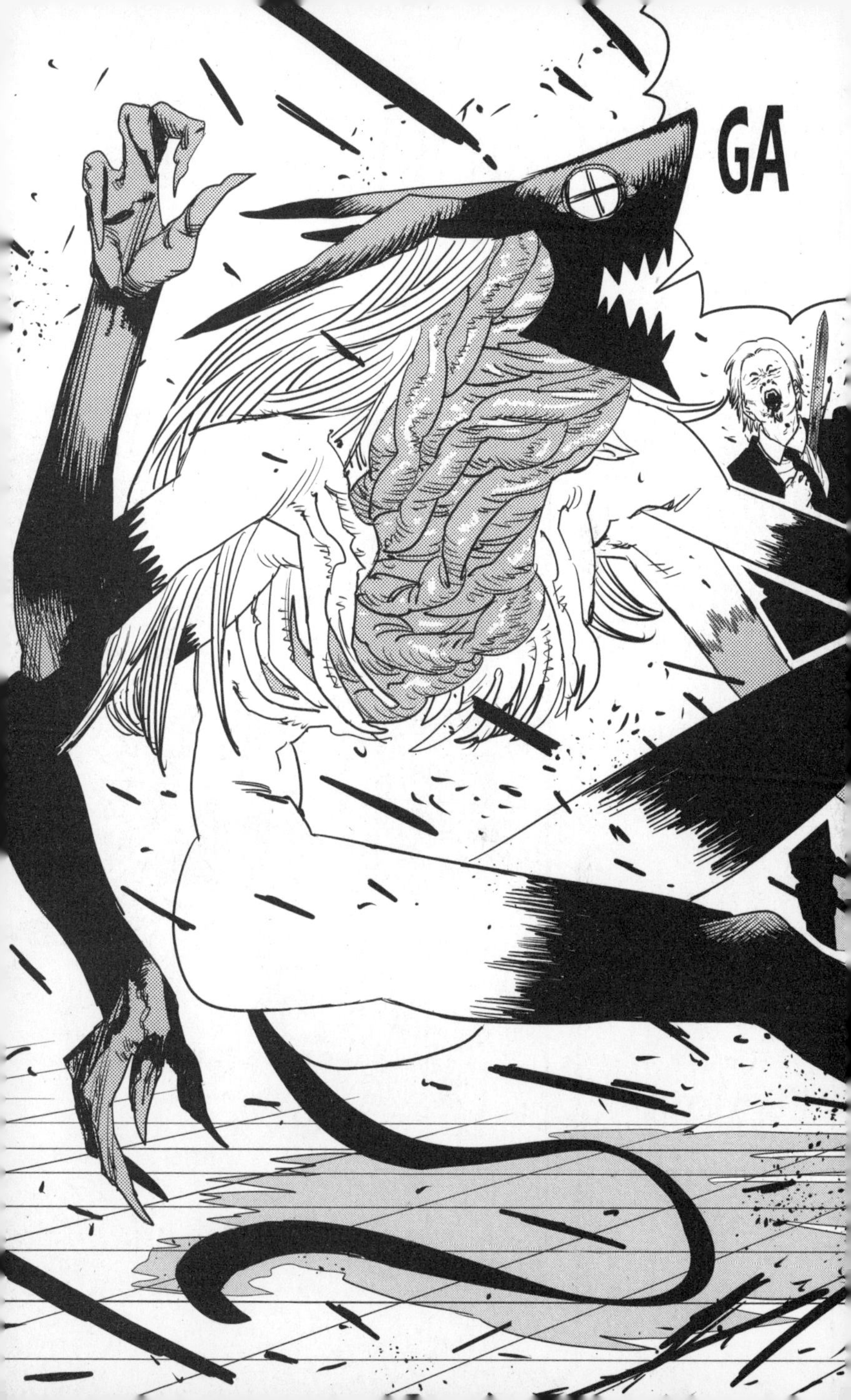
GA

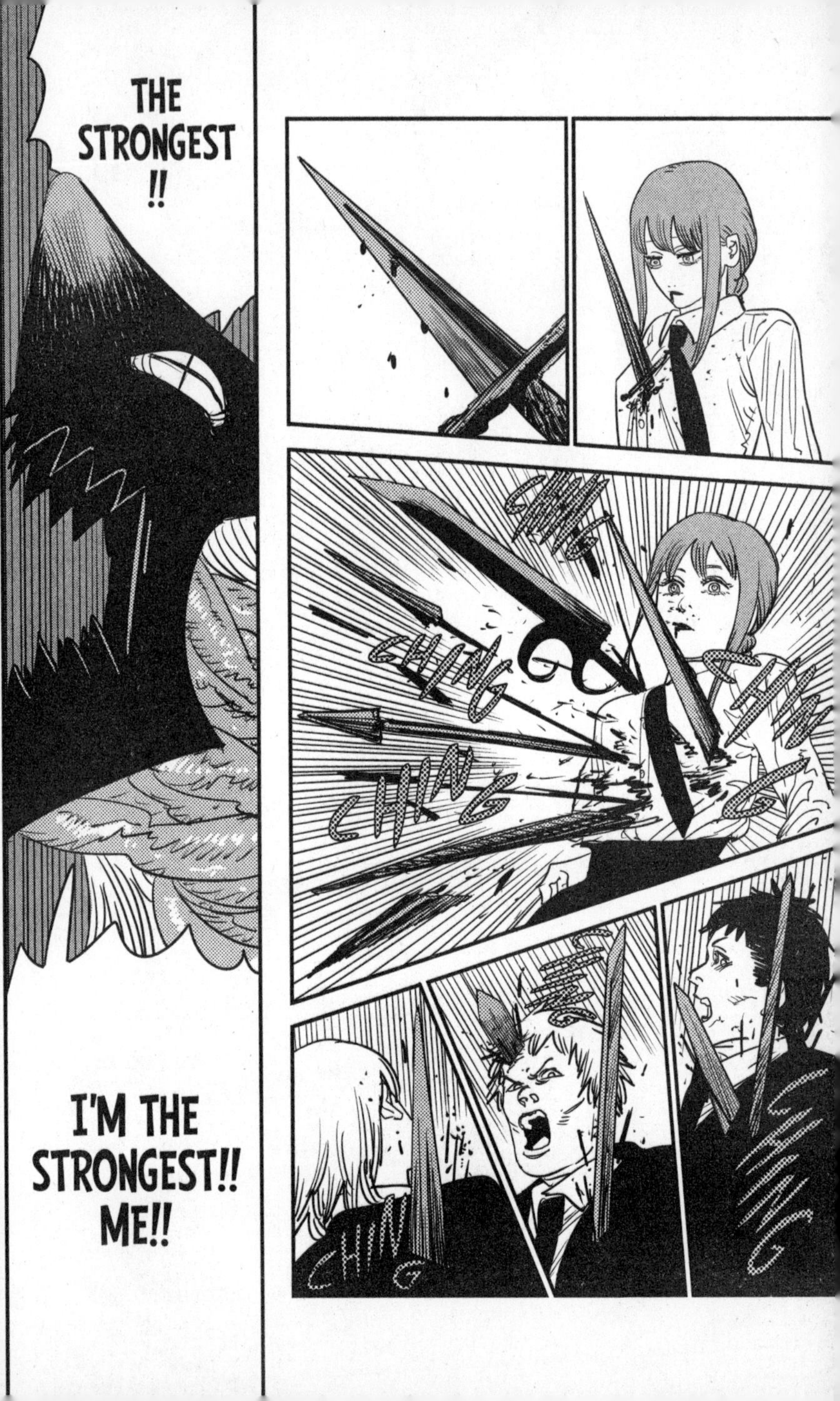
CHING
CHING
CHING
CHING
CHING
CHING
CHING
THE STRONGEST!!
I'M THE STRONGEST!! ME!!

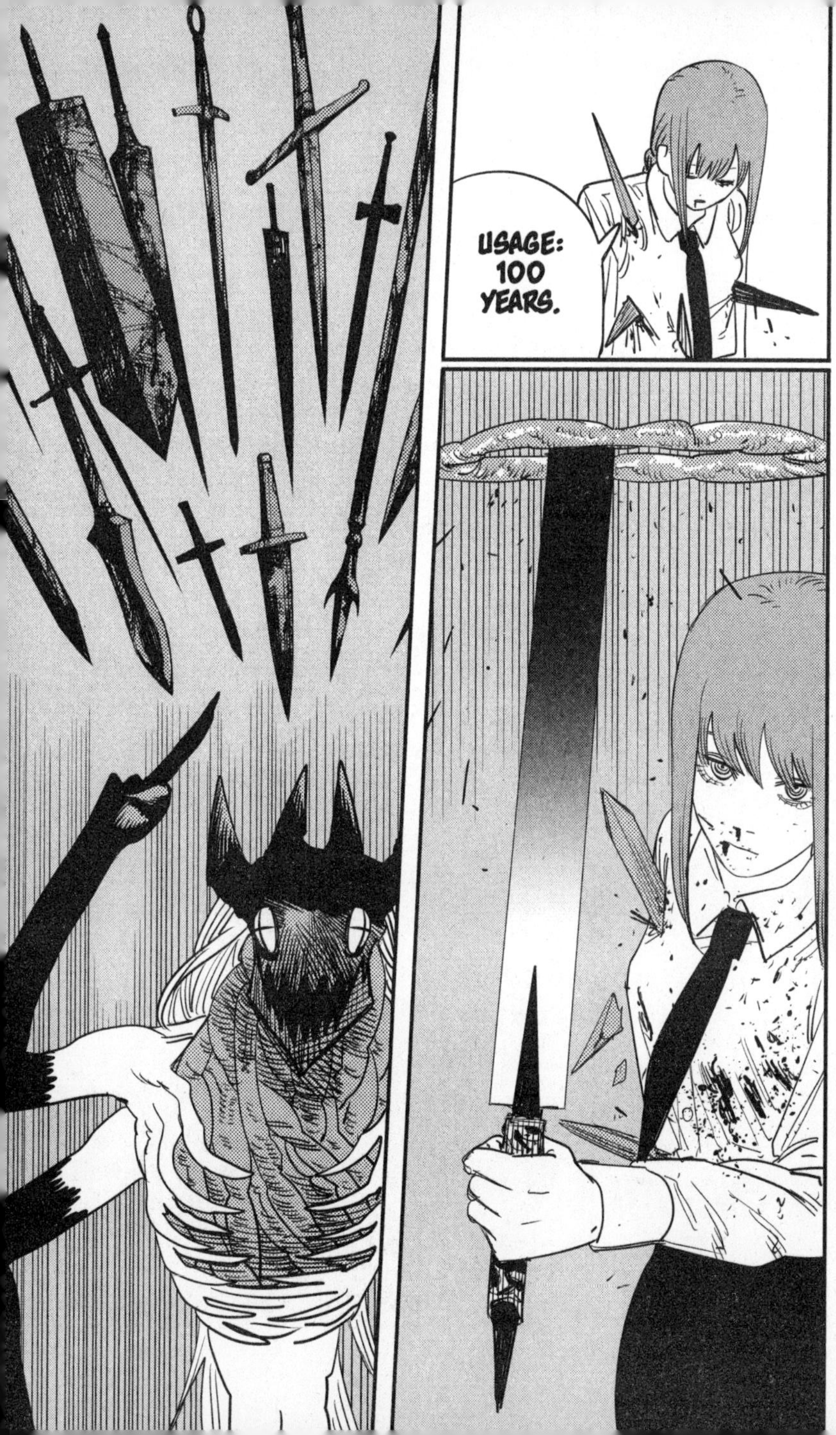
USAGE: 100 YEARS.

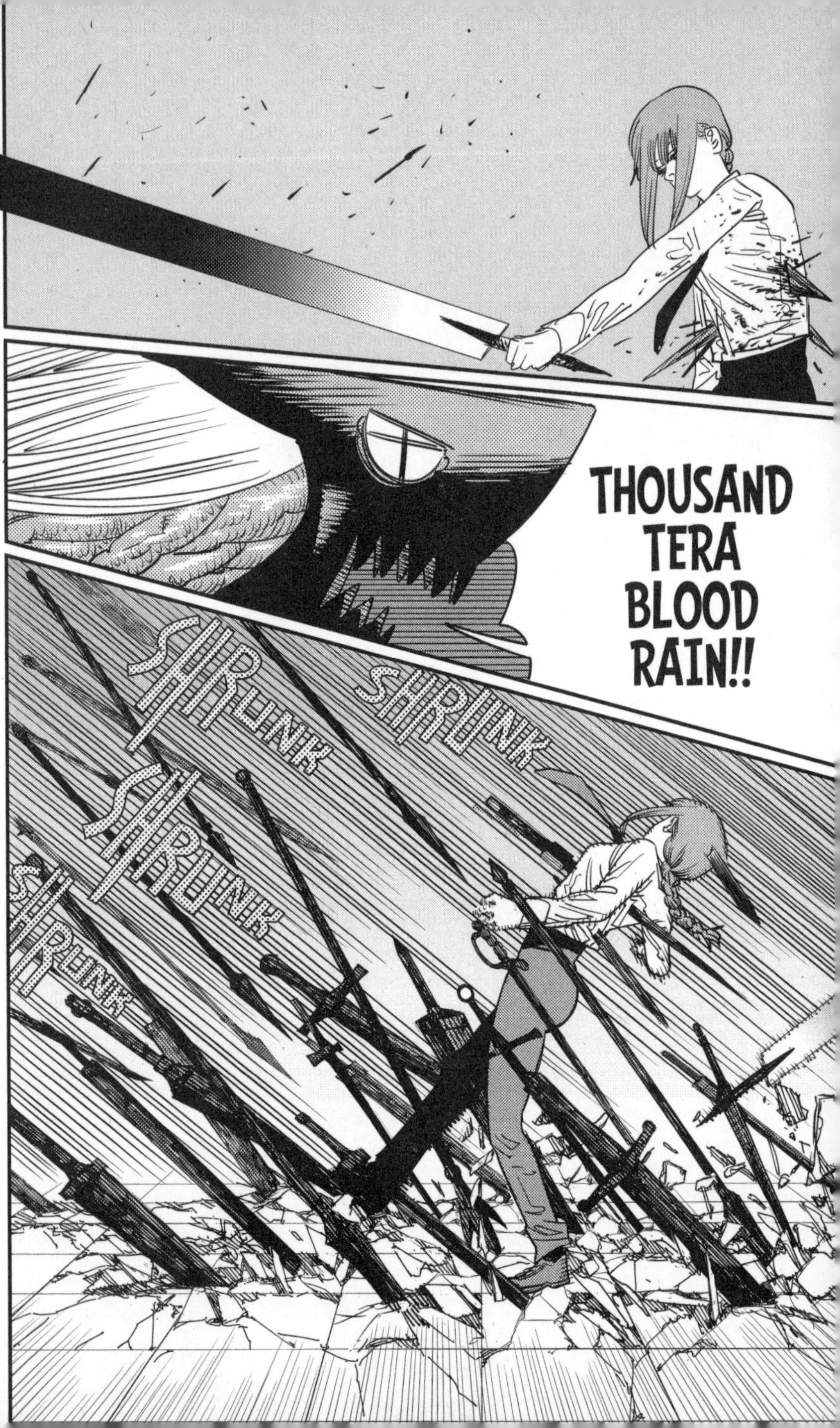
THOUSAND TERA BLOOD RAIN!!
SHRUNK
SHRUNK
SHRUNK
SHRUNK

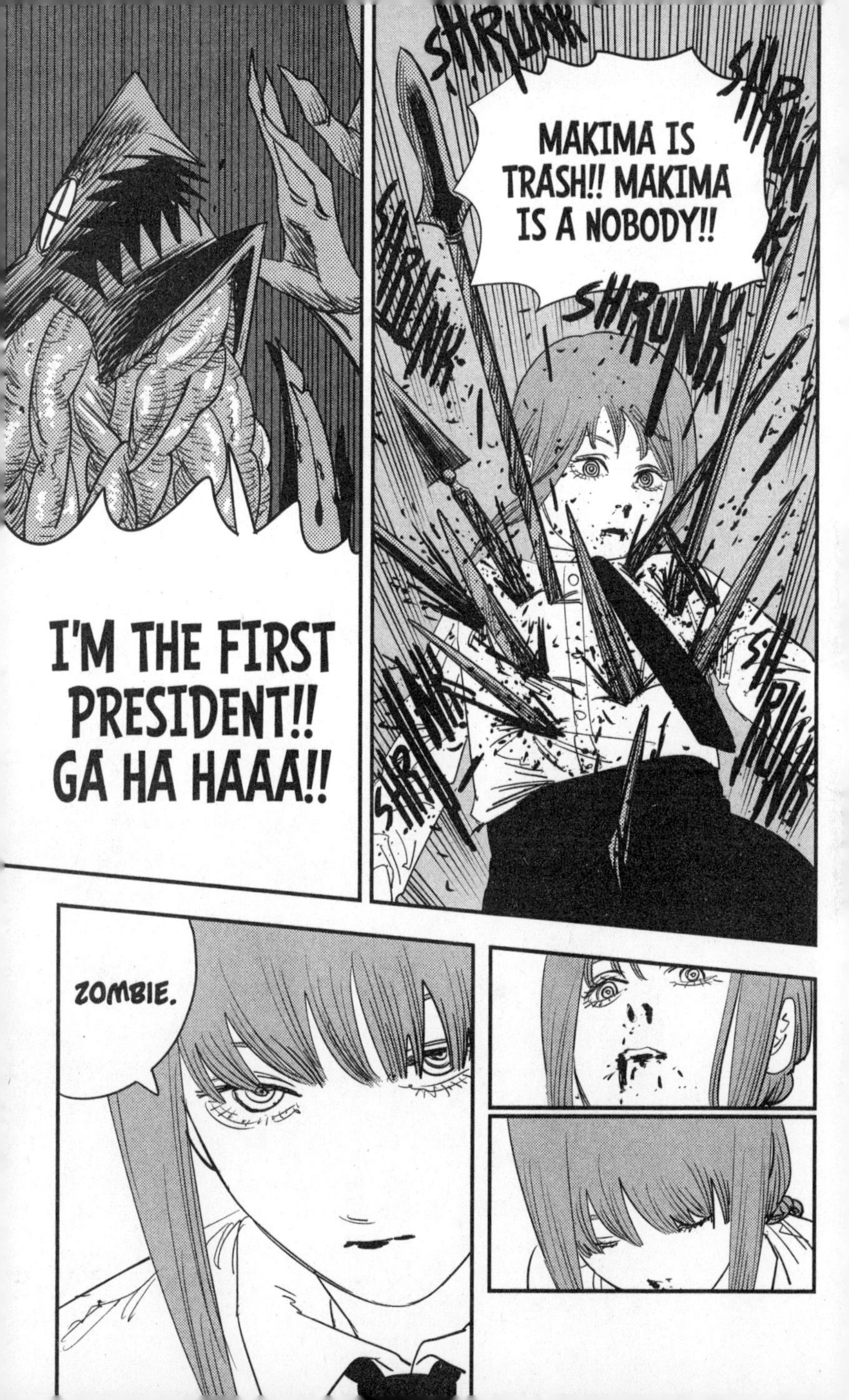
SHRUNK
SHRUNK
MAKIMA IS TRASH!! MAKIMA IS A NOBODY!!
SHRUNK
SHRUNK
SHRUNK
SHRUNK
I'M THE FIRST PRESIDENT!! GA HA HAAAA!!
ZOMBIE.

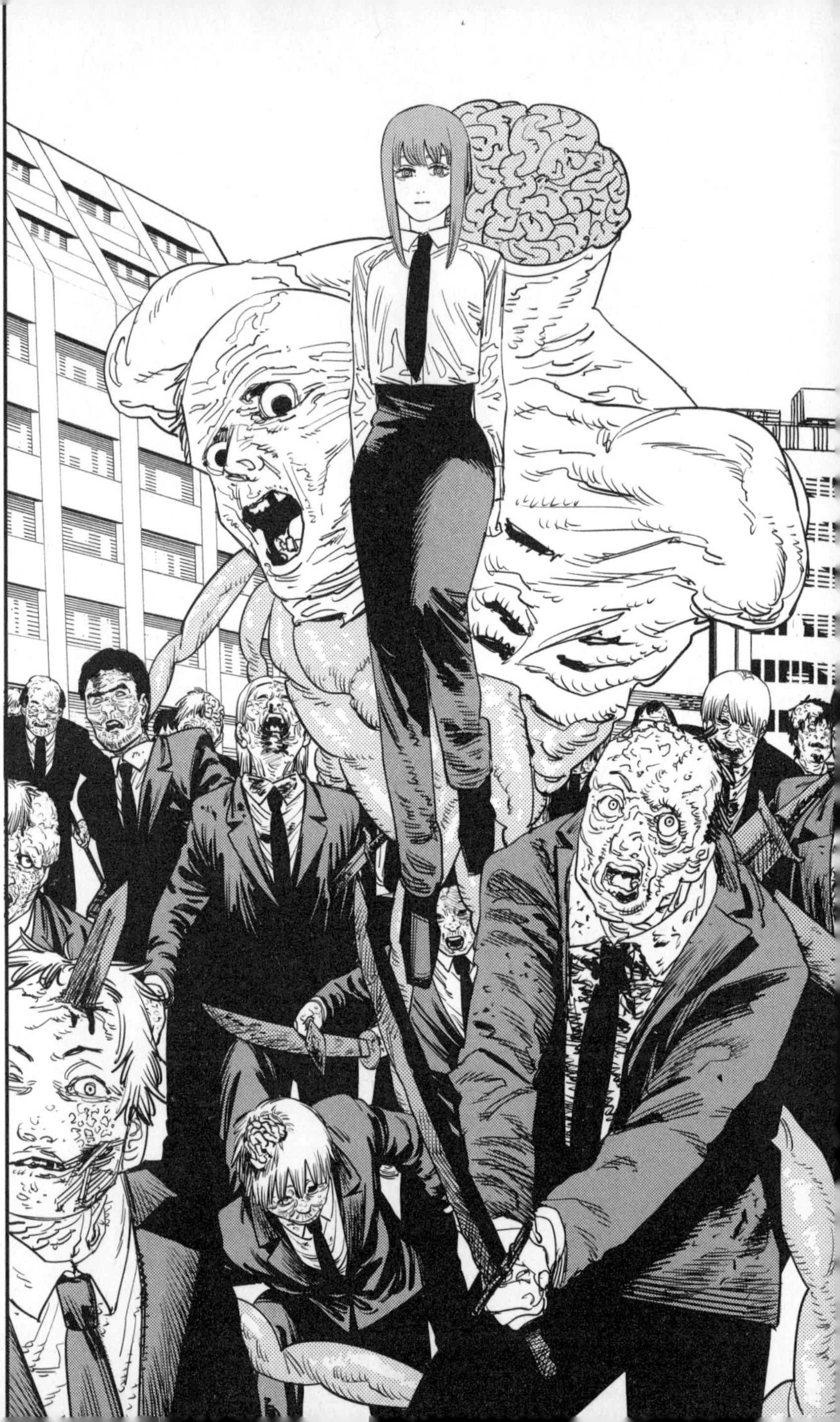

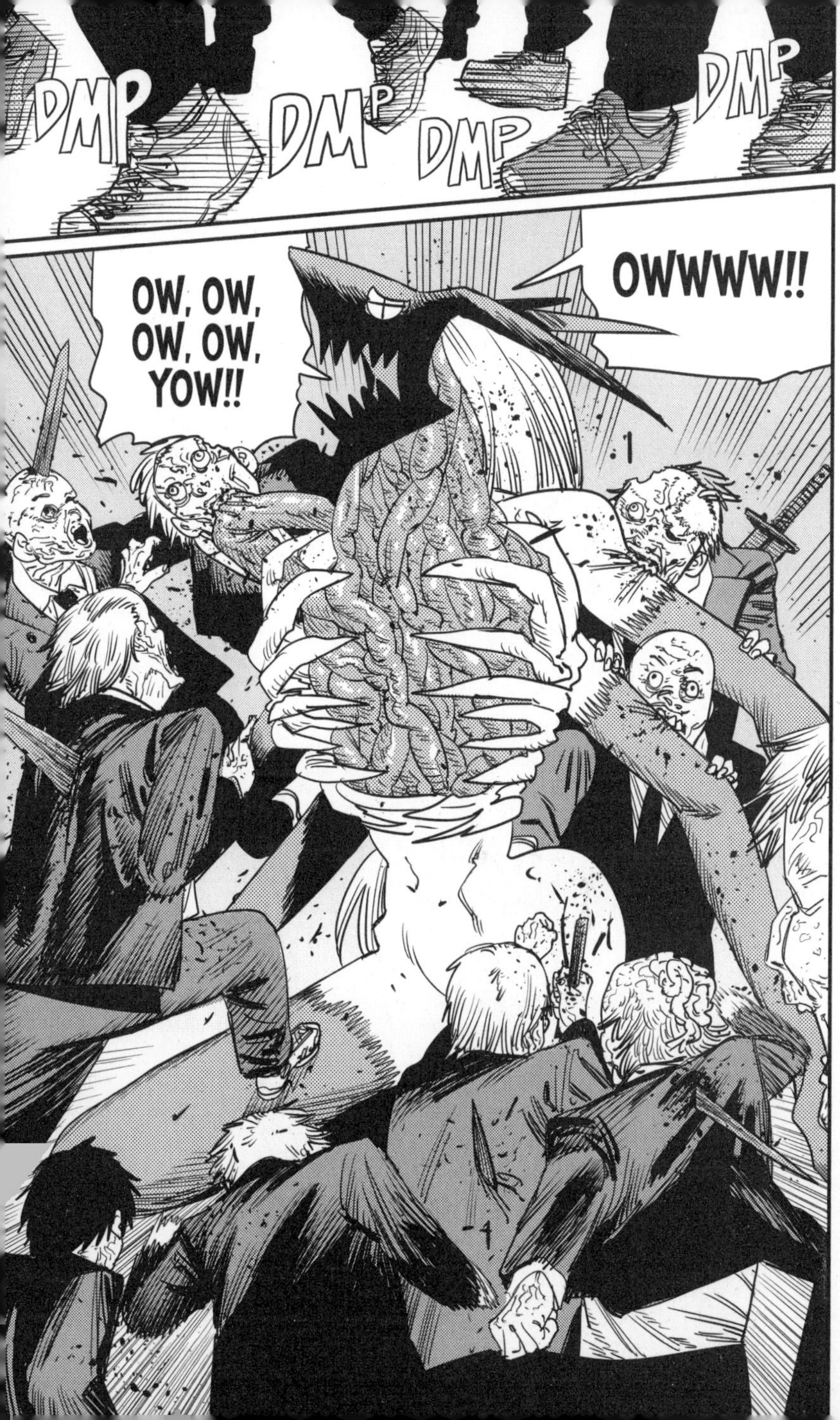
DMP
DMP
DMP
DMP
OWWWW!!
OW, OW, OW, OW, YOW!!

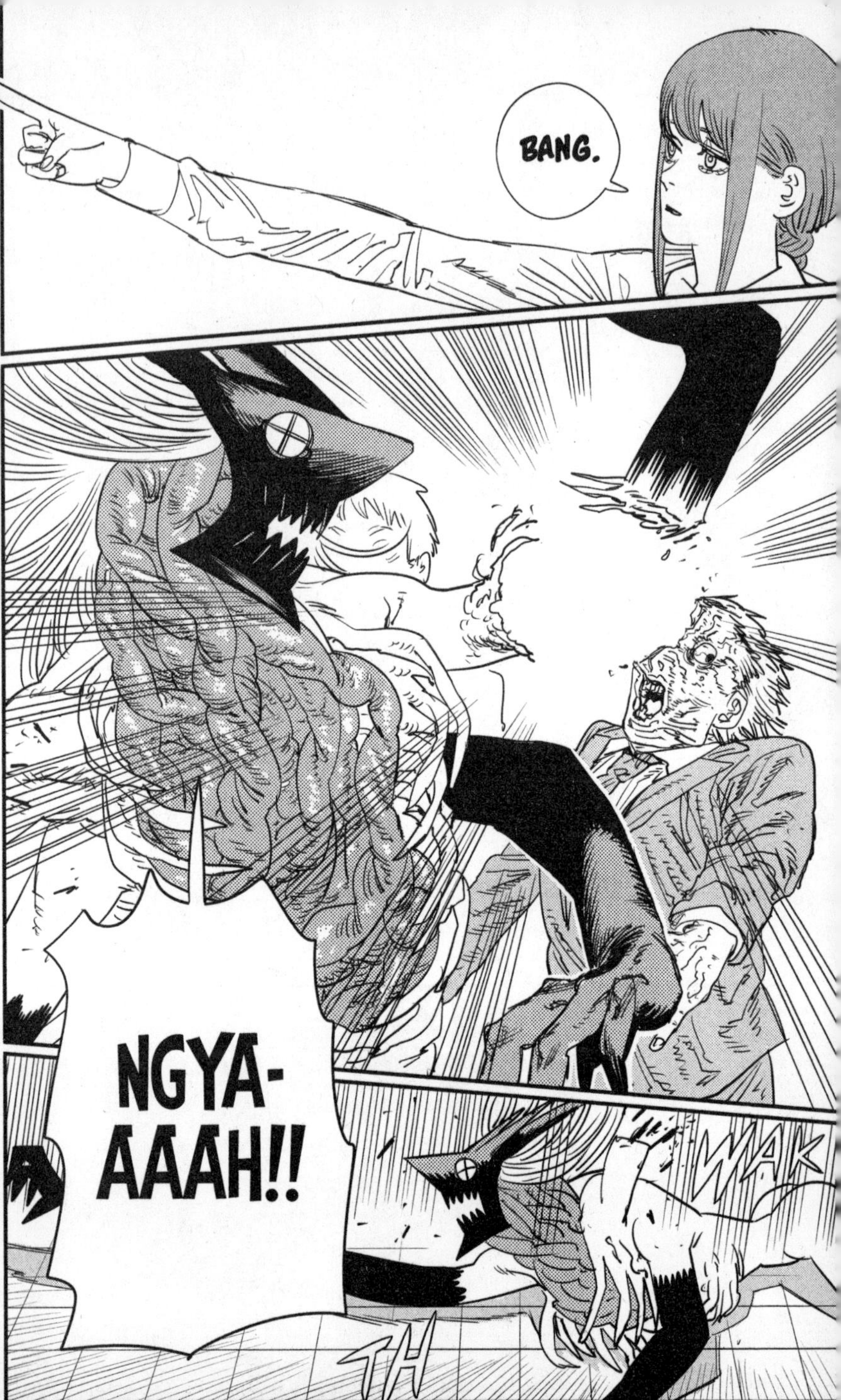
BANG.
NGYA-AAAH!!
WAK
TH

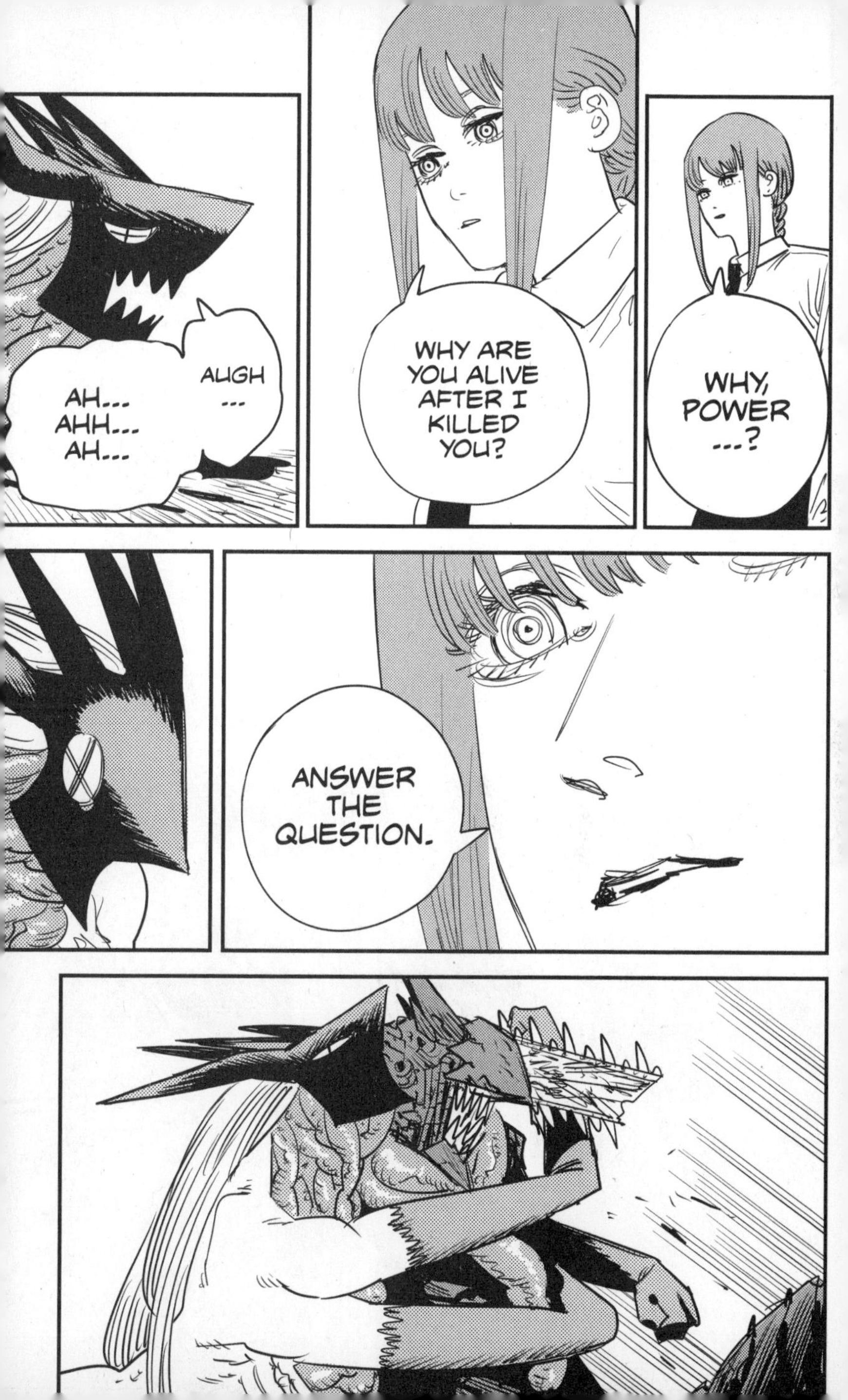
WHY, POWER ...?
WHY ARE YOU ALIVE AFTER I KILLED YOU?
AUGH ...
AH... AHH... AH...
ANSWER THE QUESTION.

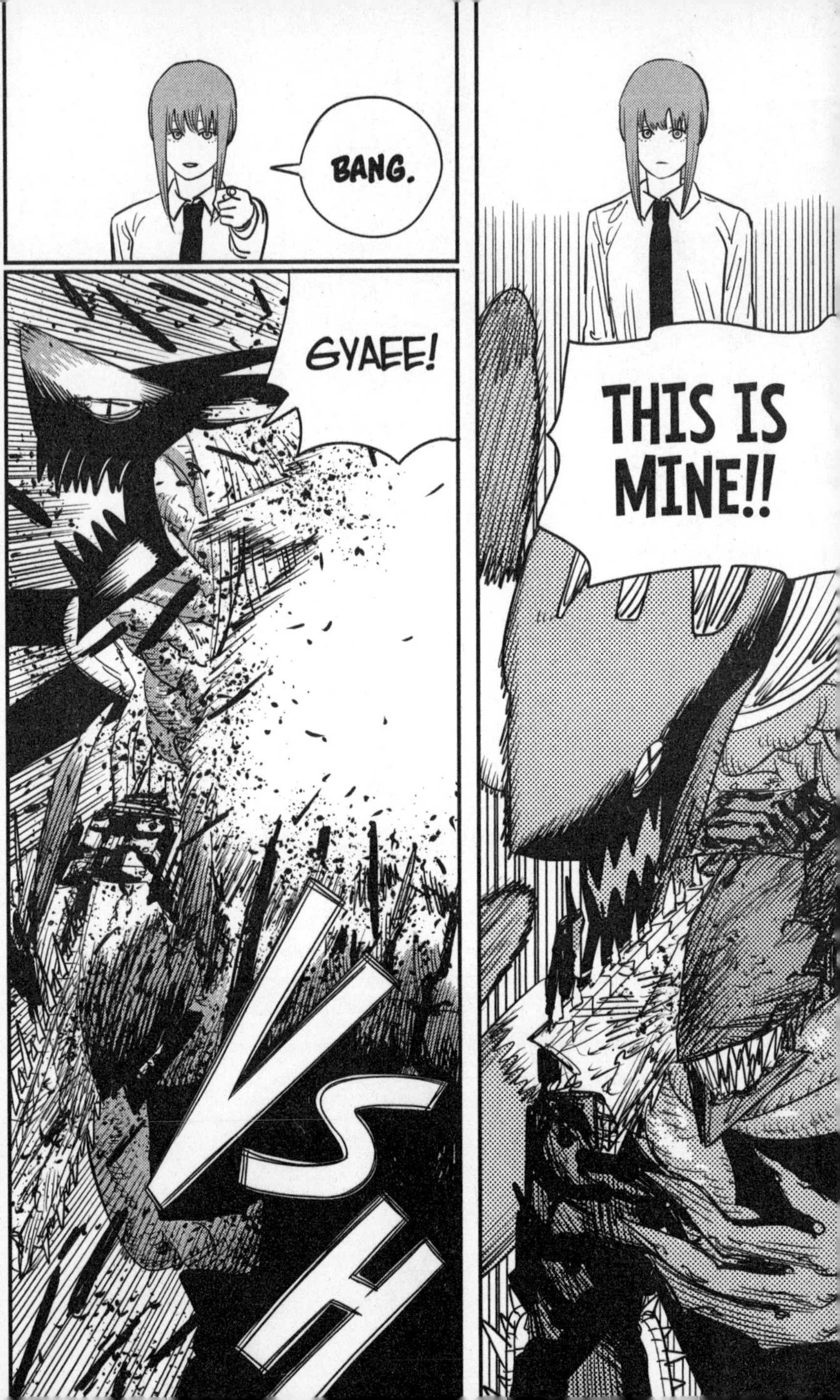
THIS IS MINE!!
BANG.
GYAEE!
VSH

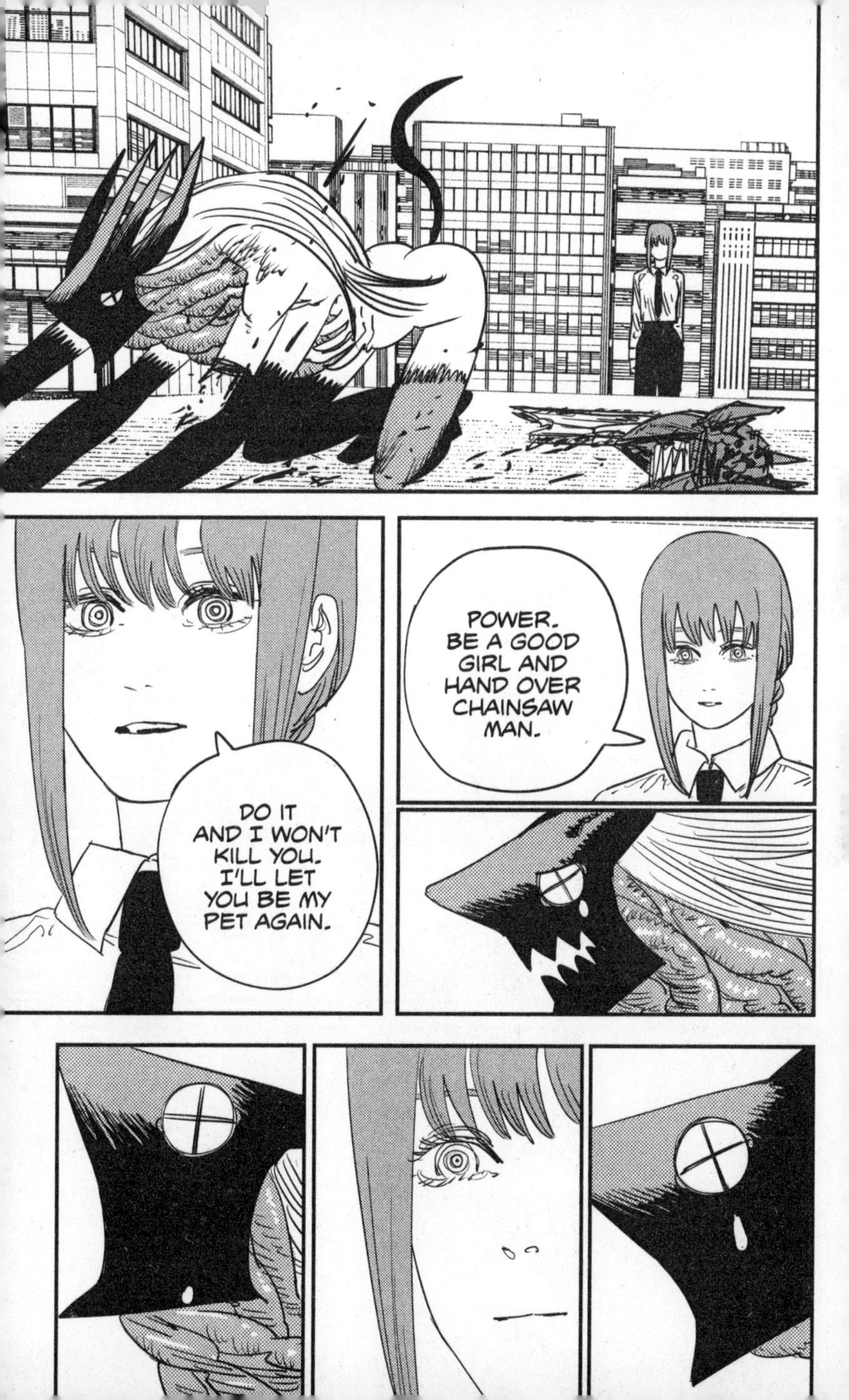
POWER. BE A GOOD GIRL AND HAND OVER CHAINSAW MAN.
DO IT AND I WON'T KILL YOU. I'LL LET YOU BE MY PET AGAIN.

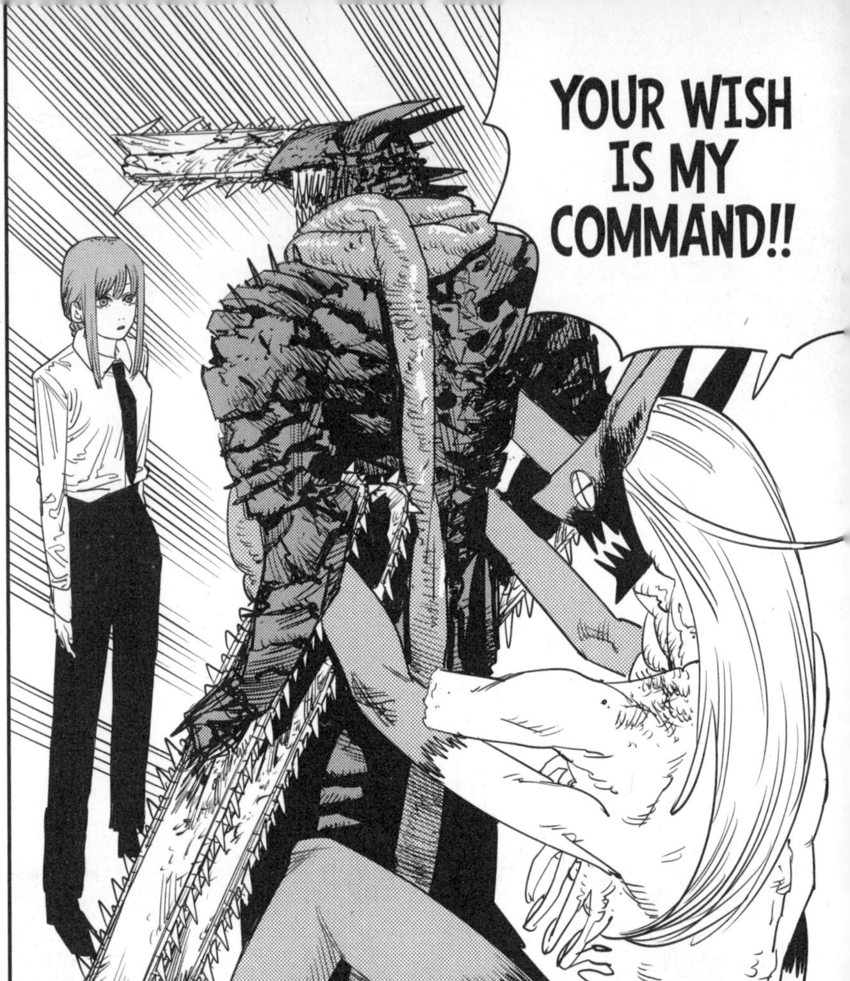
YOUR WISH IS MY COMMAND!!
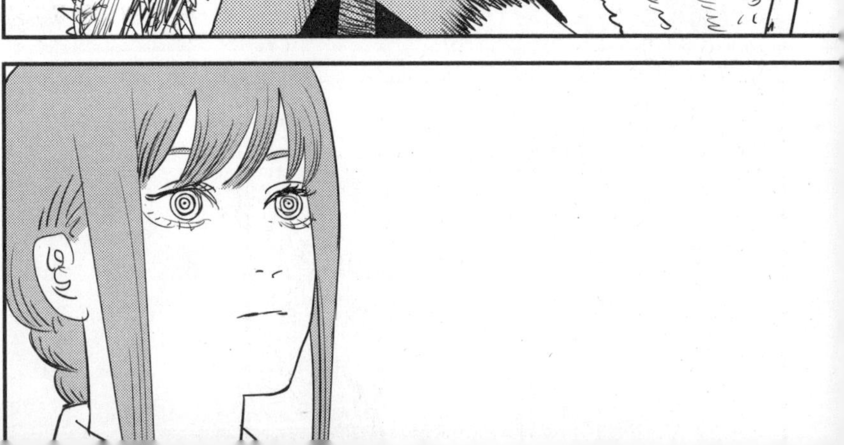

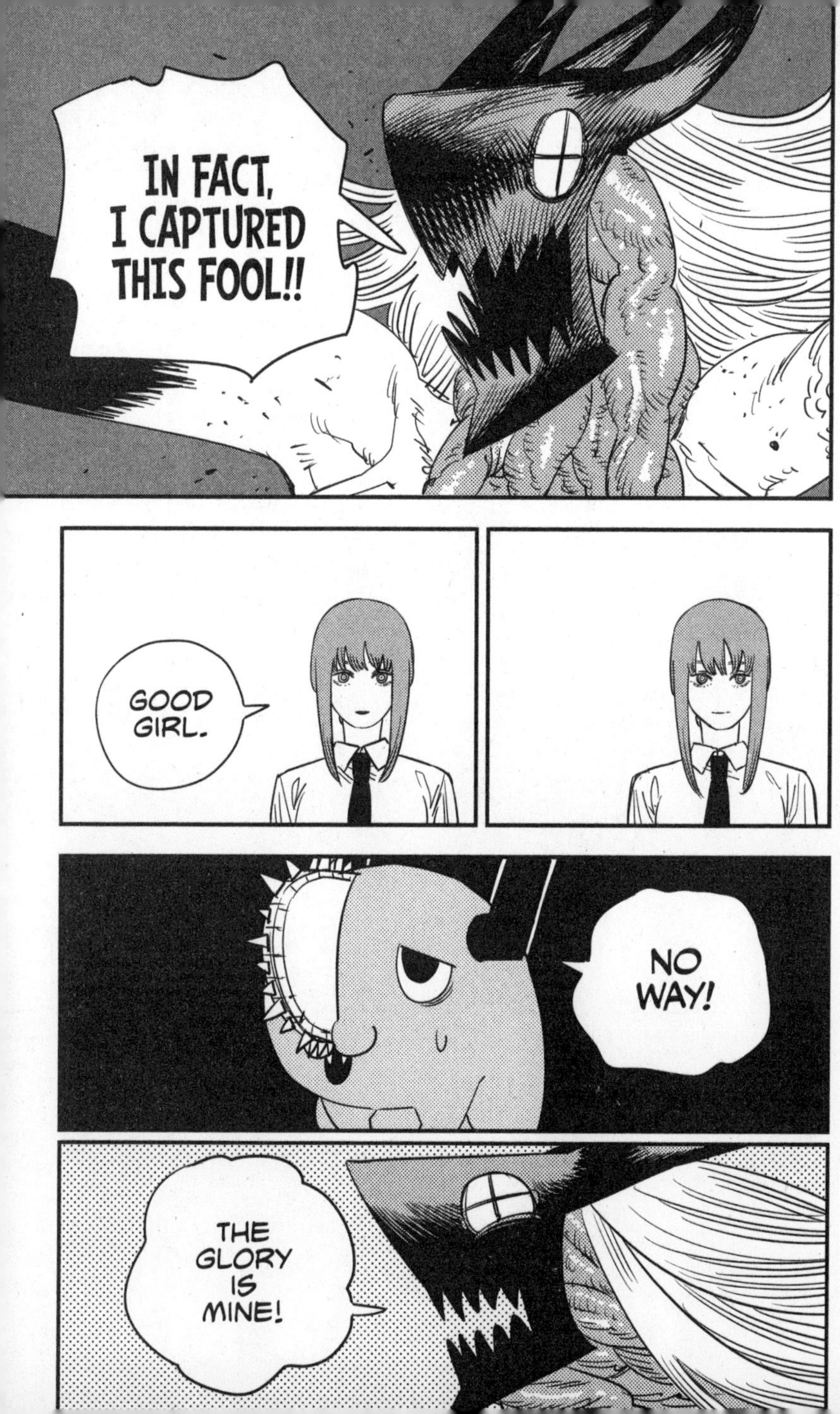
IN FACT, I CAPTURED THIS FOOL!!
GOOD GIRL.
NO WAY!
THE GLORY IS MINE!

CHAINSAW MAN

Chapter 91: Power, Power, Power

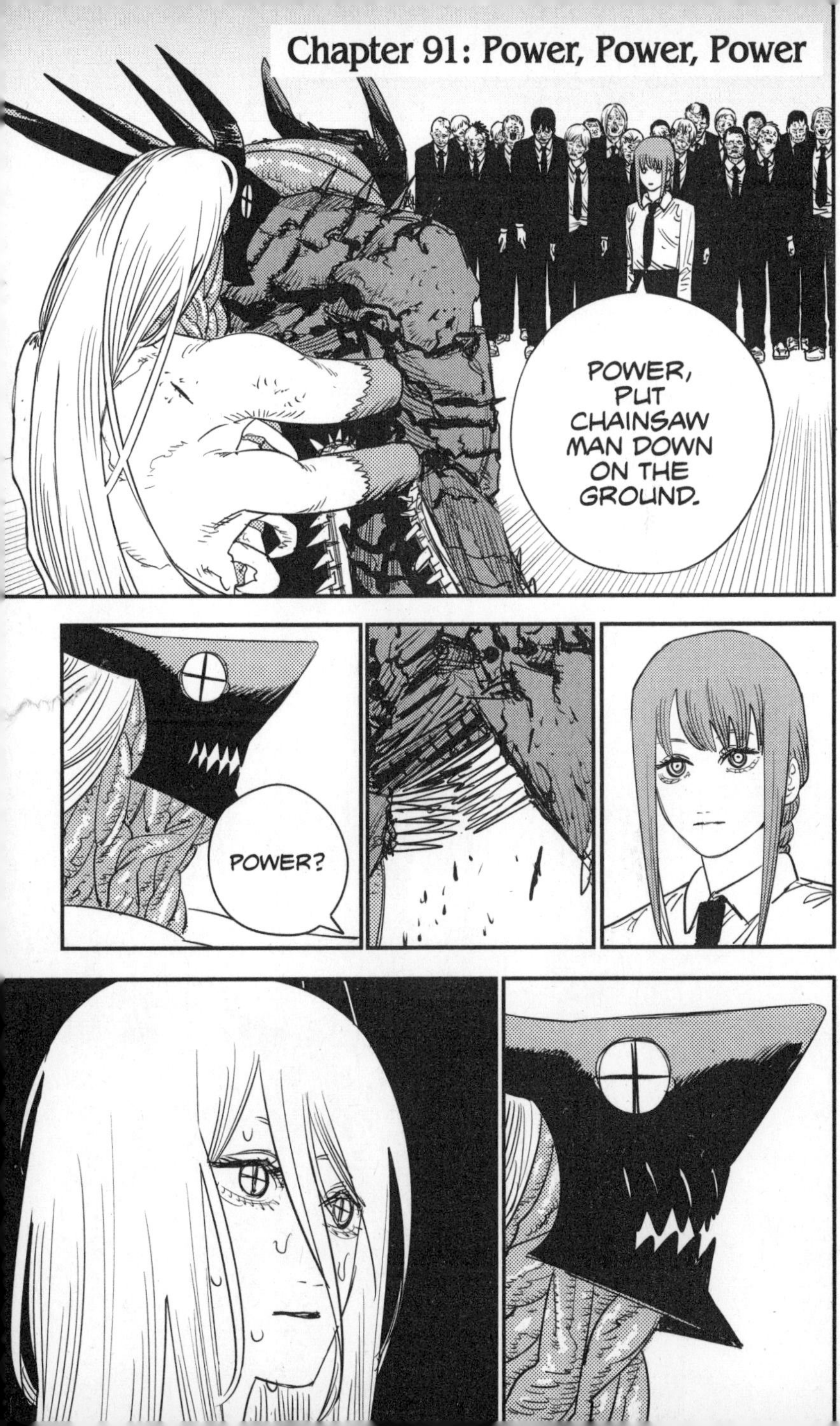
POWER, PUT CHAINSAW MAN DOWN ON THE GROUND.
POWER?

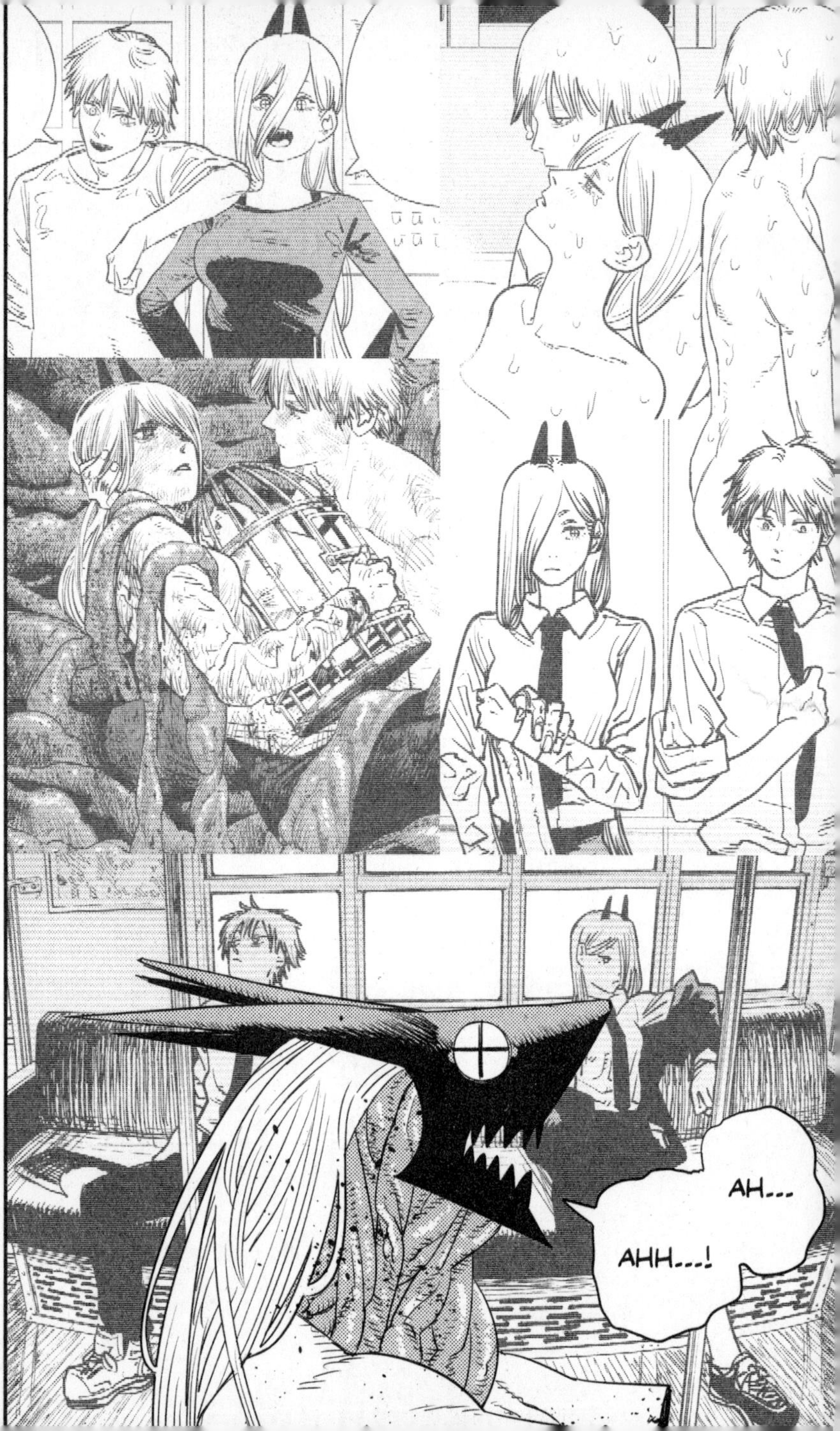
AH...
AHH...!

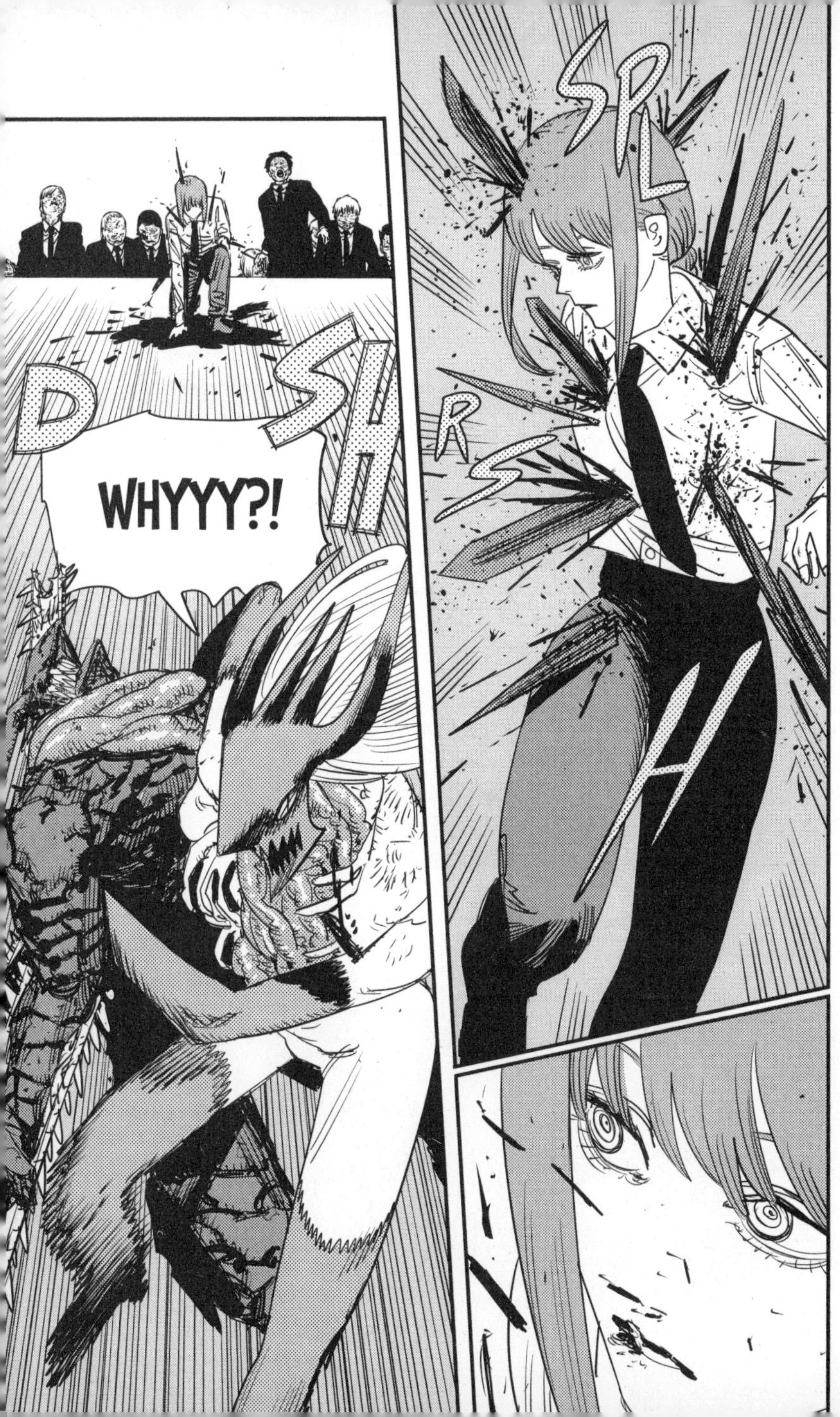
SPL
RSH
DSH
WHYYY?!

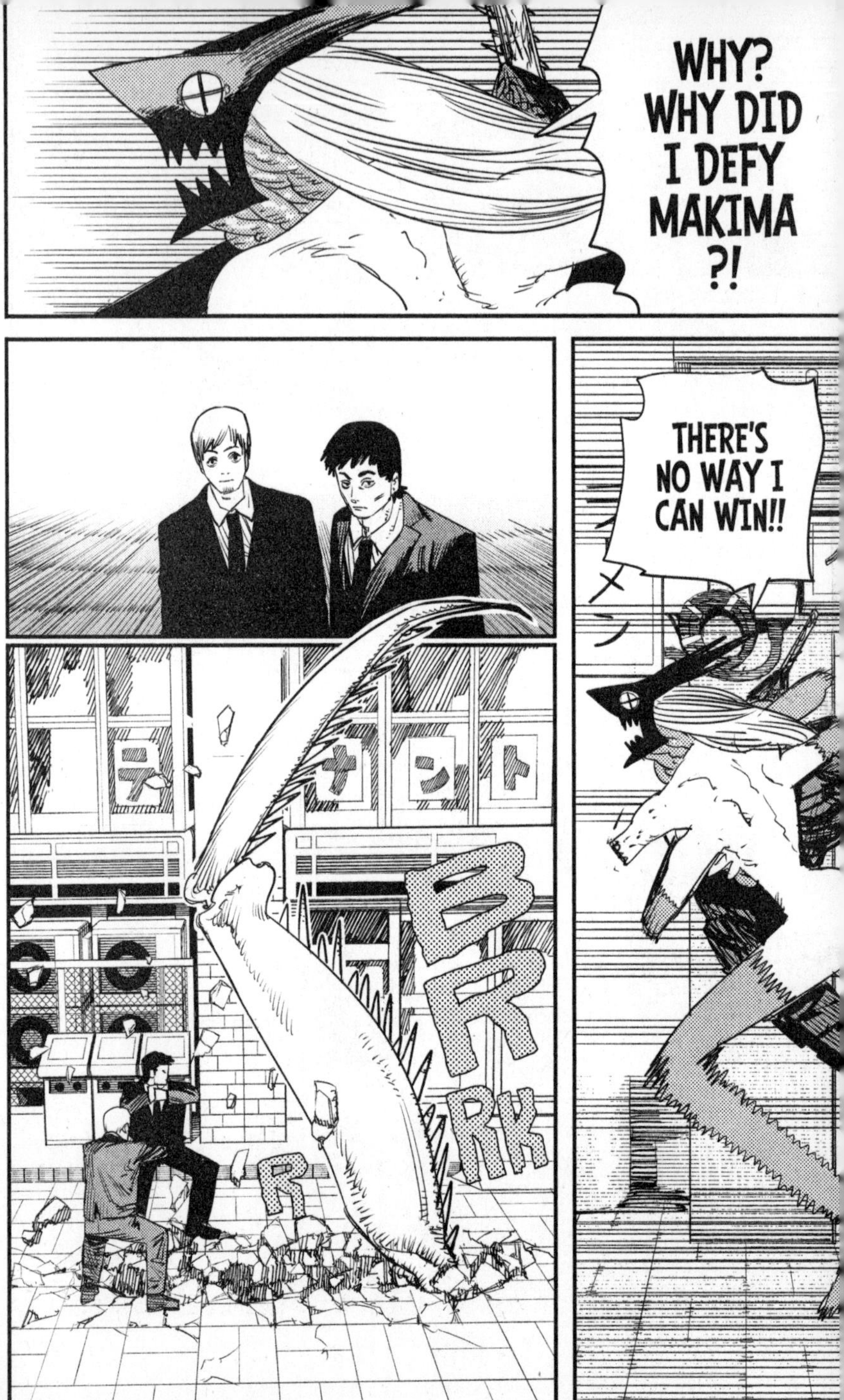
WHY? WHY DID I DEFY MAKIMA?!
THERE'S NO WAY I CAN WIN!!
BRRRK

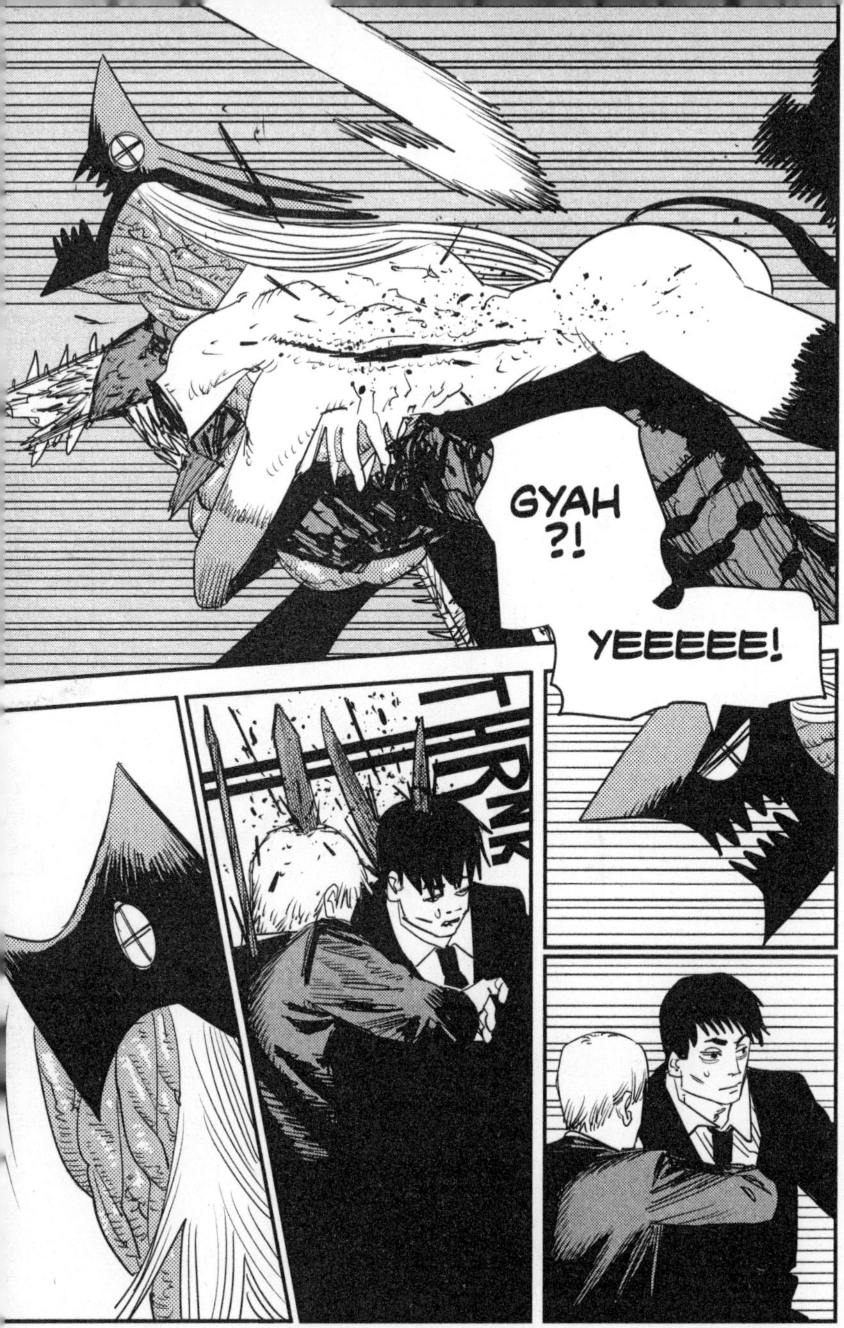
GYAH ?!
YEEEEEE!
TRNK

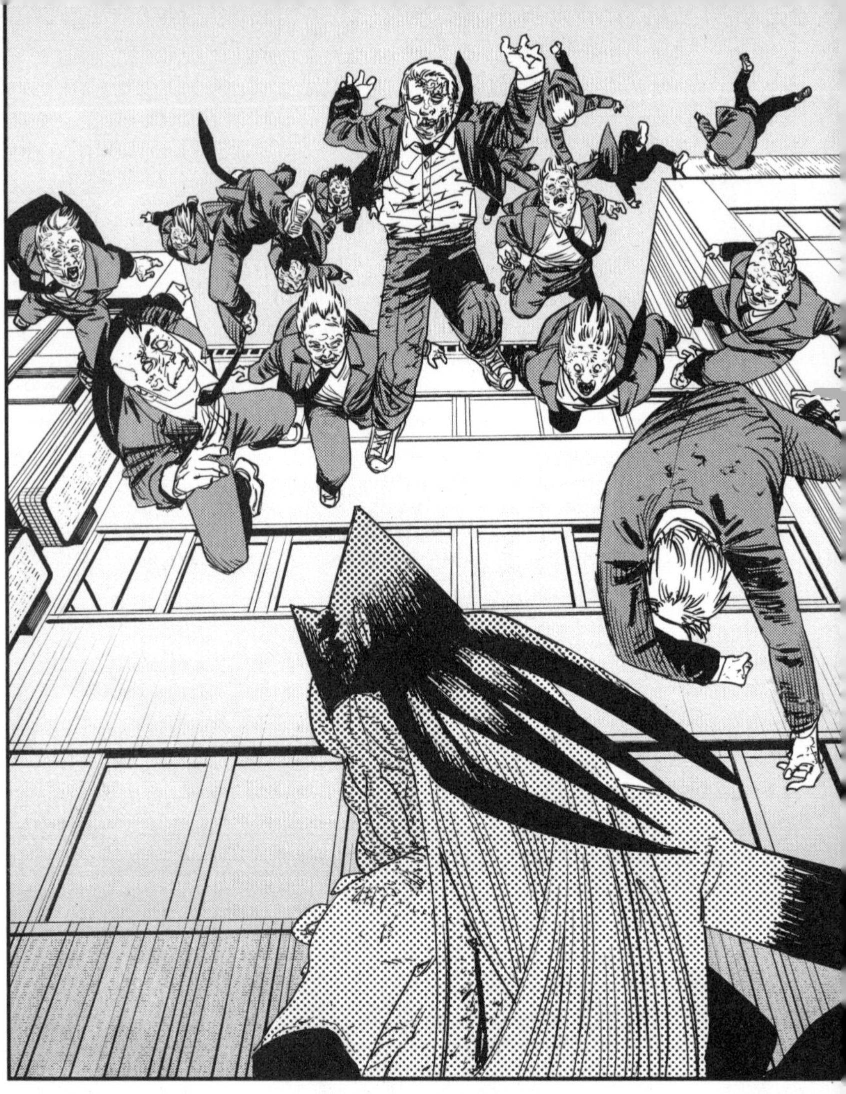
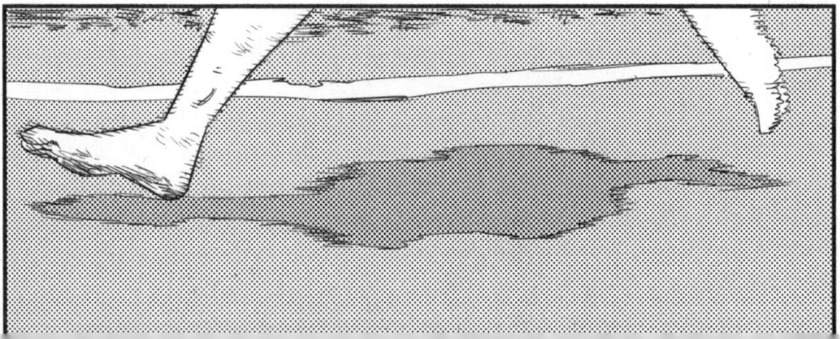

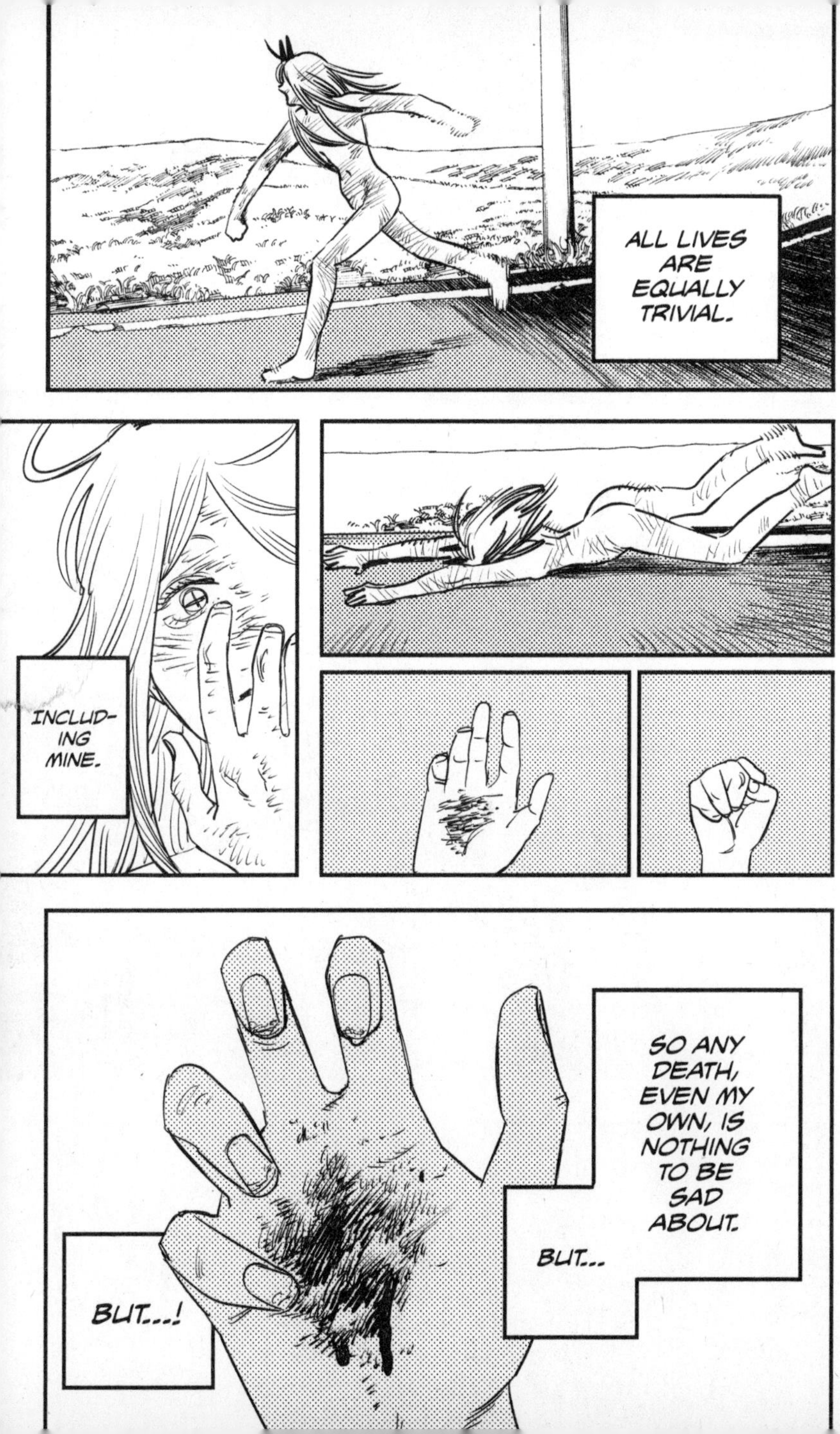
ALL LIVES ARE EQUALLY TRIVIAL.
INCLUD-ING MINE.
SO ANY DEATH, EVEN MY OWN, IS NOTHING TO BE SAD ABOUT.
BUT...
BUT...!

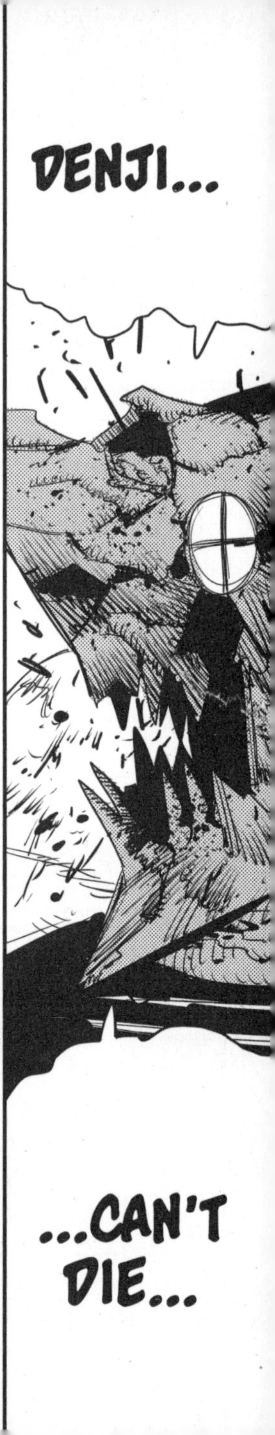
DENJI...
...CAN'T DIE...
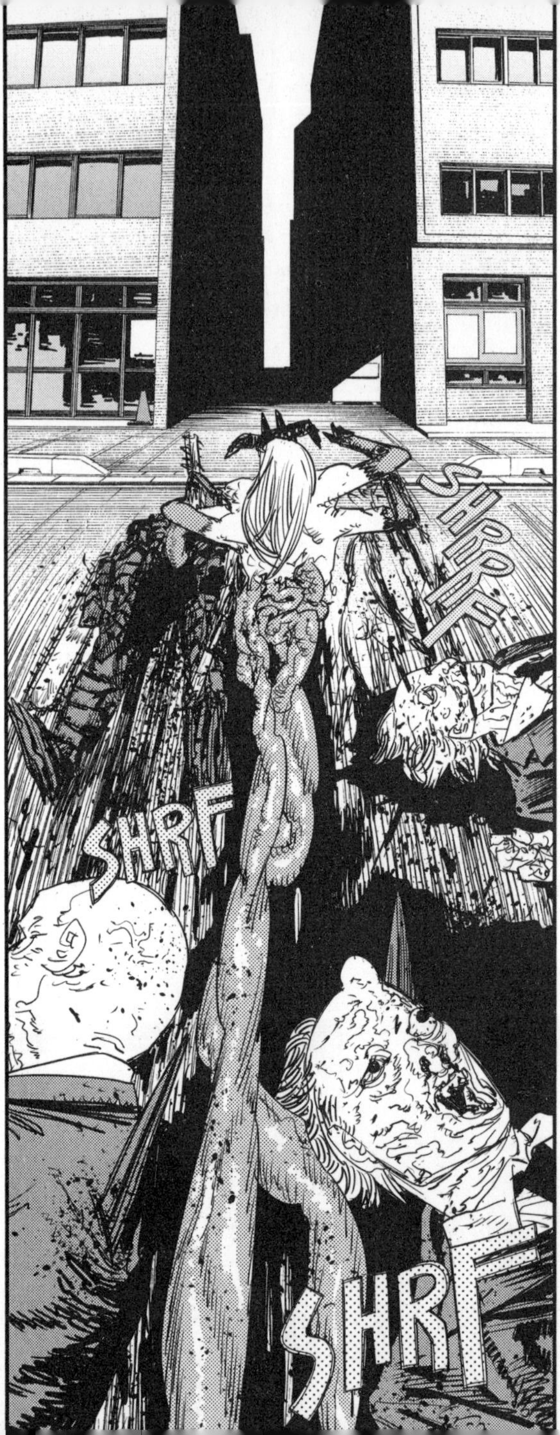
SHRF
SHRF
SHRF

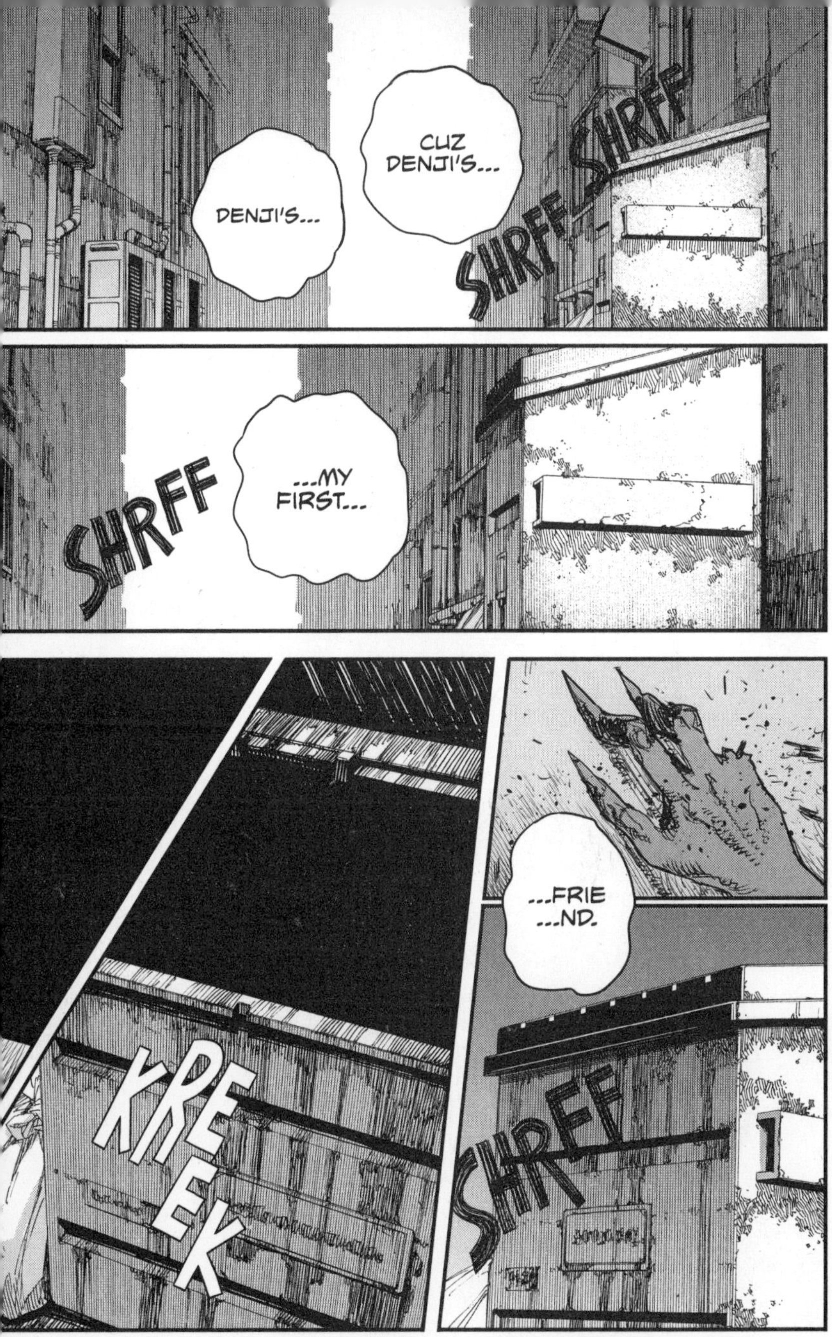
SHRFF SHRFF
CUZ DENJI'S...
DENJI'S...
SHRFF
...MY FIRST...
SHRFF
...FRIE ...ND.
SHRFF
KREEK

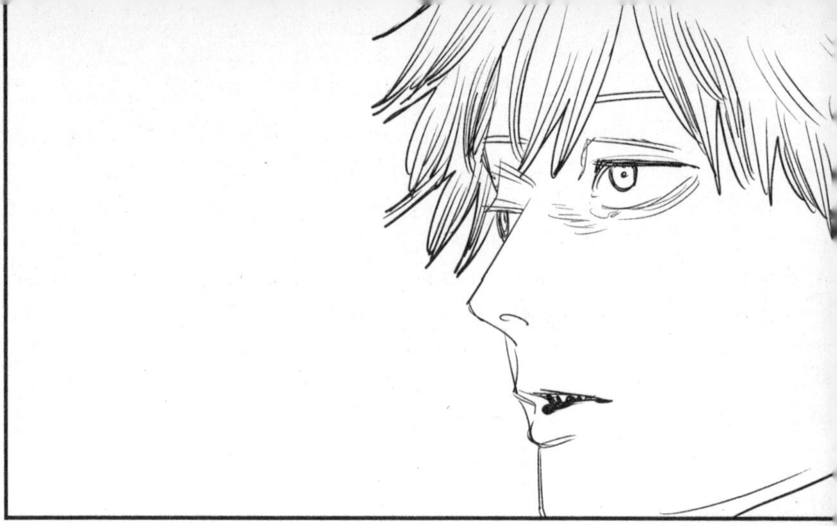
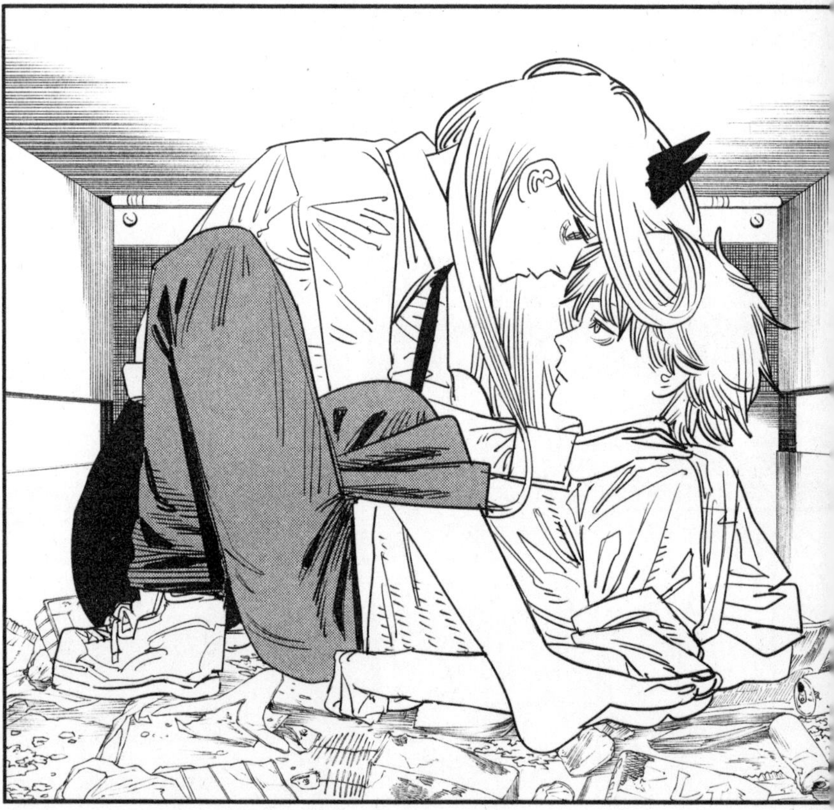

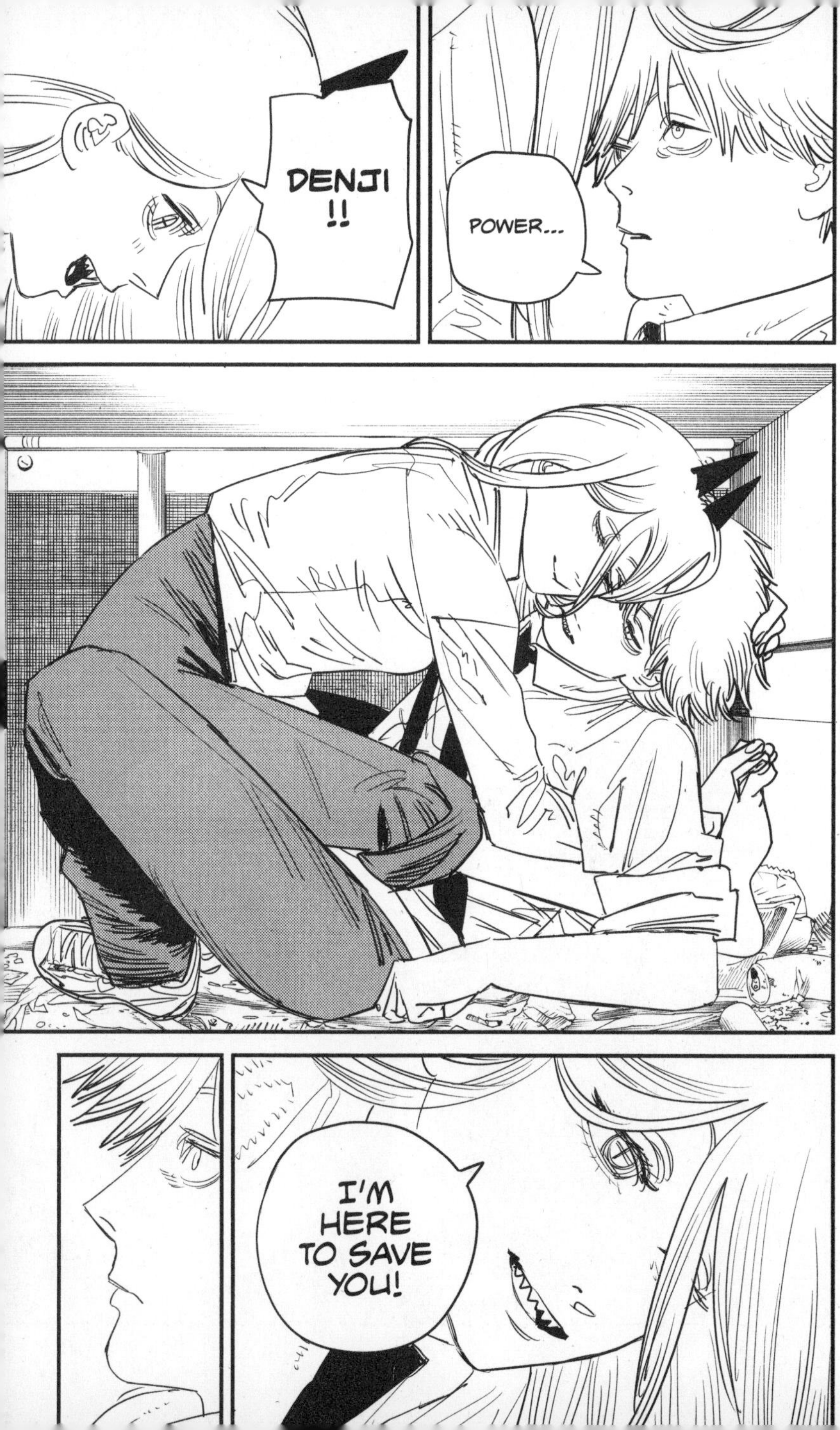
POWER...
DENJI !!
I'M HERE TO SAVE YOU!

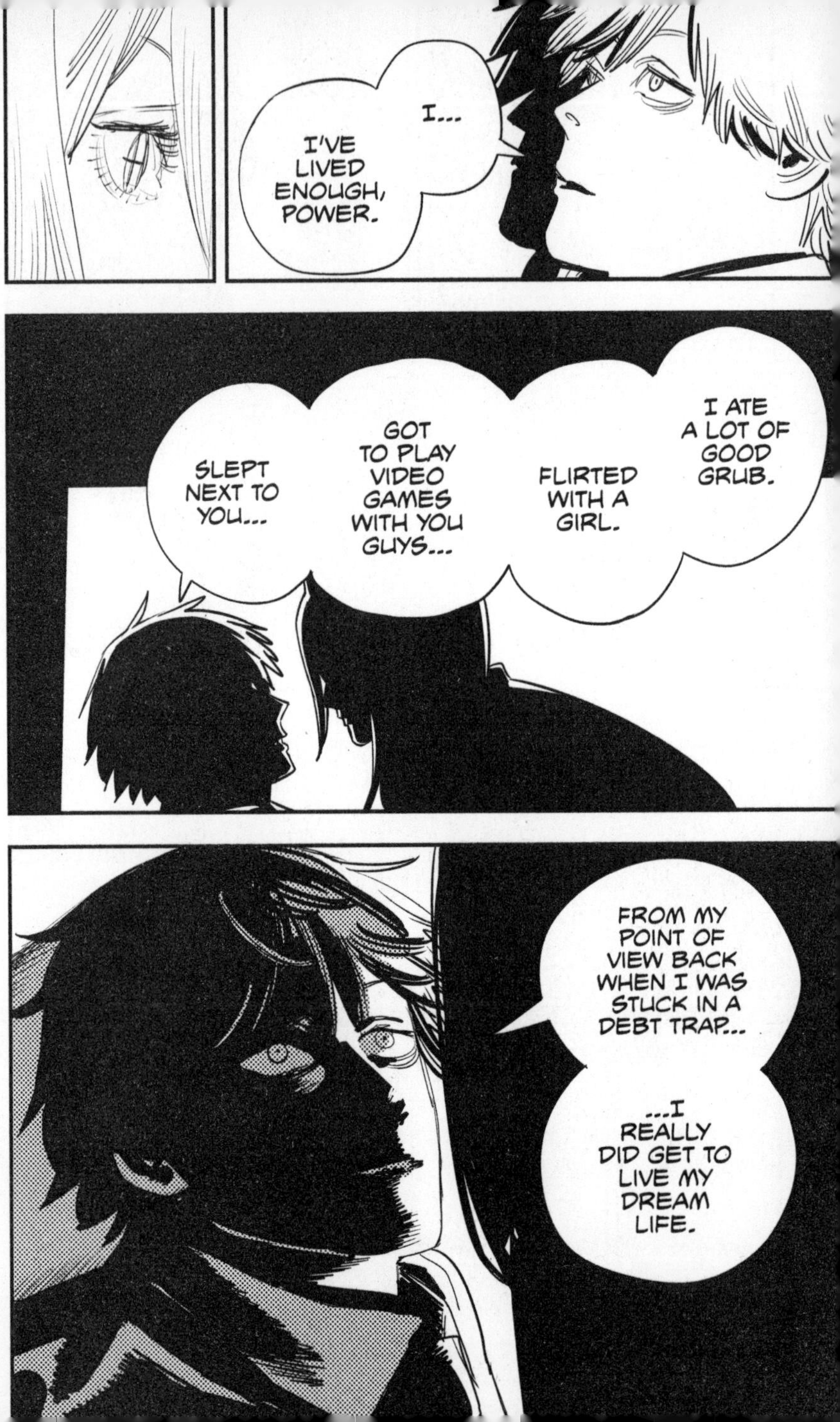
I...
I'VE LIVED ENOUGH, POWER.
I ATE A LOT OF GOOD GRUB.
FLIRTED WITH A GIRL.
GOT TO PLAY VIDEO GAMES WITH YOU GUYS...
SLEPT NEXT TO YOU...
FROM MY POINT OF VIEW BACK WHEN I WAS STUCK IN A DEBT TRAP...
...I REALLY DID GET TO LIVE MY DREAM LIFE.

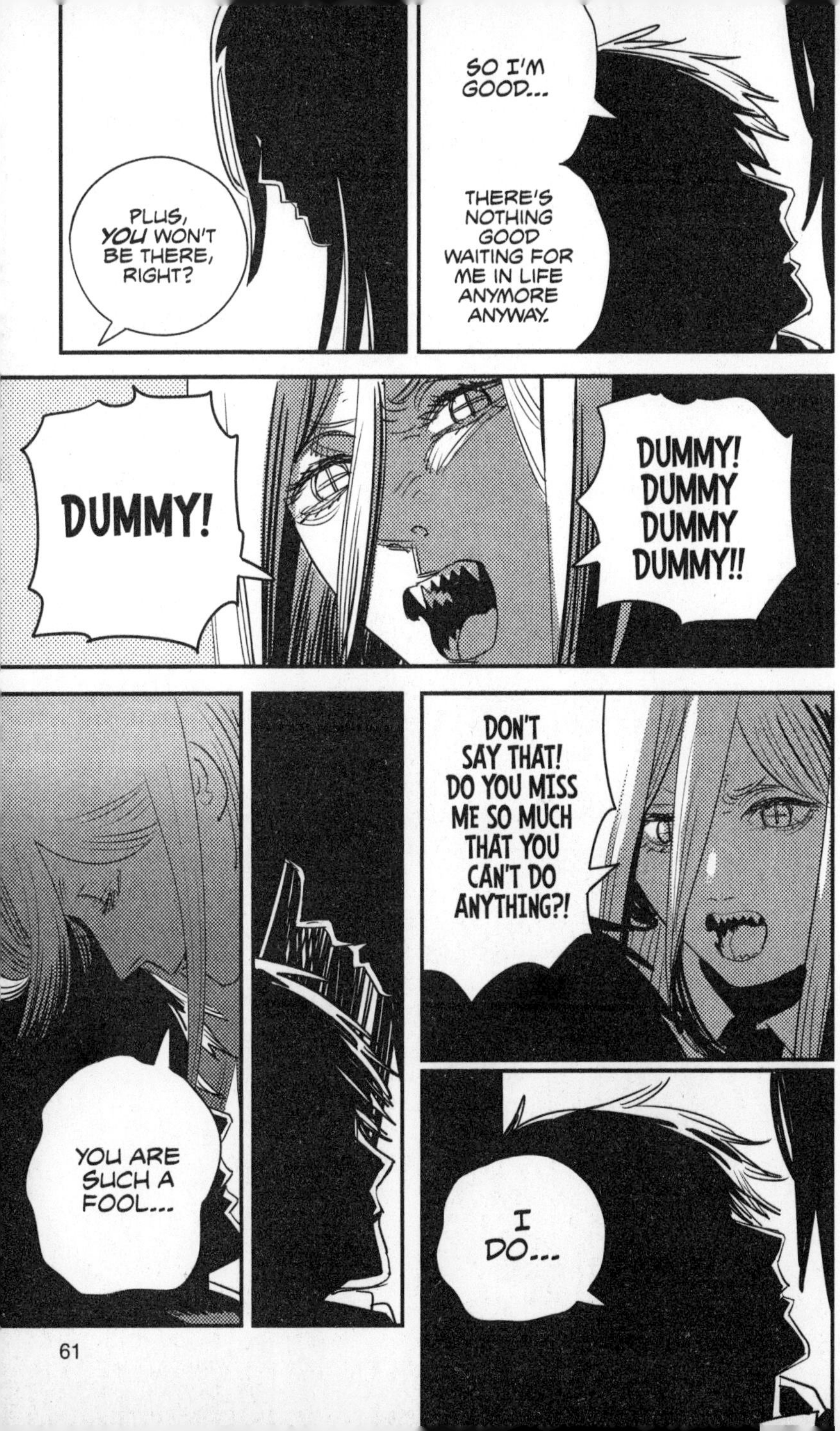
SO I'M GOOD...
THERE'S NOTHING GOOD WAITING FOR ME IN LIFE ANYMORE ANYWAY.
PLUS, YOU WON'T BE THERE, RIGHT?
DUMMY! DUMMY DUMMY DUMMY!!
DUMMY!
DON'T SAY THAT! DO YOU MISS ME SO MUCH THAT YOU CAN'T DO ANYTHING?!
I DO...
YOU ARE SUCH A FOOL...

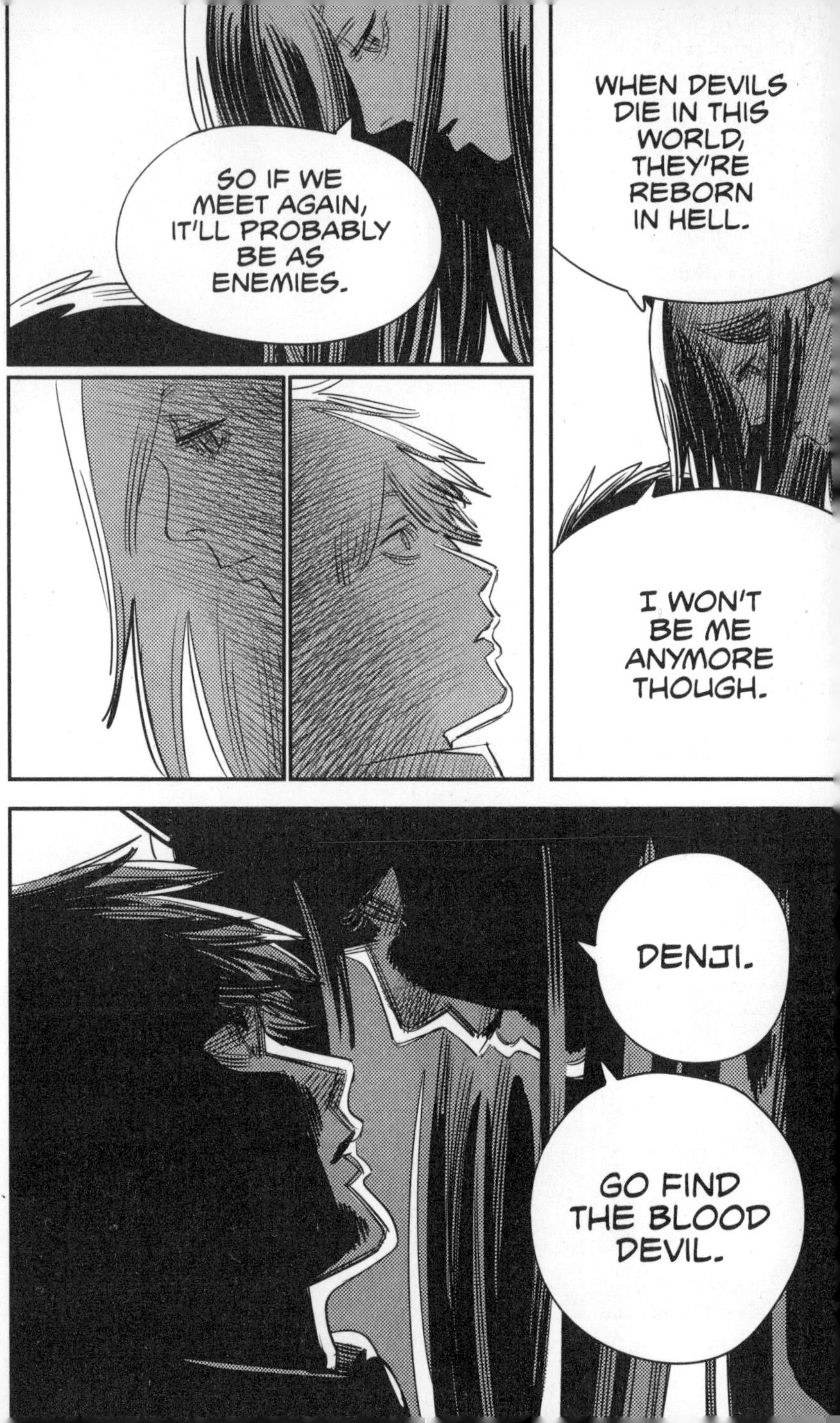
WHEN DEVILS DIE IN THIS WORLD, THEY'RE REBORN IN HELL.
I WON'T BE ME ANYMORE THOUGH.
SO IF WE MEET AGAIN, IT'LL PROBABLY BE AS ENEMIES.
DENJI.
GO FIND THE BLOOD DEVIL.

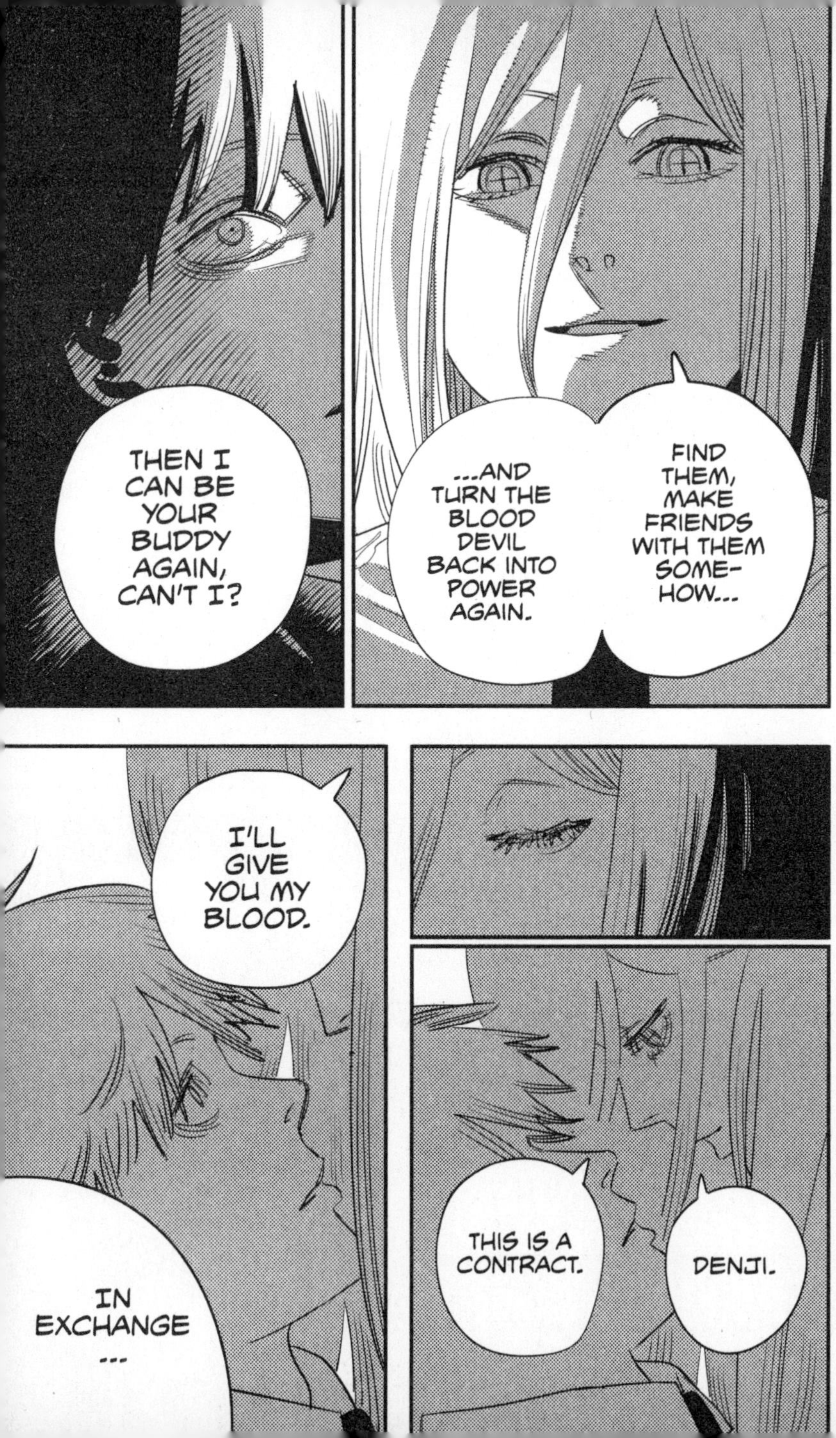
FIND THEM, MAKE FRIENDS WITH THEM SOME-HOW...
...AND TURN THE BLOOD DEVIL BACK INTO POWER AGAIN.
THEN I CAN BE YOUR BUDDY AGAIN, CAN'T I?
DENJI.
THIS IS A CONTRACT.
I'LL GIVE YOU MY BLOOD.
IN EXCHANGE ...

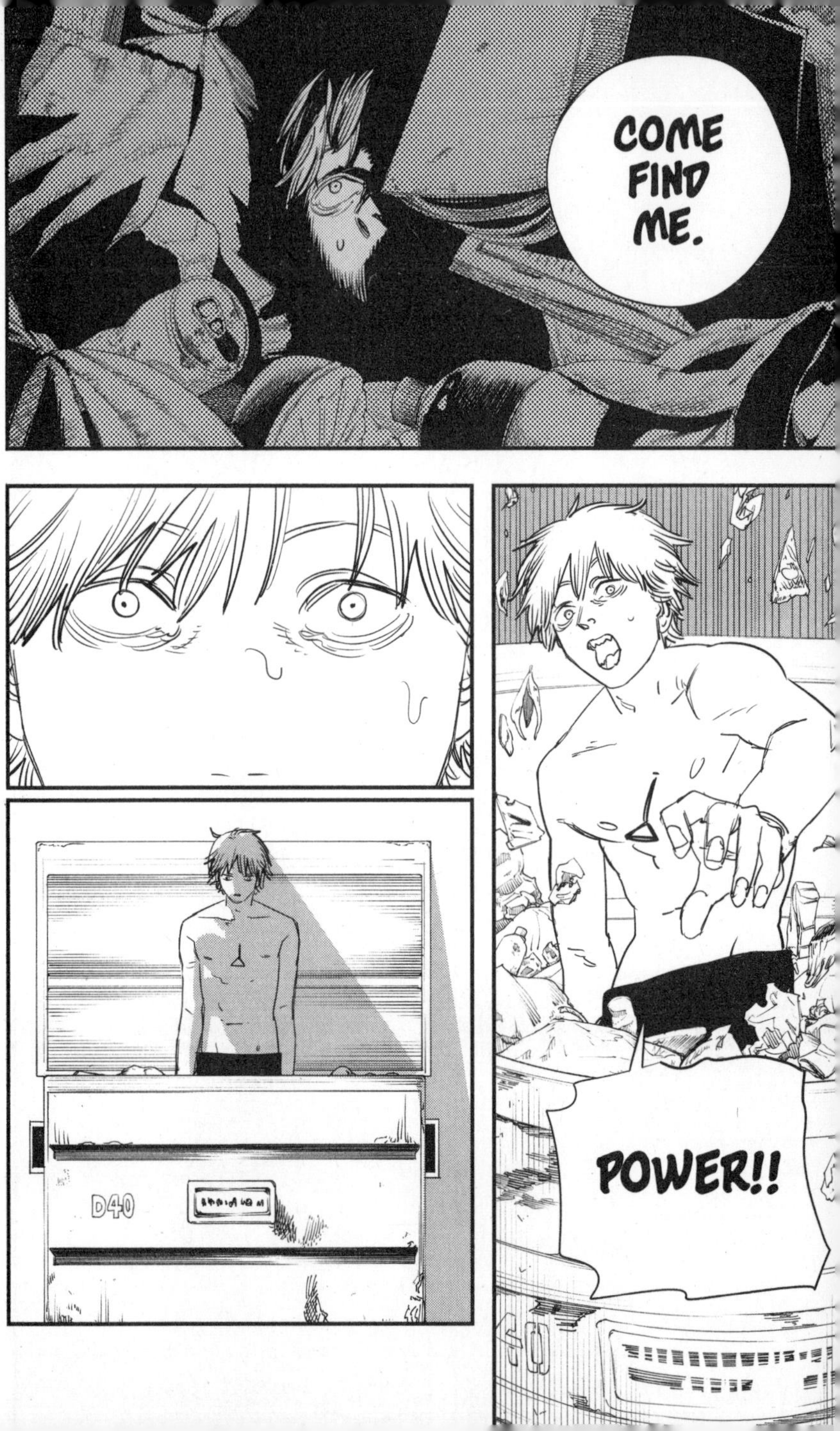
COME FIND ME.
POWER!!
D40

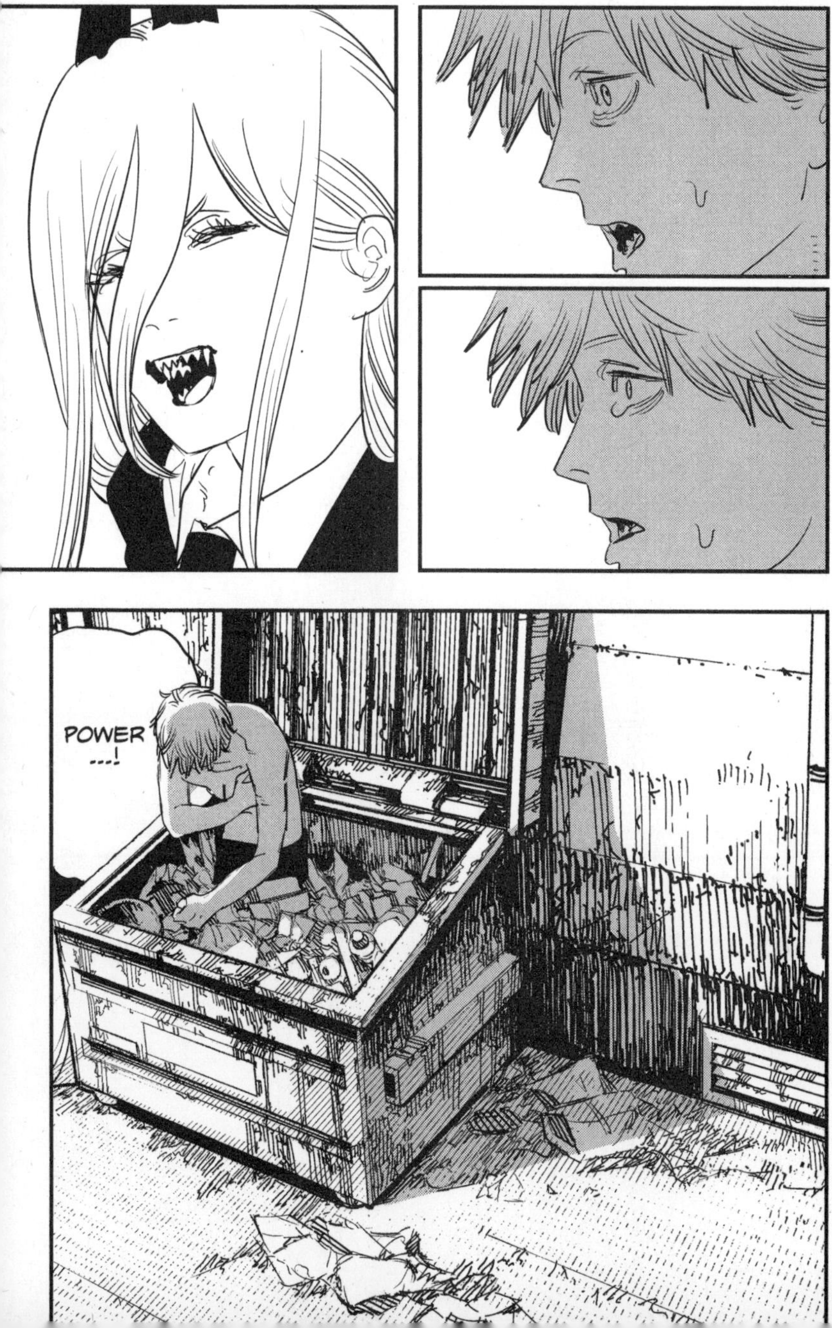
POWER
---!

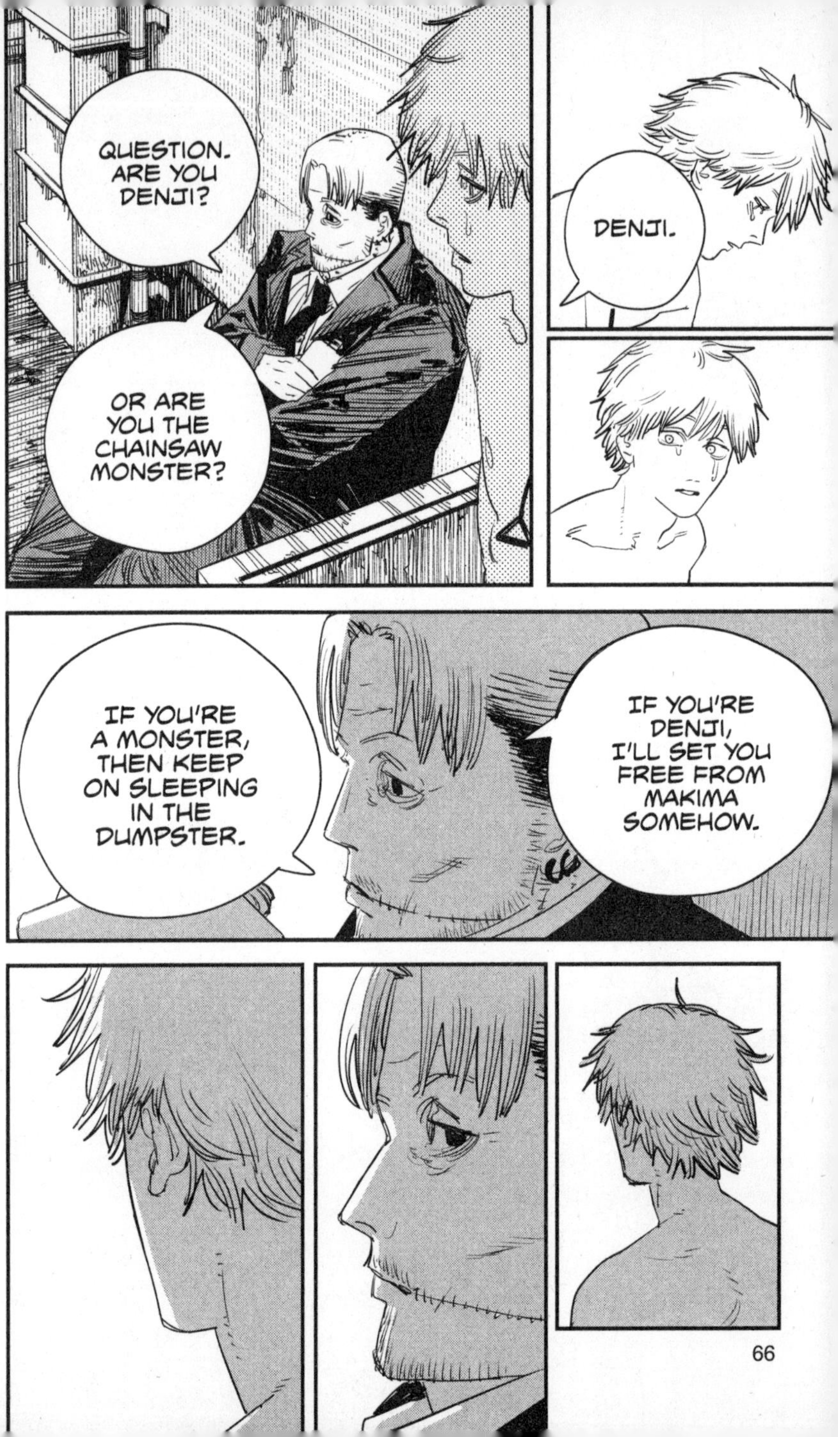
DENJI.
QUESTION. ARE YOU DENJI?
OR ARE YOU THE CHAINSAW MONSTER?
IF YOU'RE DENJI, I'LL SET YOU FREE FROM MAKIMA SOMEHOW.
IF YOU'RE A MONSTER, THEN KEEP ON SLEEPING IN THE DUMPSTER.

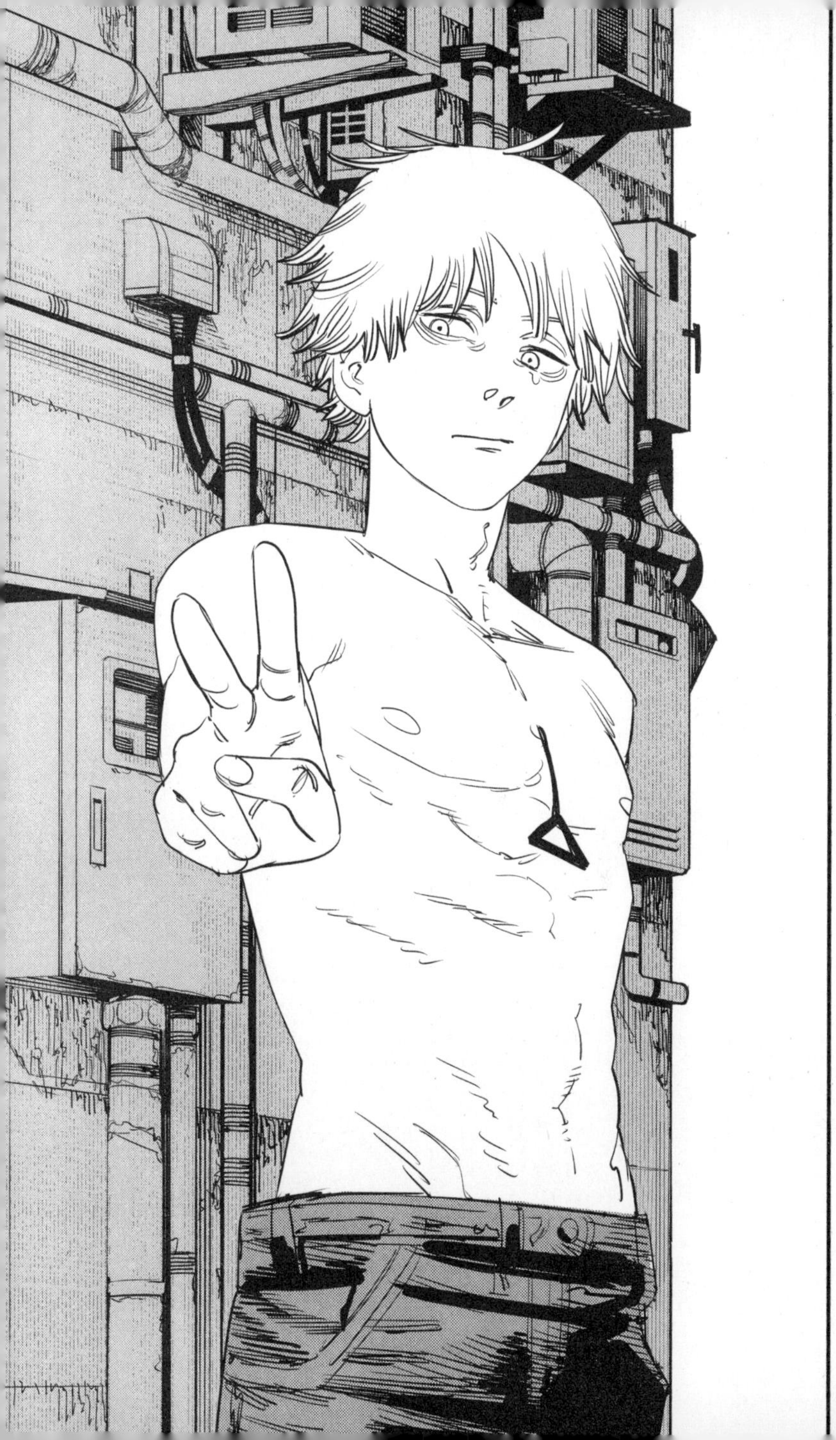

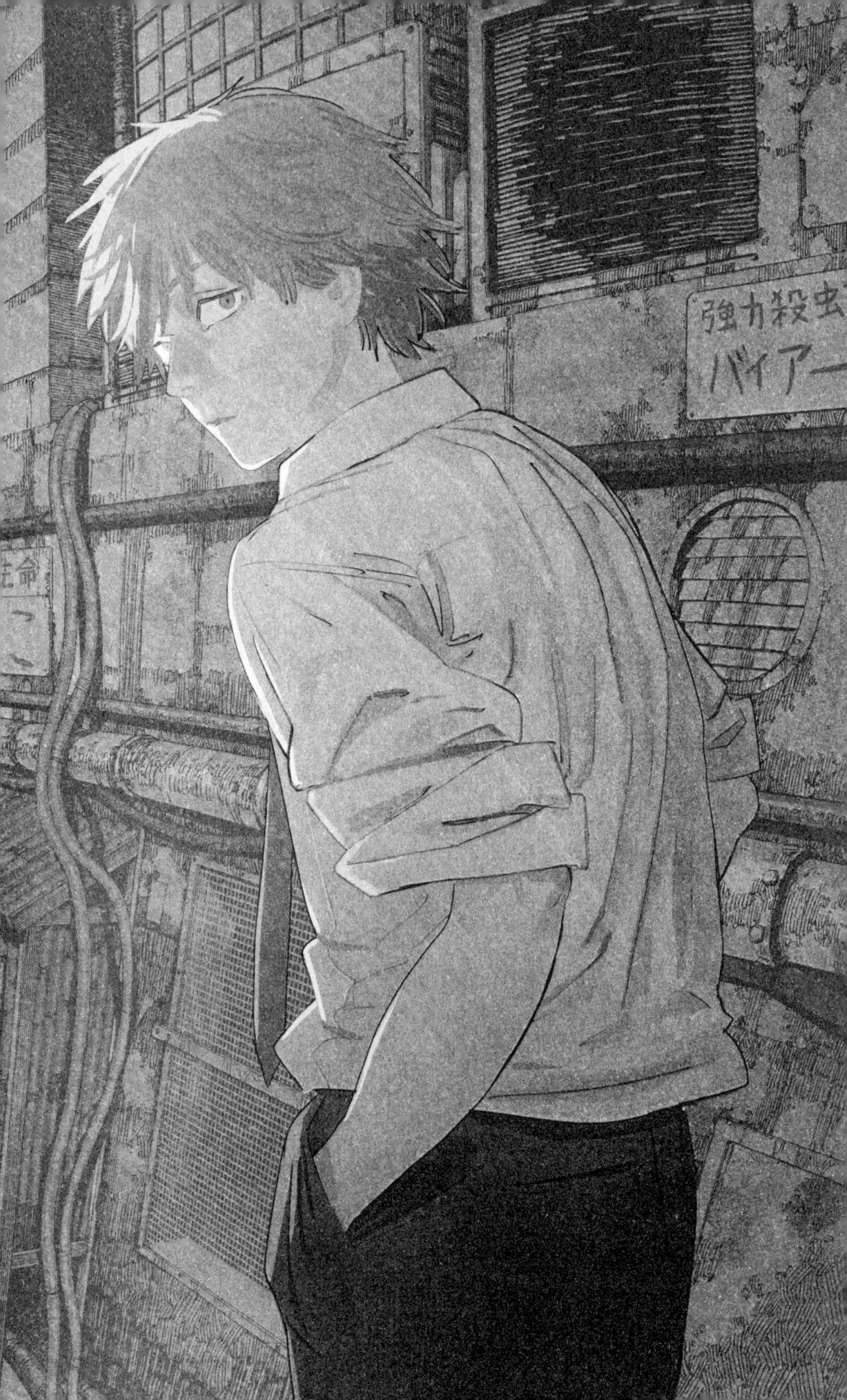
強力殺虫
バイアー

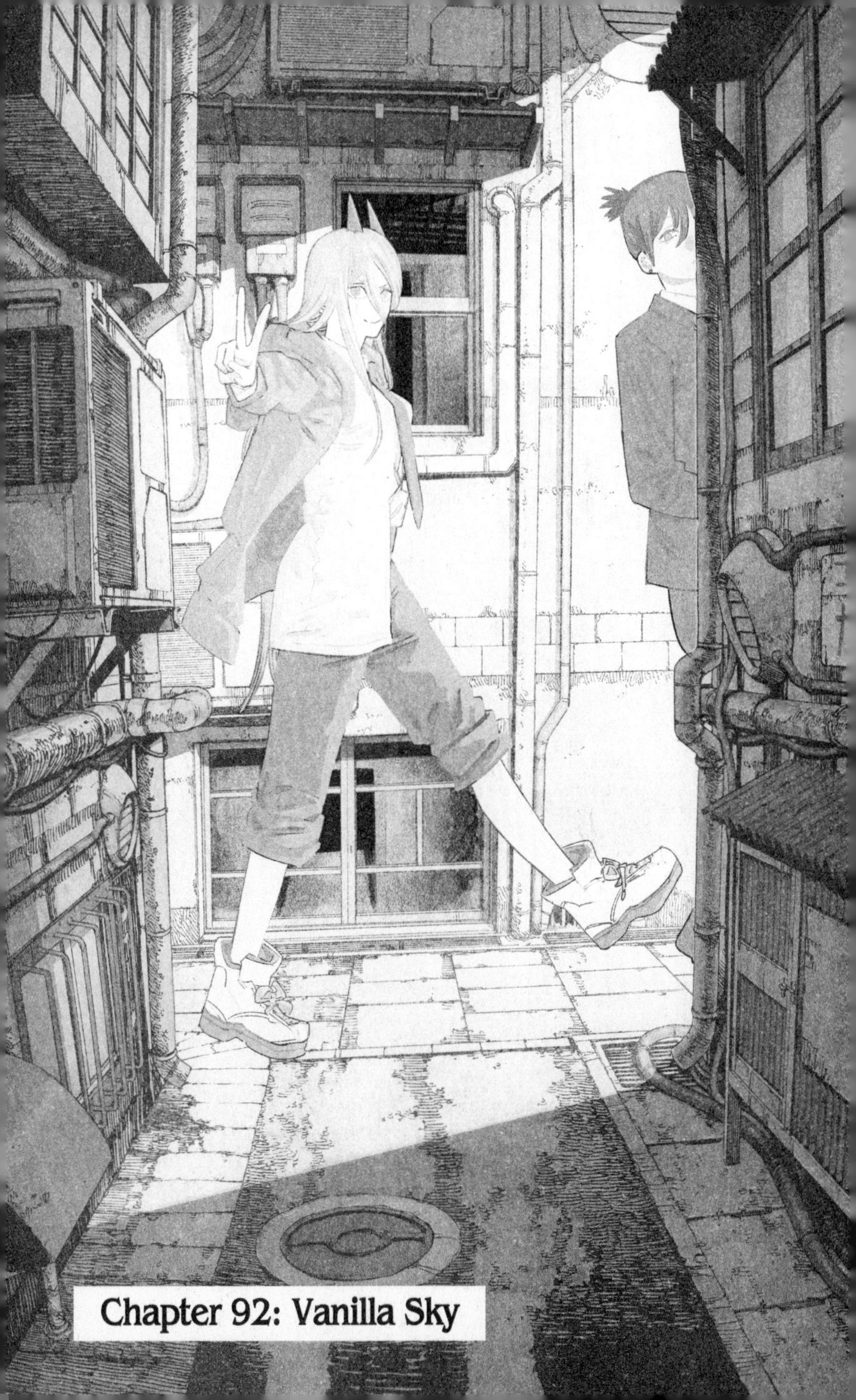

Chapter 92: Vanilla Sky

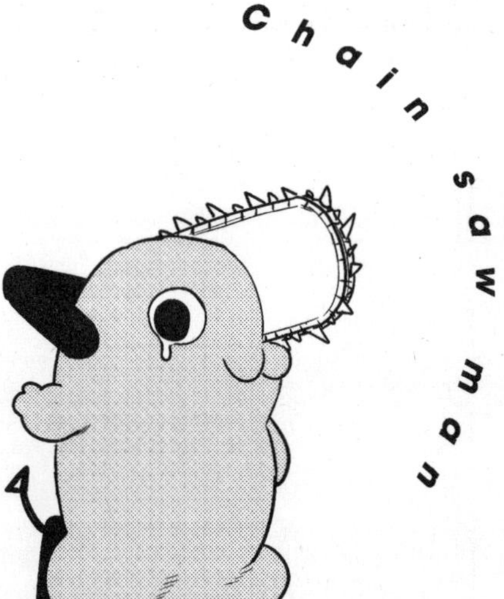
Chainsaw man

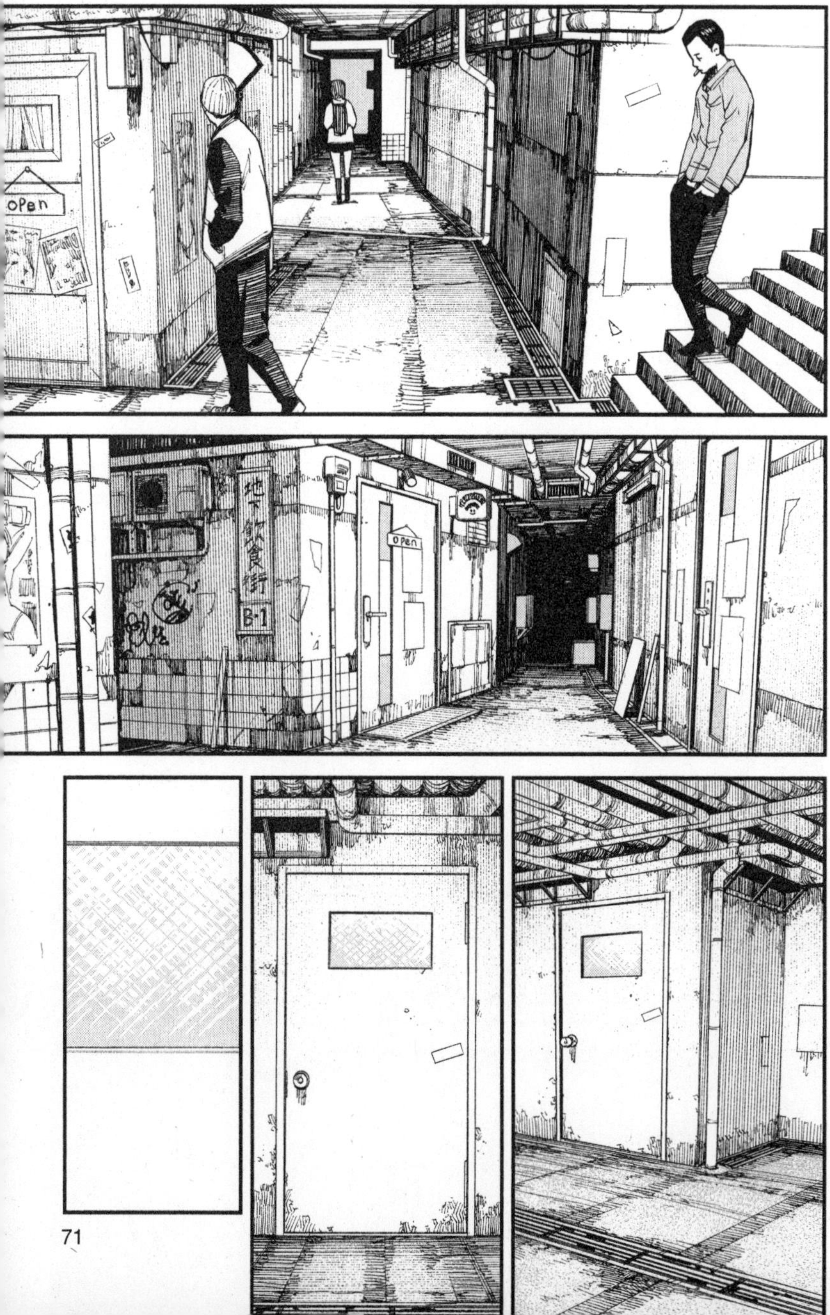
Open
地下飲食街
B-1
Open

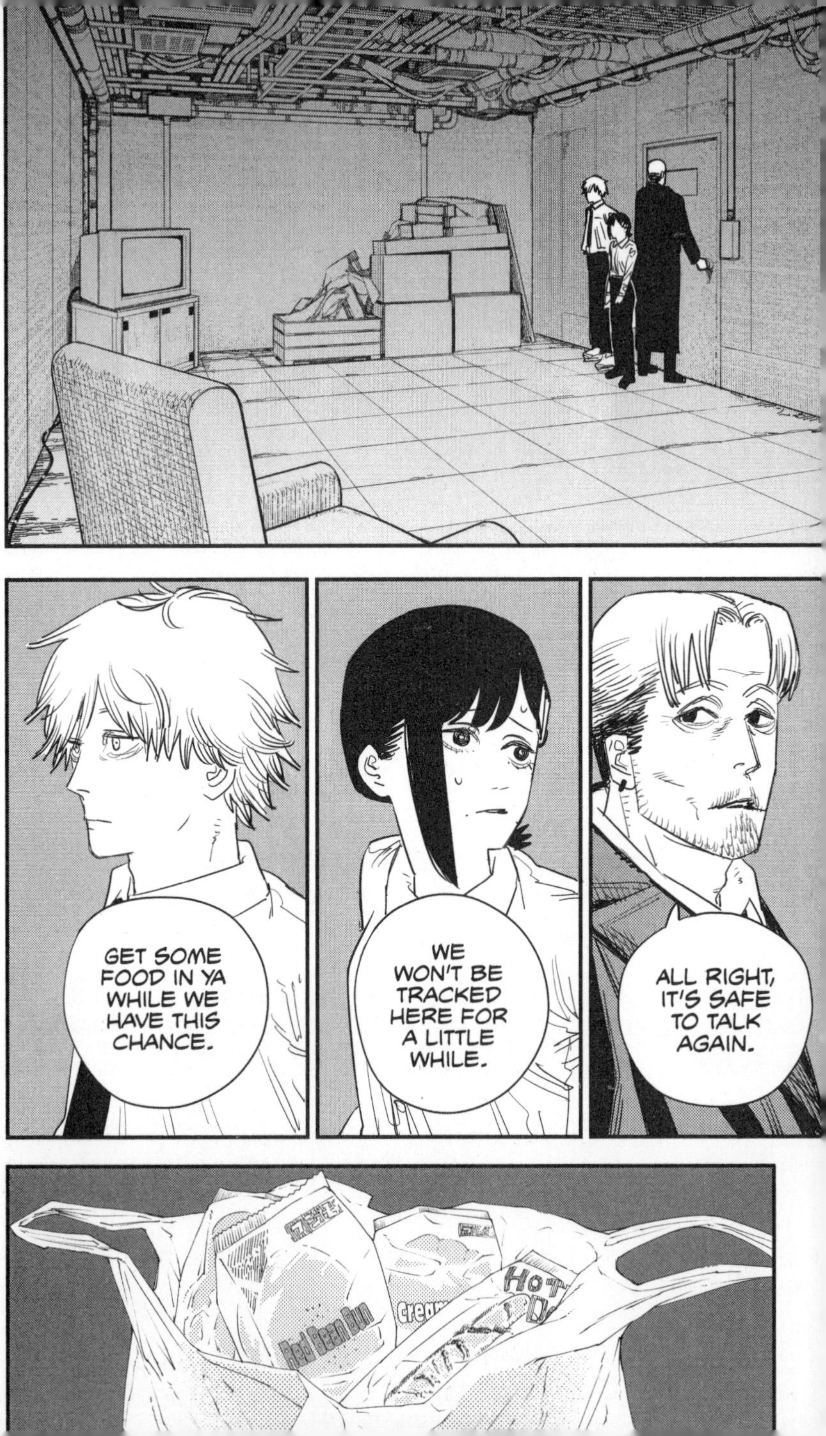
ALL RIGHT, IT'S SAFE TO TALK AGAIN.
WE WON'T BE TRACKED HERE FOR A LITTLE WHILE.
GET SOME FOOD IN YA WHILE WE HAVE THIS CHANCE.
Red Bean Bun

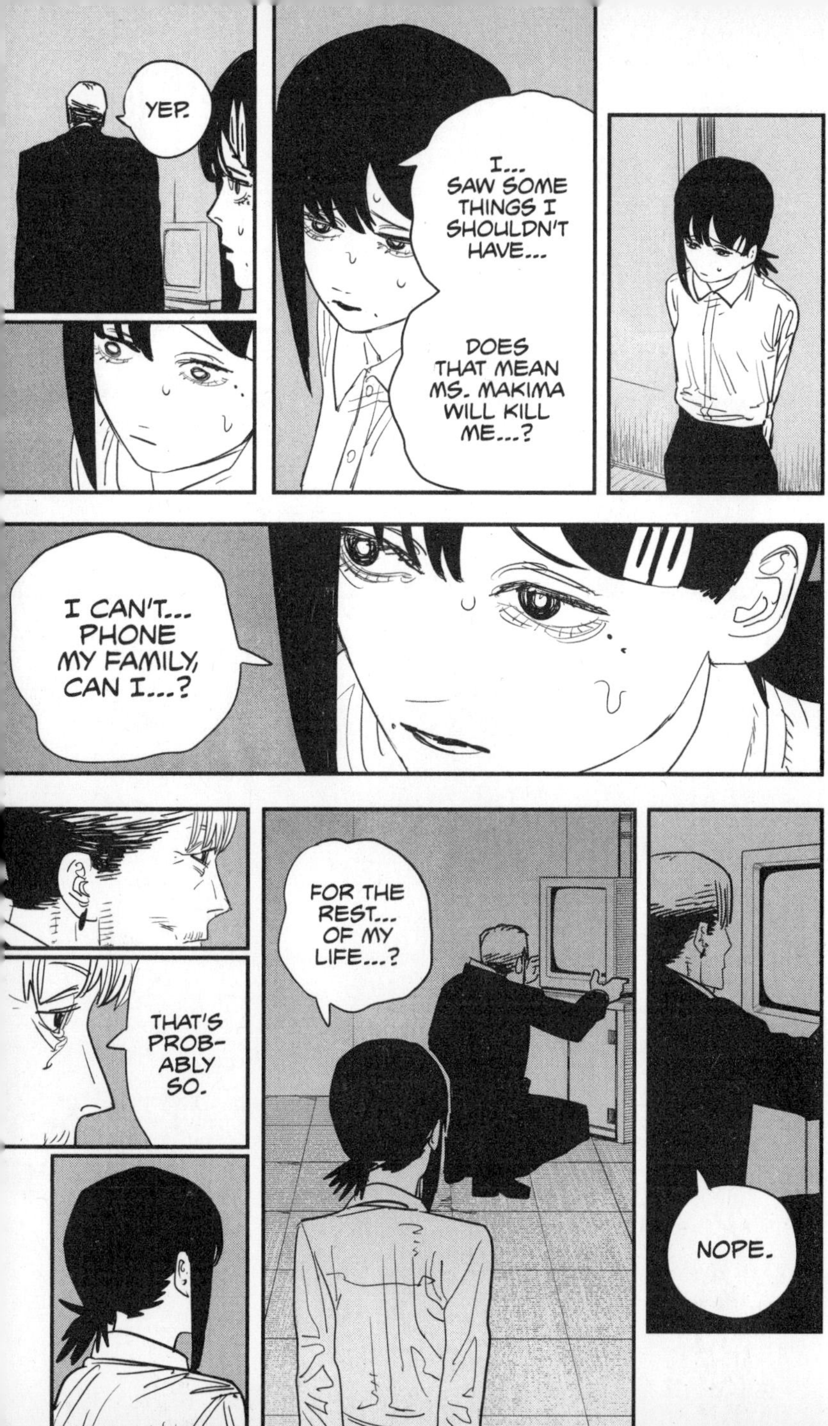
I... SAW SOME THINGS I SHOULDN'T HAVE...
DOES THAT MEAN MS. MAKIMA WILL KILL ME...?
YEP.
I CAN'T... PHONE MY FAMILY, CAN I...?
NOPE.
FOR THE REST... OF MY LIFE...?
THAT'S PROB-ABLY SO.

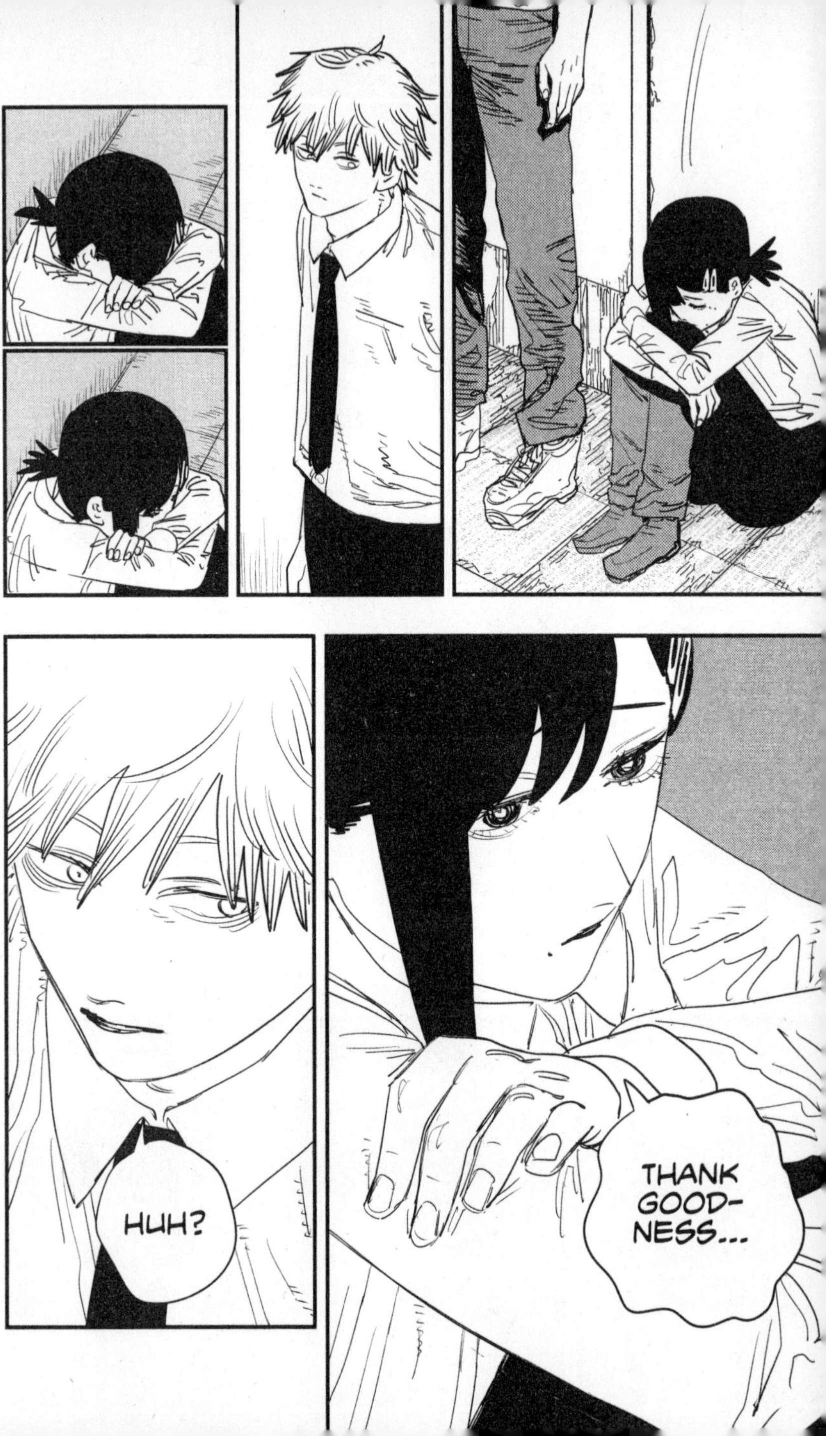
THANK GOOD-NESS...
HUH?

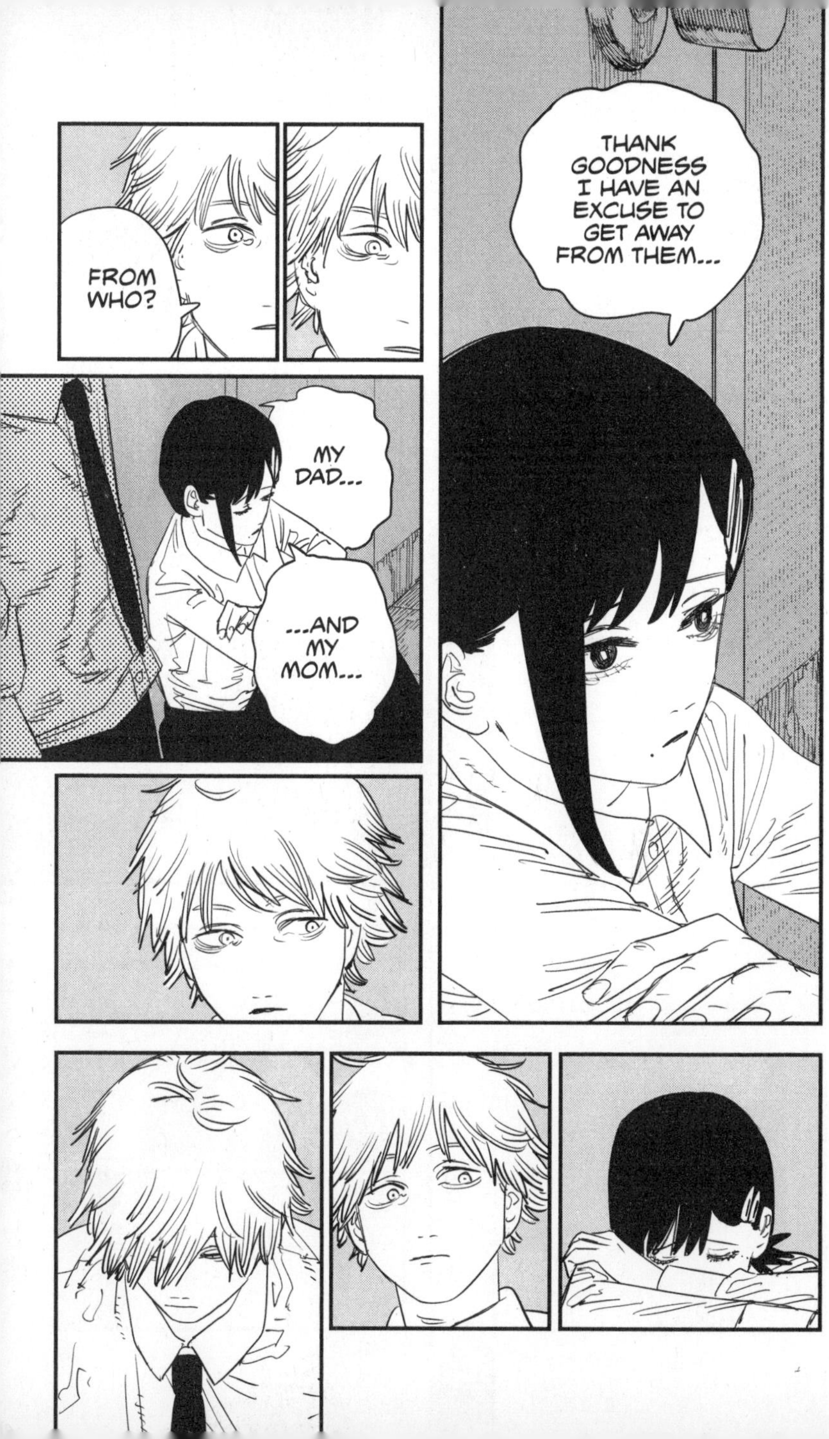
THANK GOODNESS I HAVE AN EXCUSE TO GET AWAY FROM THEM...
FROM WHO?
MY DAD...
...AND MY MOM...

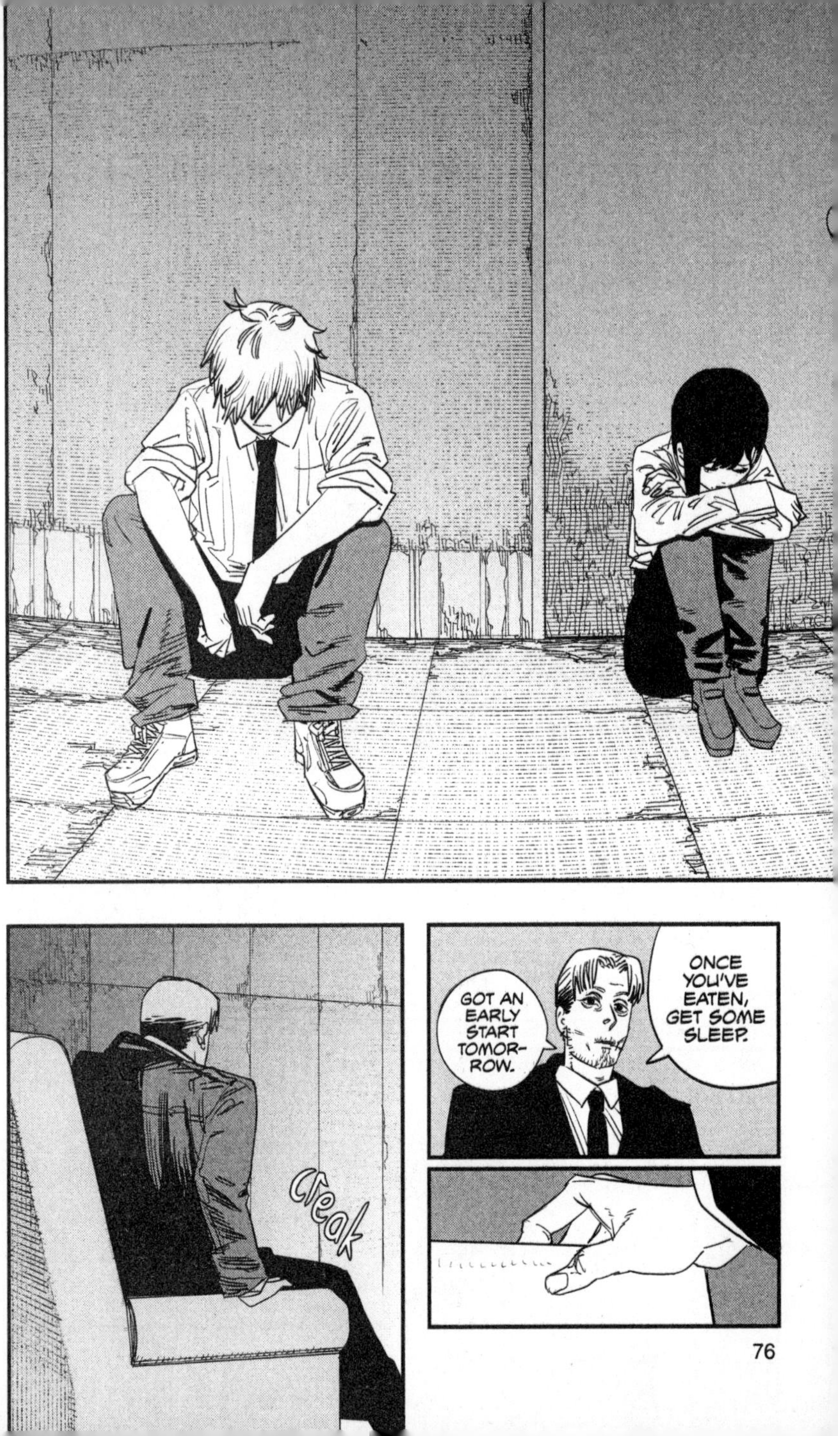
ONCE YOU'VE EATEN, GET SOME SLEEP.
GOT AN EARLY START TOMORROW.
creak

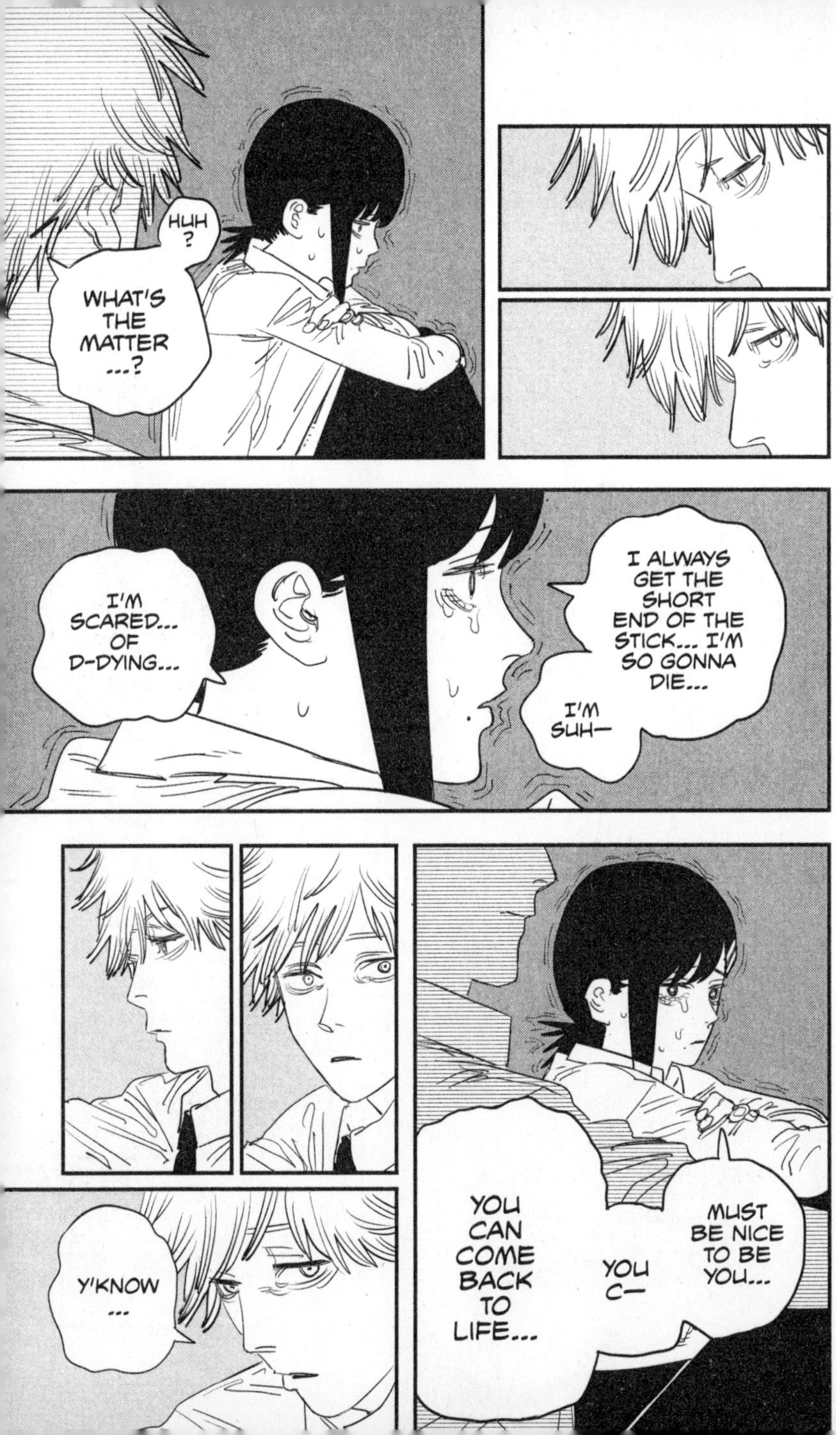
HUH?
WHAT'S THE MATTER...?
I ALWAYS GET THE SHORT END OF THE STICK... I'M SO GONNA DIE...
I'M SUH—
I'M SCARED... OF D-DYING...
MUST BE NICE TO BE YOU...
YOU C—
YOU CAN COME BACK TO LIFE...
Y'KNOW...

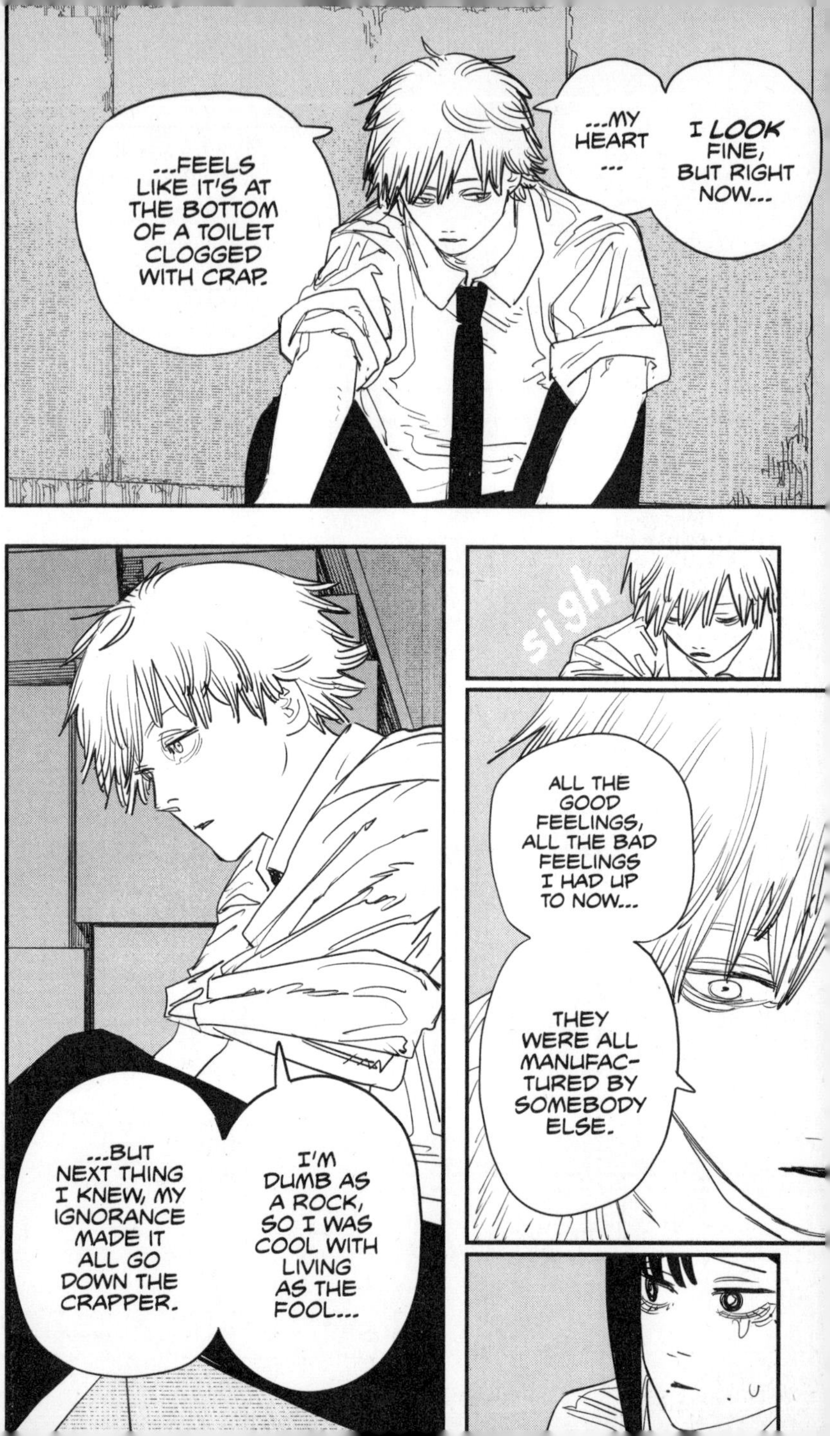
I *LOOK* FINE, BUT RIGHT NOW...
...MY HEART ...
...FEELS LIKE IT'S AT THE BOTTOM OF A TOILET CLOGGED WITH CRAP.
sigh
ALL THE GOOD FEELINGS, ALL THE BAD FEELINGS I HAD UP TO NOW...
THEY WERE ALL MANUFAC-TURED BY SOMEBODY ELSE.
I'M DUMB AS A ROCK, SO I WAS COOL WITH LIVING AS THE FOOL...
...BUT NEXT THING I KNEW, MY IGNORANCE MADE IT ALL GO DOWN THE CRAPPER.

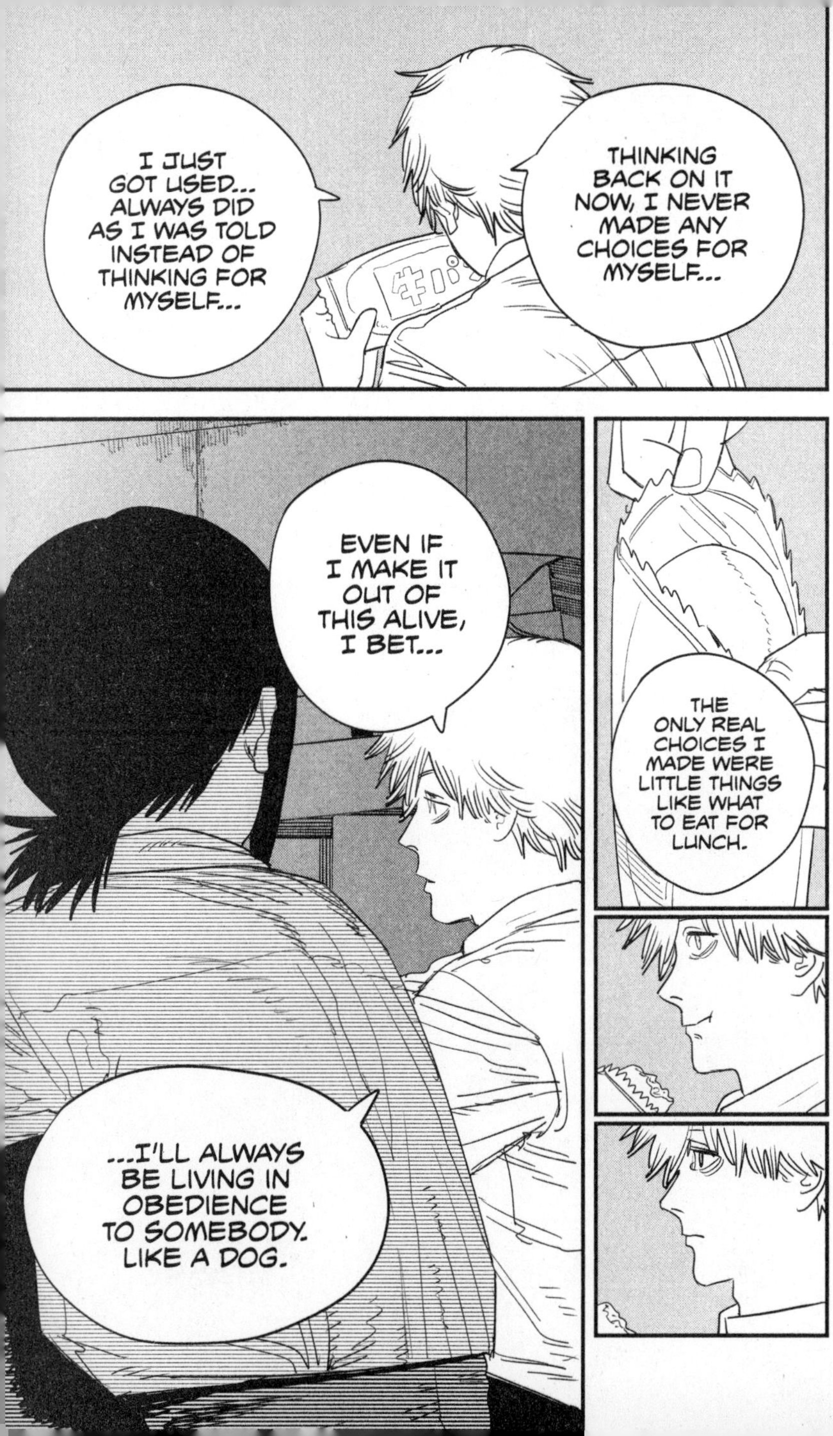
THINKING BACK ON IT NOW, I NEVER MADE ANY CHOICES FOR MYSELF...
I JUST GOT USED... ALWAYS DID AS I WAS TOLD INSTEAD OF THINKING FOR MYSELF...
THE ONLY REAL CHOICES I MADE WERE LITTLE THINGS LIKE WHAT TO EAT FOR LUNCH.
EVEN IF I MAKE IT OUT OF THIS ALIVE, I BET...
...I'LL ALWAYS BE LIVING IN OBEDIENCE TO SOMEBODY. LIKE A DOG.

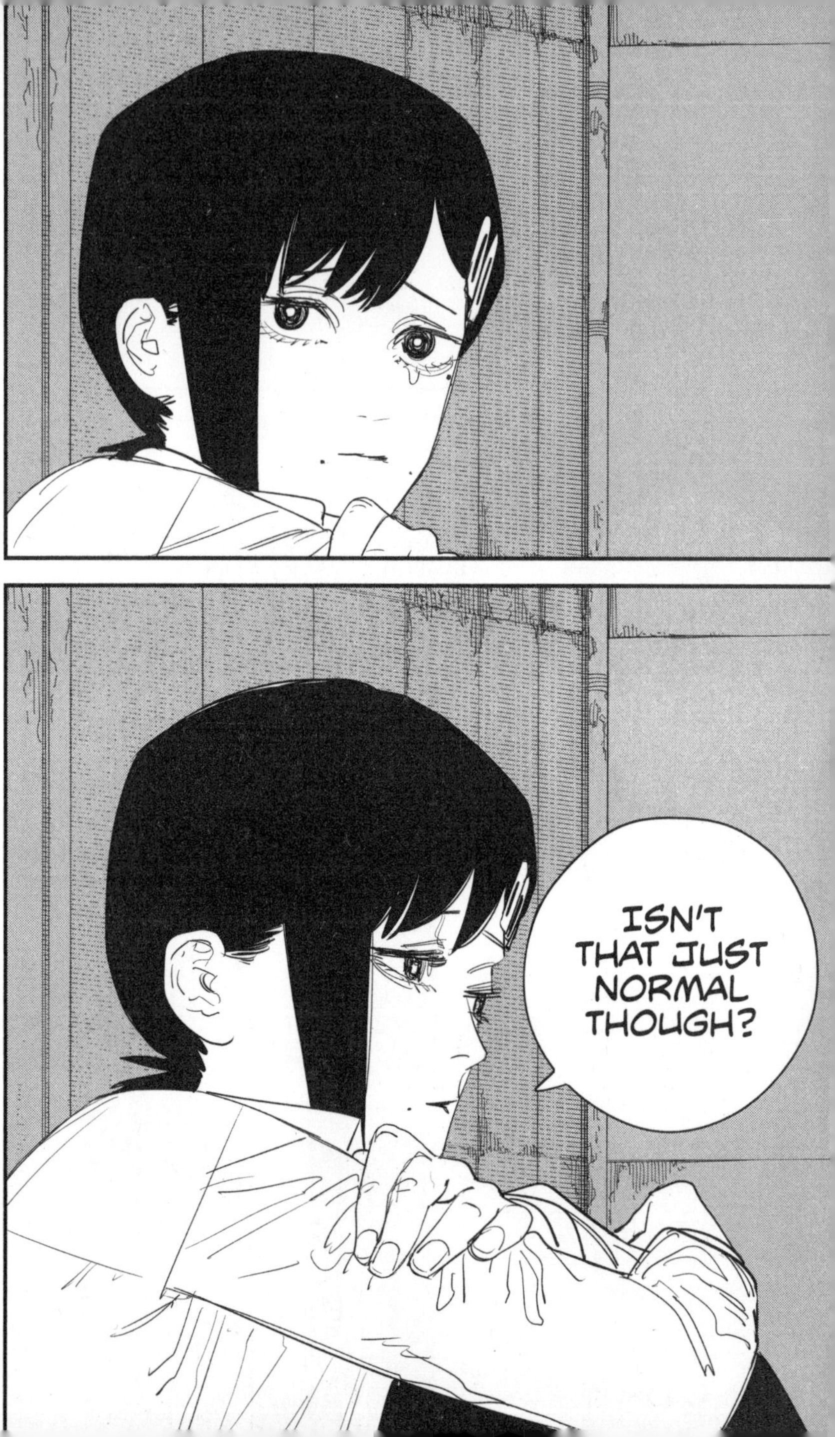
ISN'T THAT JUST NORMAL THOUGH?

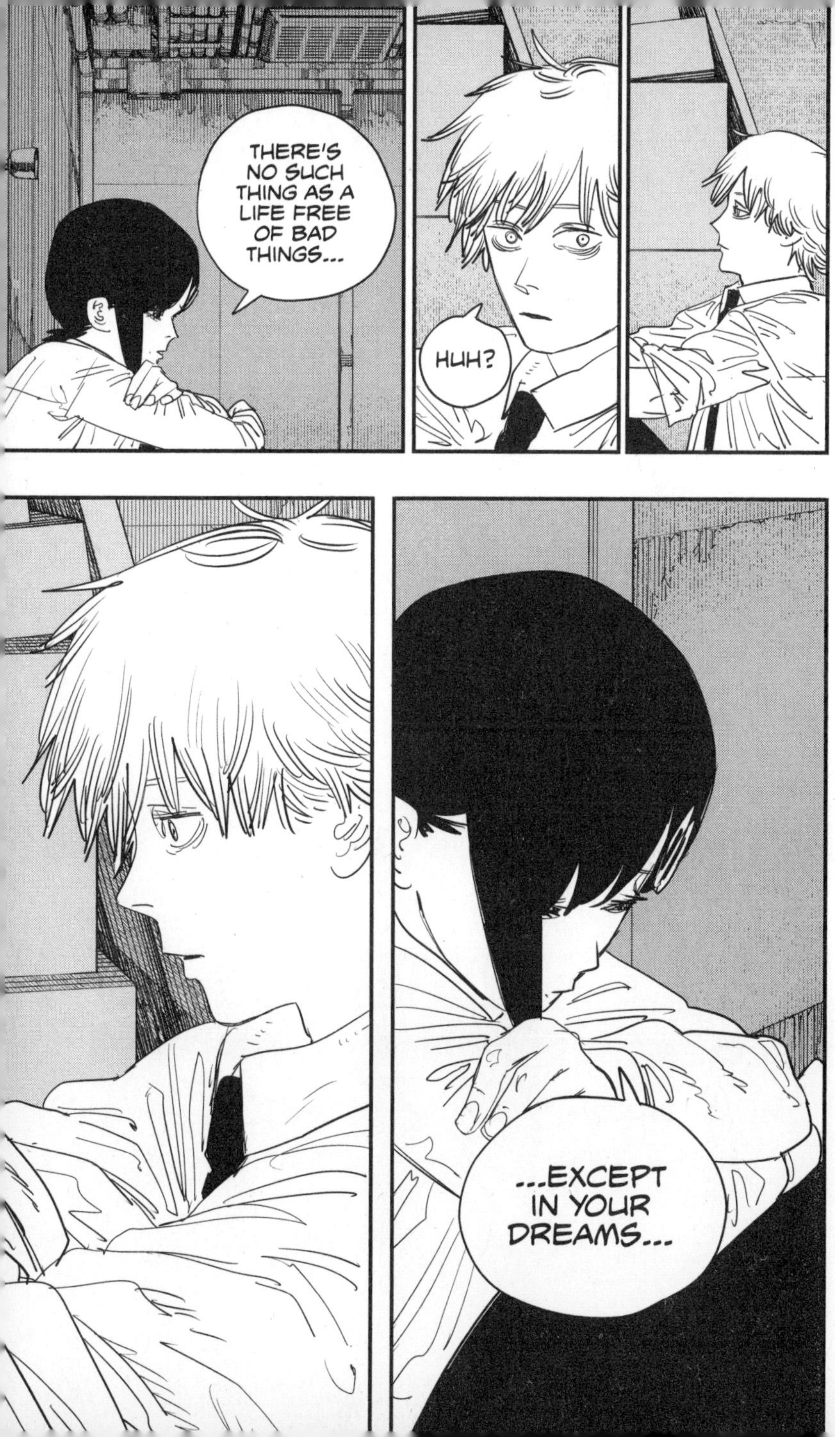
HUH?
THERE'S NO SUCH THING AS A LIFE FREE OF BAD THINGS...
...EXCEPT IN YOUR DREAMS...

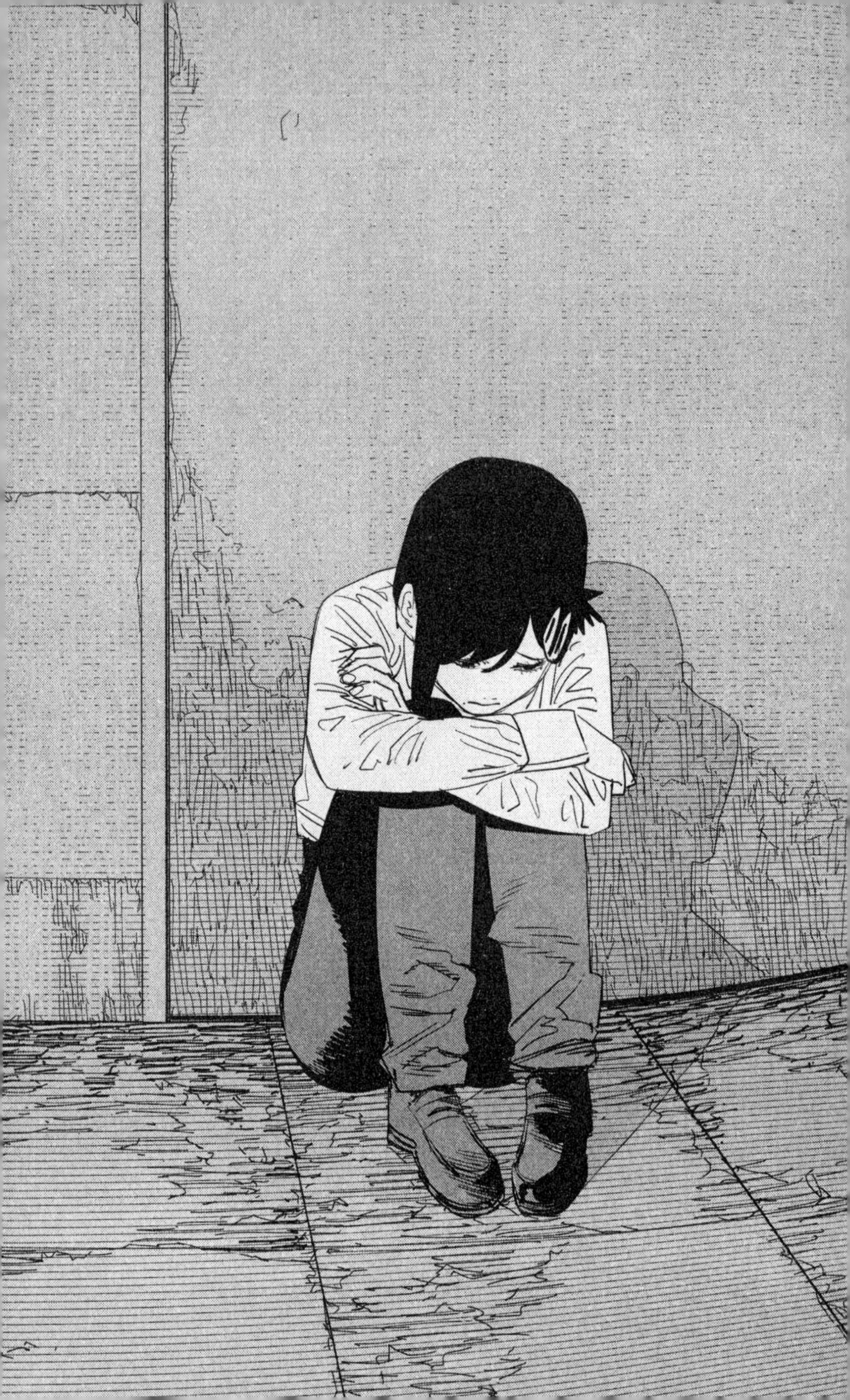

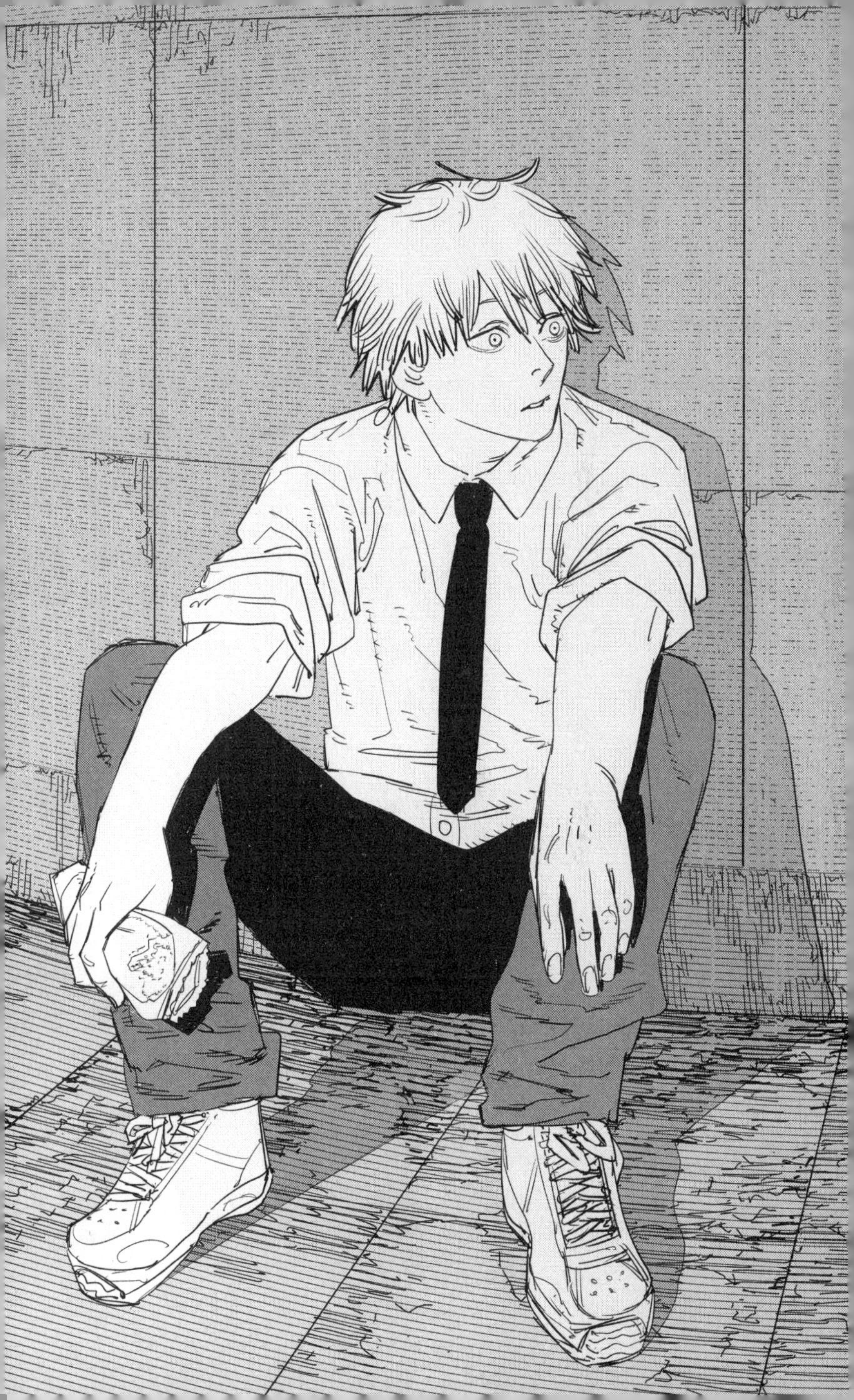

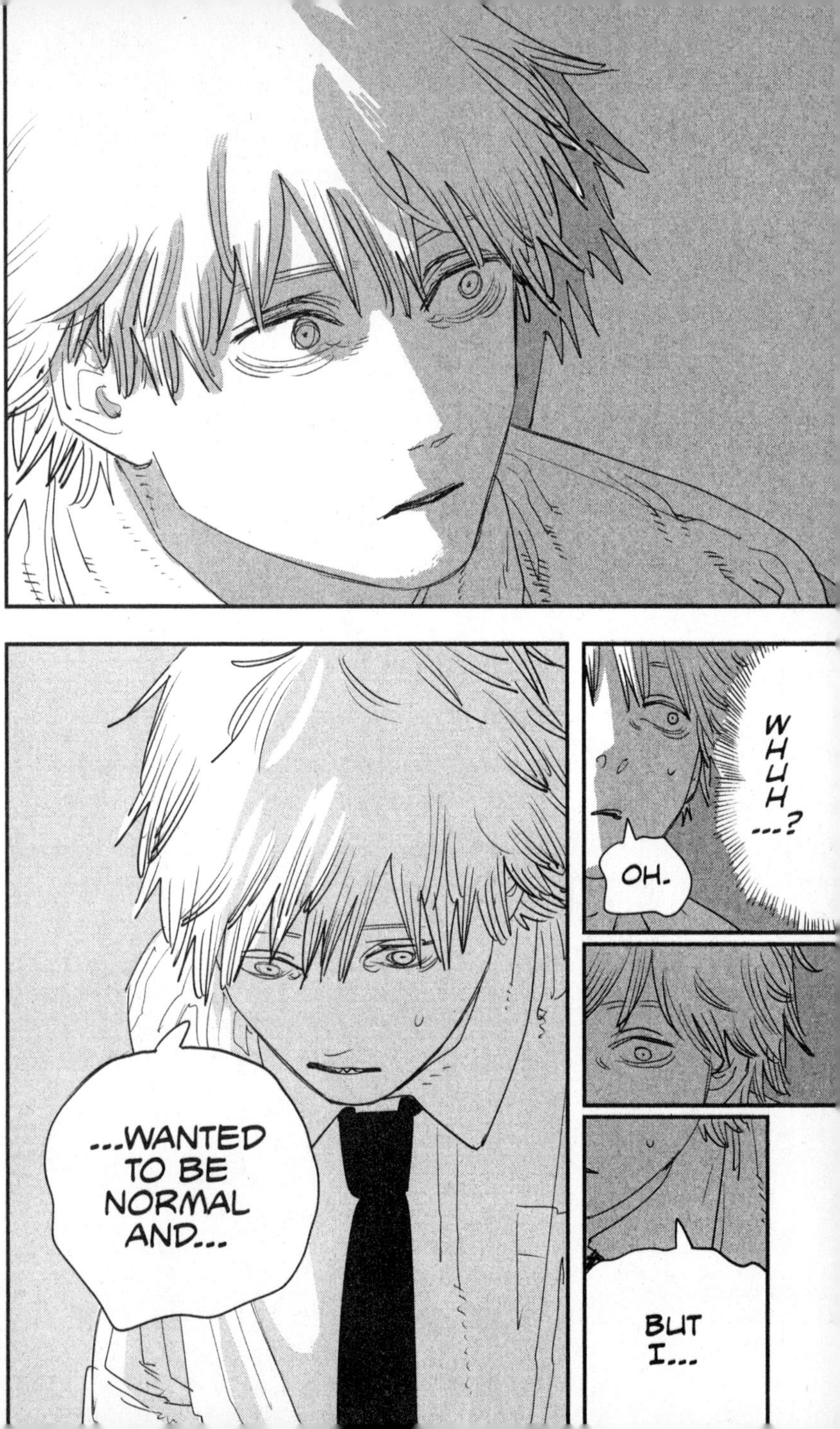
WHUH...?
OH.
BUT I...
...WANTED TO BE NORMAL AND...

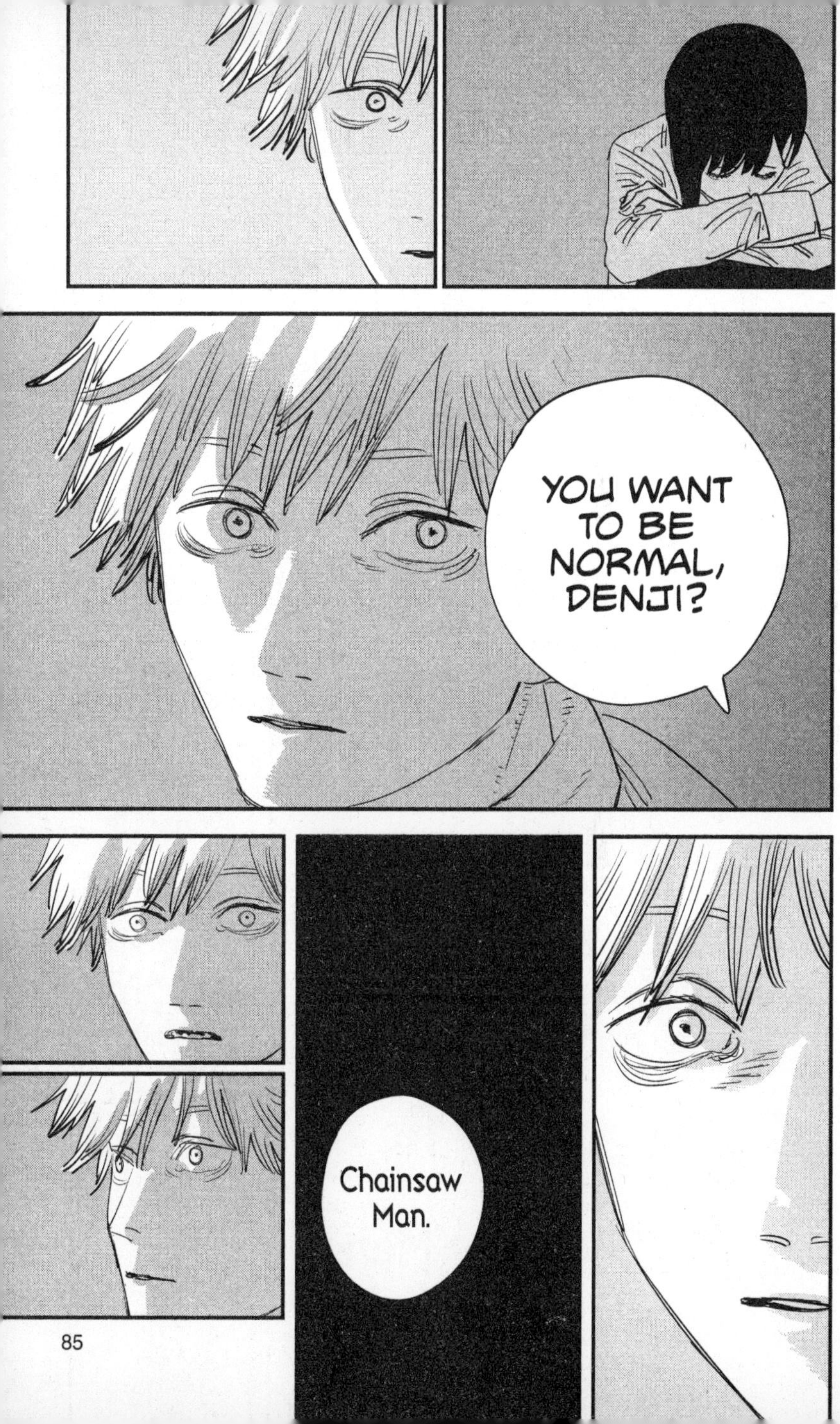
YOU WANT TO BE NORMAL, DENJI?
Chainsaw Man.

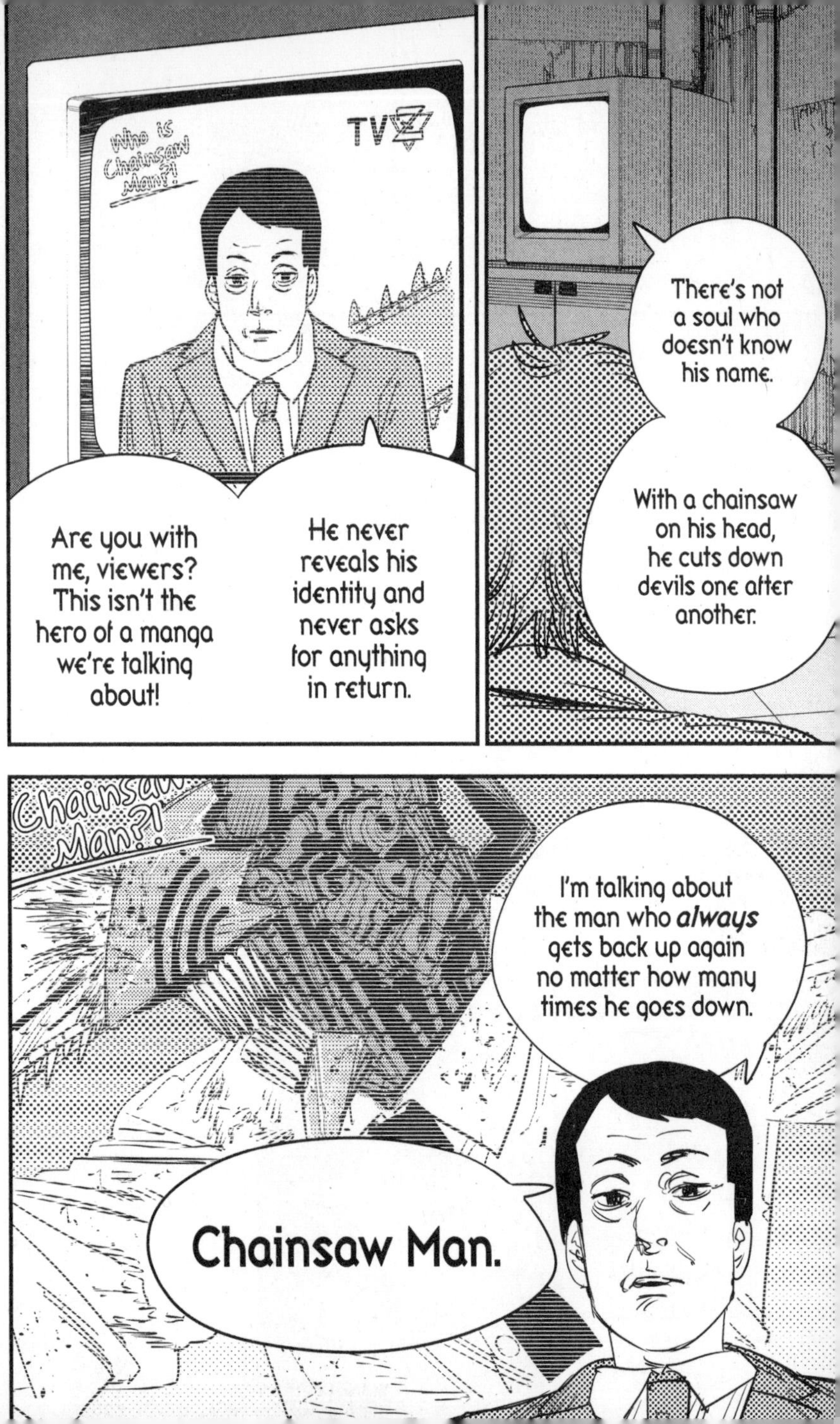
There's not a soul who doesn't know his name.
With a chainsaw on his head, he cuts down devils one after another.
Who is Chainsaw Man?!
He never reveals his identity and never asks for anything in return.
Are you with me, viewers? This isn't the hero of a manga we're talking about!
I'm talking about the man who *always* gets back up again no matter how many times he goes down.
Chainsaw Man?!
Chainsaw Man.

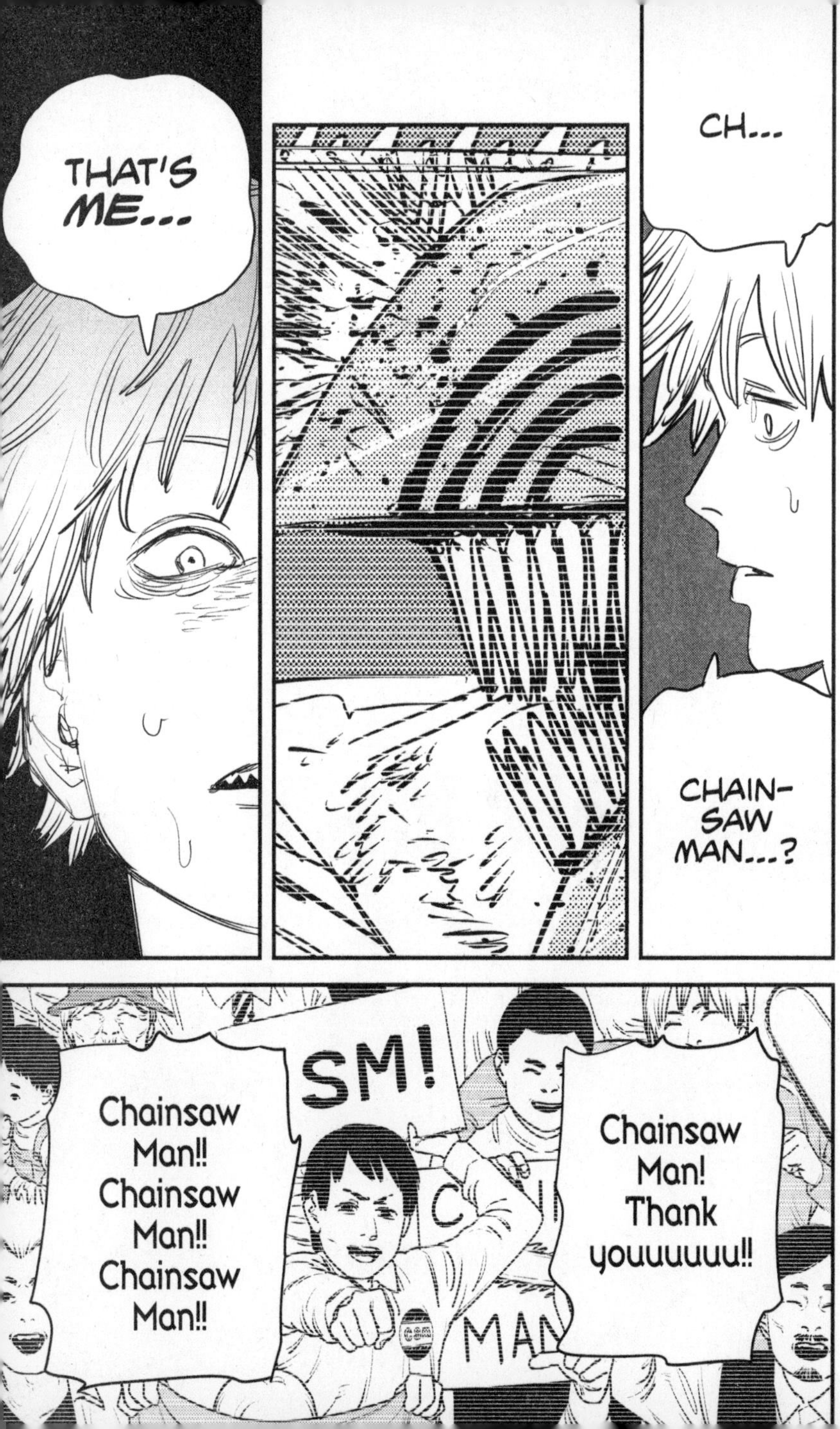
CH...
CHAIN-SAW MAN...?
THAT'S ME...
Chainsaw Man! Thank youuuuuu!!
SM!
Chainsaw Man!! Chainsaw Man!! Chainsaw Man!!

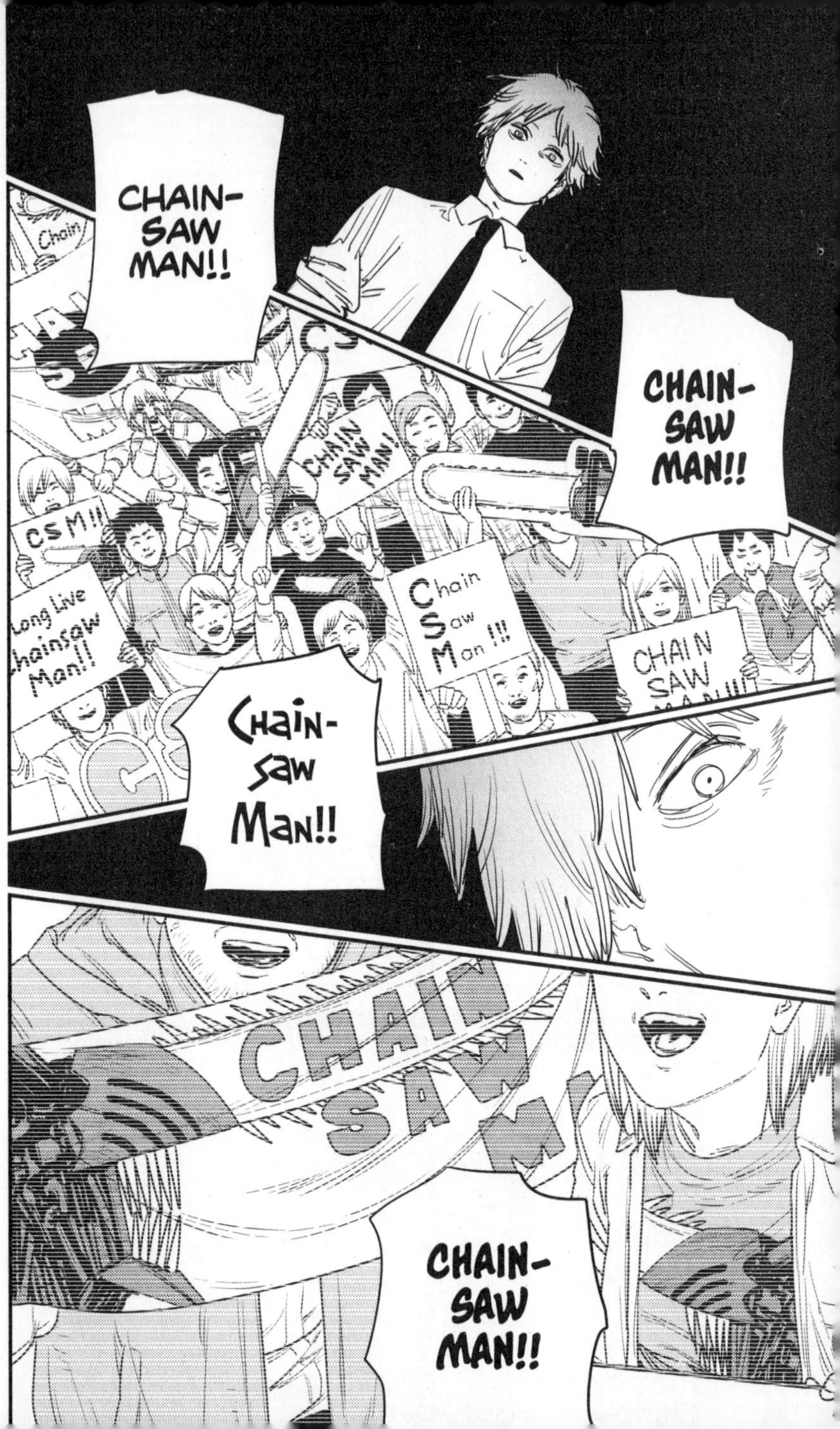
CHAIN-SAW MAN!!
CHAIN-SAW MAN!!
Chain
CHAIN SAW MAN!
CSM!!
Chain Saw Man!!!
CHAIN SAW
Long Live Chainsaw Man!!
Chain-saw Man!!
CHAIN SAW
CHAIN-SAW MAN!!

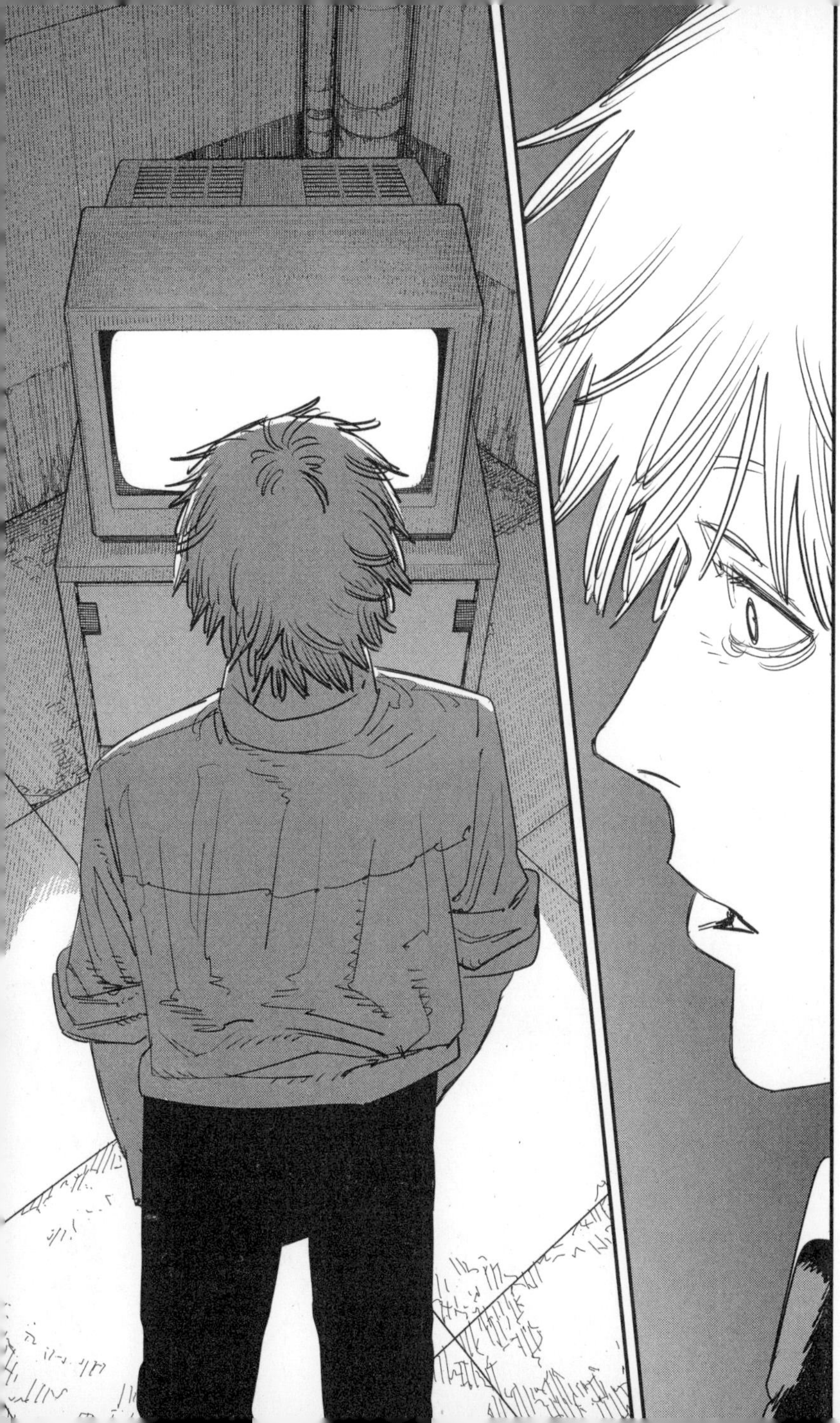

Chainsaw man

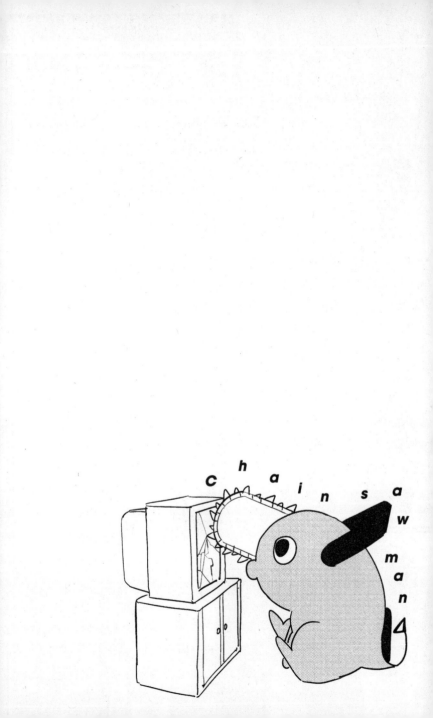

Chapter 93: You & Crappy Movies

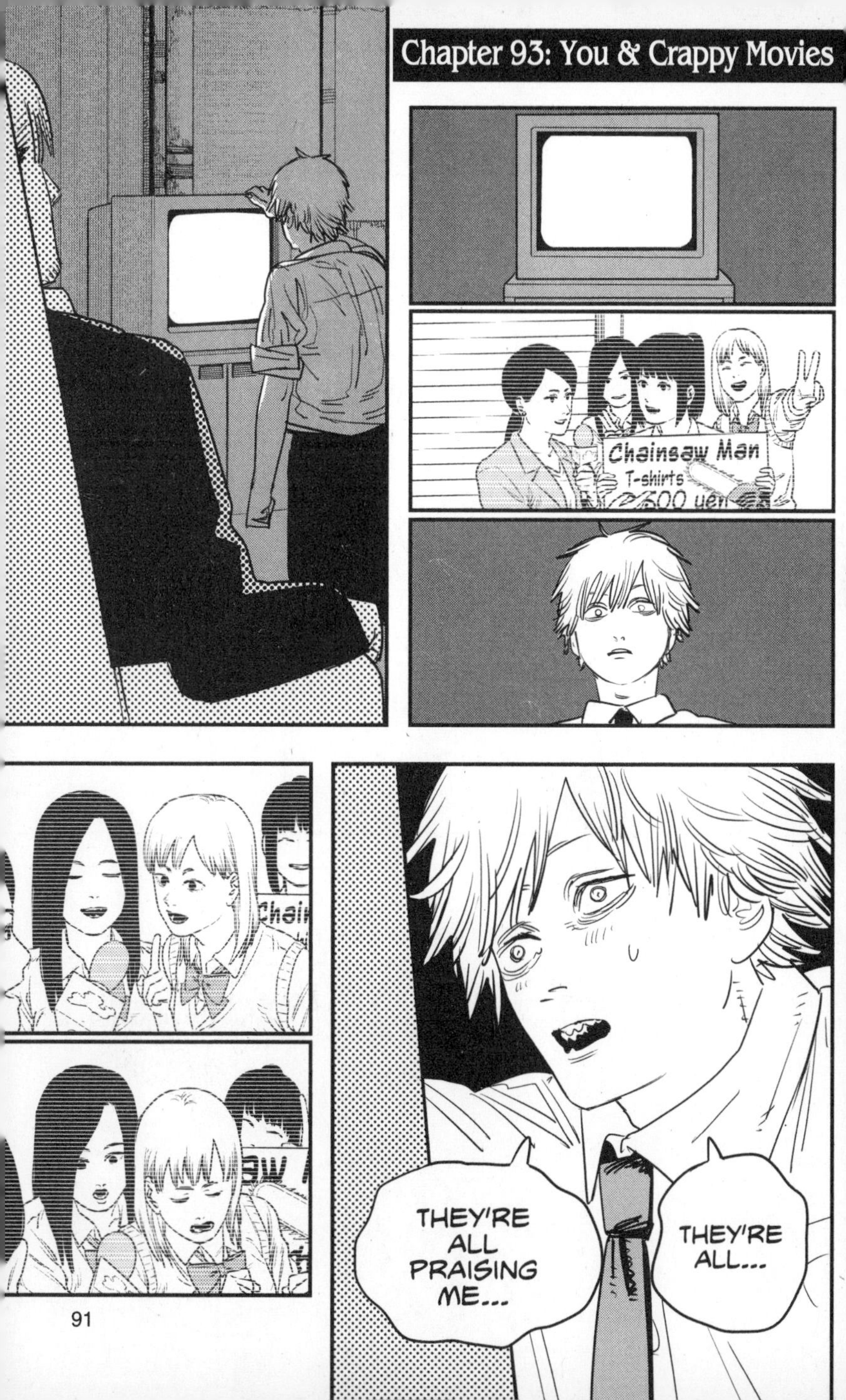
Chainsaw Man
T-shirts
THEY'RE ALL...
THEY'RE ALL PRAISING ME...

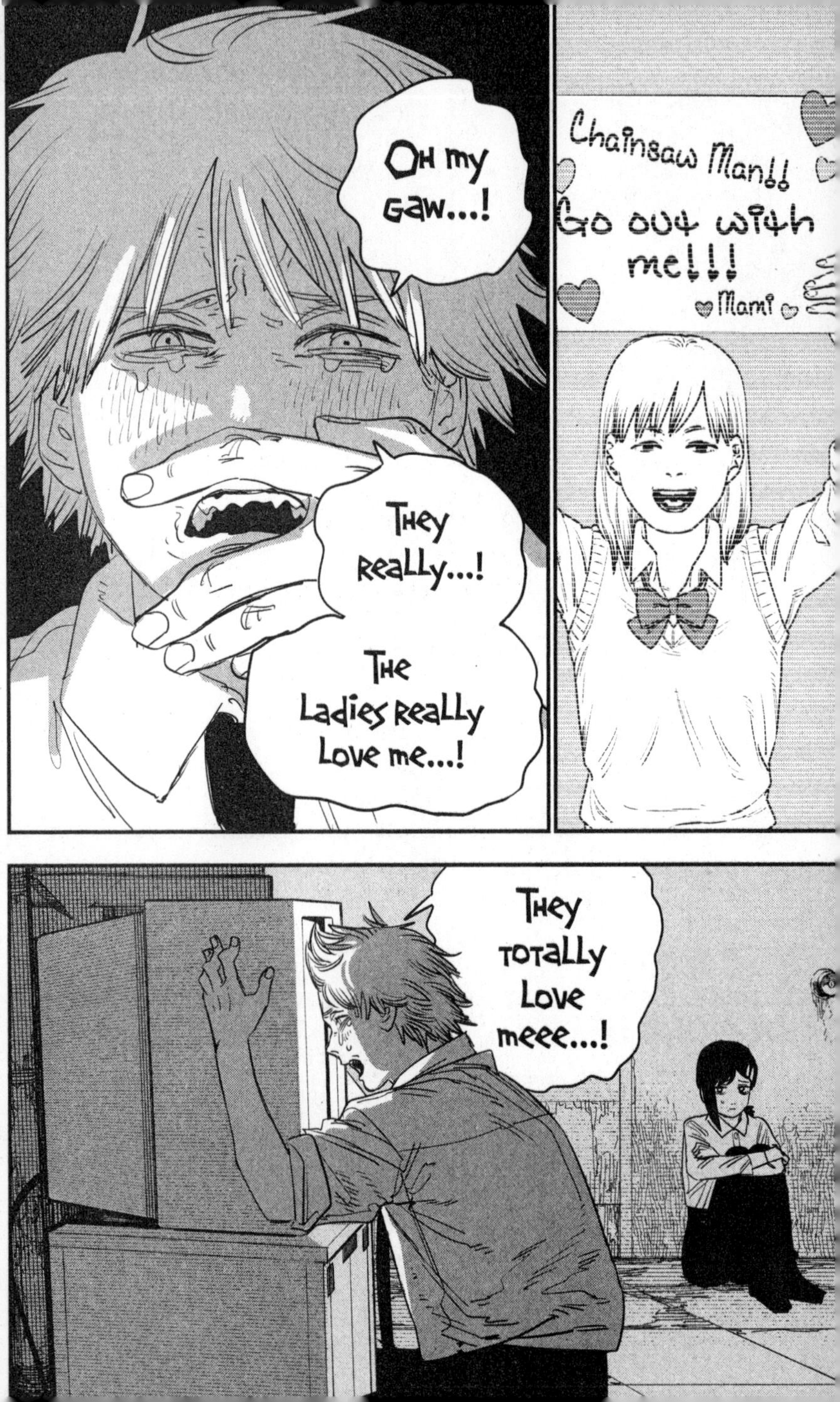
Chainsaw Man!!
Go out with me!!!
Mami
Oh my gaw...!
They really...!
The Ladies really Love me...!
They totally Love meee...!

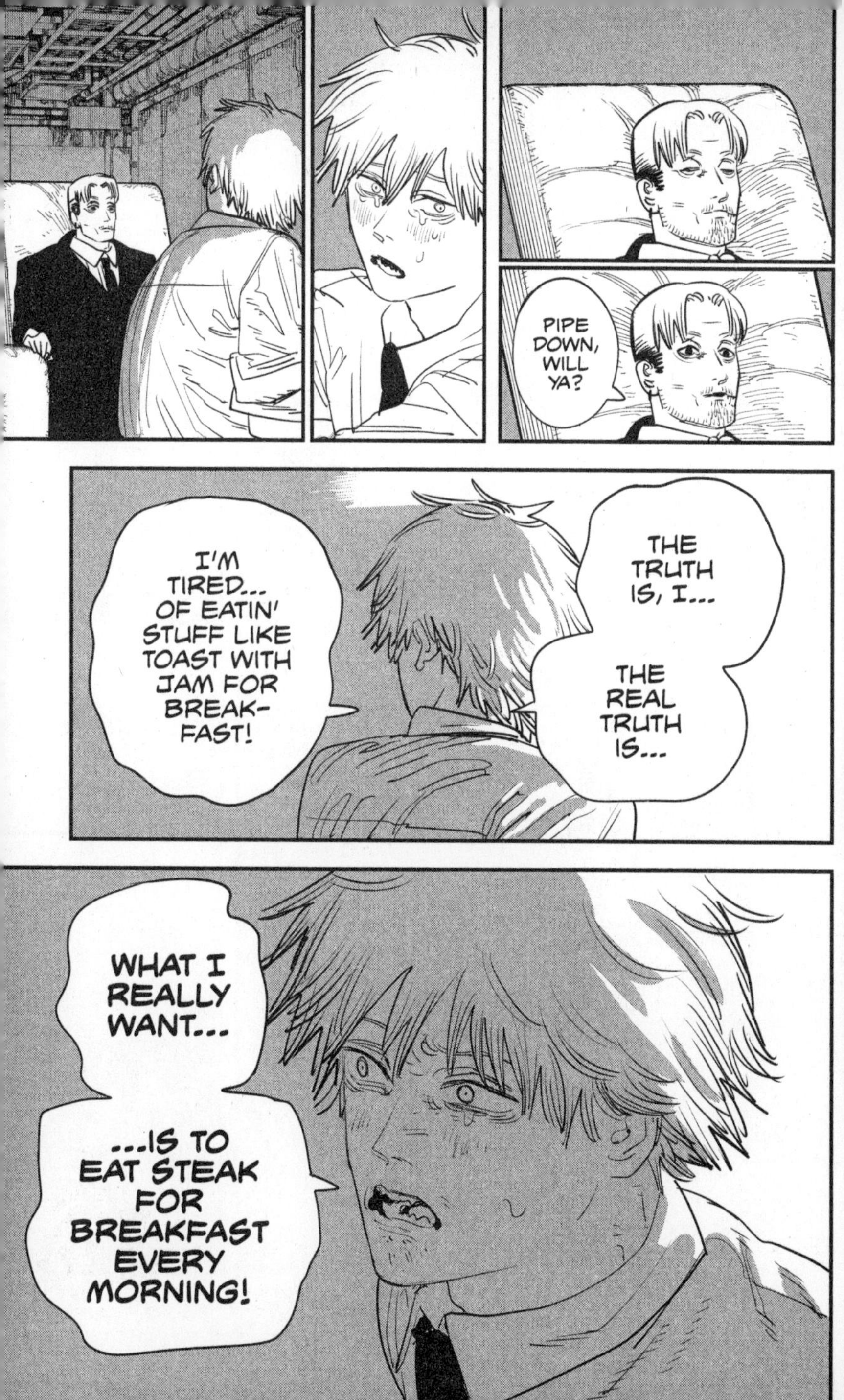
PIPE DOWN, WILL YA?
THE TRUTH IS, I...
THE REAL TRUTH IS...
I'M TIRED... OF EATIN' STUFF LIKE TOAST WITH JAM FOR BREAK-FAST!
WHAT I REALLY WANT...
...IS TO EAT STEAK FOR BREAKFAST EVERY MORNING!

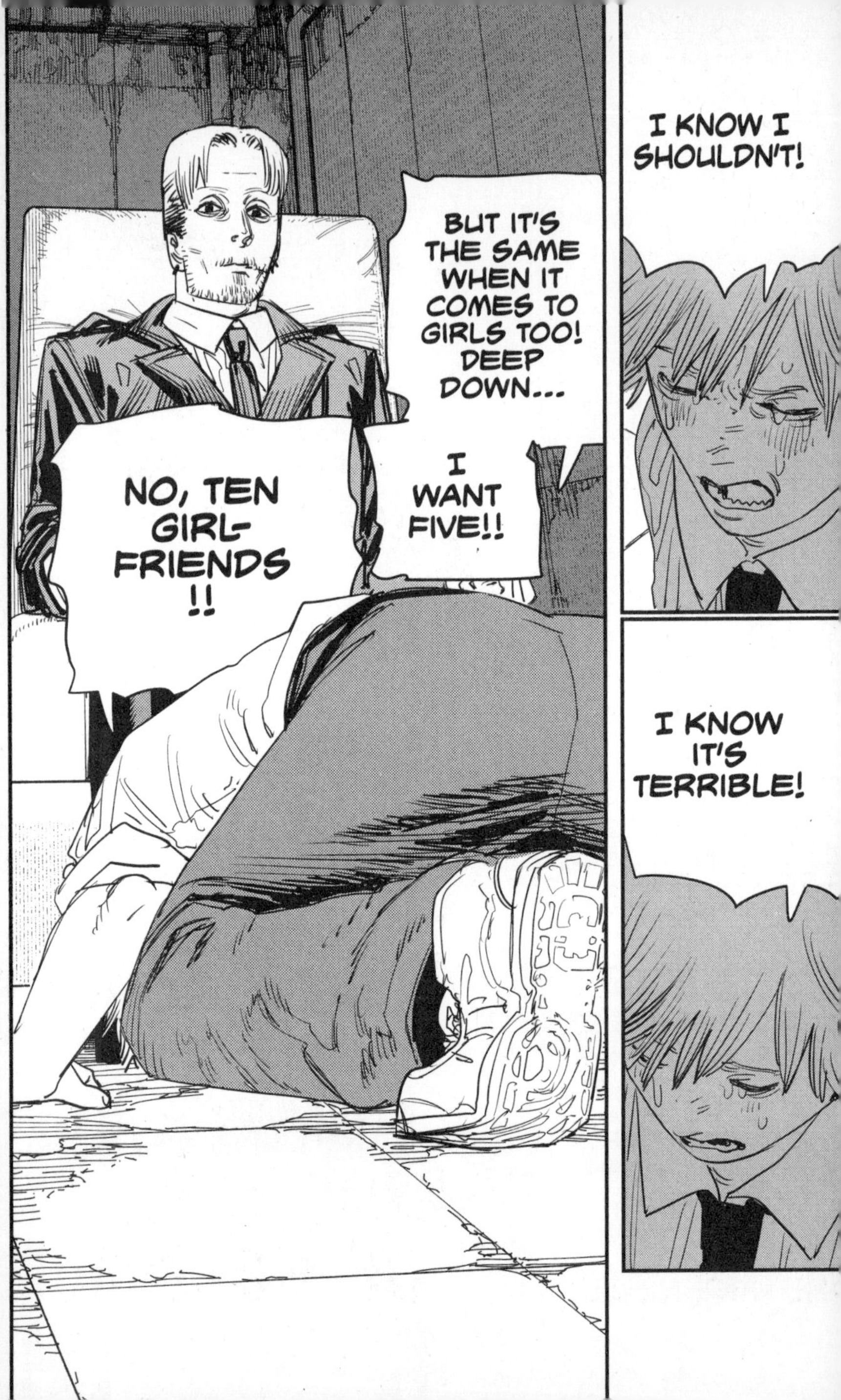
I KNOW I SHOULDN'T!
I KNOW IT'S TERRIBLE!
BUT IT'S THE SAME WHEN IT COMES TO GIRLS TOO! DEEP DOWN...
I WANT FIVE!!
NO, TEN GIRL-FRIENDS !!

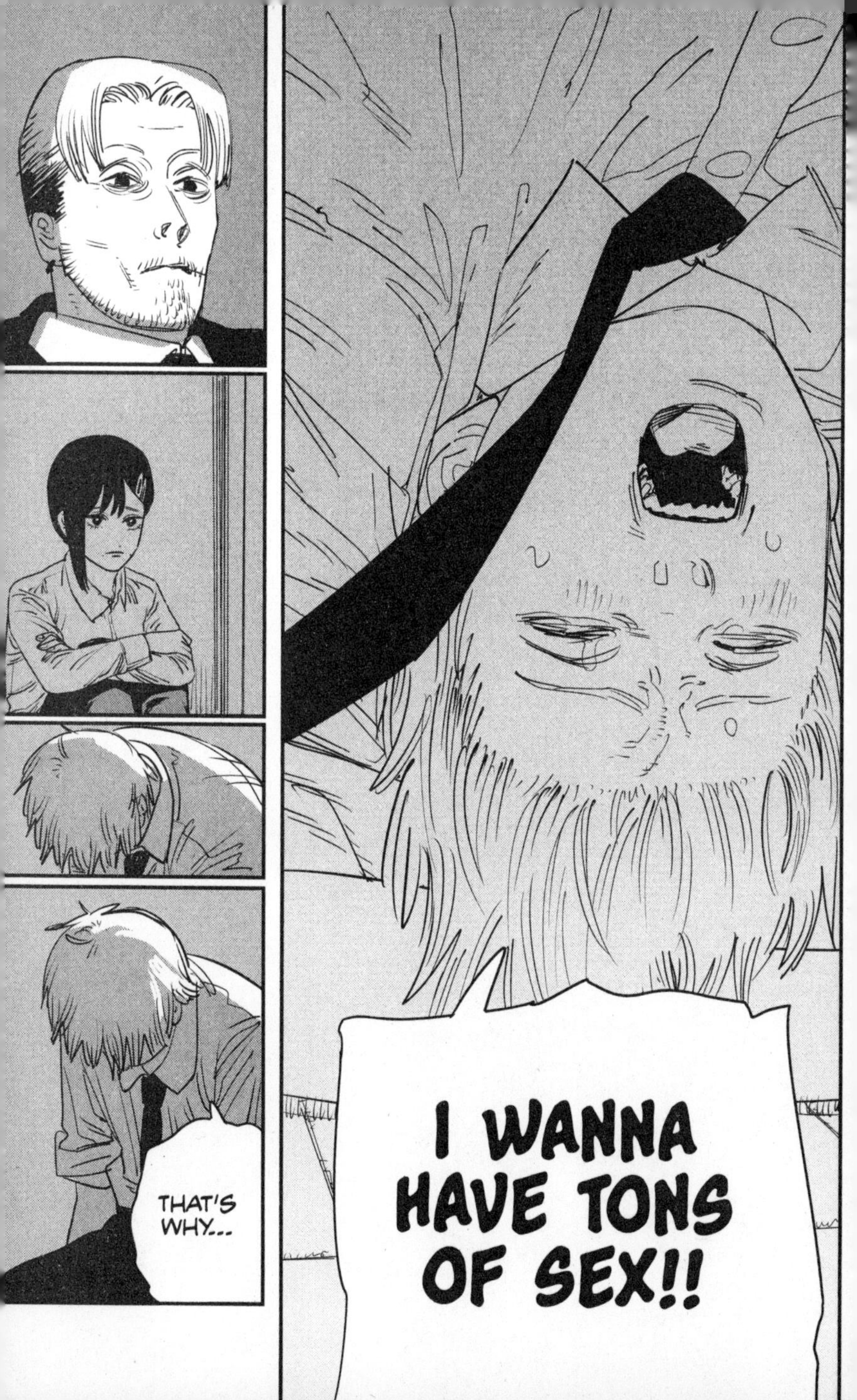
I WANNA HAVE TONS OF SEX!!
THAT'S WHY...

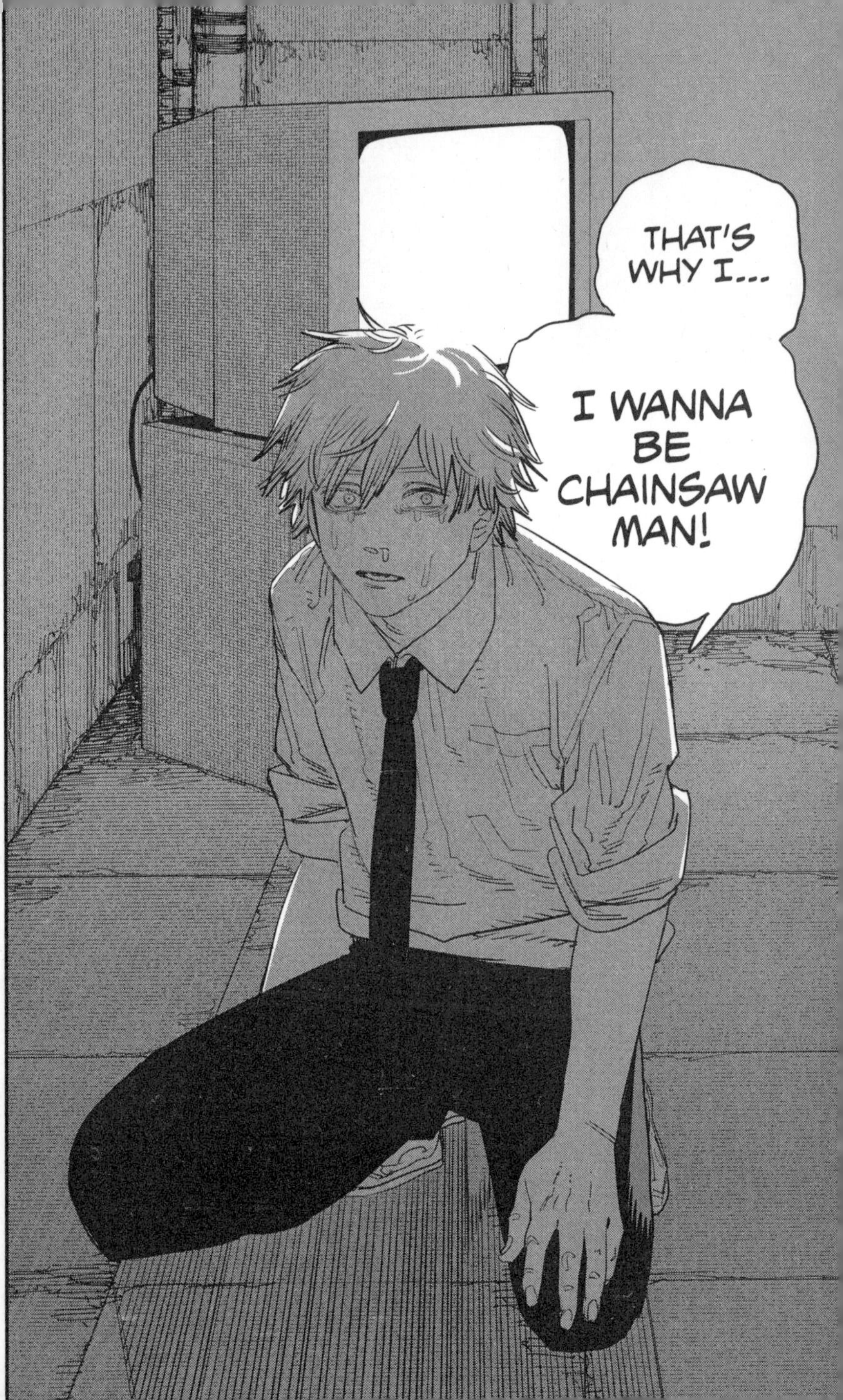
THAT'S WHY I...
I WANNA BE CHAINSAW MAN!

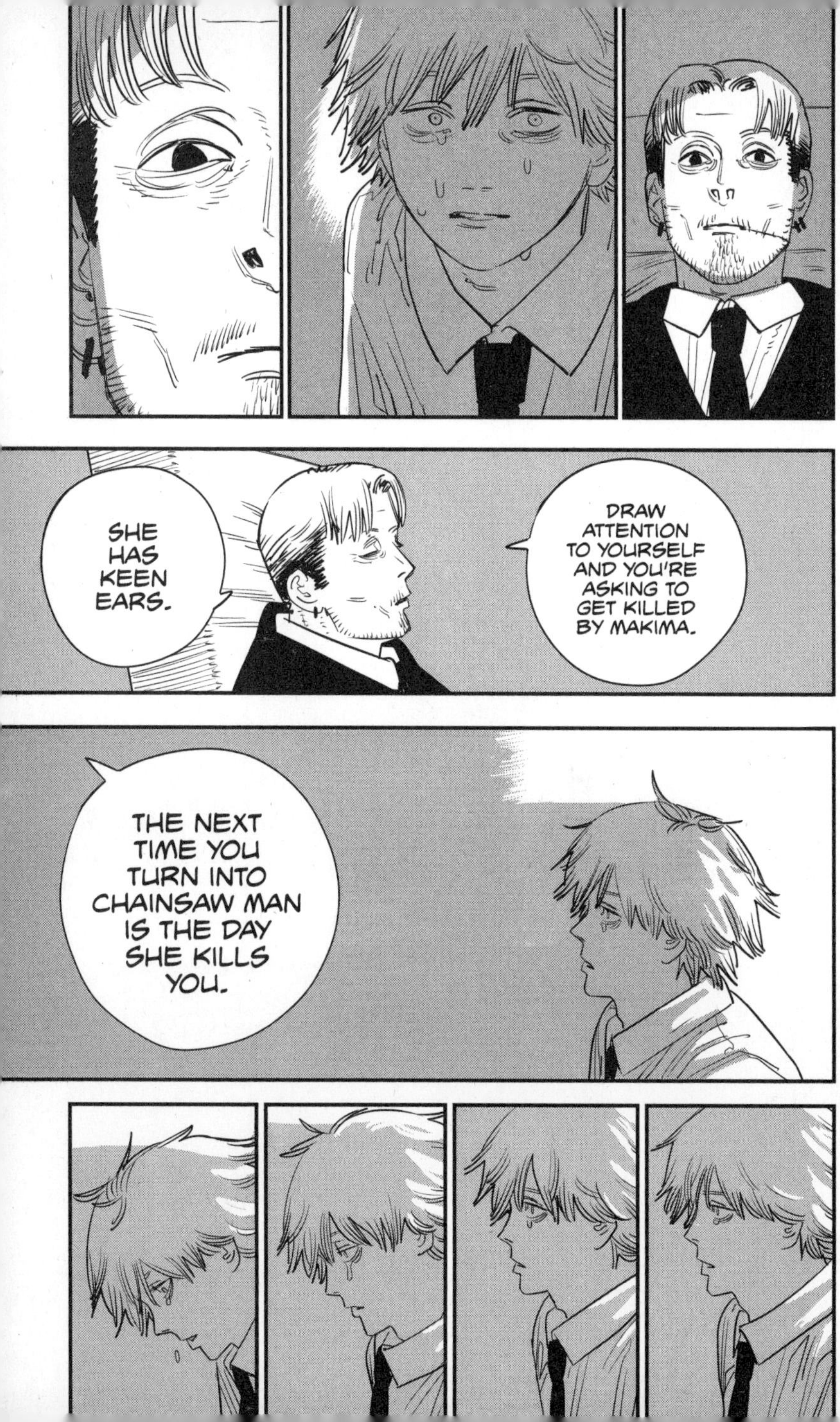
DRAW ATTENTION TO YOURSELF AND YOU'RE ASKING TO GET KILLED BY MAKIMA.
SHE HAS KEEN EARS.
THE NEXT TIME YOU TURN INTO CHAINSAW MAN IS THE DAY SHE KILLS YOU.

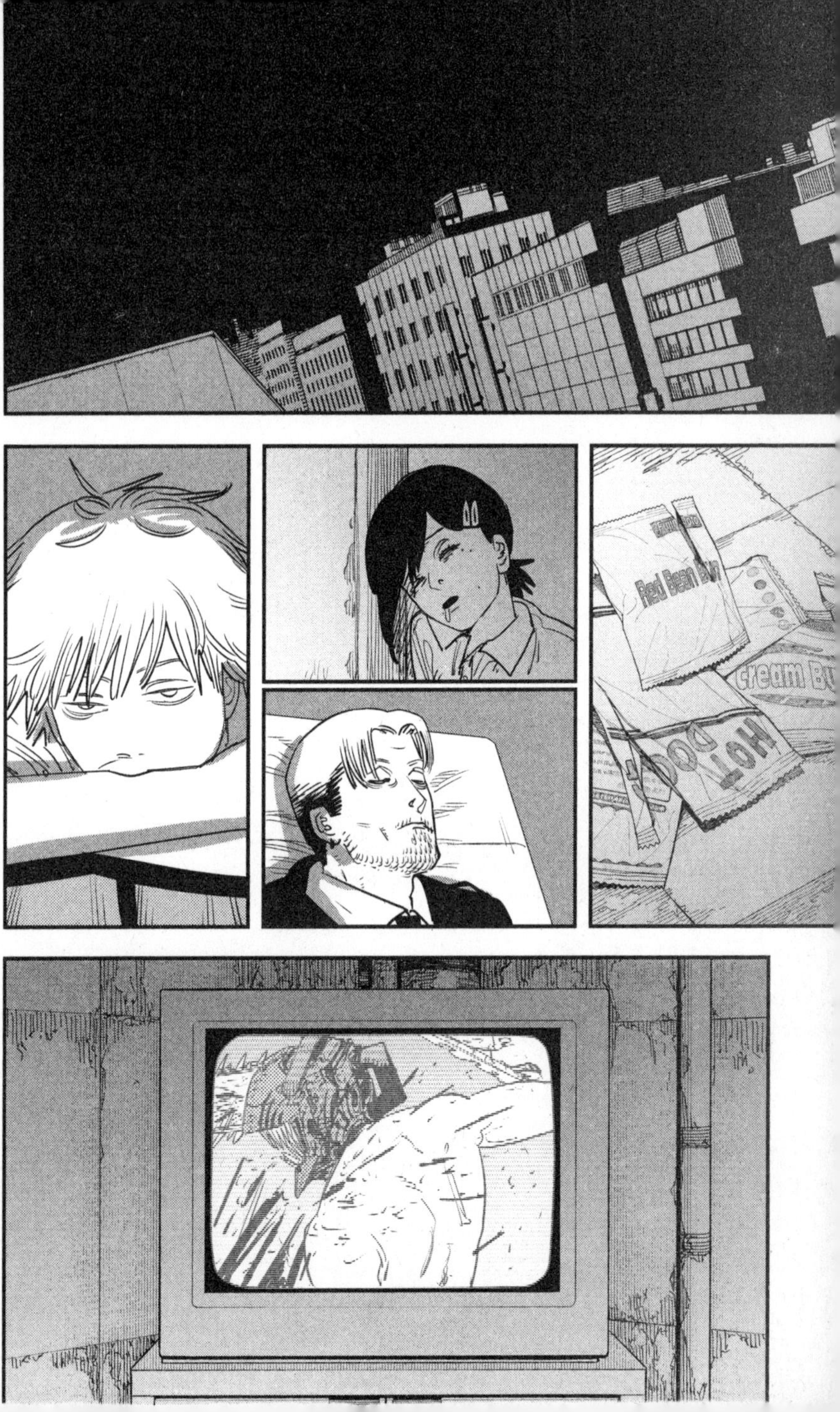

Red Bean Bun
cream Bu
HOT DOG

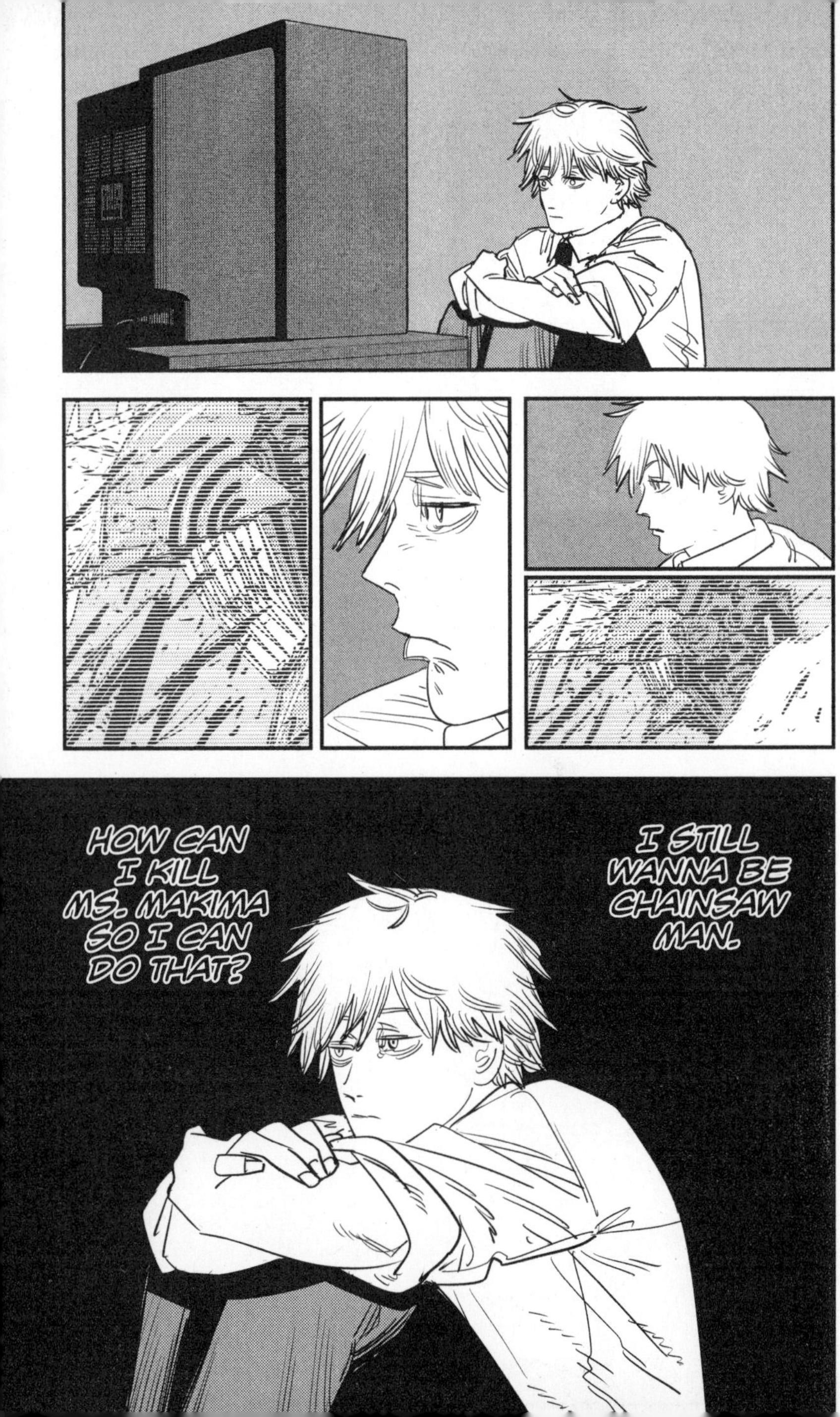
I STILL WANNA BE CHAINSAW MAN.
HOW CAN I KILL MS. MAKIMA SO I CAN DO THAT?

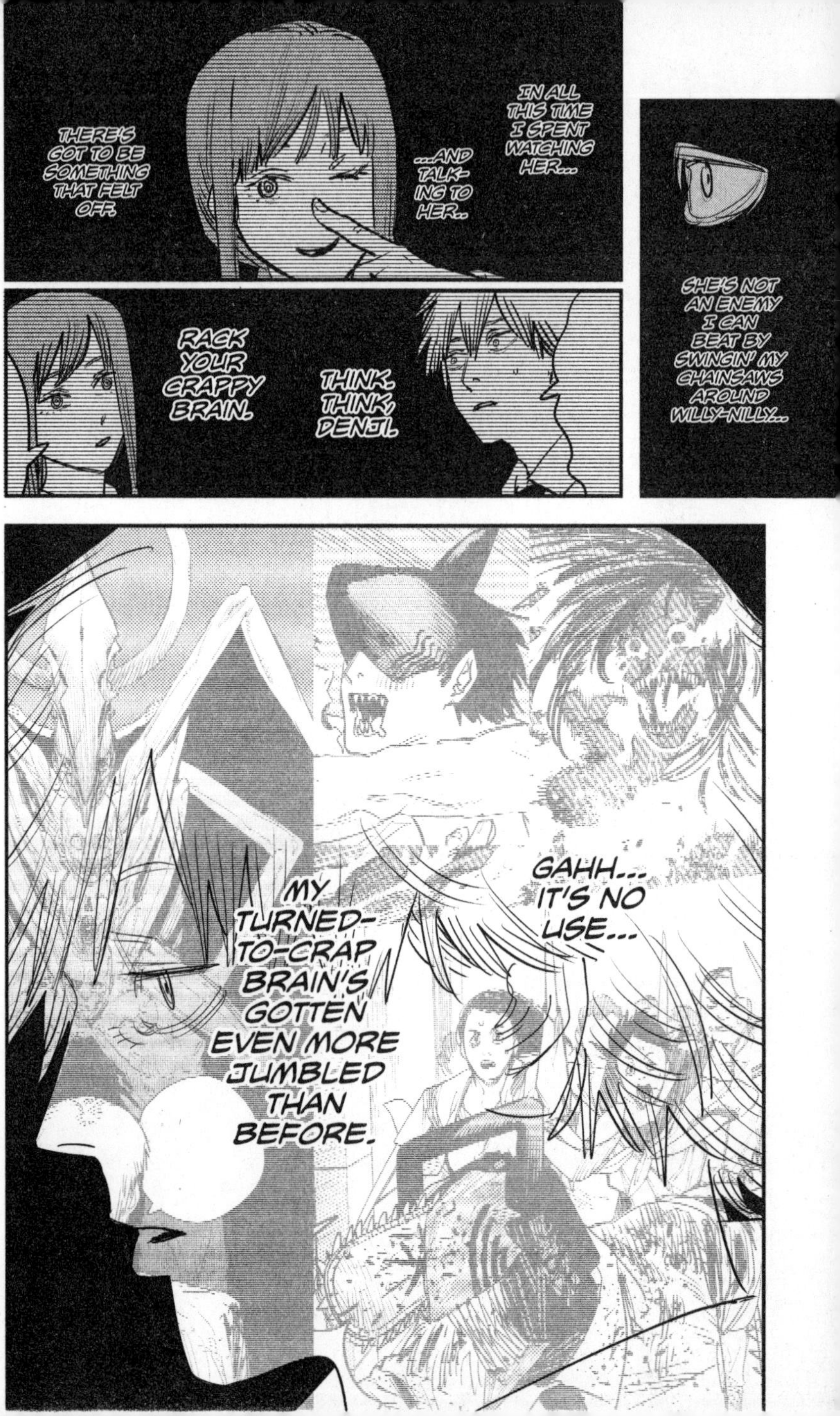
SHE'S NOT AN ENEMY I CAN BEAT BY SWINGIN' MY CHAINSAWS AROUND WILLY-NILLY...
IN ALL THIS TIME I SPENT WATCHING HER...
...AND TALKING TO HER..
THERE'S GOT TO BE SOMETHING THAT FELT OFF.
THINK. THINK, DENJI.
RACK YOUR CRAPPY BRAIN.
GAHH... IT'S NO USE...
MY TURNED-TO-CRAP BRAIN'S GOTTEN EVEN MORE JUMBLED THAN BEFORE.

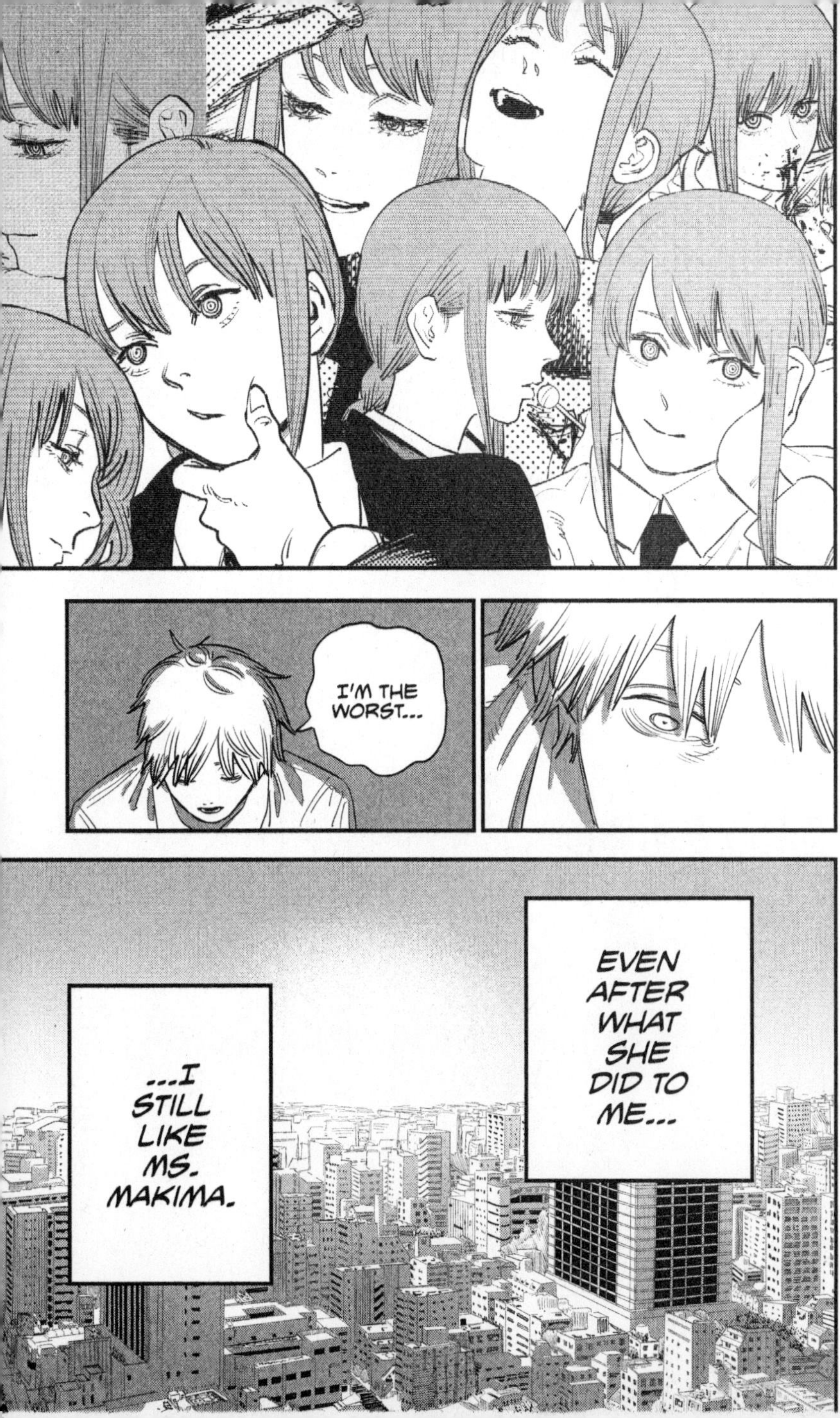
I'M THE WORST...
EVEN AFTER WHAT SHE DID TO ME...
...I STILL LIKE MS. MAKIMA.

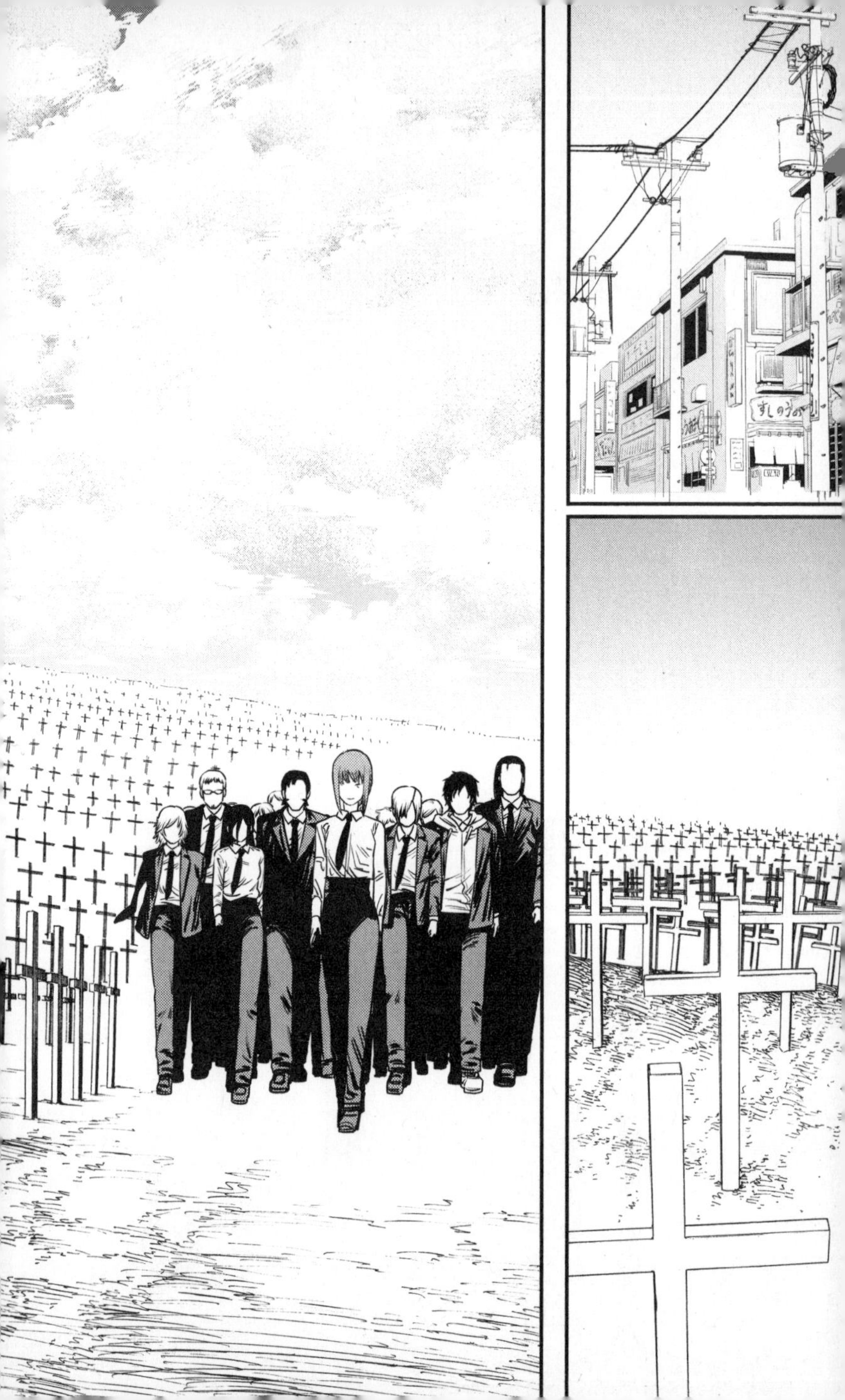

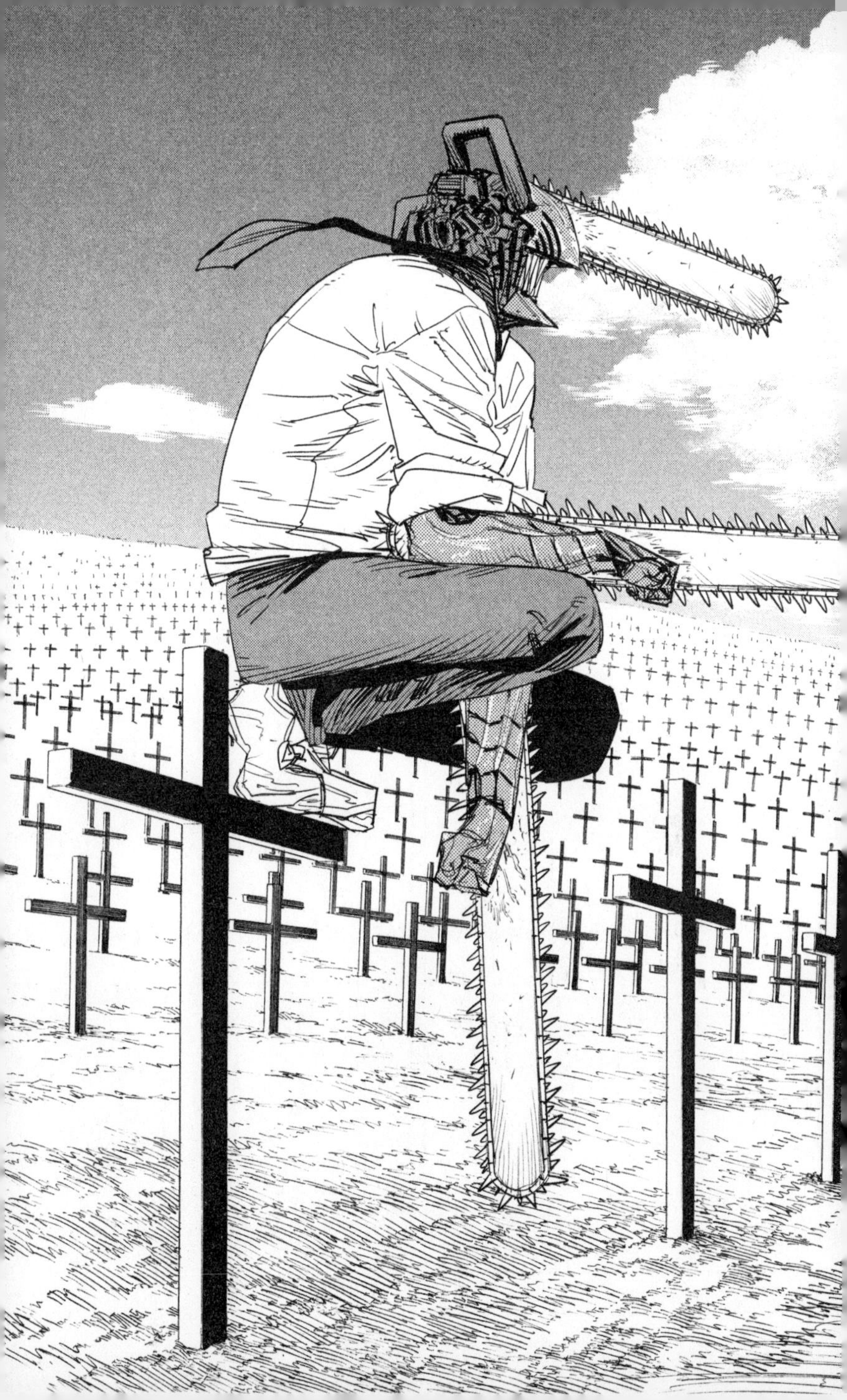

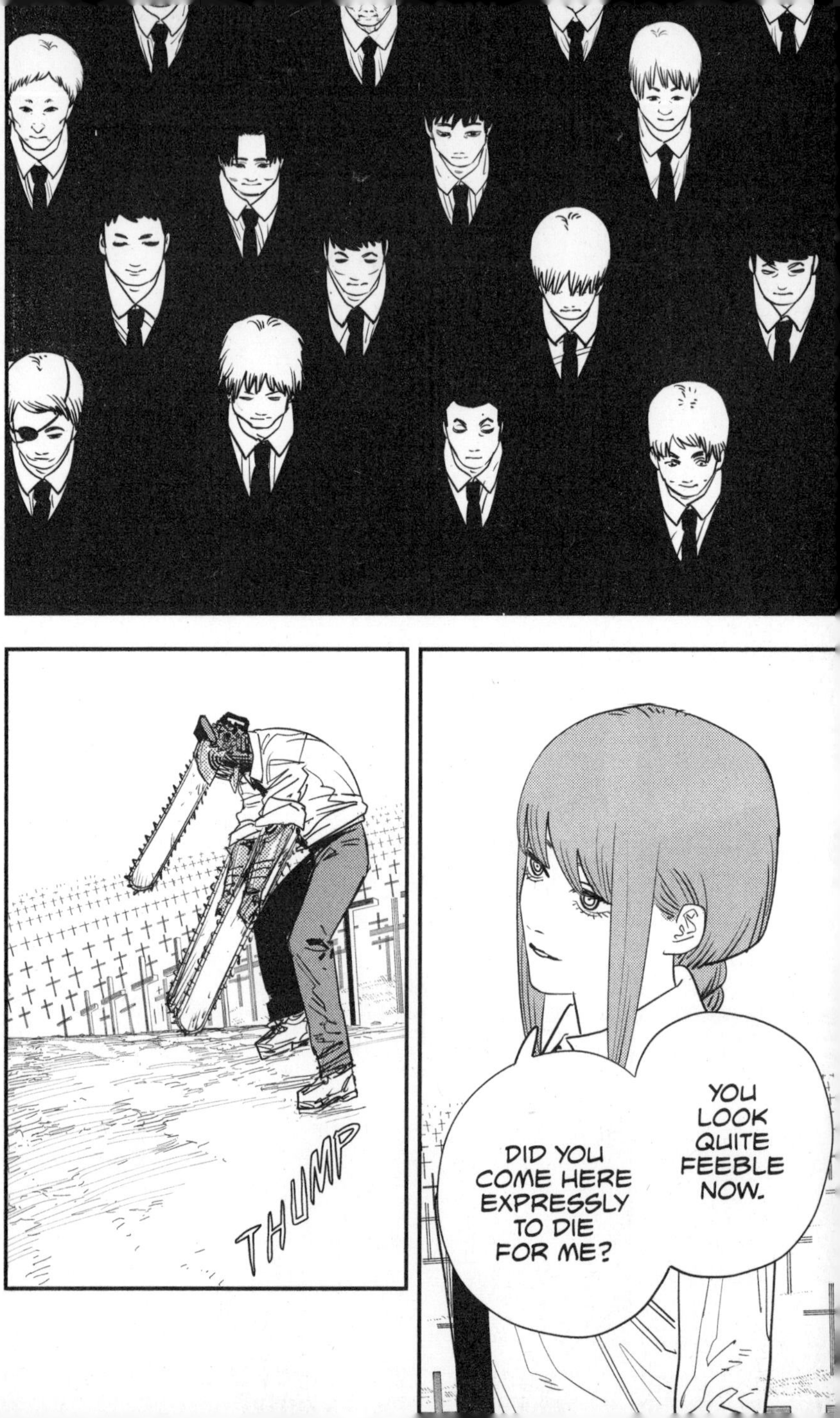
YOU LOOK QUITE FEEBLE NOW.
DID YOU COME HERE EXPRESSLY TO DIE FOR ME?
THUMP

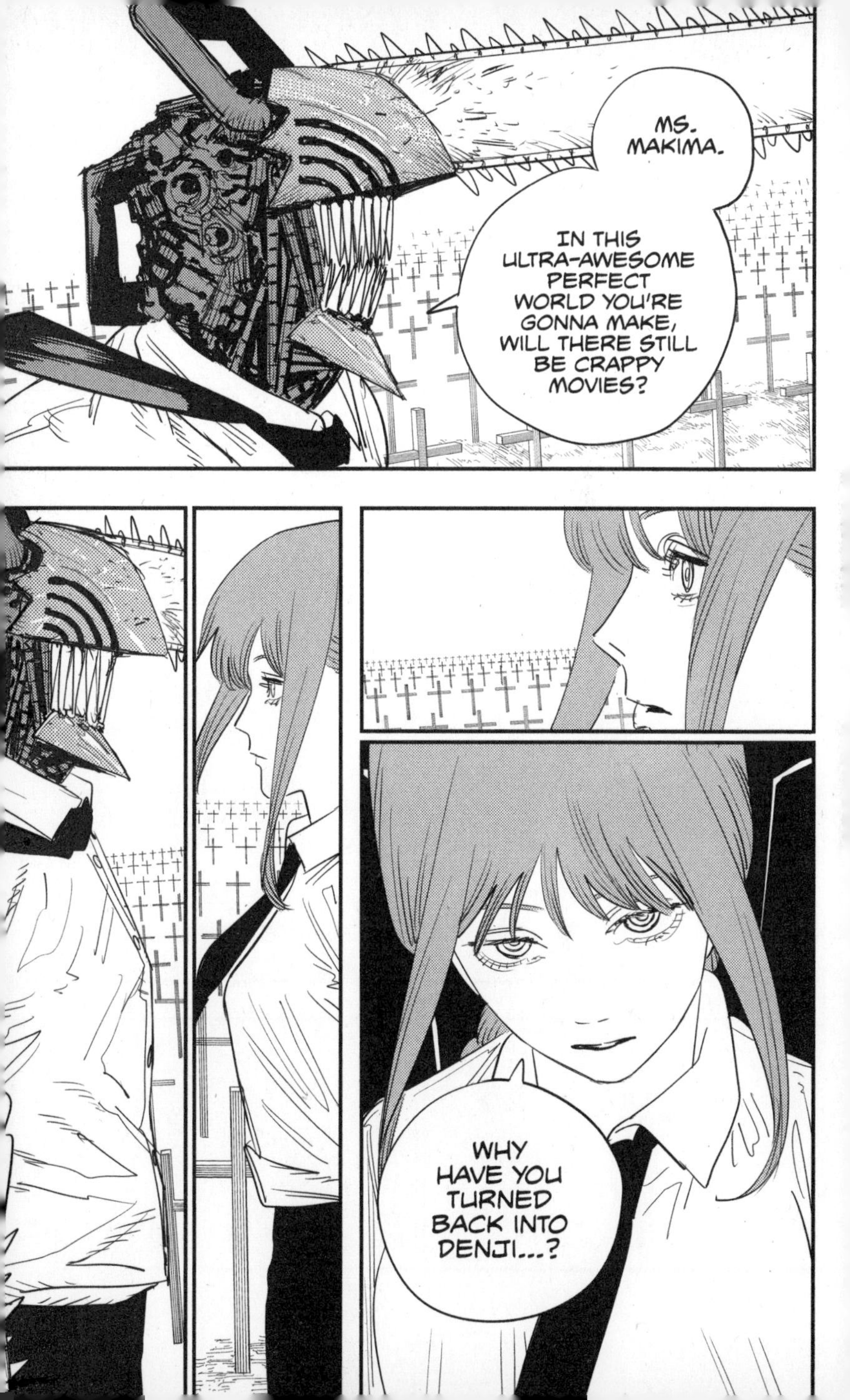
MS. MAKIMA.
IN THIS ULTRA-AWESOME PERFECT WORLD YOU'RE GONNA MAKE, WILL THERE STILL BE CRAPPY MOVIES?
WHY HAVE YOU TURNED BACK INTO DENJI...?

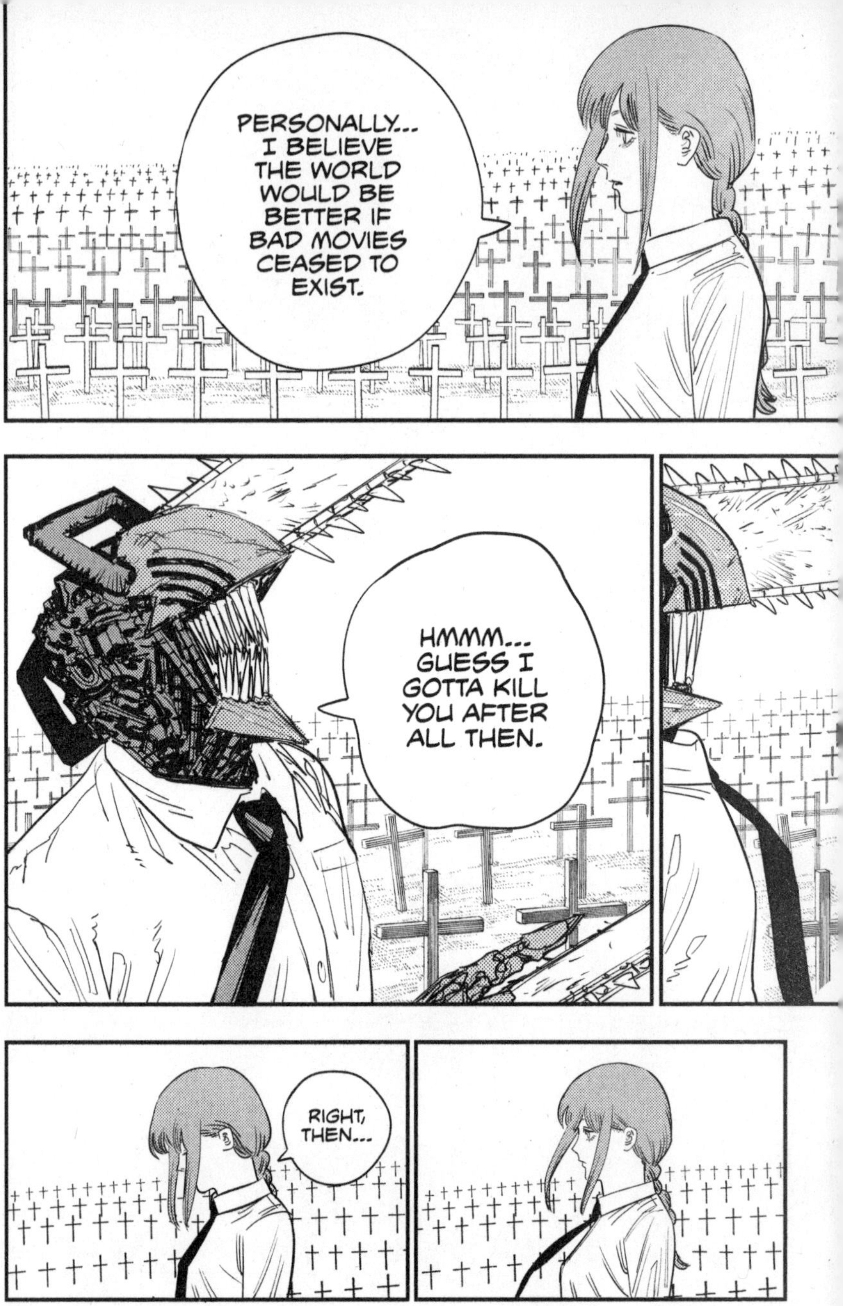
PERSONALLY... I BELIEVE THE WORLD WOULD BE BETTER IF BAD MOVIES CEASED TO EXIST.
HMMM... GUESS I GOTTA KILL YOU AFTER ALL THEN.
RIGHT, THEN...

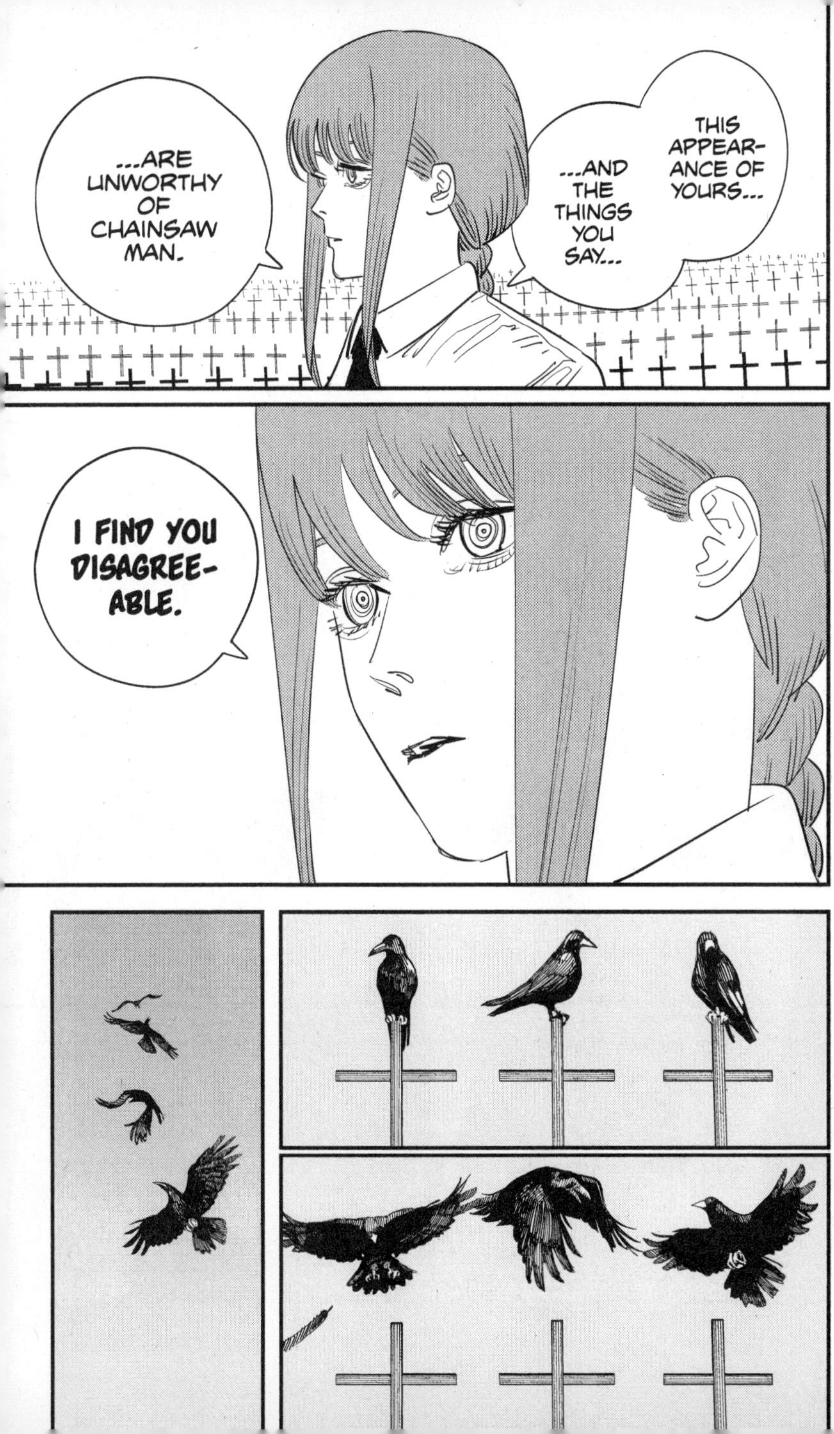
THIS APPEARANCE OF YOURS...
...AND THE THINGS YOU SAY...
...ARE UNWORTHY OF CHAINSAW MAN.
I FIND YOU DISAGREEABLE.

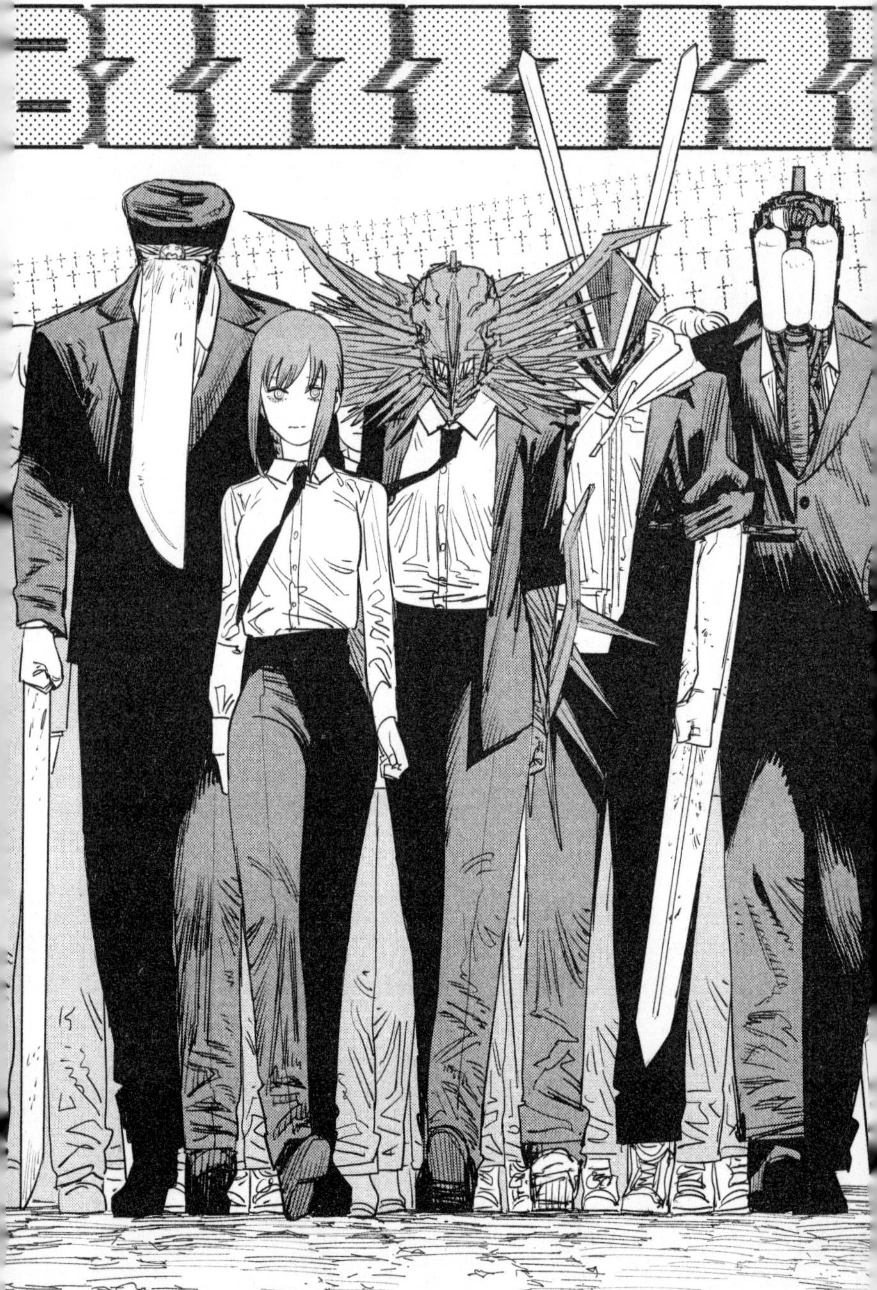

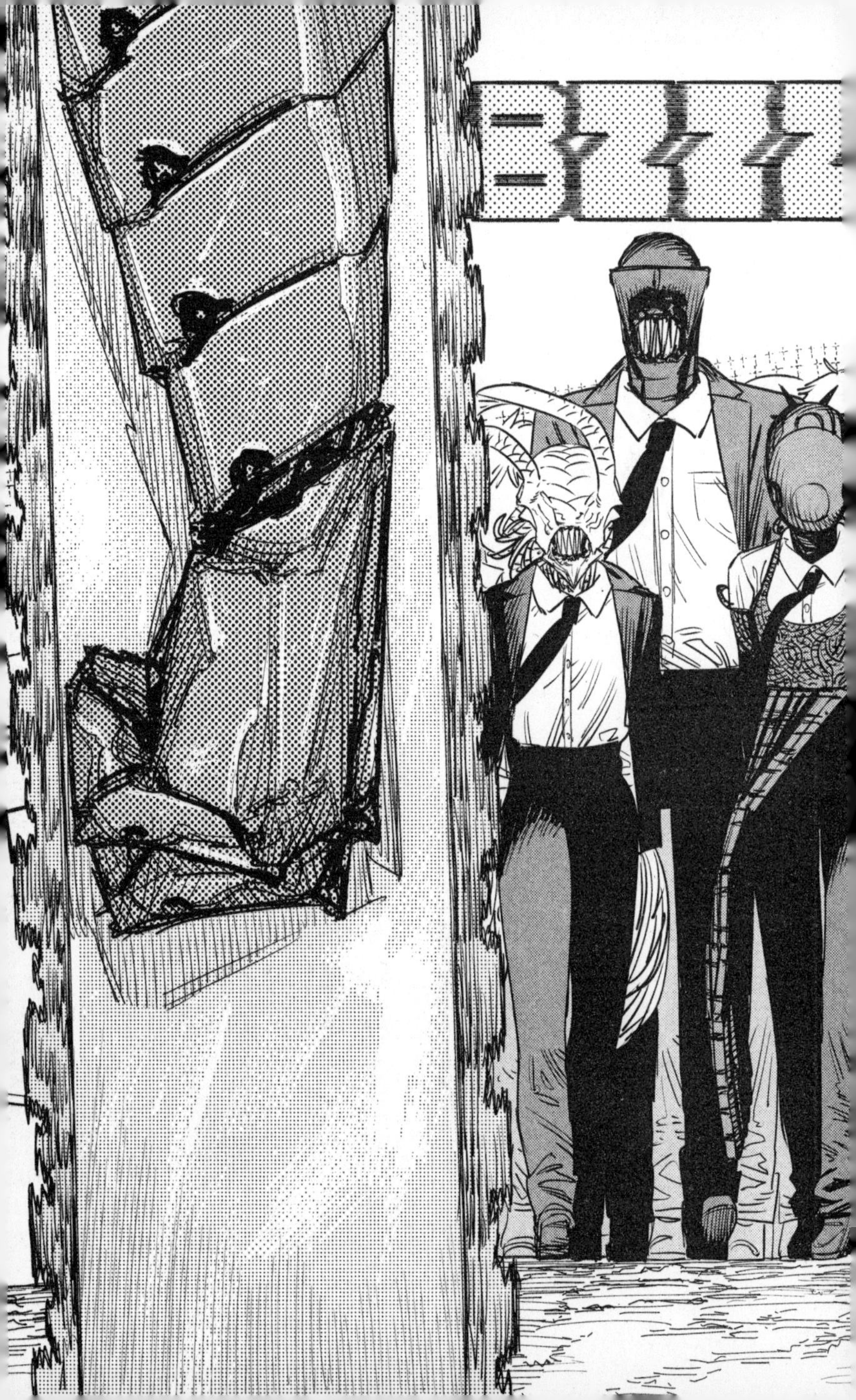

Chain saw man

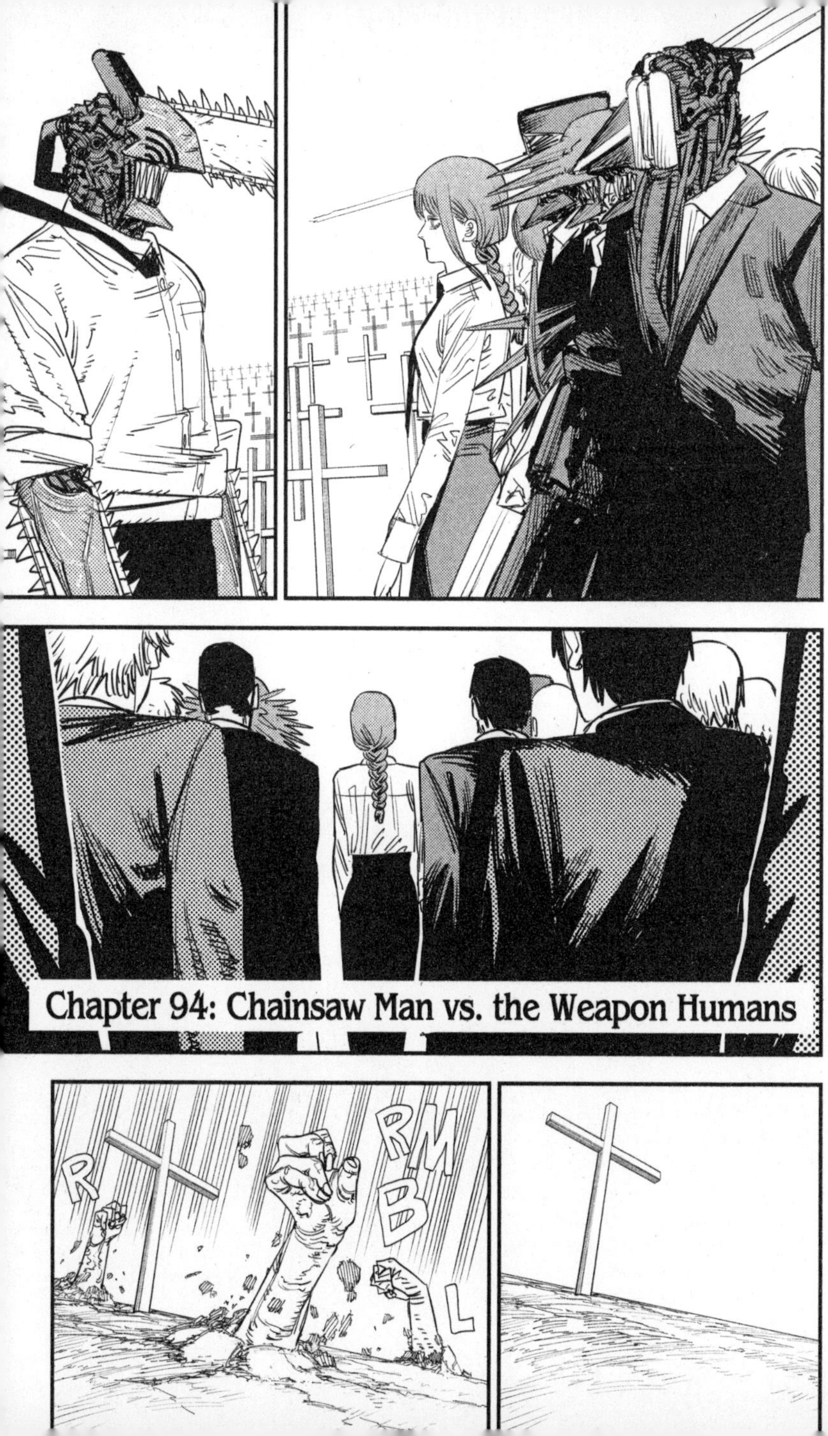
Chapter 94: Chainsaw Man vs. the Weapon Humans
R
RMBL

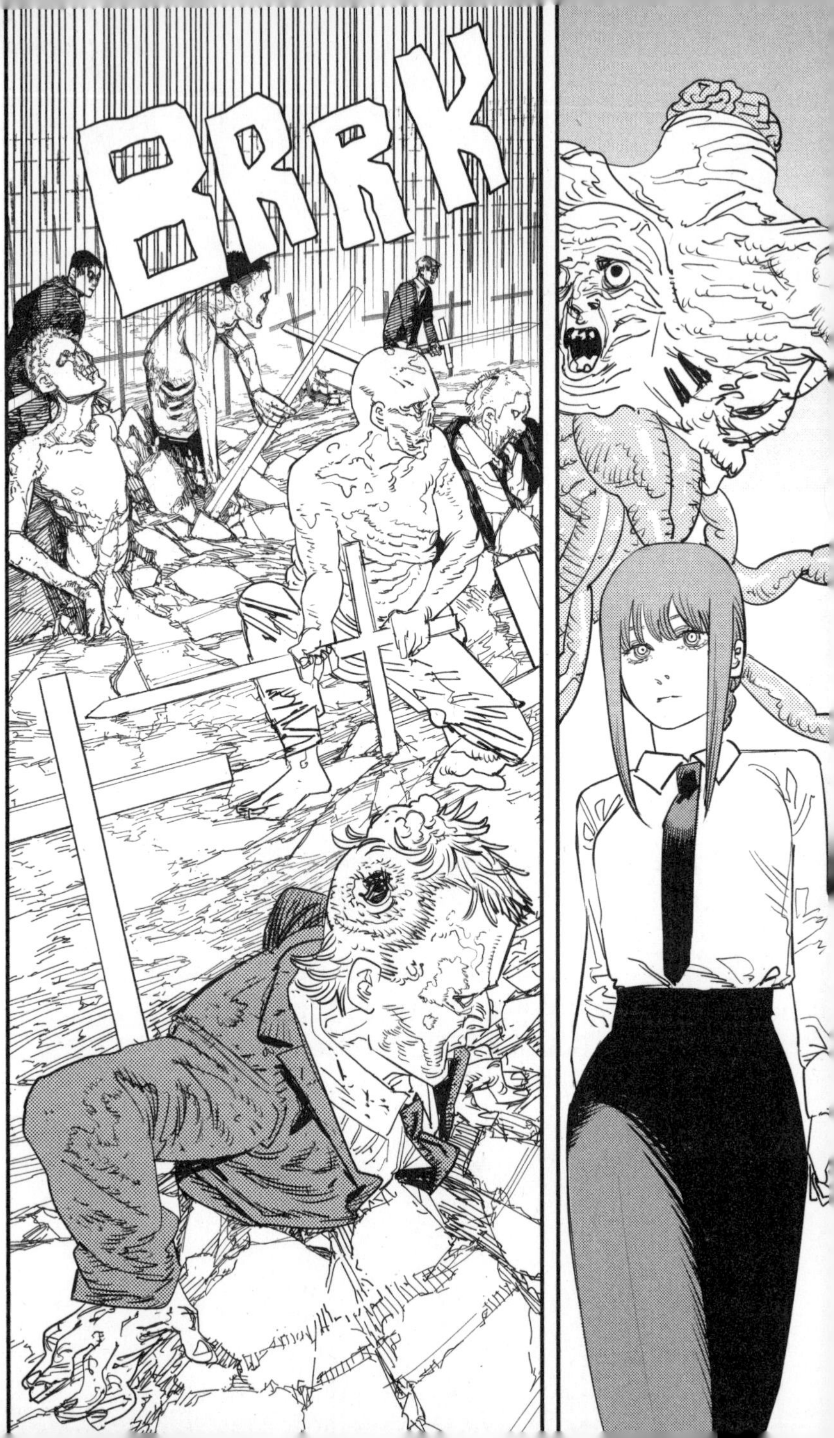
BRRK

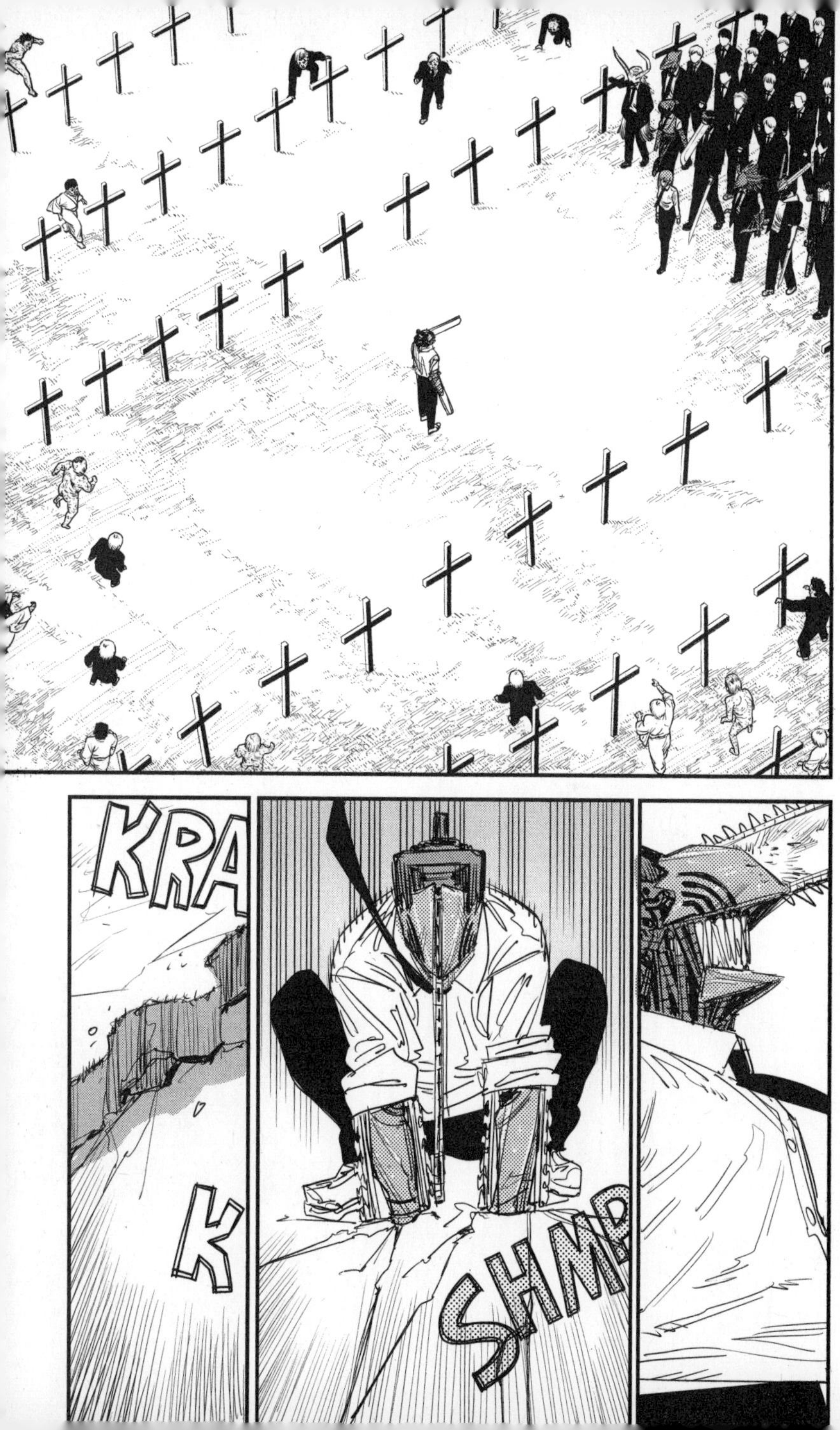
SHMP
KRA
K

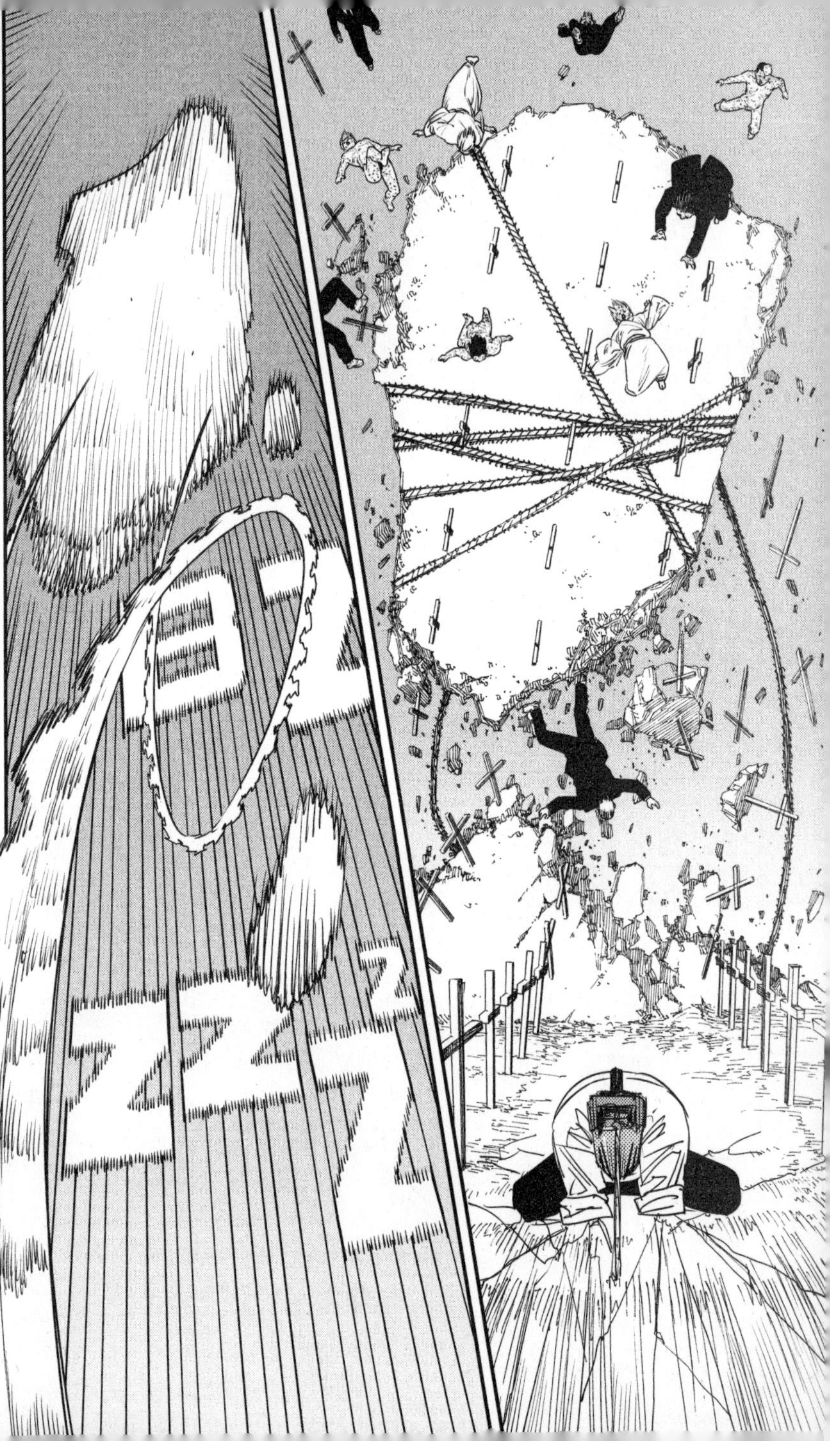

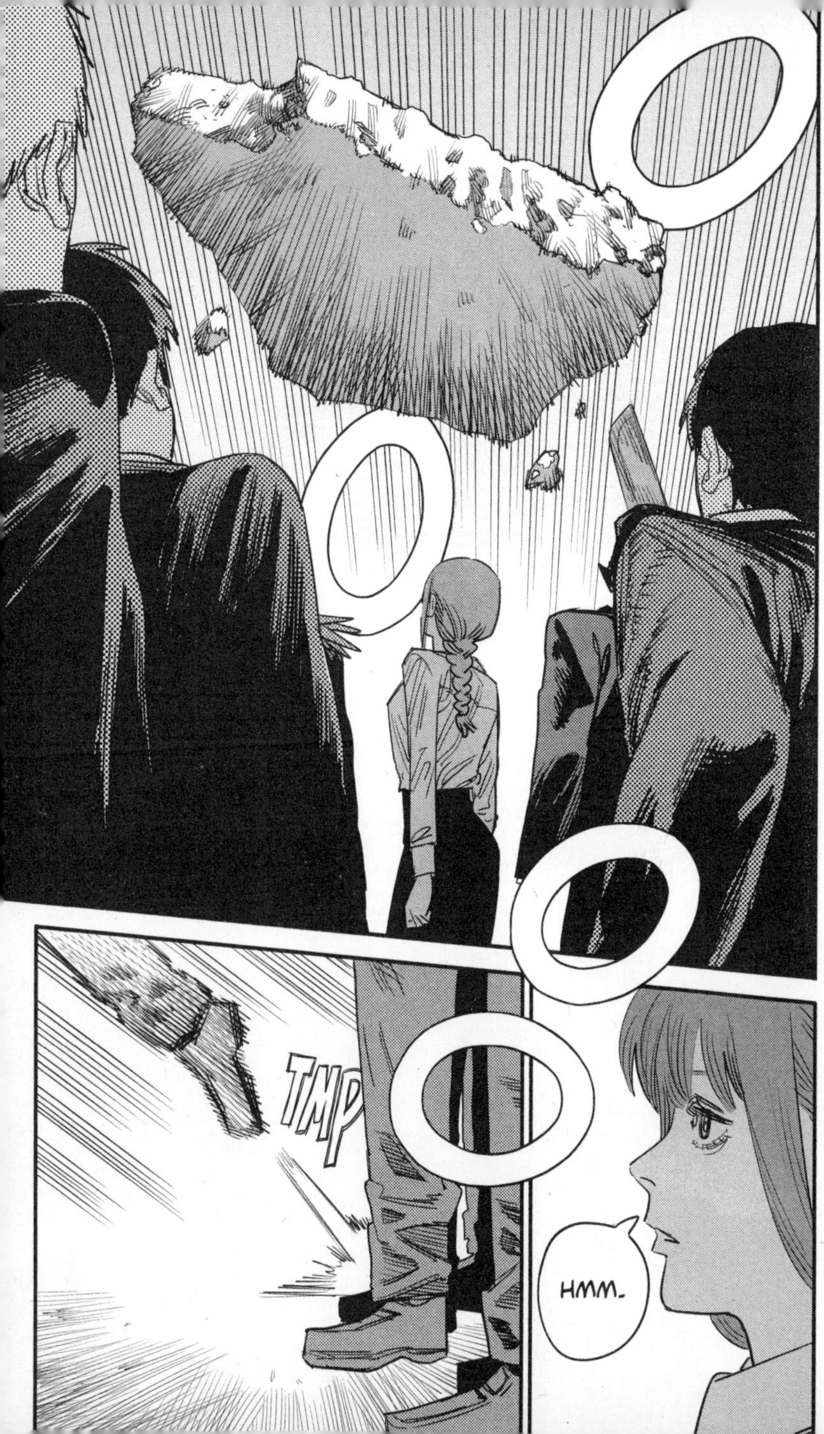
HMM.
TMP

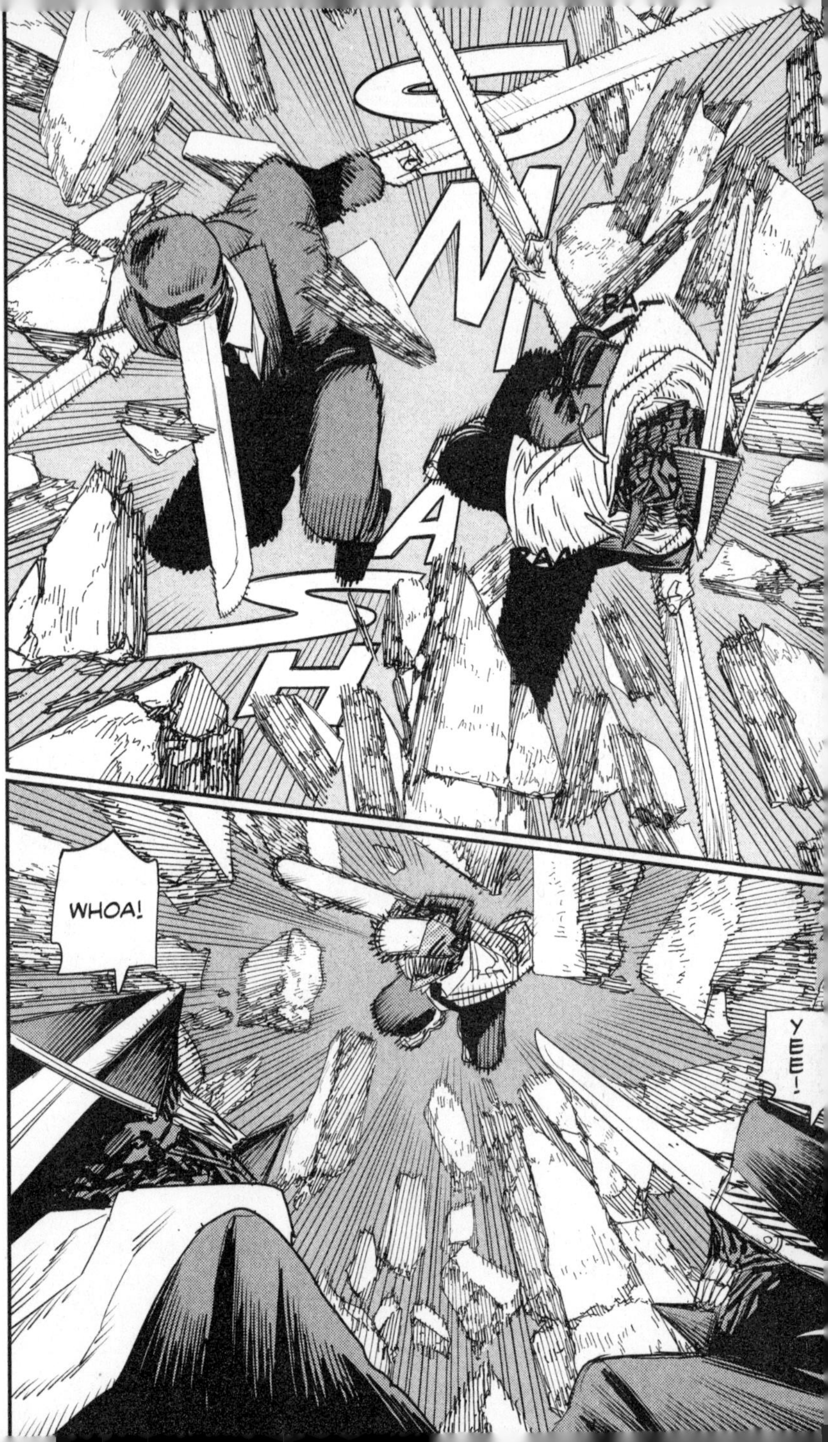
SMASH
BA—
BAA
YEE!
WHOA!

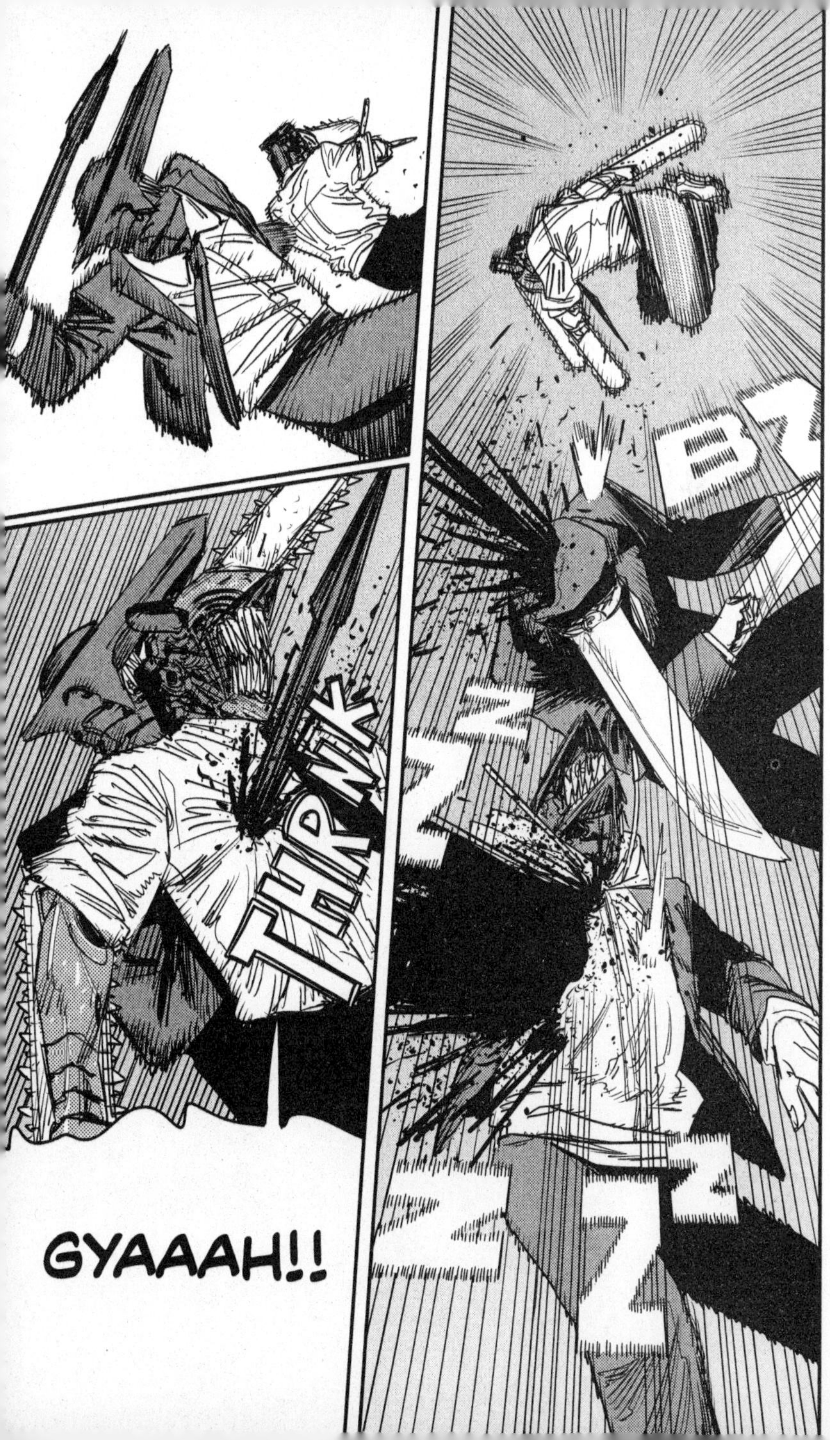
THRNK
GYAAAH!!

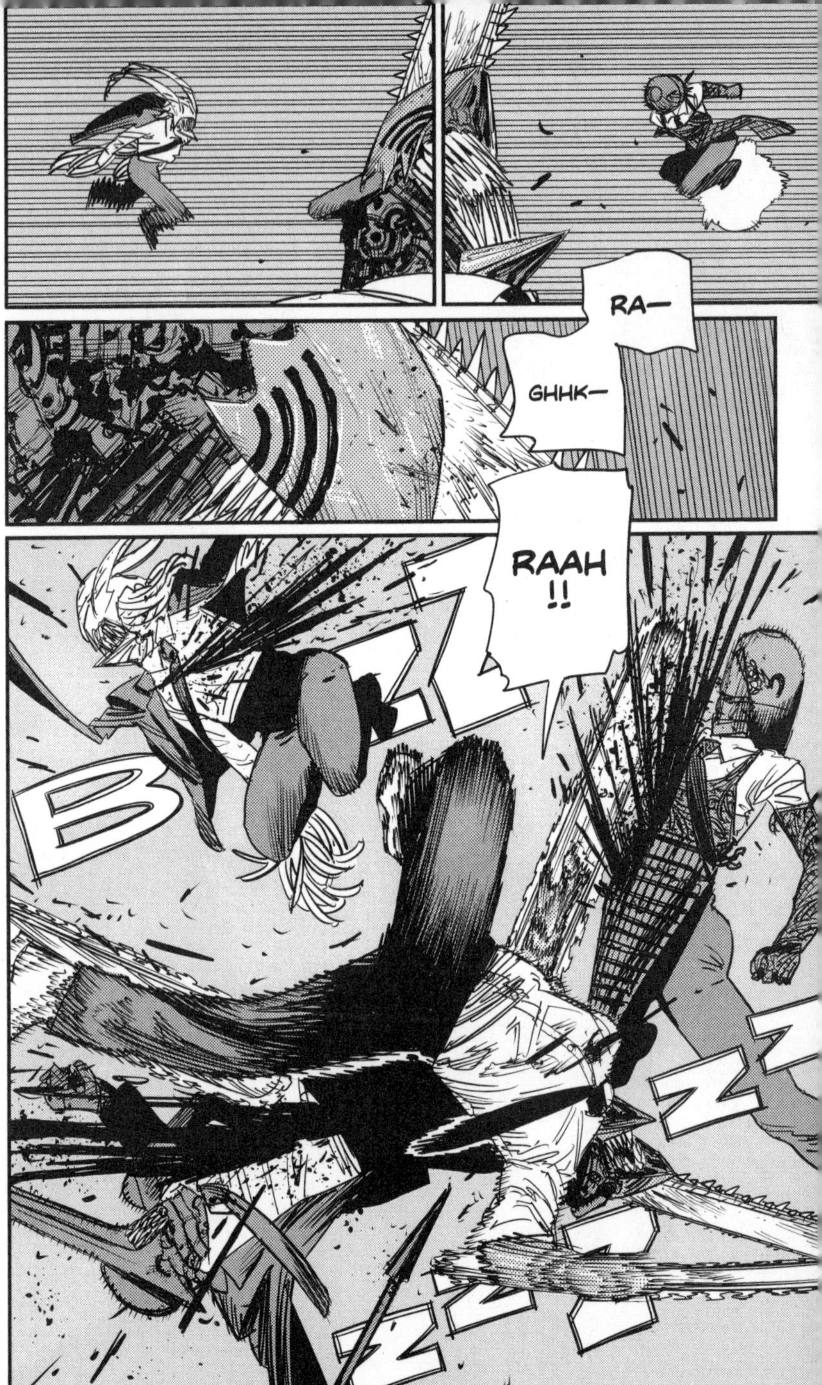
RA—
GHHK—
RAAH!!
BZZZZ

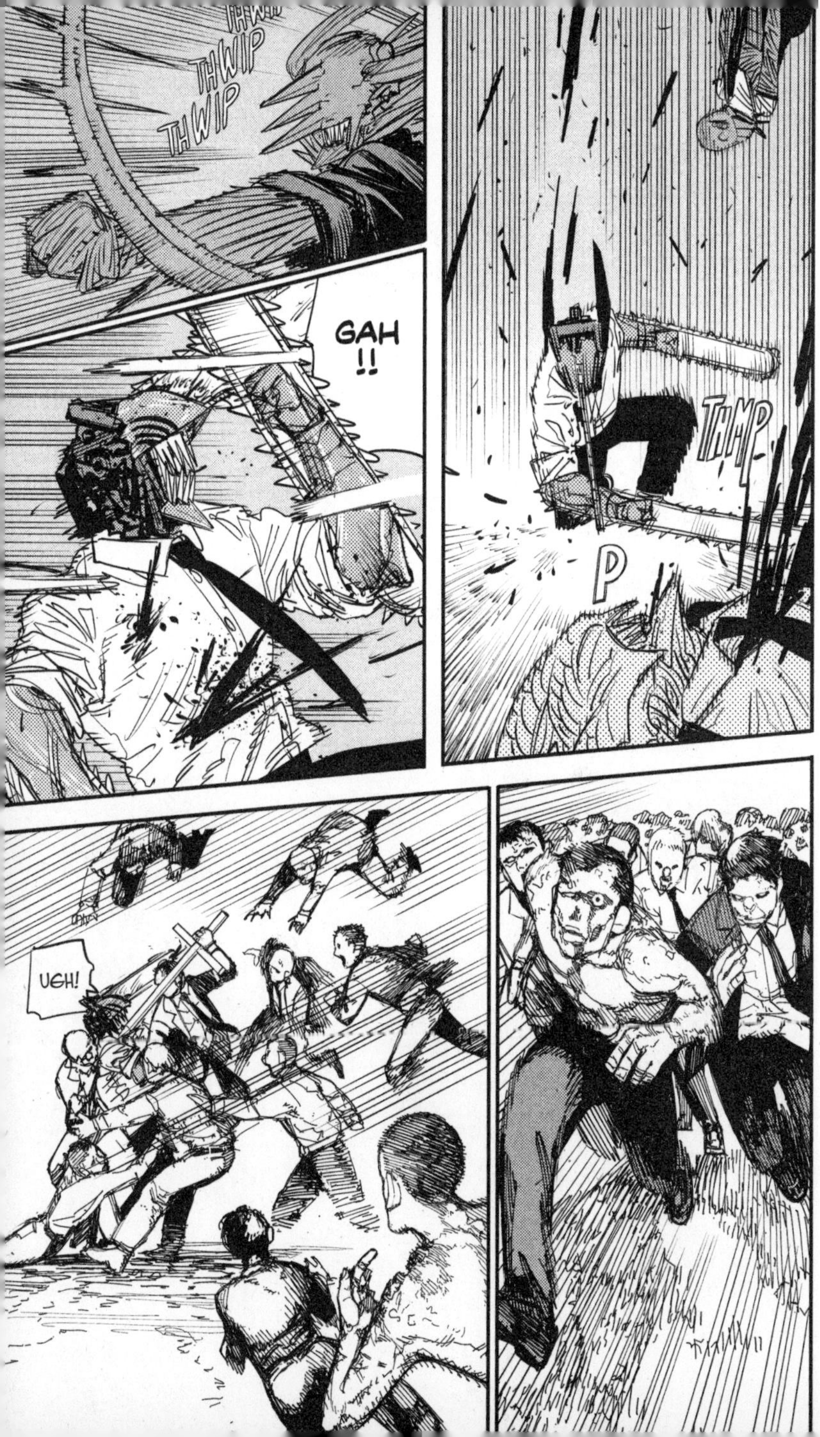
THMP
P
THWIP
THWIP
THWIP
GAH !!
UGH!

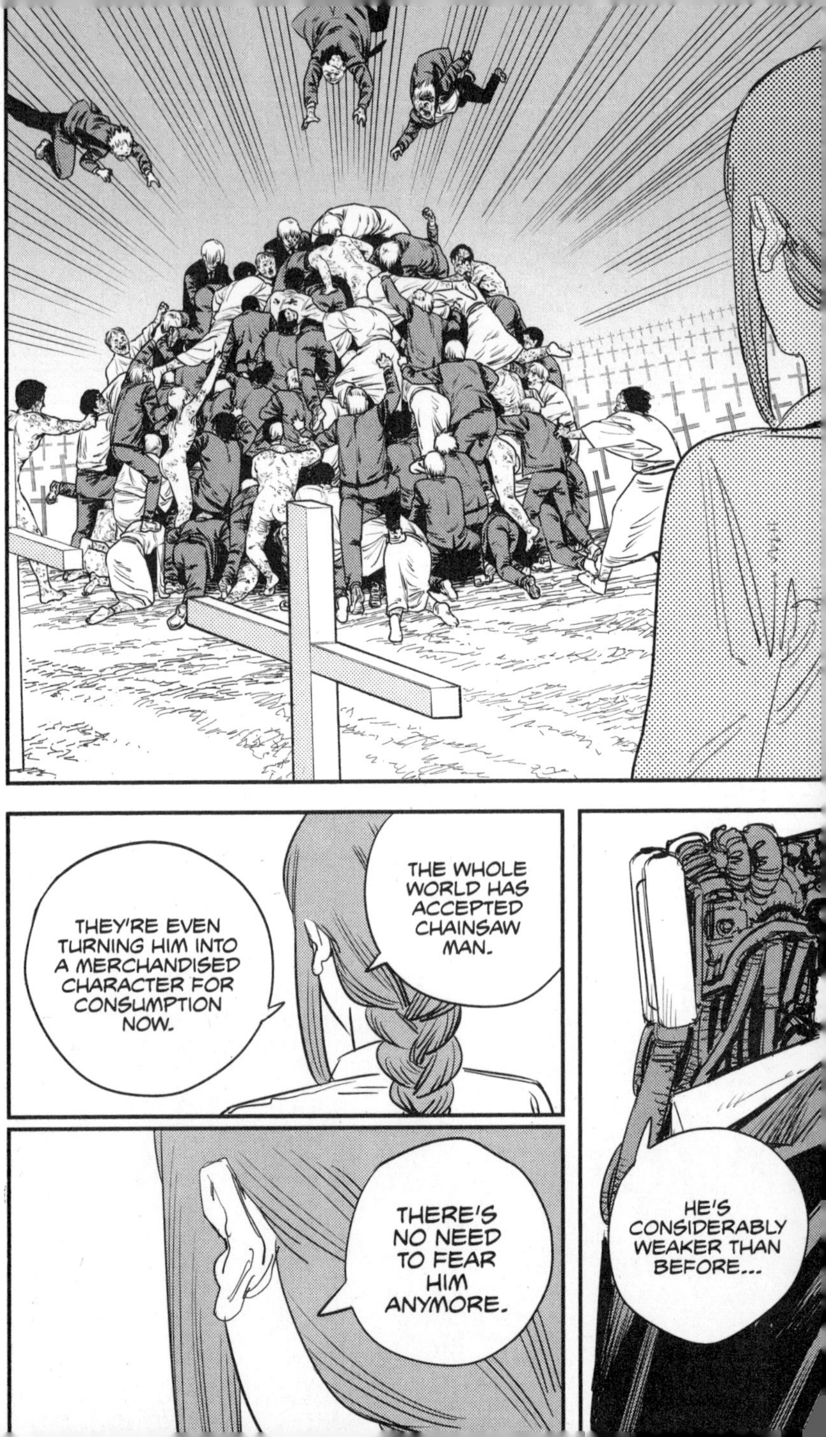
HE'S CONSIDERABLY WEAKER THAN BEFORE...
THE WHOLE WORLD HAS ACCEPTED CHAINSAW MAN.
THEY'RE EVEN TURNING HIM INTO A MERCHANDISED CHARACTER FOR CONSUMPTION NOW.
THERE'S NO NEED TO FEAR HIM ANYMORE.

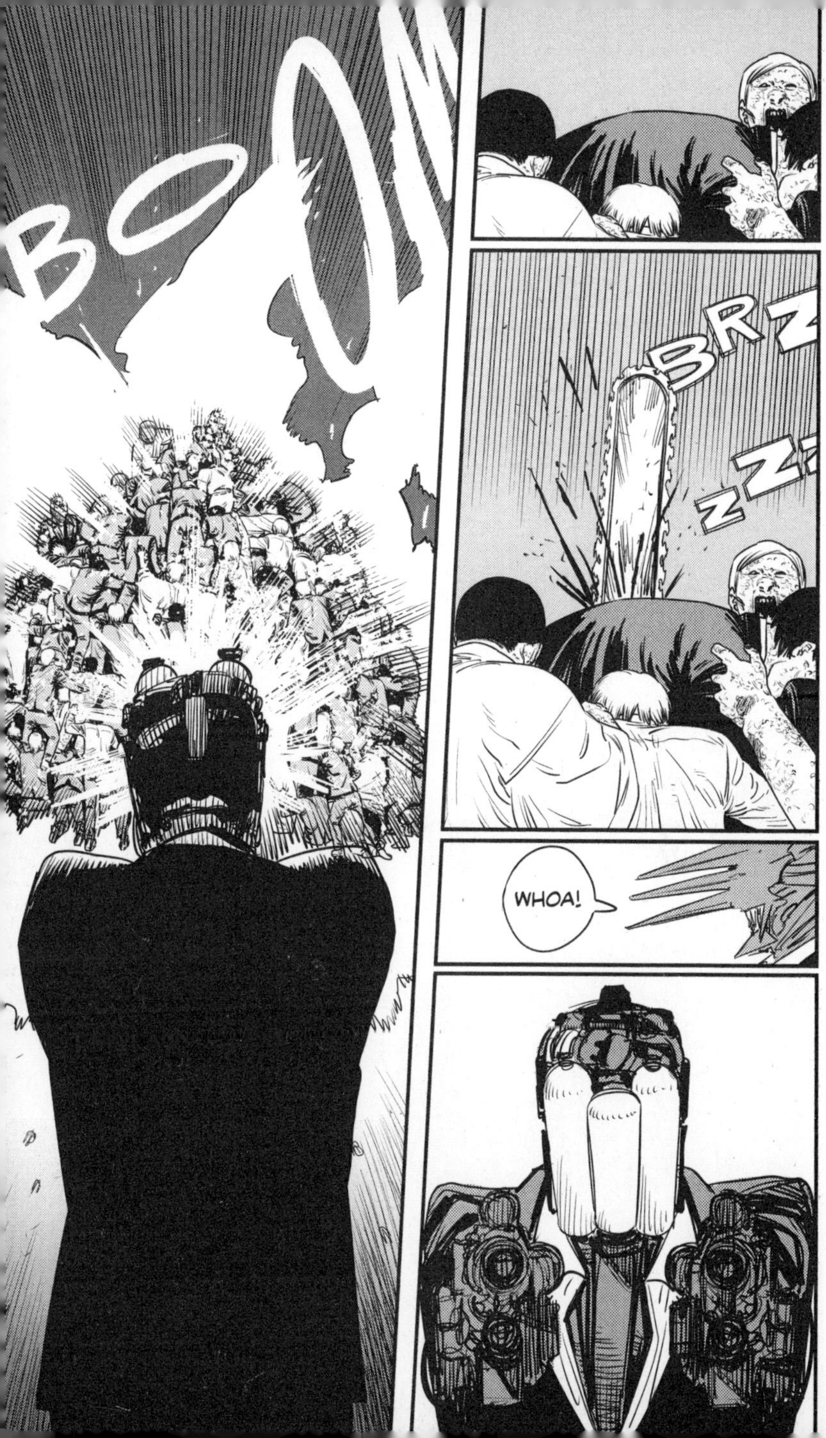
BRZZZZ
WHOA!
BOOM

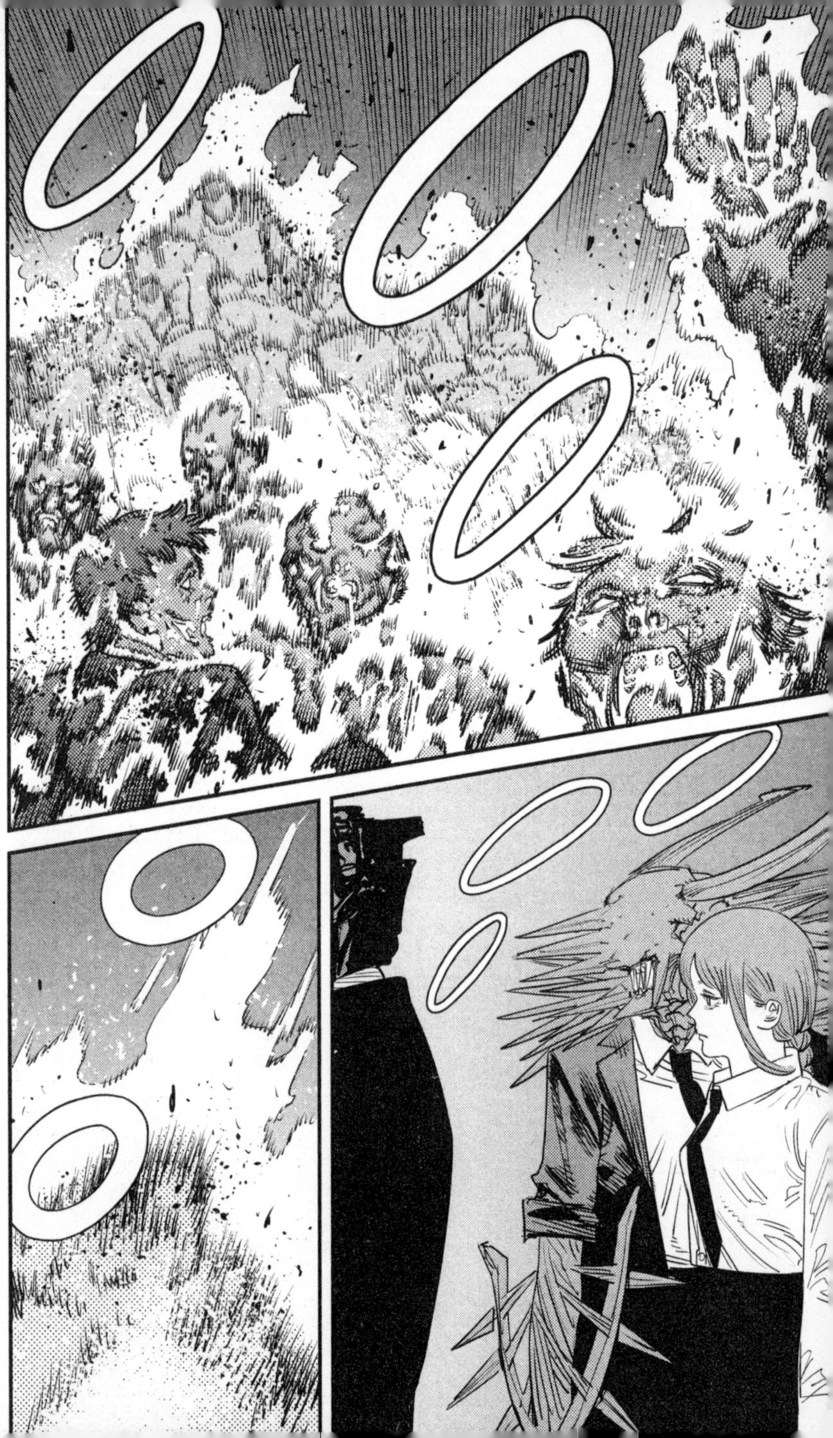

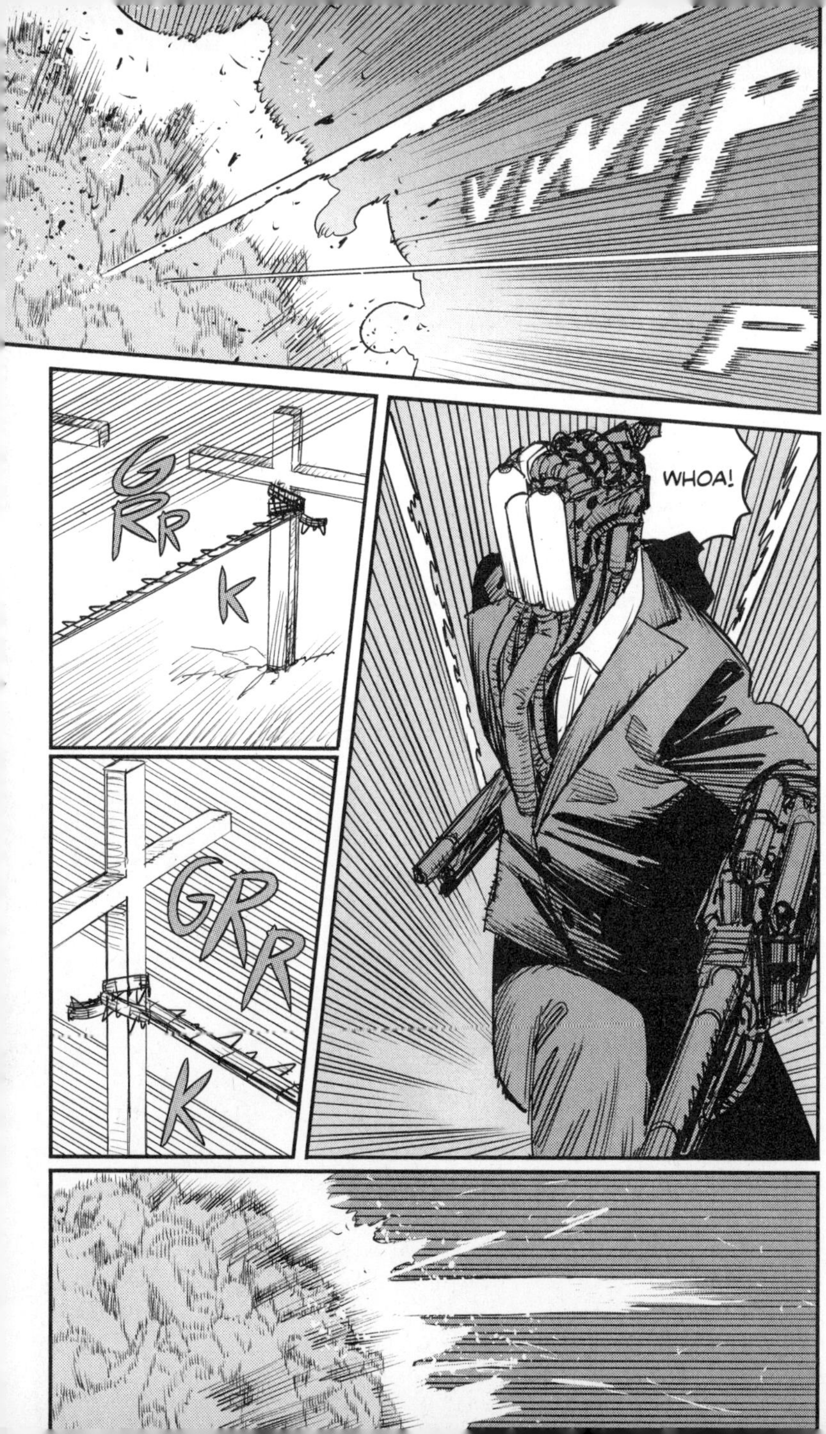
WHOA!
GRRK
GRRRK

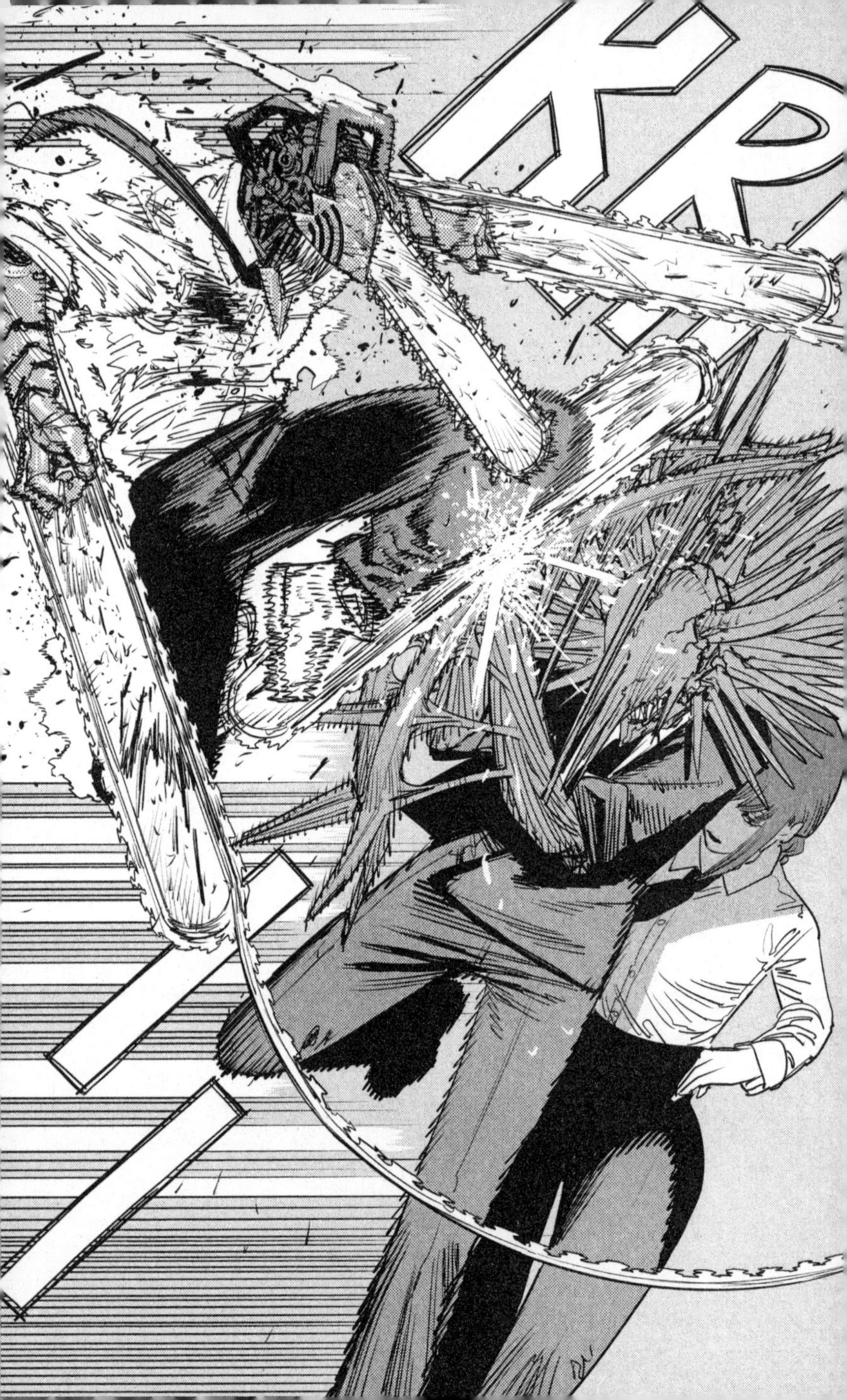

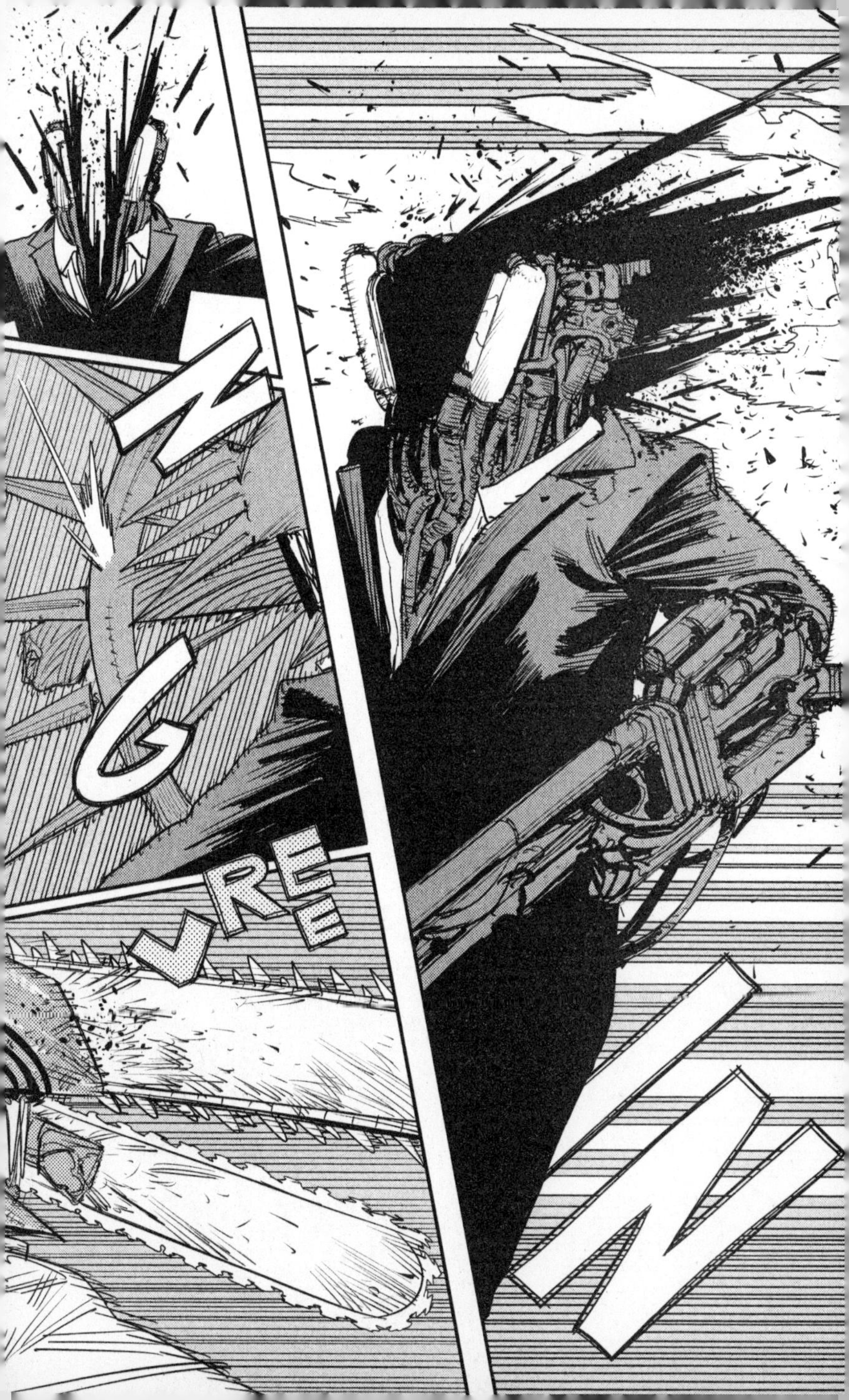
VREE
N
G
N

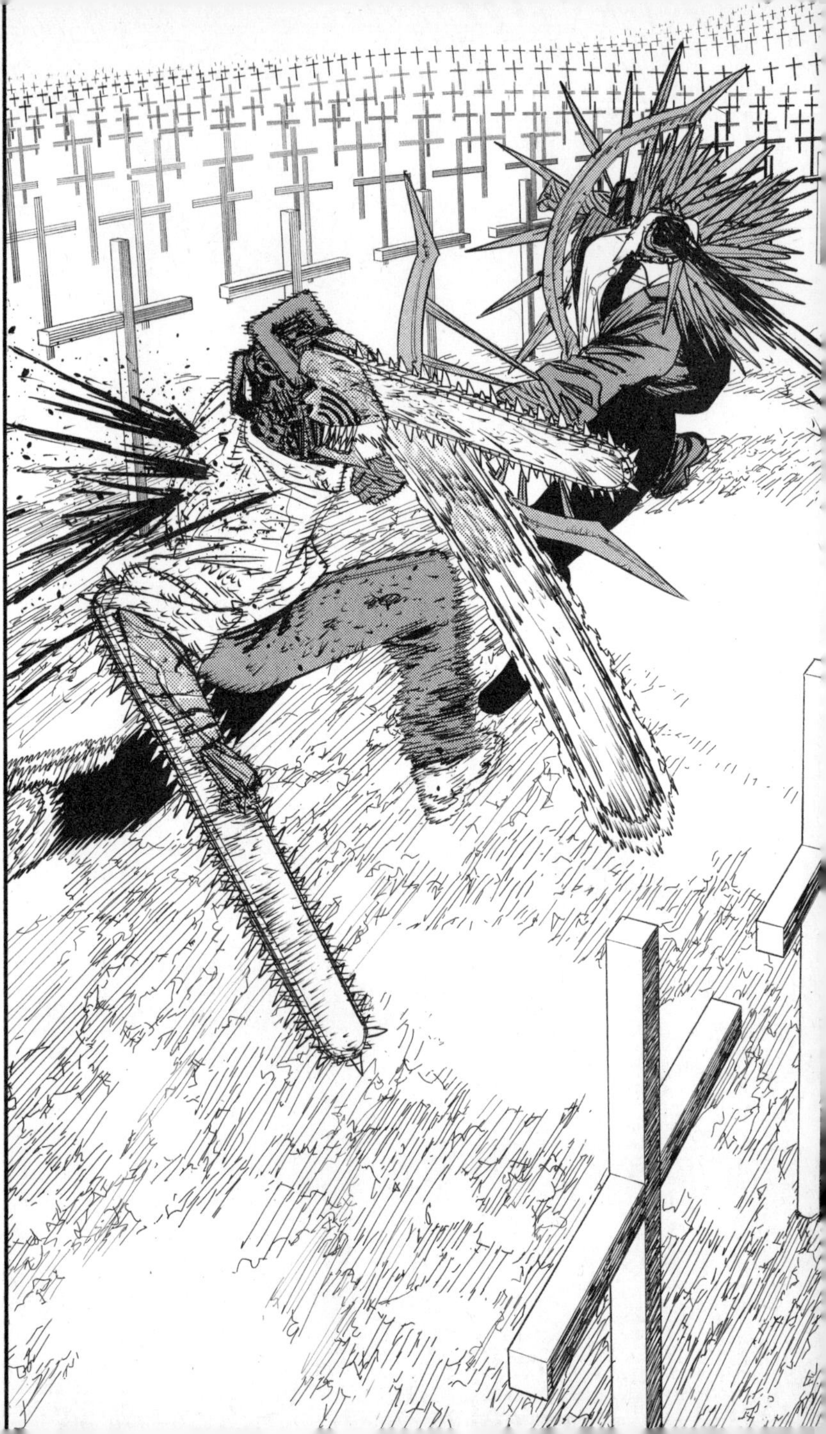

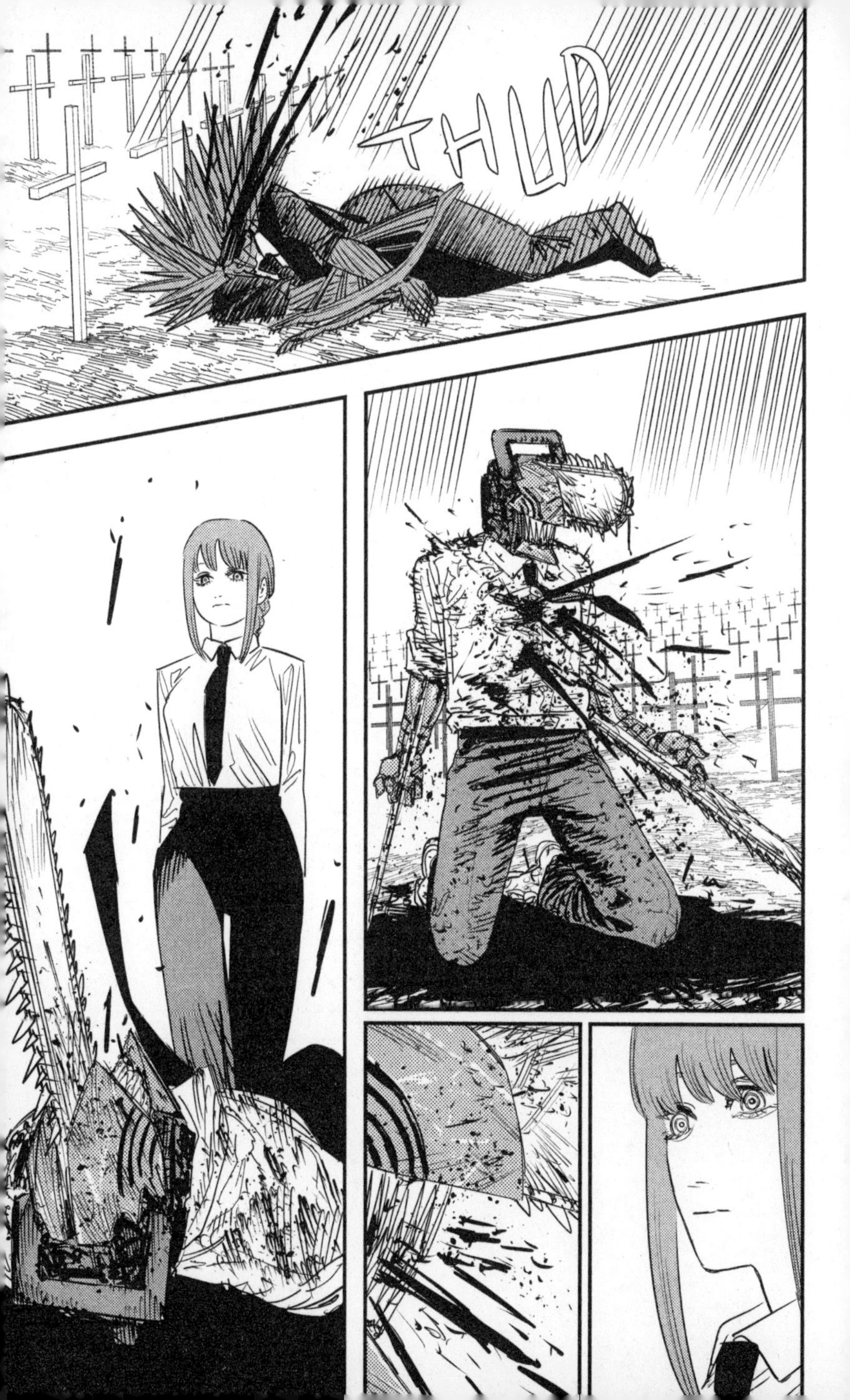
THUD

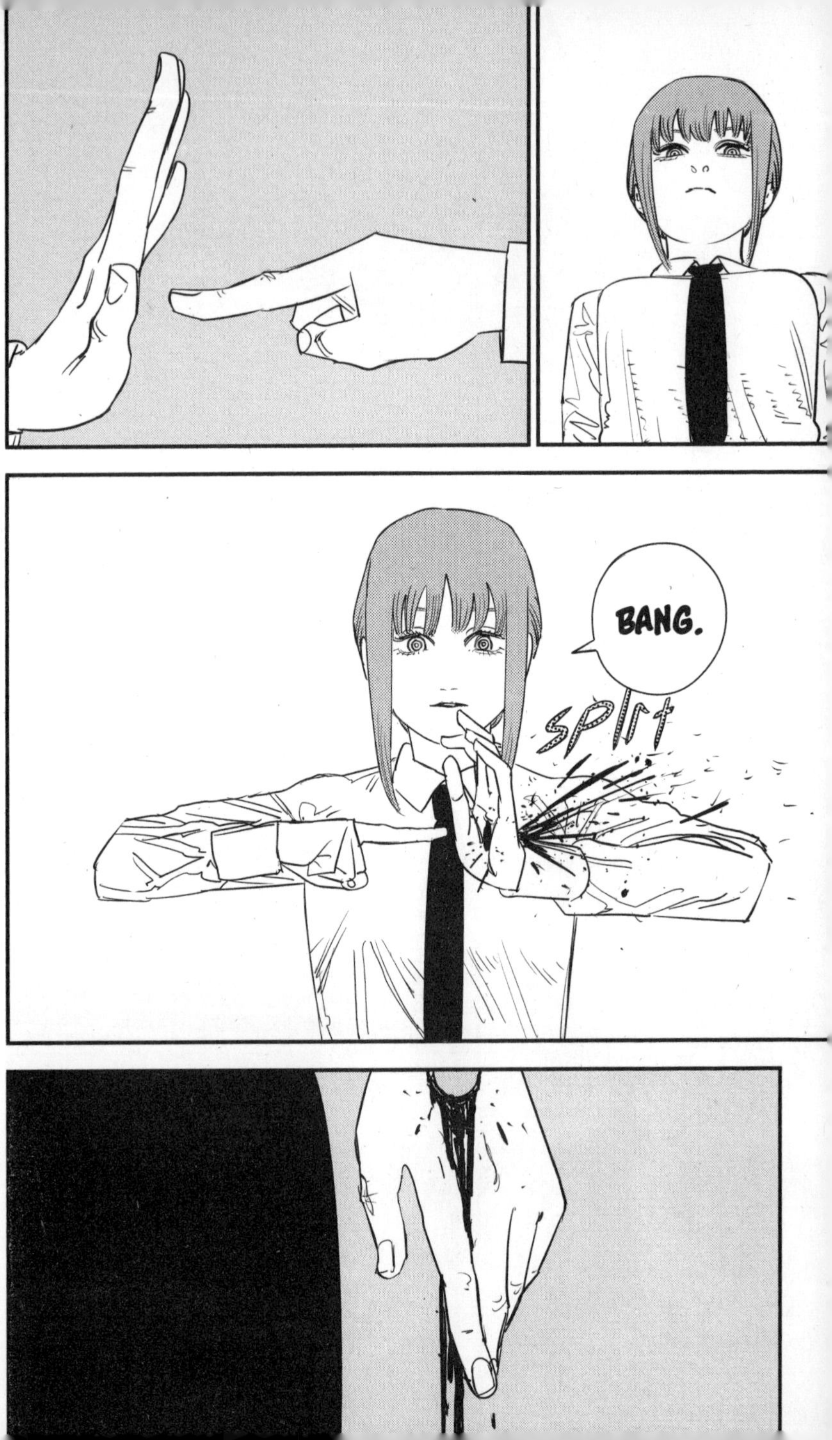
BANG.
splrt

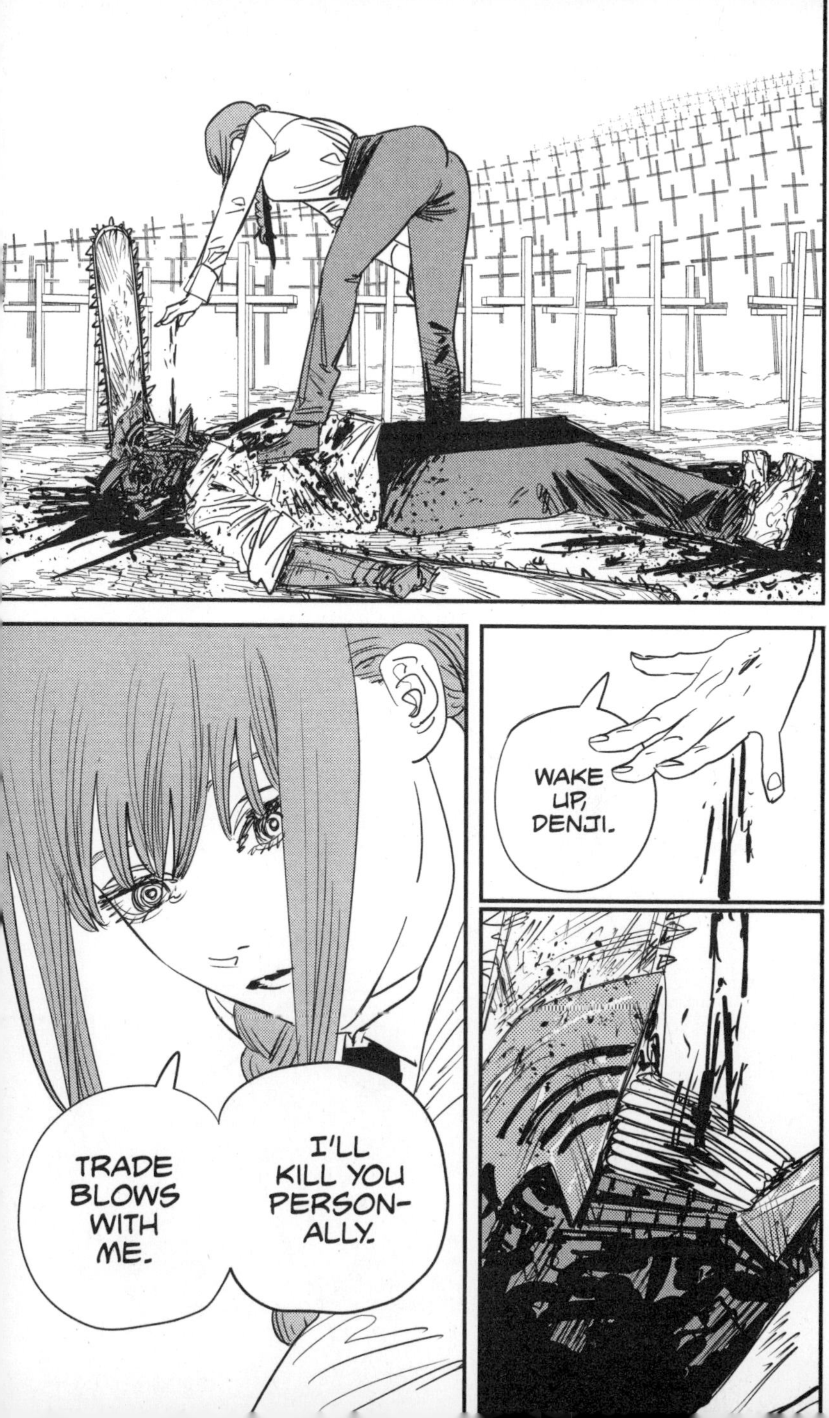
WAKE UP, DENJI.
I'LL KILL YOU PERSON-ALLY.
TRADE BLOWS WITH ME.

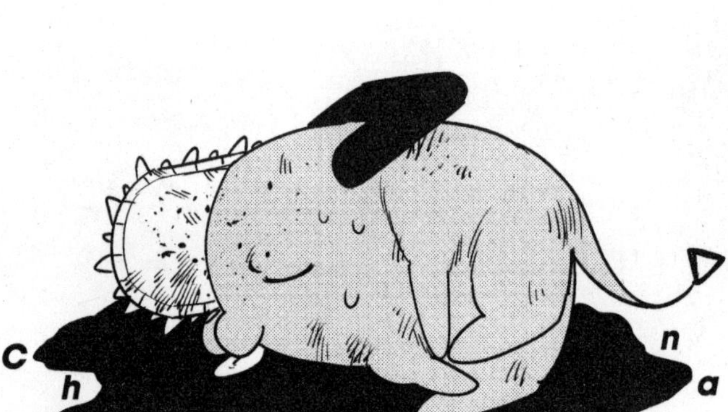
Chainsaw man

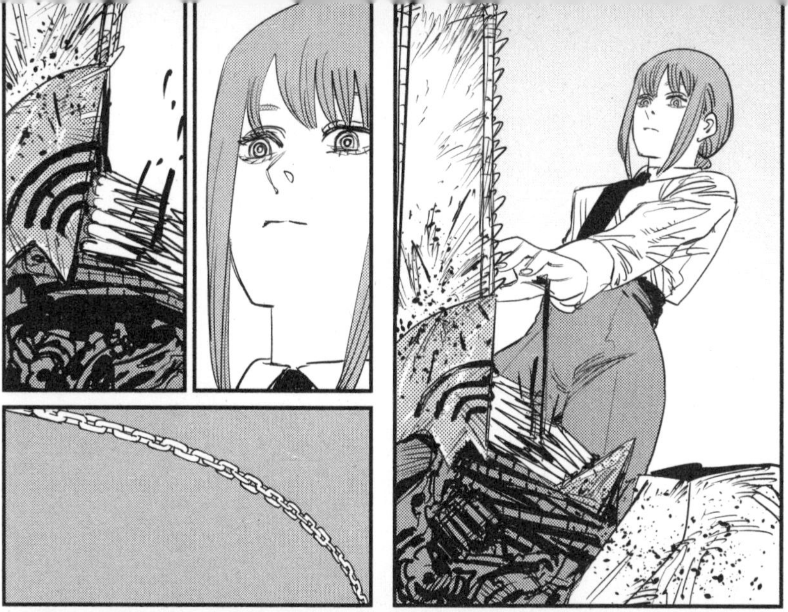

Chapter 95: Chainsaw Man vs. Control Devil

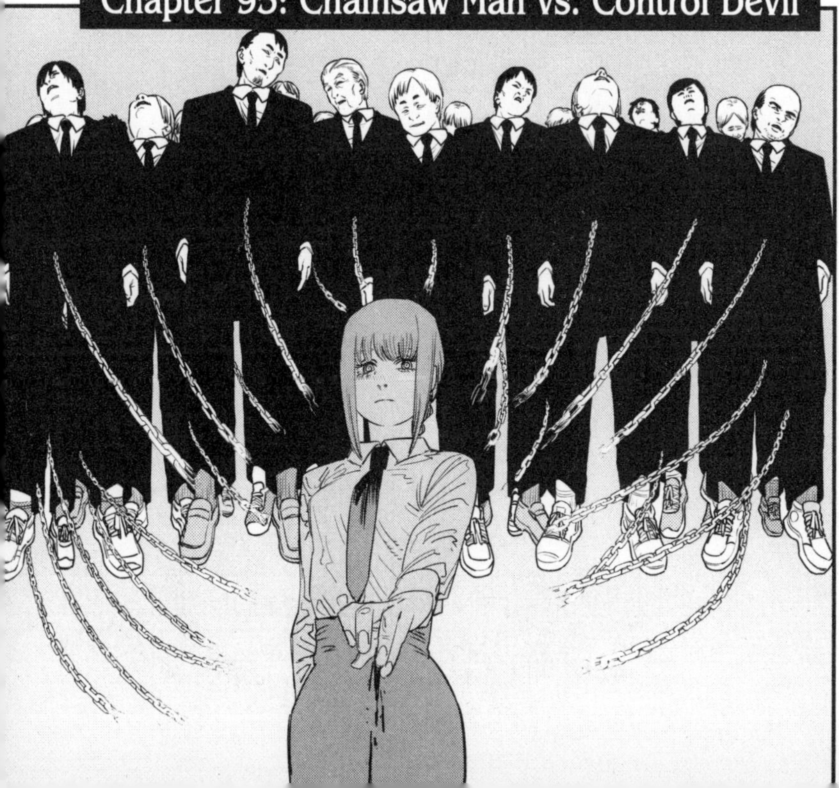

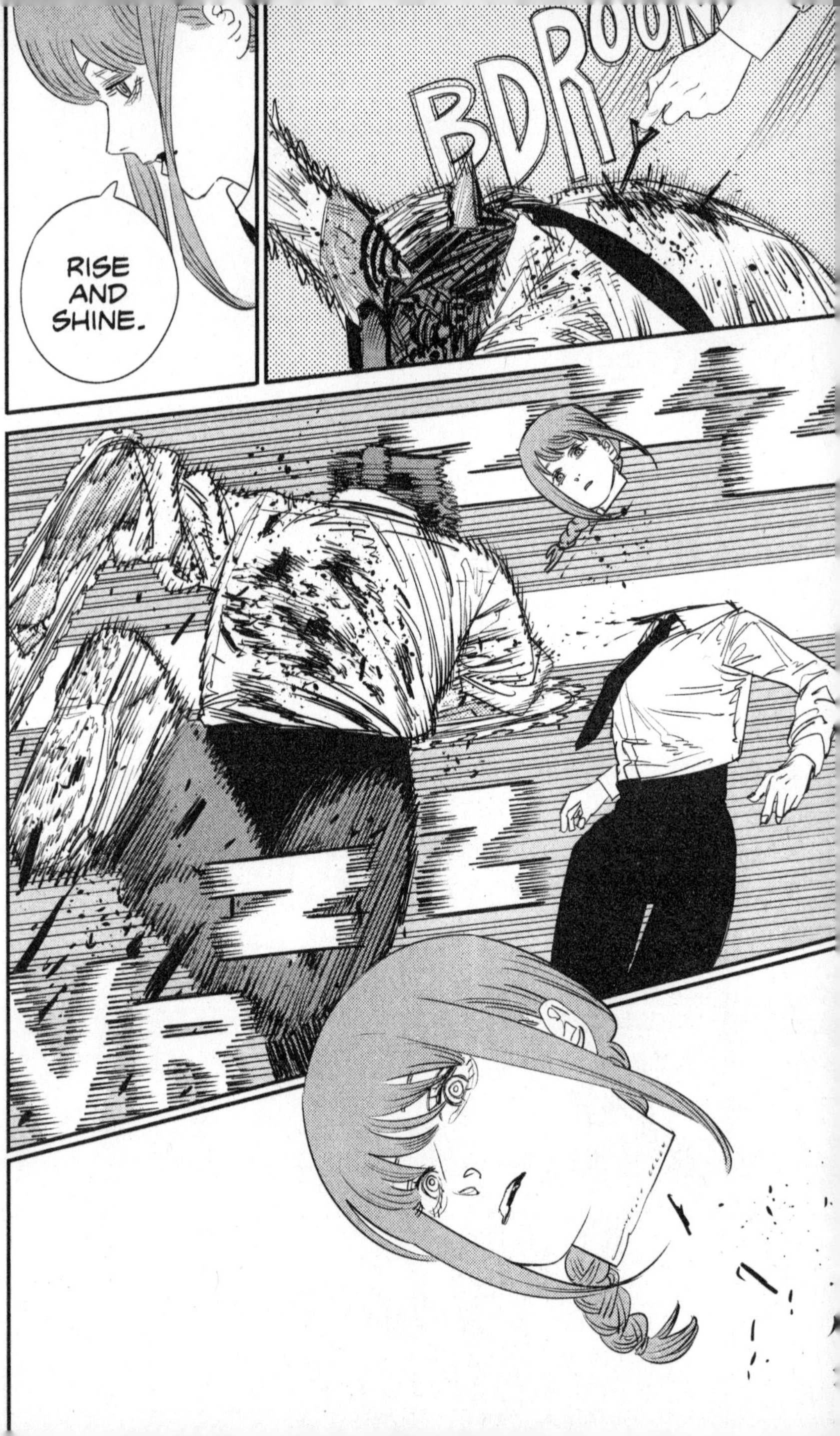
BDROOM
RISE AND SHINE.
VR

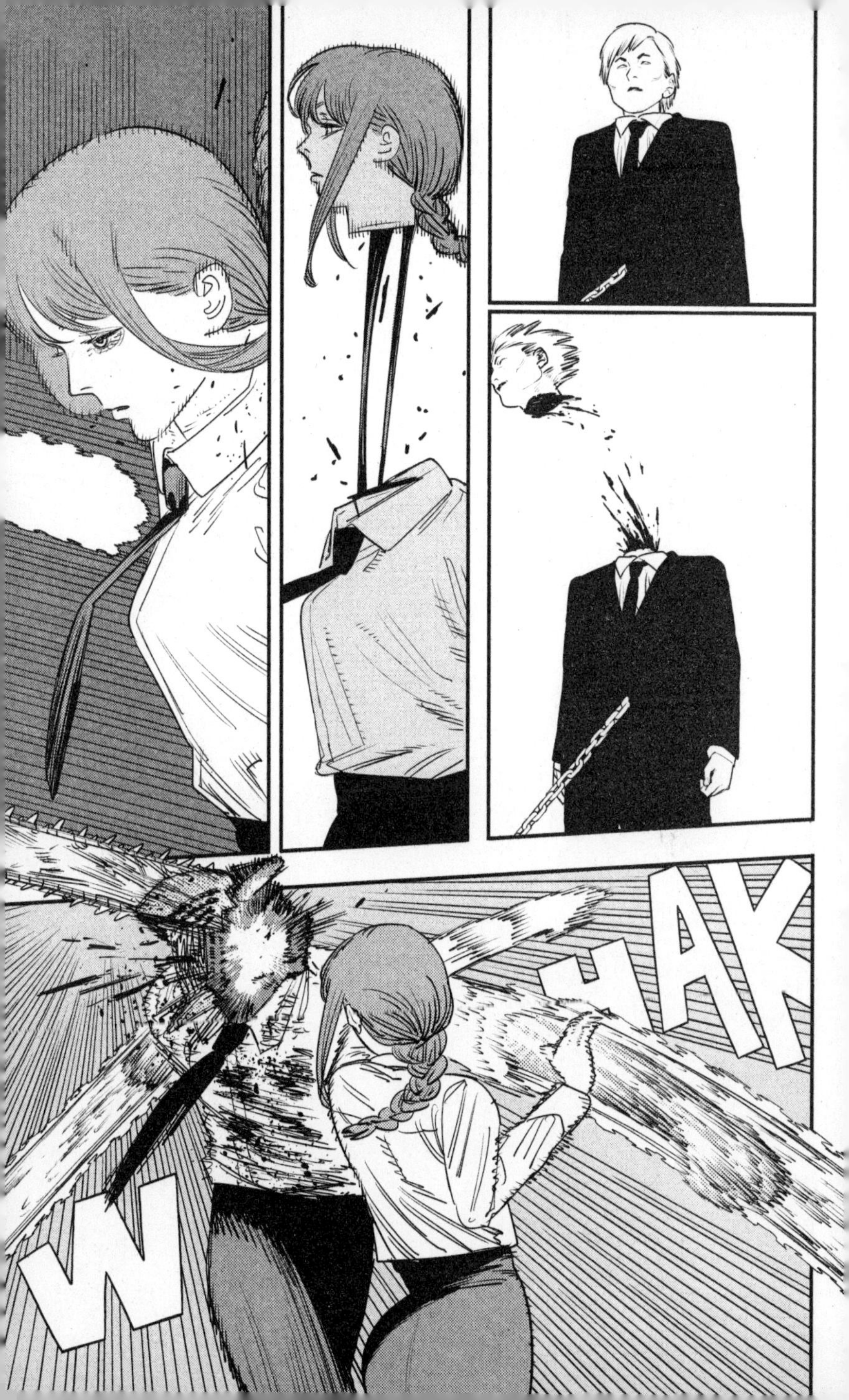
WHAK

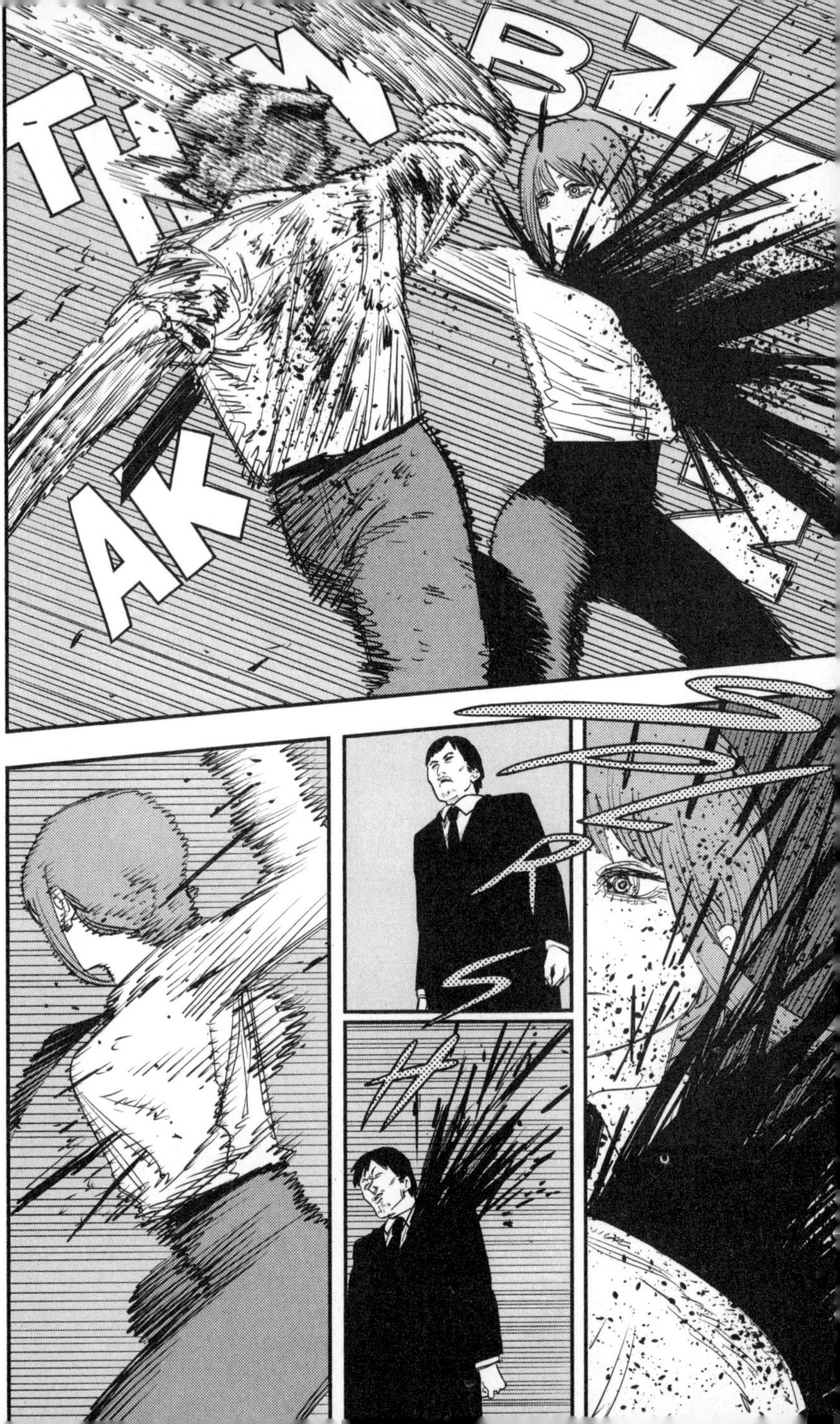
THWB
AK

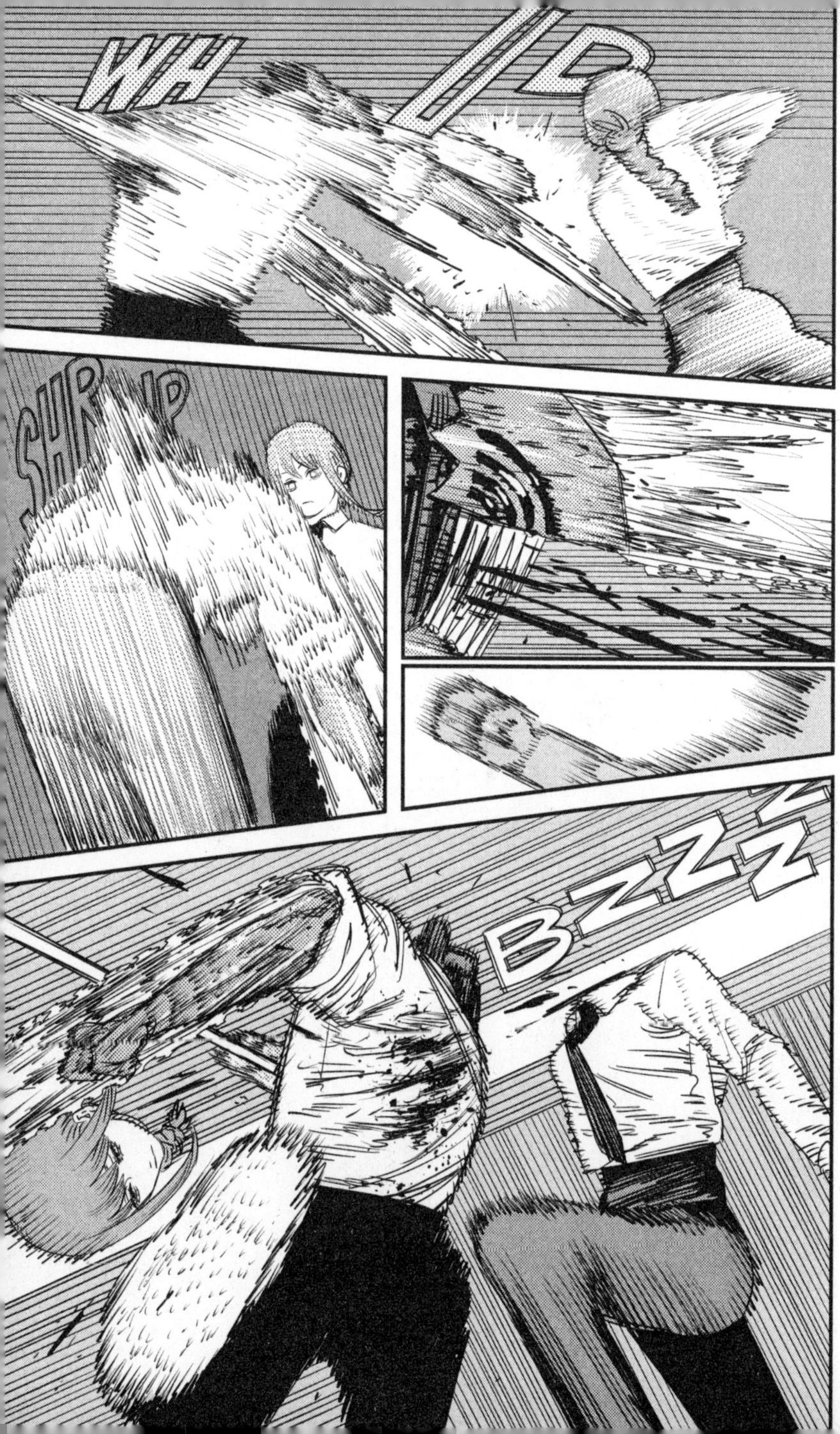
WH UD
SHR IP
BZZZZ

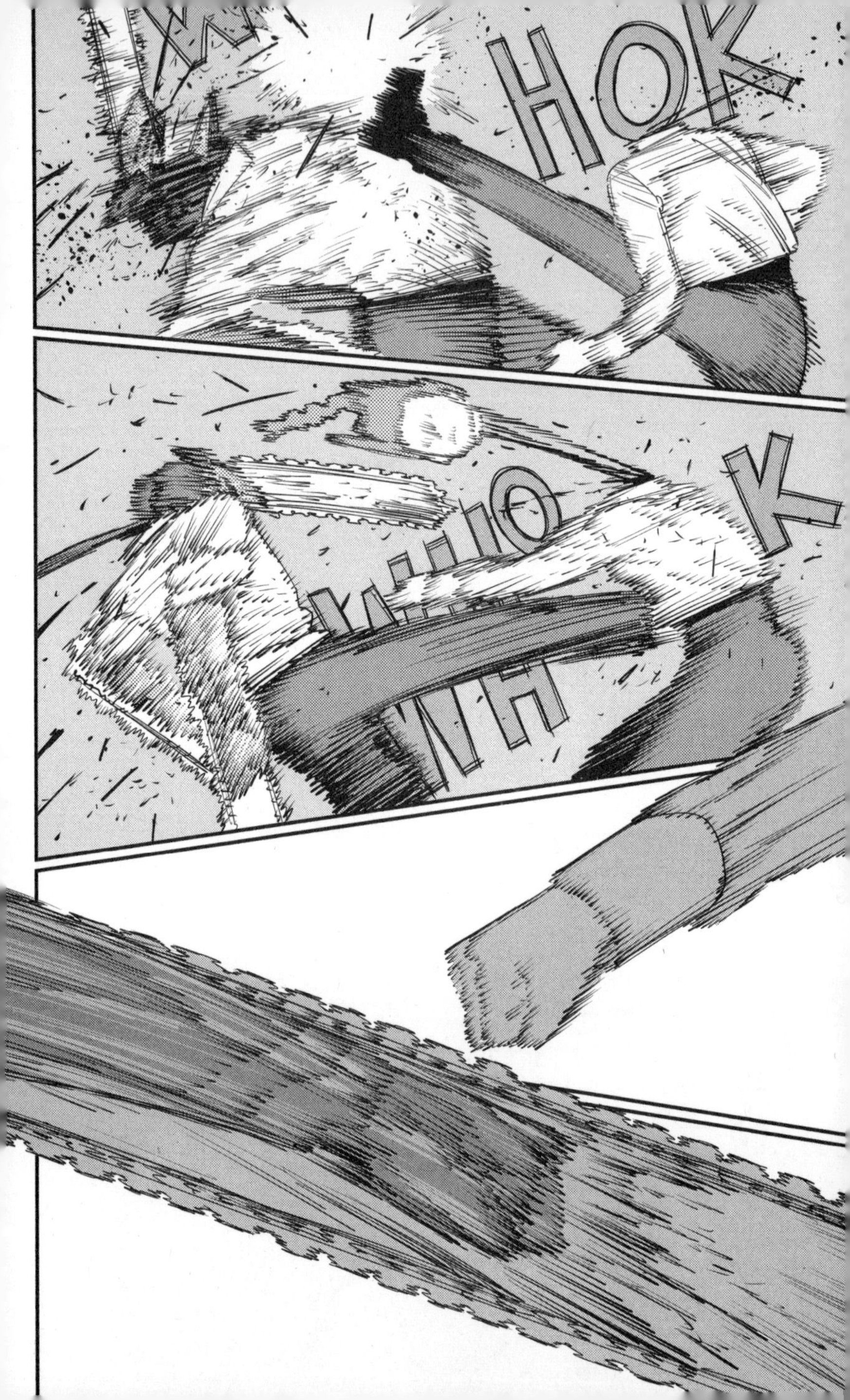
HOK
WHOK

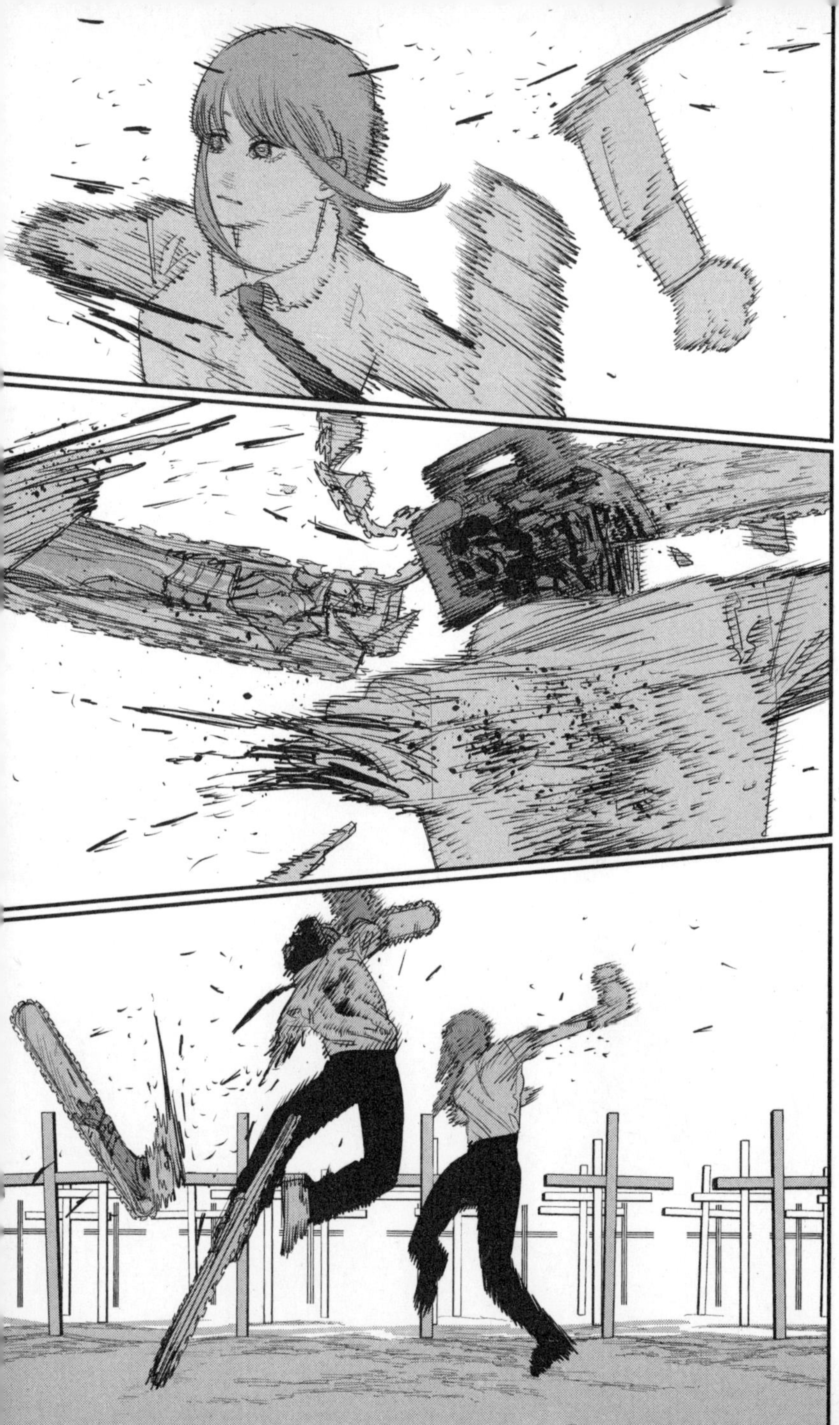

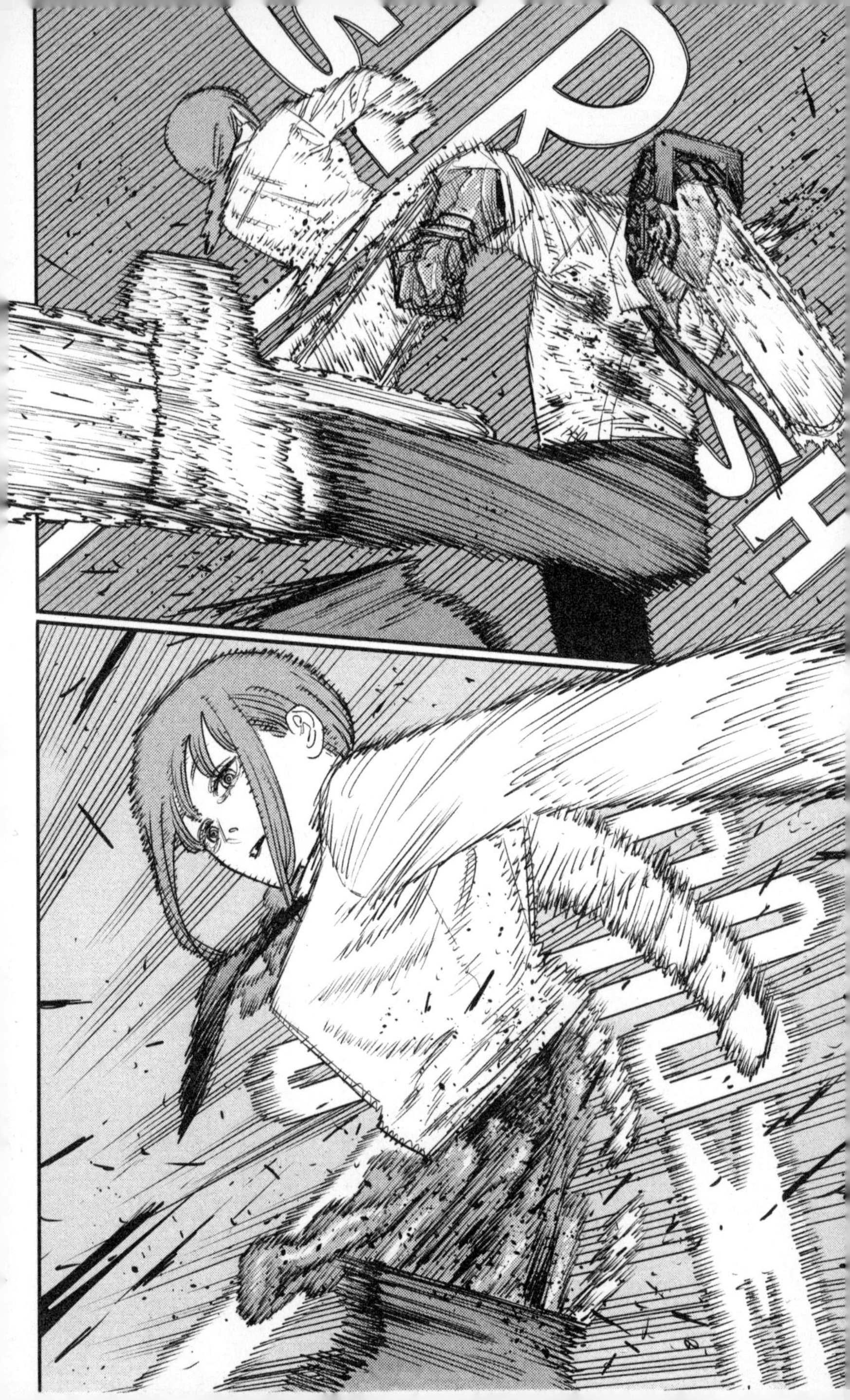

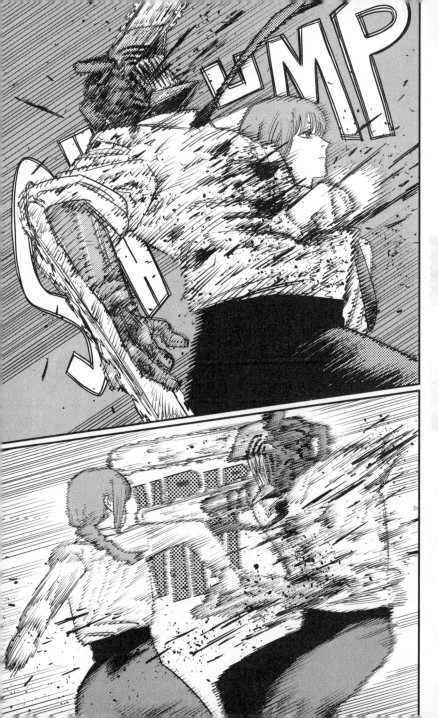

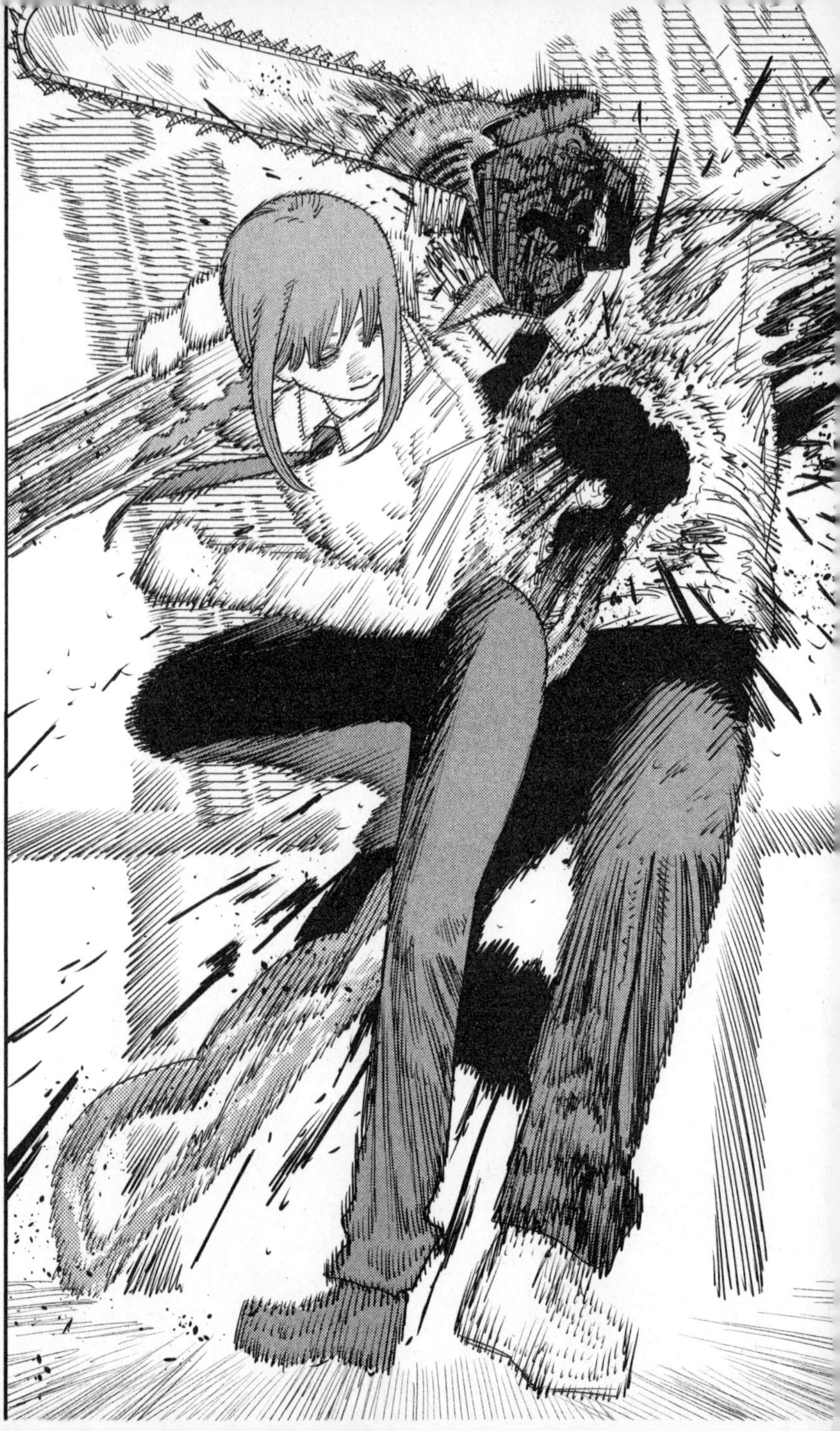

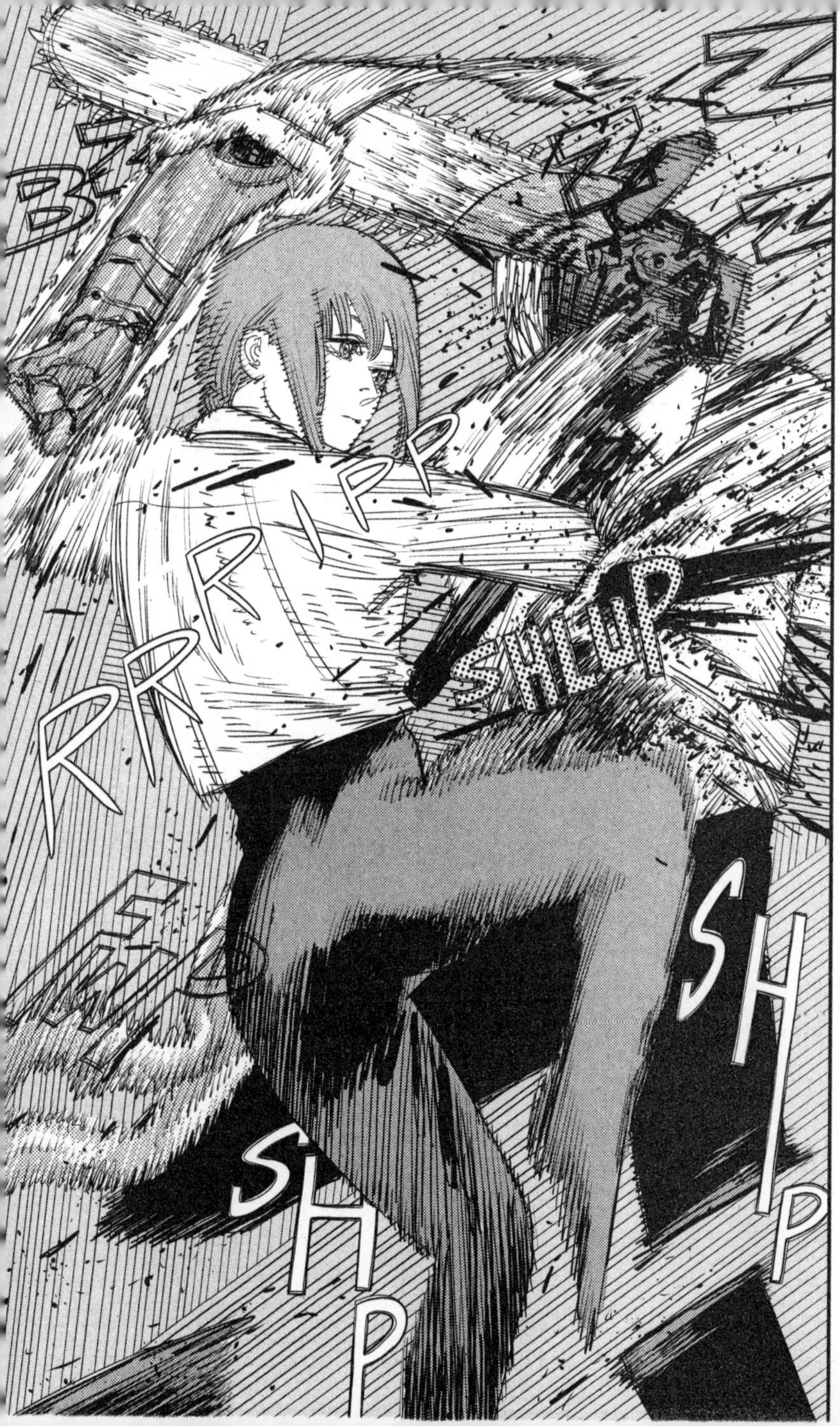
SHLUP
RRRIPP
SHIP
SHIP

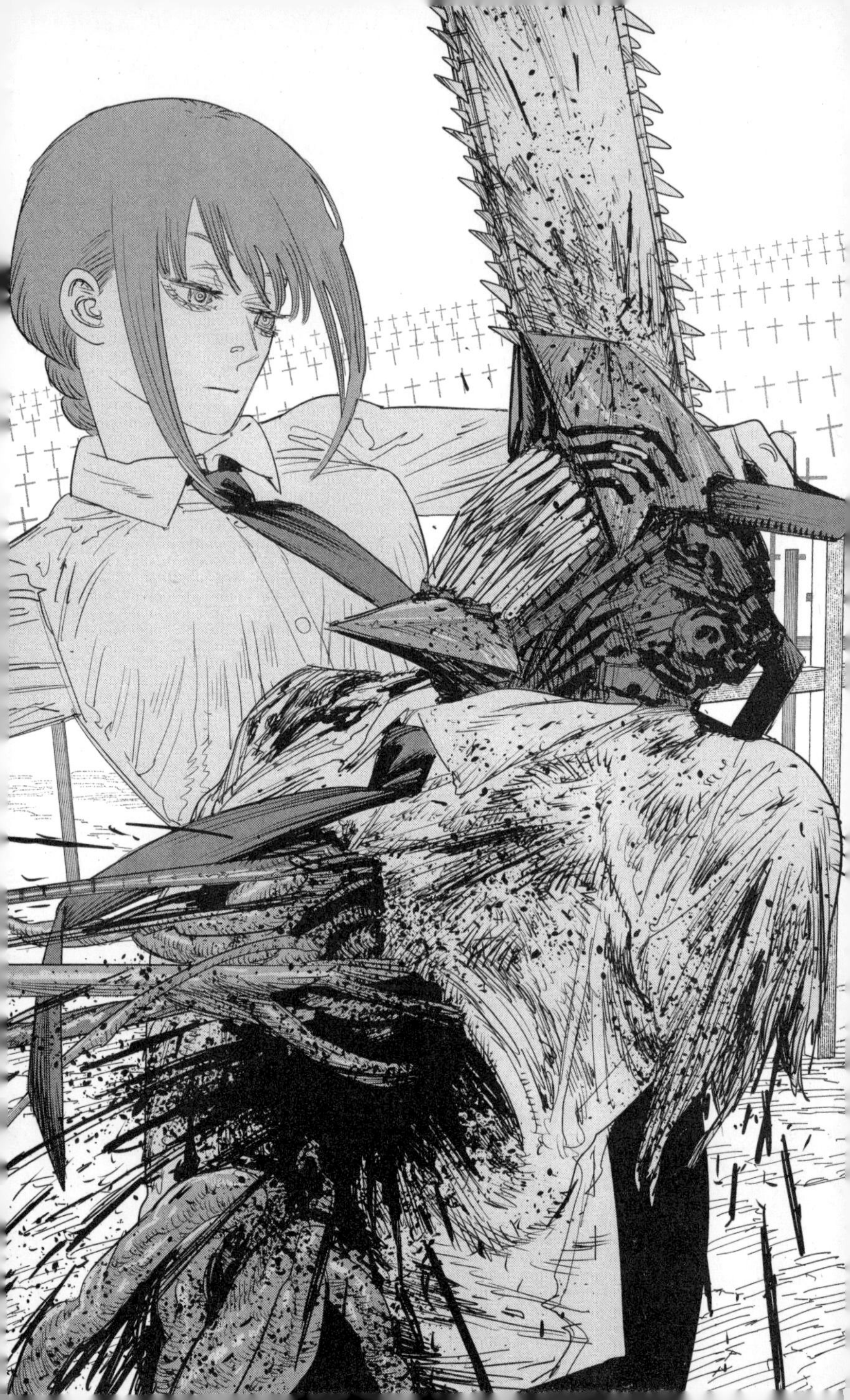

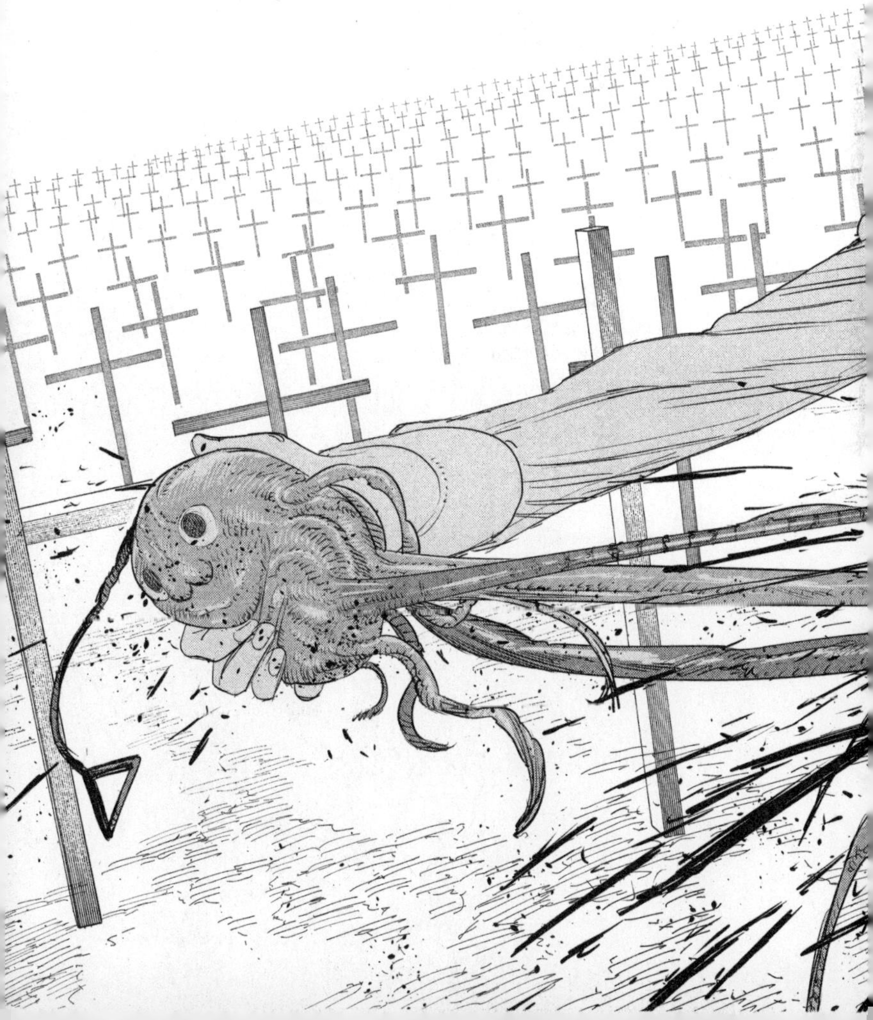

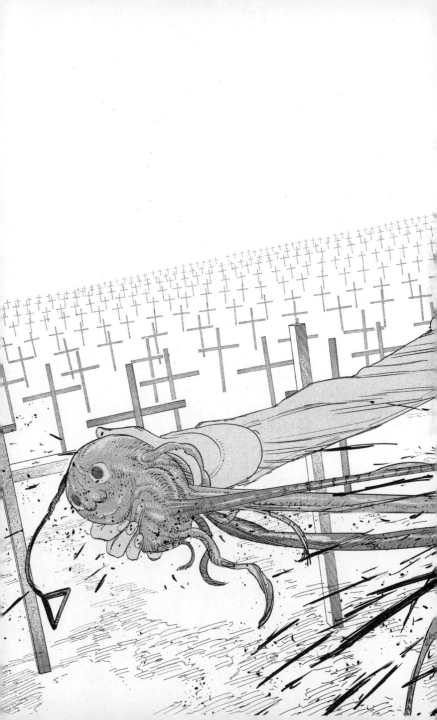

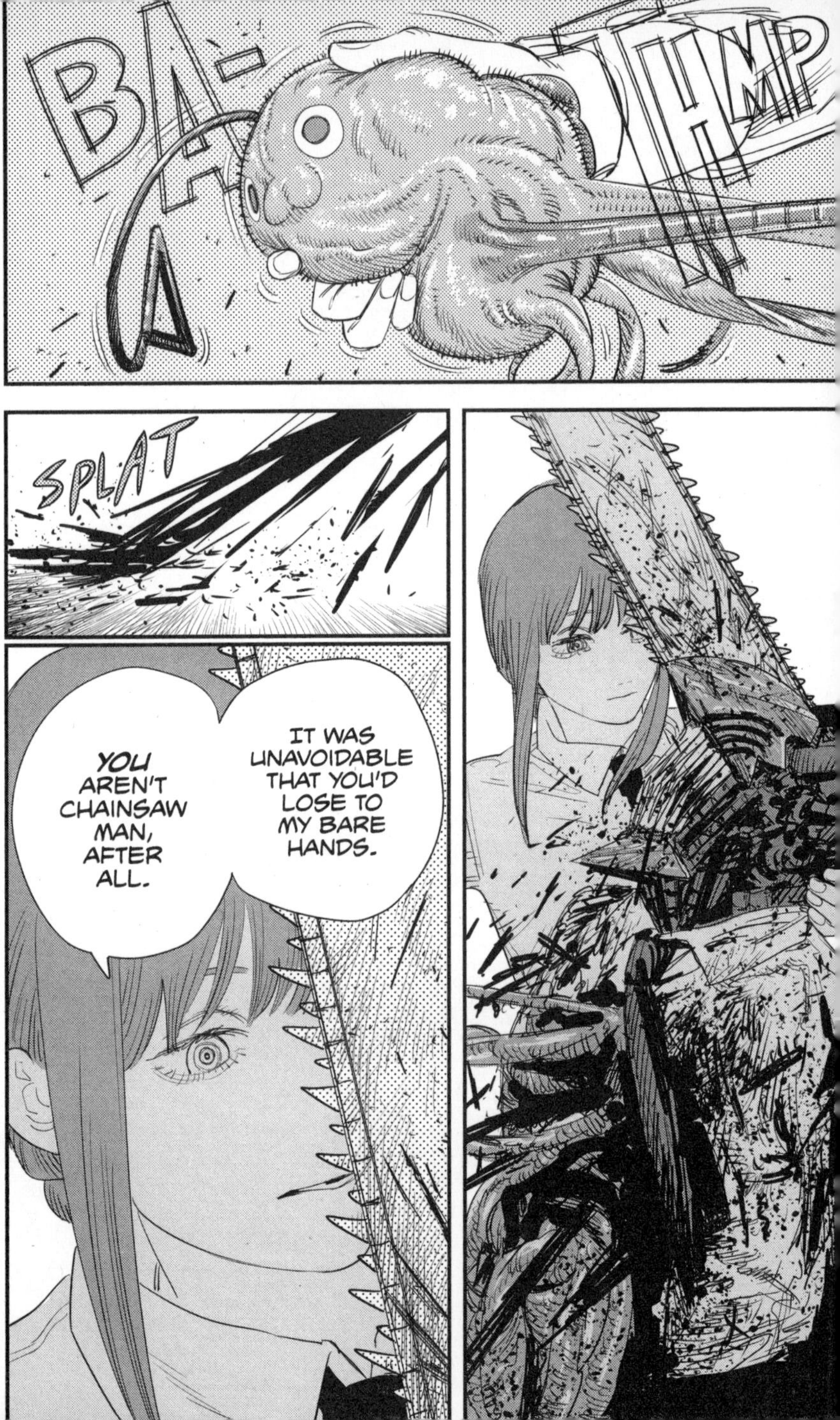
BA-A
THMP
SPLAT
IT WAS UNAVOIDABLE THAT YOU'D LOSE TO MY BARE HANDS.
YOU AREN'T CHAINSAW MAN, AFTER ALL.

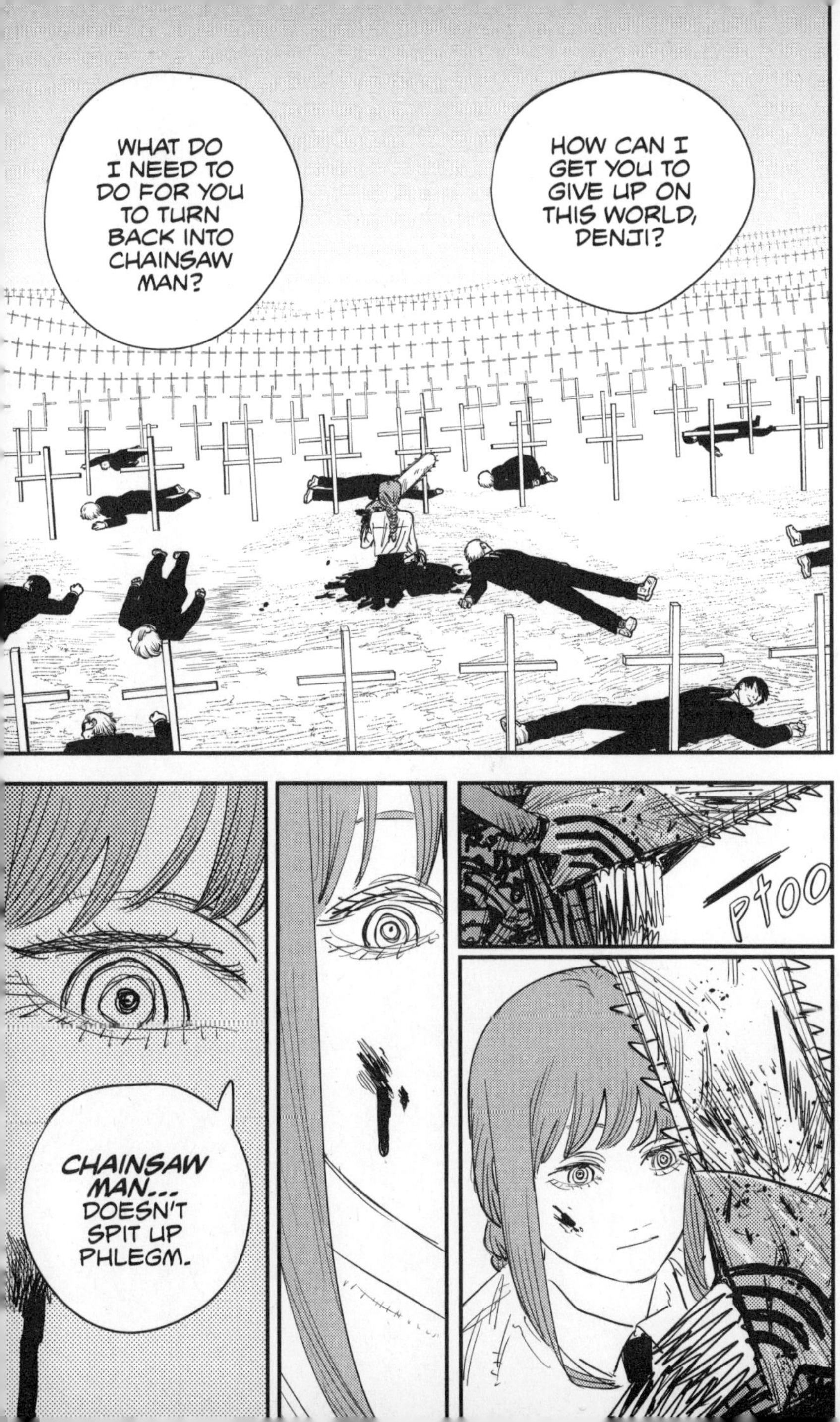
HOW CAN I GET YOU TO GIVE UP ON THIS WORLD, DENJI?
WHAT DO I NEED TO DO FOR YOU TO TURN BACK INTO CHAINSAW MAN?
PTOO
CHAINSAW MAN... DOESN'T SPIT UP PHLEGM.

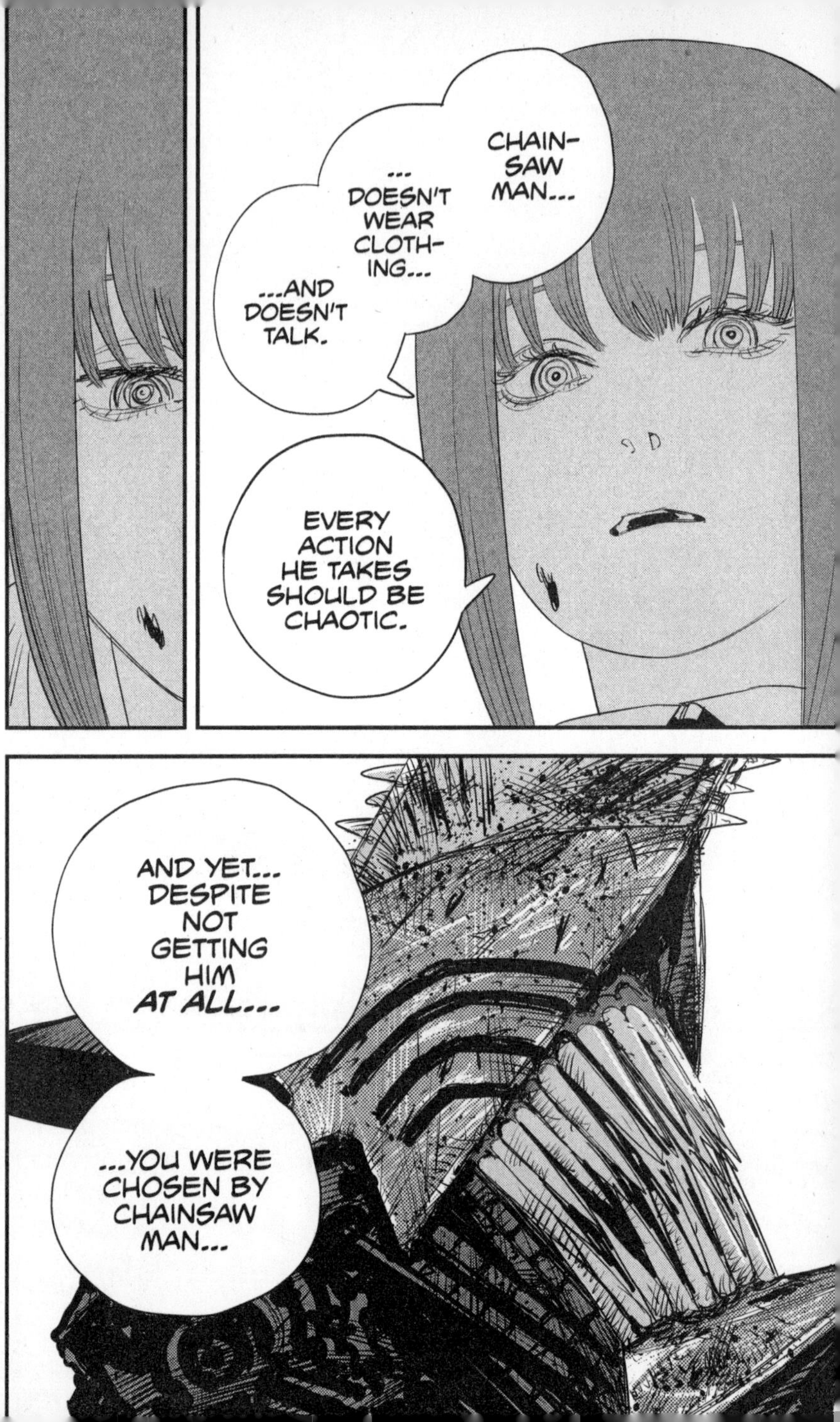
CHAIN-SAW MAN...
...DOESN'T WEAR CLOTH-ING...
...AND DOESN'T TALK.
EVERY ACTION HE TAKES SHOULD BE CHAOTIC.
AND YET... DESPITE NOT GETTING HIM *AT ALL...*
...YOU WERE CHOSEN BY CHAINSAW MAN...

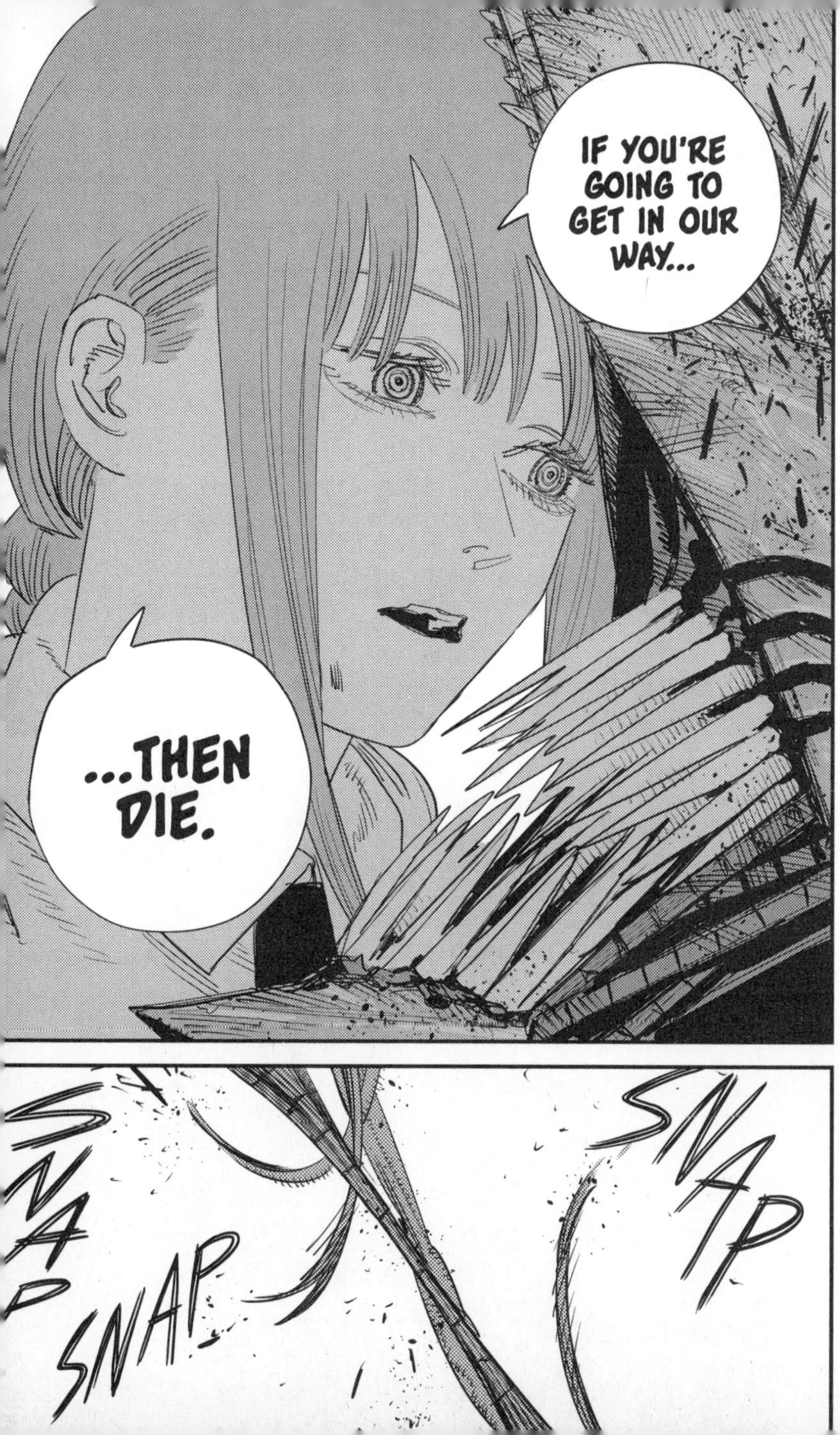
IF YOU'RE GOING TO GET IN OUR WAY...
...THEN DIE.
SNAP
SNAP
SNAP

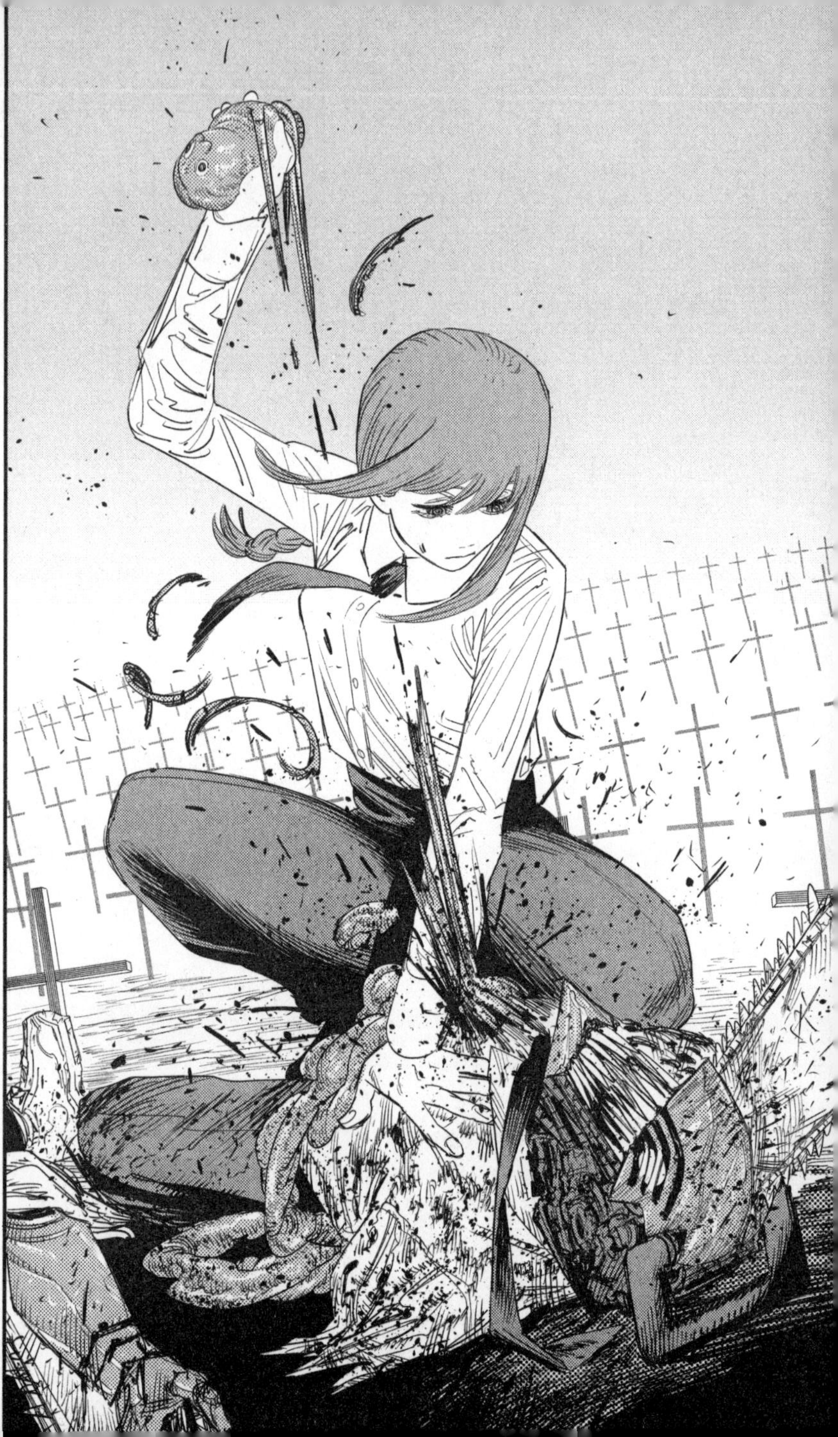

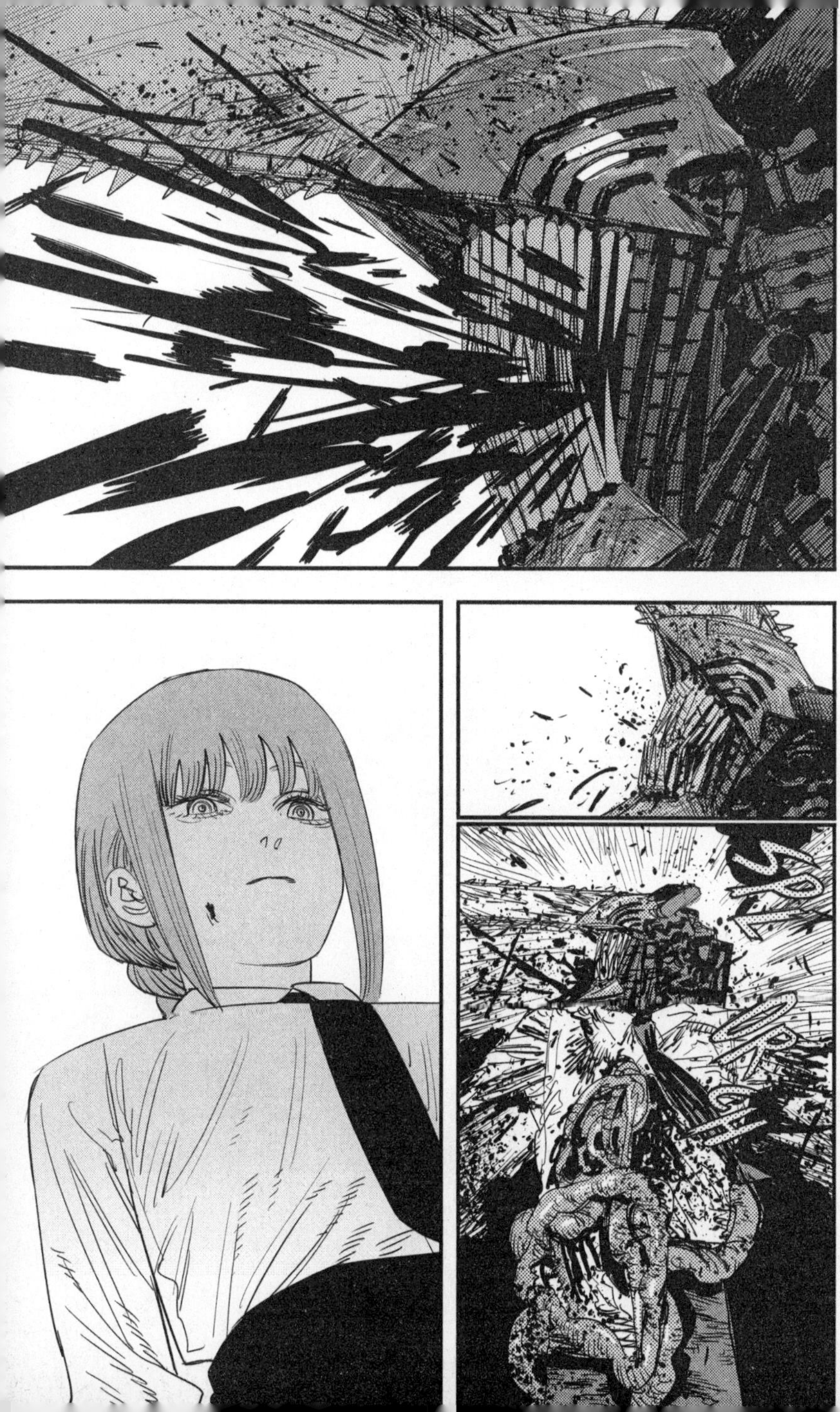
SPLORCH

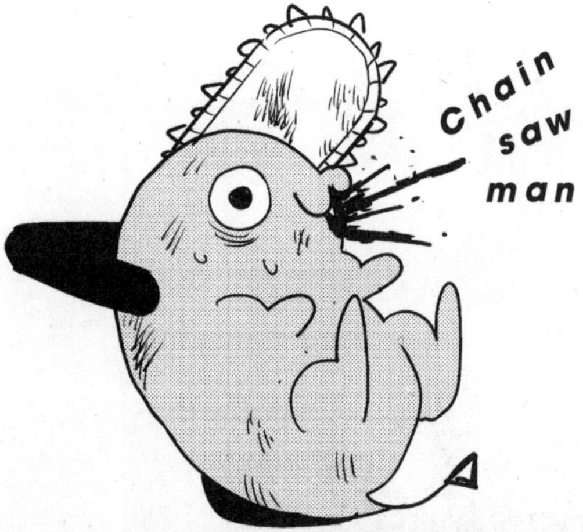
Chain
saw
man

Chapter 96: This Kind of Taste

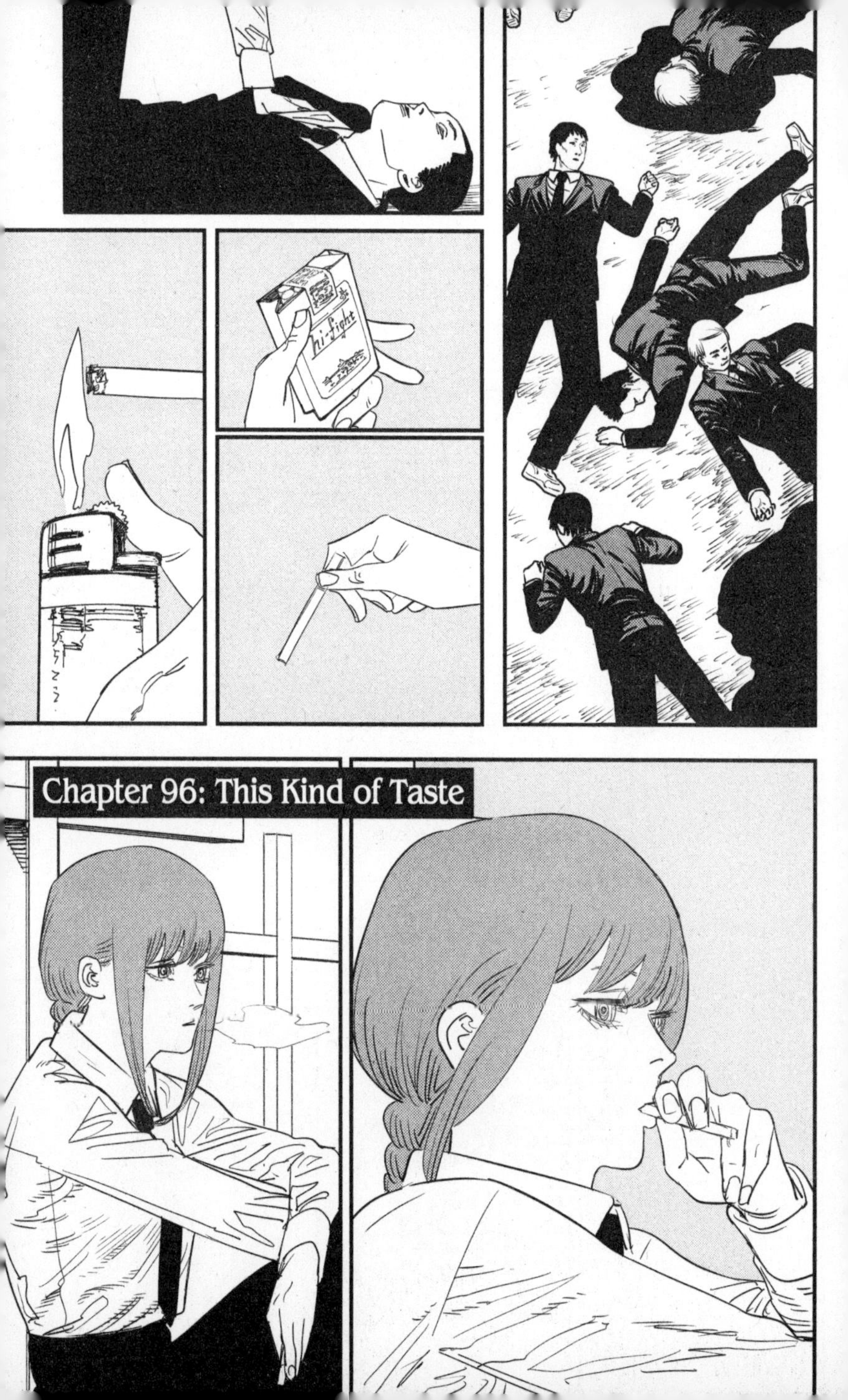

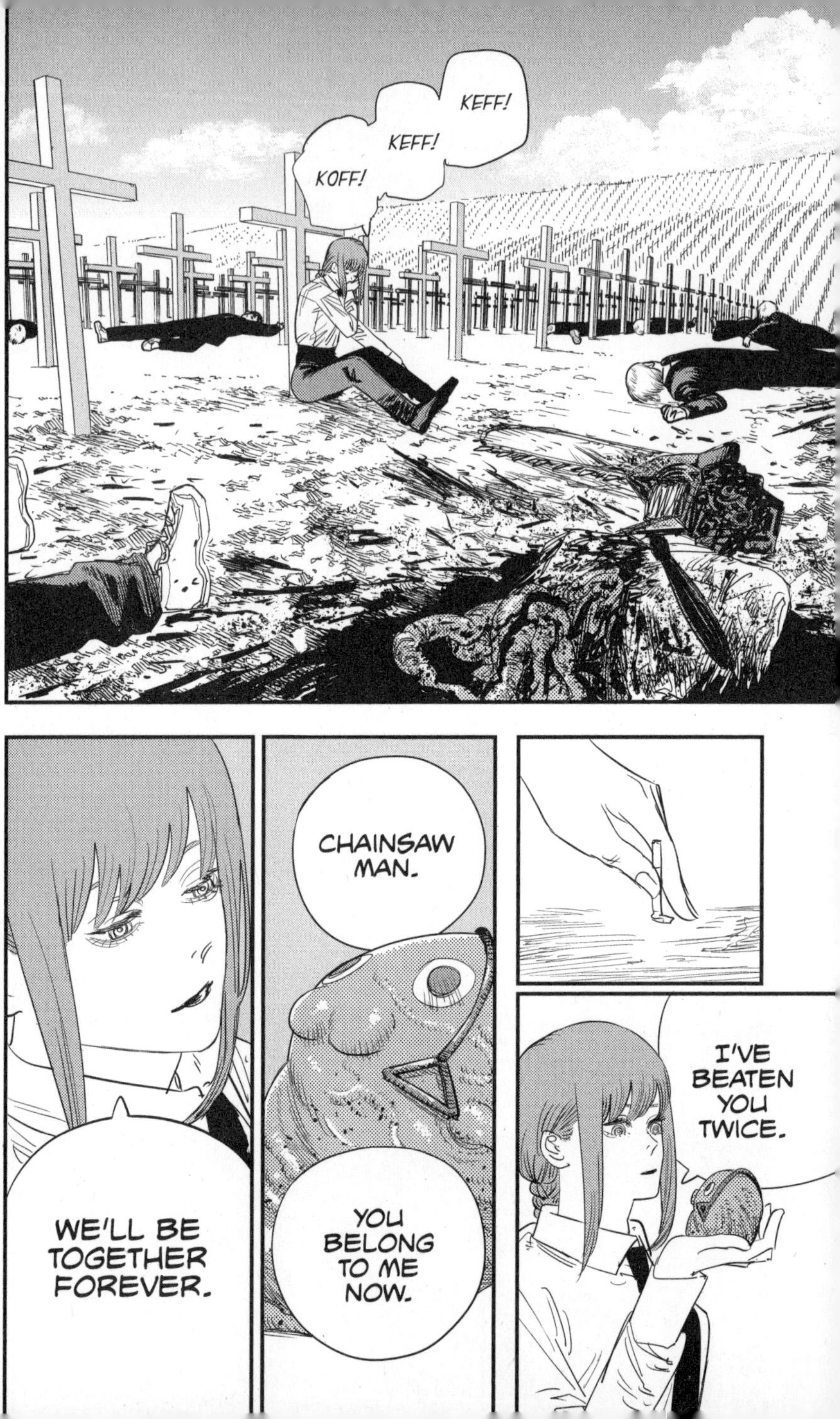
KEFF!
KEFF!
KOFF!
I'VE BEATEN YOU TWICE.
CHAINSAW MAN.
YOU BELONG TO ME NOW.
WE'LL BE TOGETHER FOREVER.

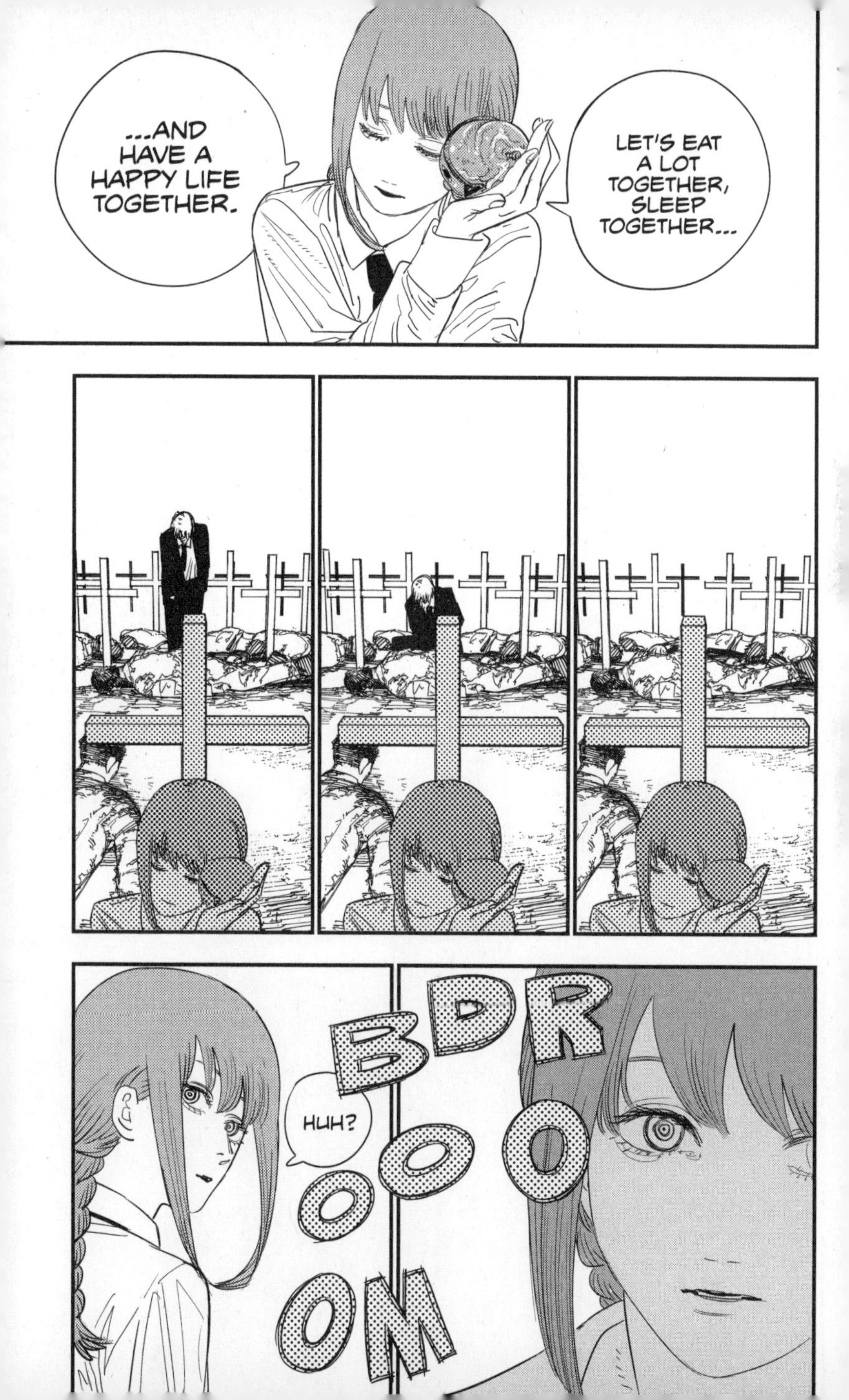
LET'S EAT A LOT TOGETHER, SLEEP TOGETHER...
...AND HAVE A HAPPY LIFE TOGETHER.
BDROOOOM
HUH?

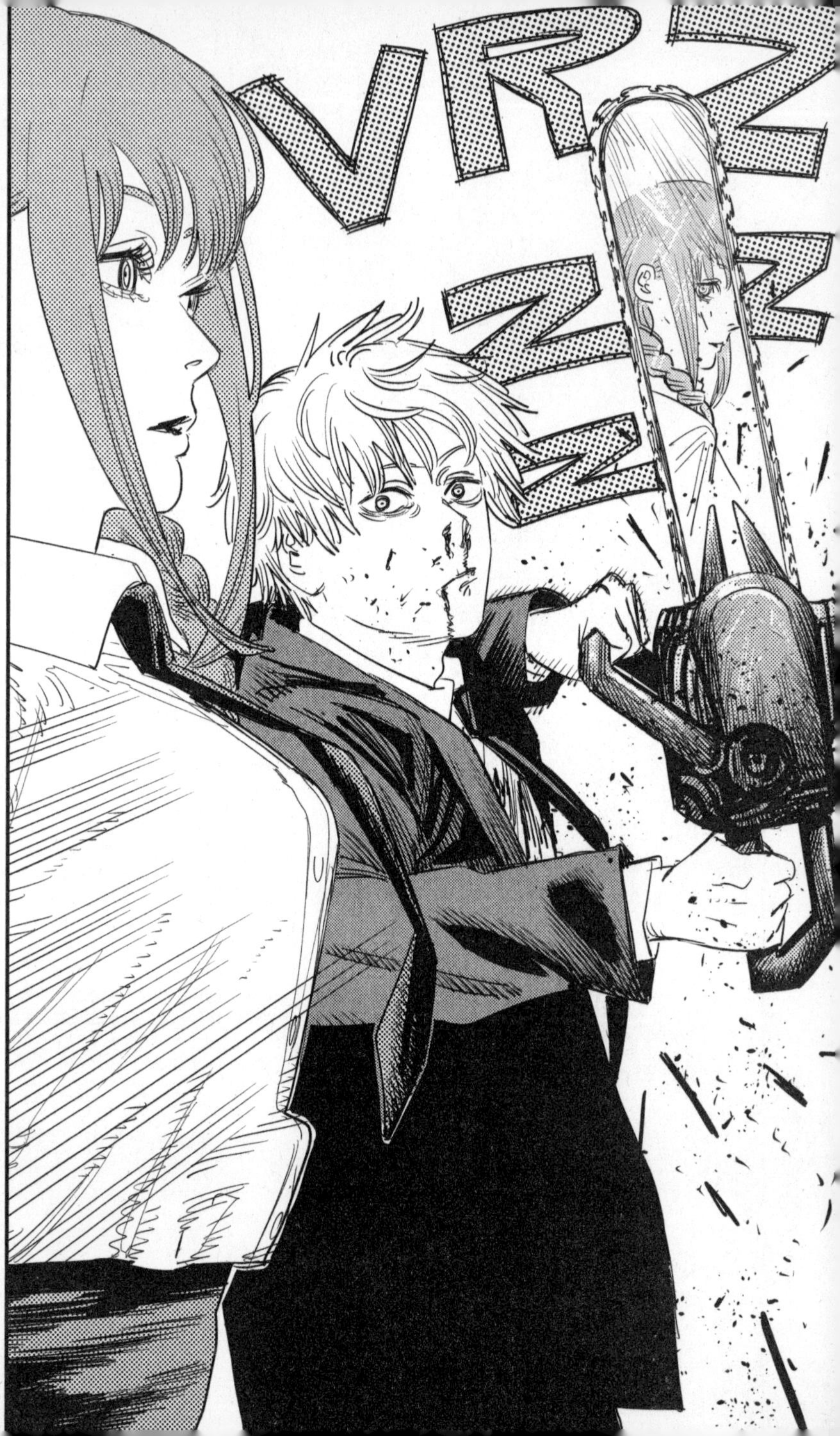
VRZZZZ

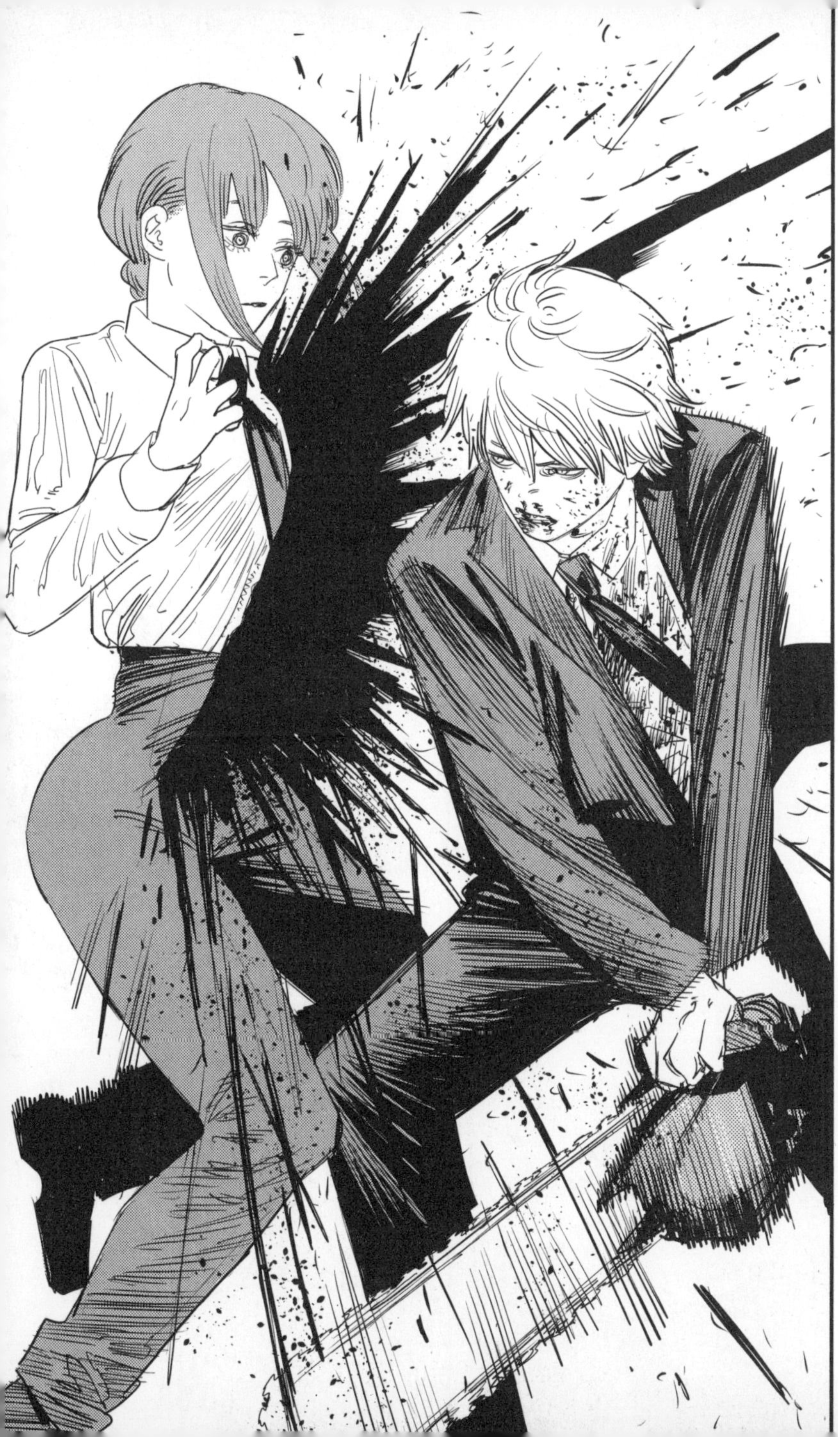

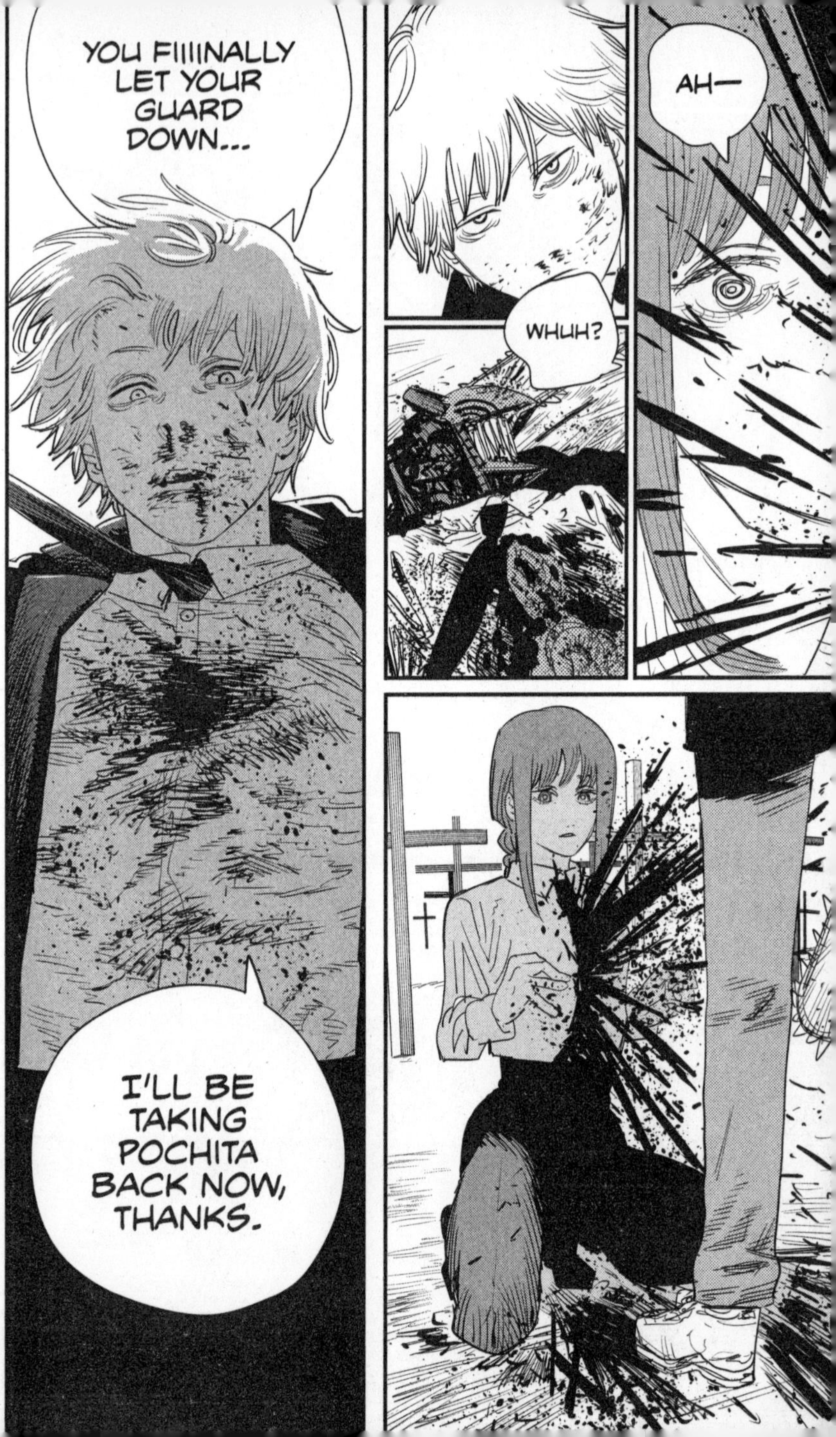
AH—
WHUH?
YOU FIIIINALLY LET YOUR GUARD DOWN...
I'LL BE TAKING POCHITA BACK NOW, THANKS.

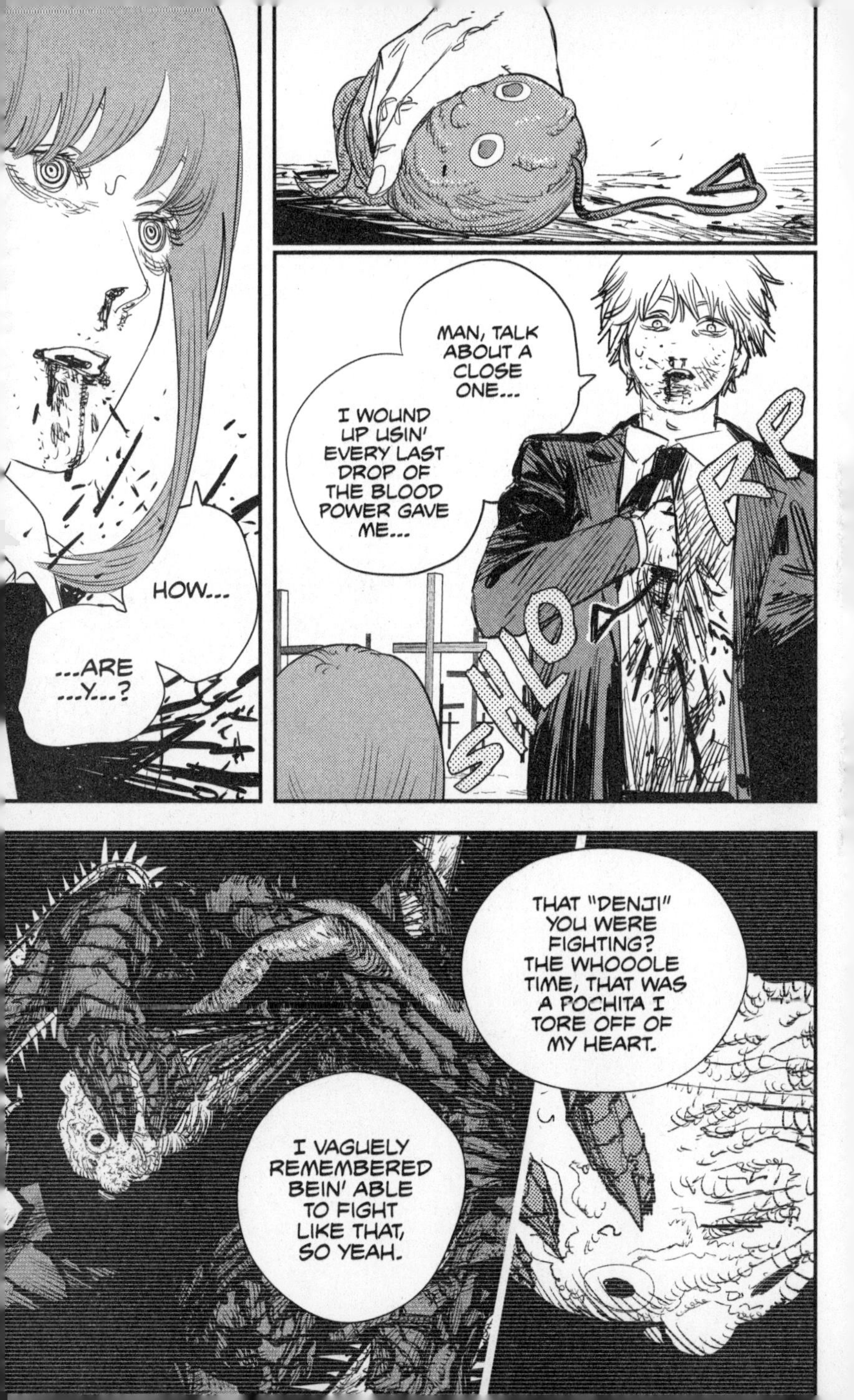
MAN, TALK ABOUT A CLOSE ONE...
I WOUND UP USIN' EVERY LAST DROP OF THE BLOOD POWER GAVE ME...
SHLORP
HOW...
...ARE ...Y...?
THAT "DENJI" YOU WERE FIGHTING? THE WHOOOLE TIME, THAT WAS A POCHITA I TORE OFF OF MY HEART.
I VAGUELY REMEMBERED BEIN' ABLE TO FIGHT LIKE THAT, SO YEAH.

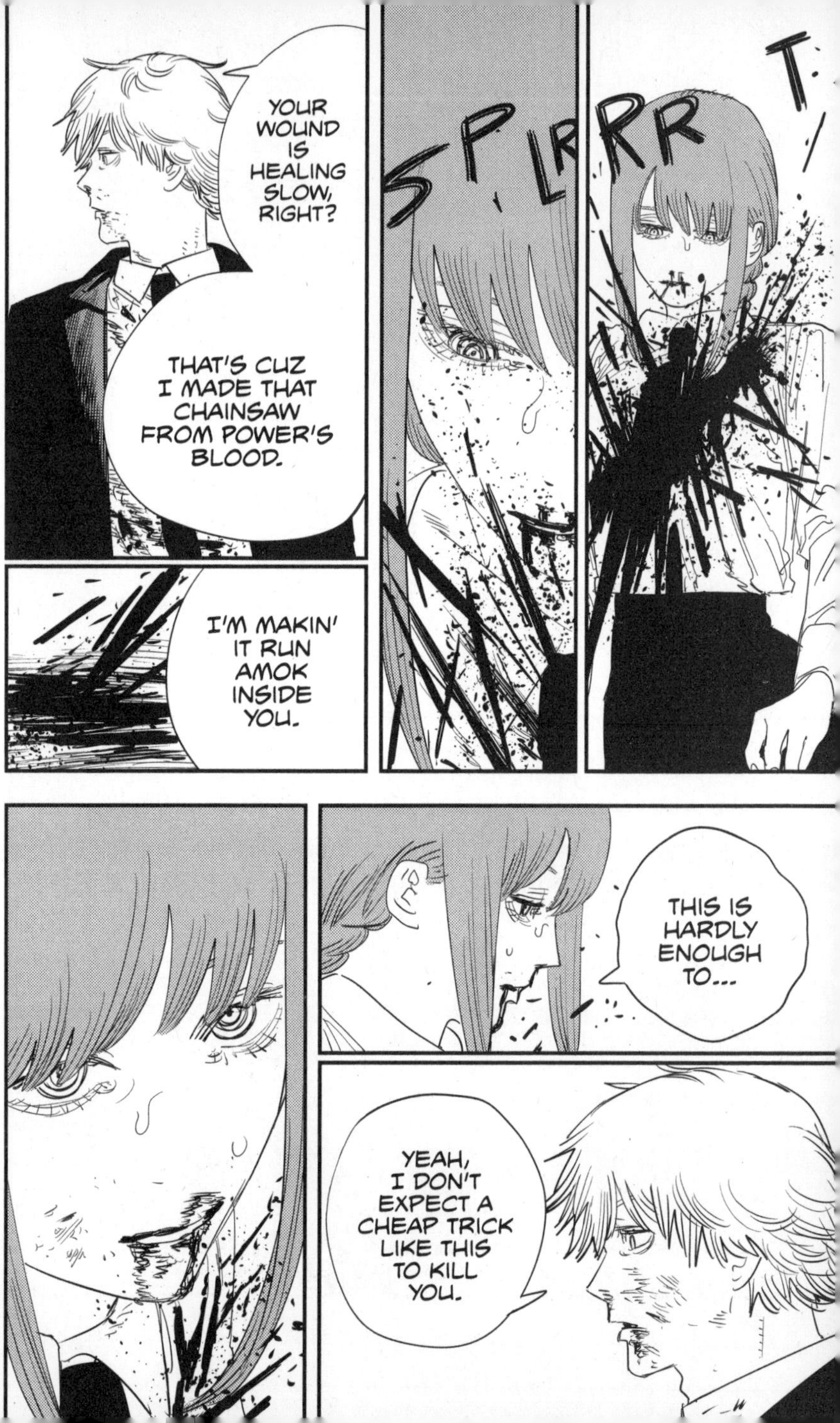
SPLRRRT
YOUR WOUND IS HEALING SLOW, RIGHT?
THAT'S CUZ I MADE THAT CHAINSAW FROM POWER'S BLOOD.
I'M MAKIN' IT RUN AMOK INSIDE YOU.
THIS IS HARDLY ENOUGH TO...
YEAH, I DON'T EXPECT A CHEAP TRICK LIKE THIS TO KILL YOU.

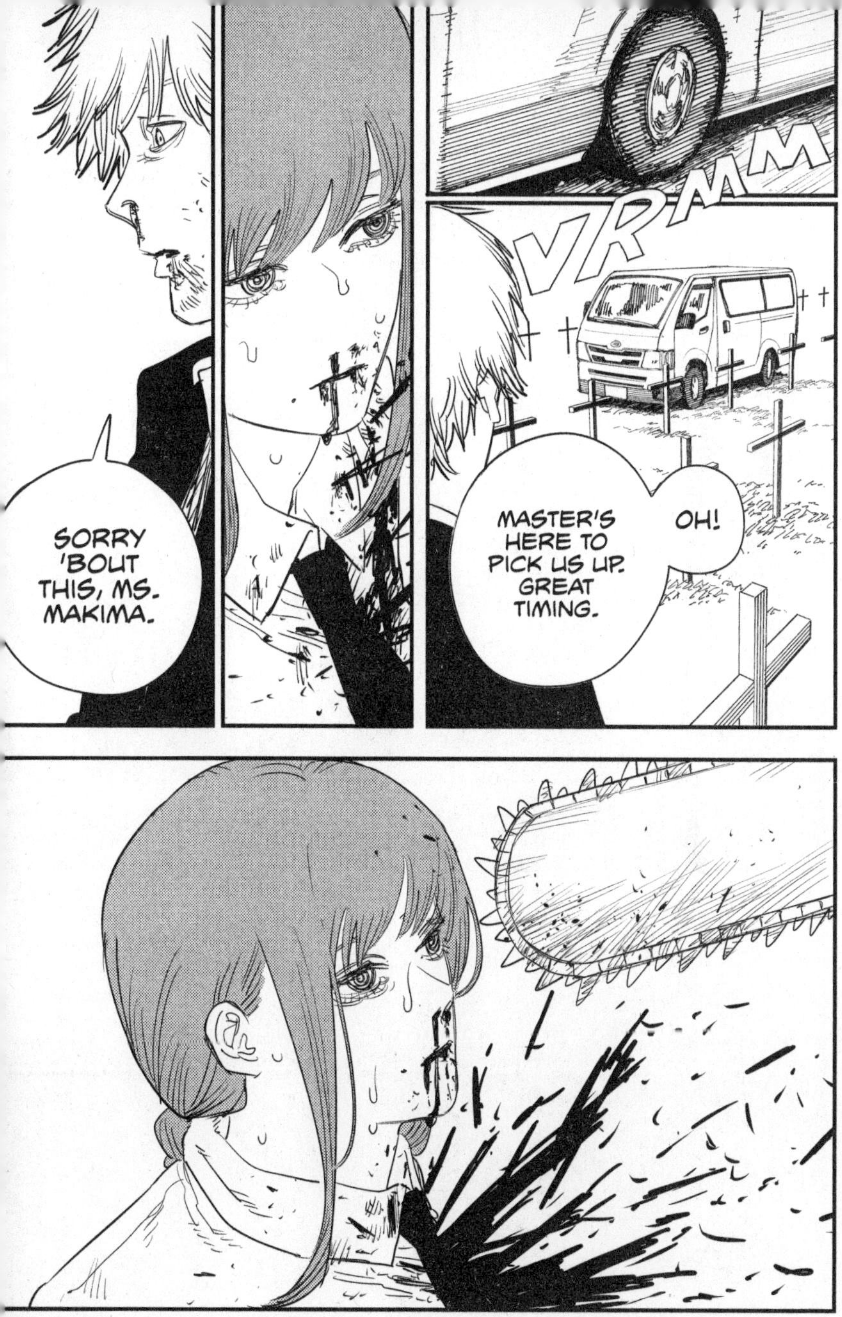
VRMM
OH!
MASTER'S HERE TO PICK US UP. GREAT TIMING.
SORRY 'BOUT THIS, MS. MAKIMA.

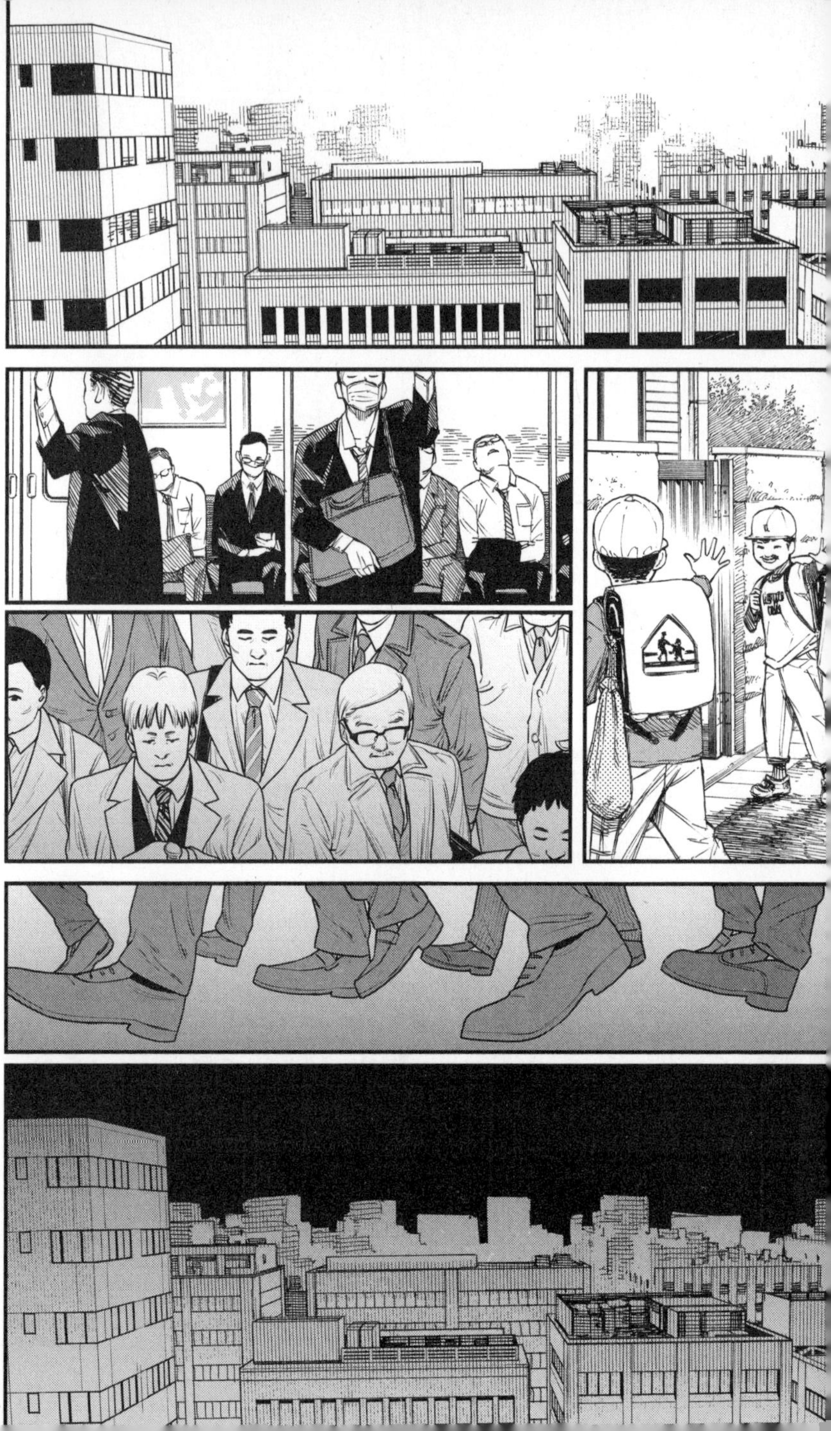

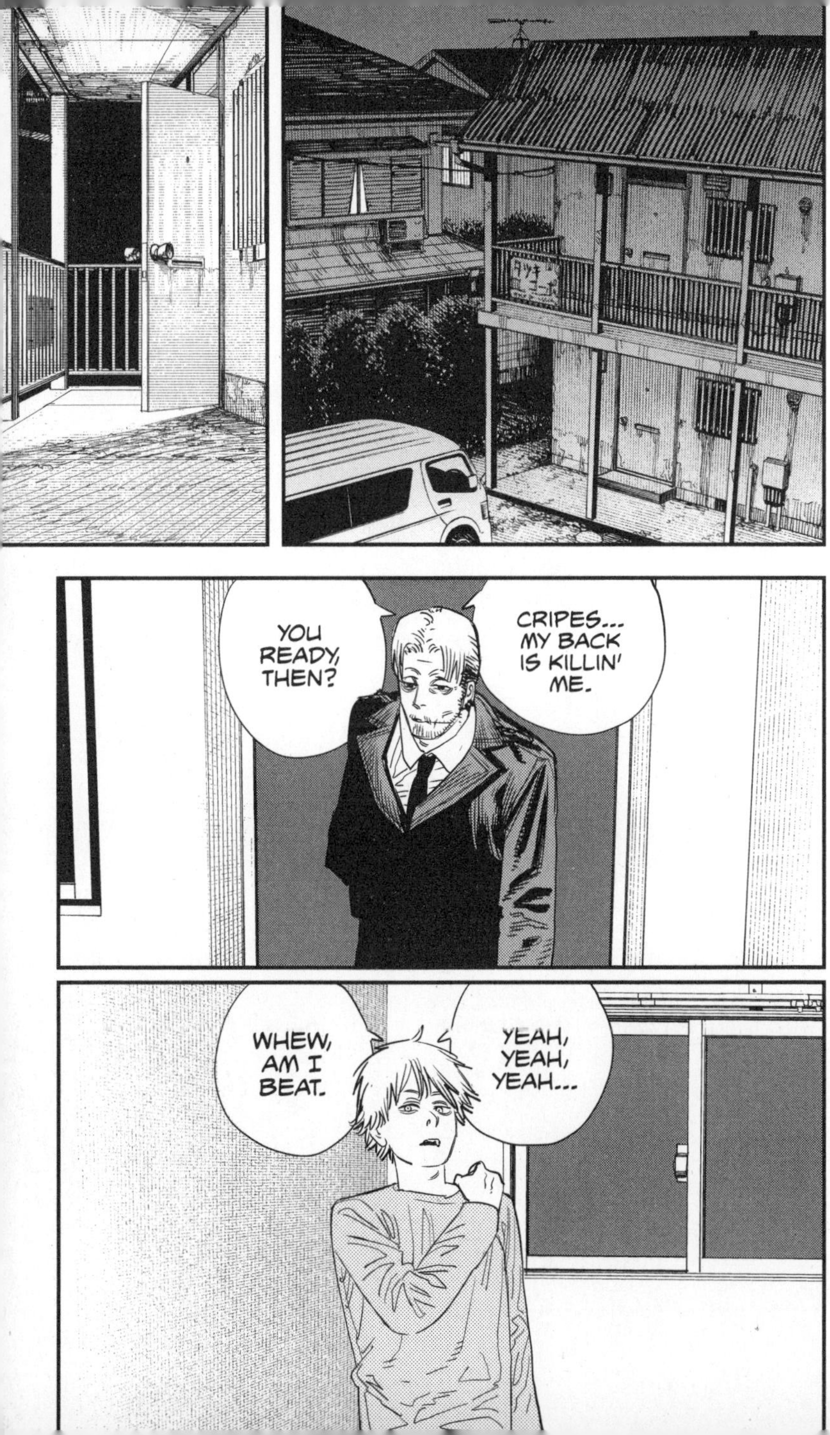
CRIPES... MY BACK IS KILLIN' ME.
YOU READY, THEN?
YEAH, YEAH, YEAH...
WHEW, AM I BEAT.

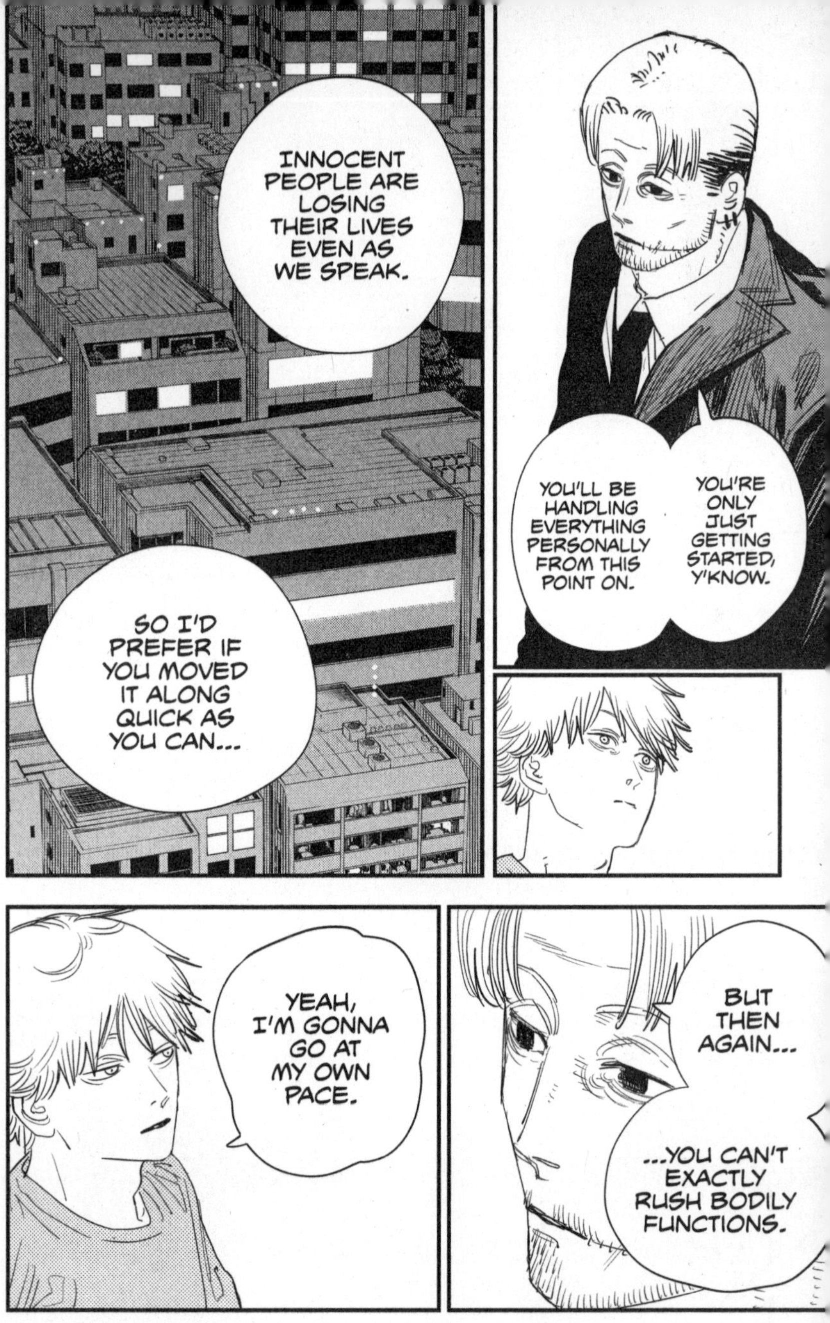
YOU'RE ONLY JUST GETTING STARTED, Y'KNOW.
YOU'LL BE HANDLING EVERYTHING PERSONALLY FROM THIS POINT ON.
INNOCENT PEOPLE ARE LOSING THEIR LIVES EVEN AS WE SPEAK.
SO I'D PREFER IF YOU MOVED IT ALONG QUICK AS YOU CAN...
BUT THEN AGAIN...
...YOU CAN'T EXACTLY RUSH BODILY FUNCTIONS.
YEAH, I'M GONNA GO AT MY OWN PACE.

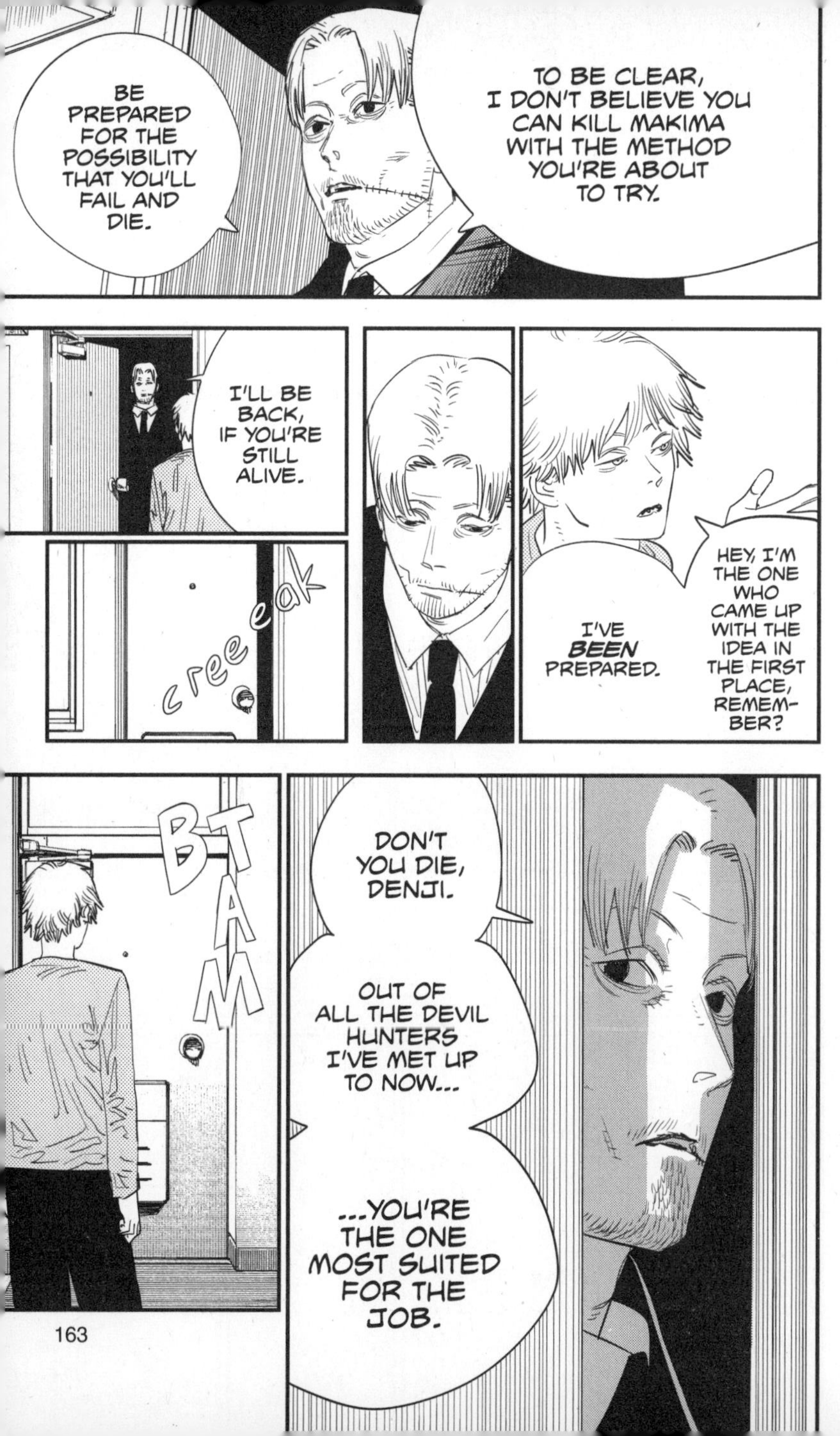
TO BE CLEAR, I DON'T BELIEVE YOU CAN KILL MAKIMA WITH THE METHOD YOU'RE ABOUT TO TRY.
BE PREPARED FOR THE POSSIBILITY THAT YOU'LL FAIL AND DIE.
HEY, I'M THE ONE WHO CAME UP WITH THE IDEA IN THE FIRST PLACE, REMEMBER?
I'VE *BEEN* PREPARED.
I'LL BE BACK, IF YOU'RE STILL ALIVE.
creeeak
DON'T YOU DIE, DENJI.
OUT OF ALL THE DEVIL HUNTERS I'VE MET UP TO NOW...
...YOU'RE THE ONE MOST SUITED FOR THE JOB.
BTAM

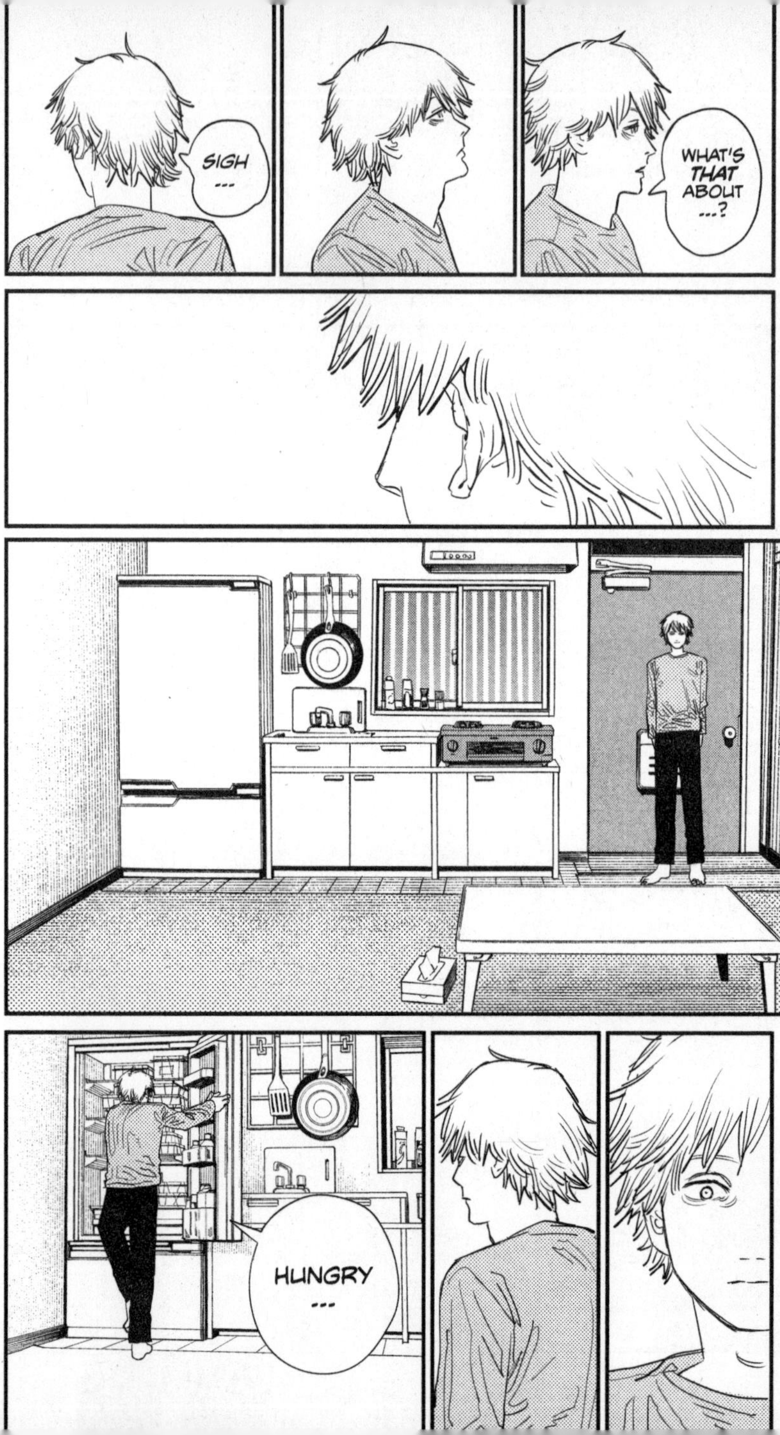
WHAT'S *THAT* ABOUT ...?
SIGH ...
HUNGRY ...

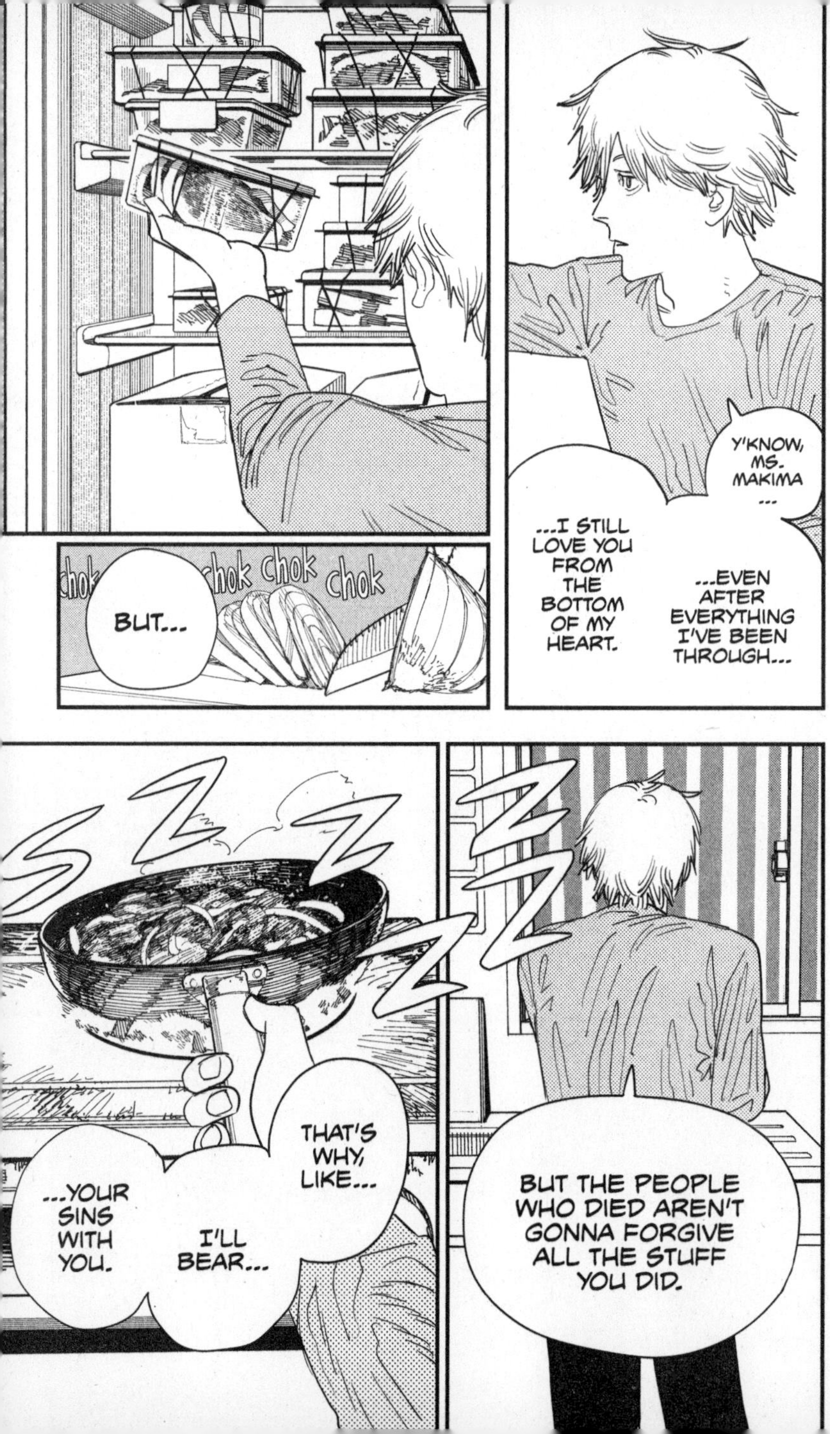

Y'KNOW, MS. MAKIMA ...
...EVEN AFTER EVERYTHING I'VE BEEN THROUGH...
...I STILL LOVE YOU FROM THE BOTTOM OF MY HEART.
chok chok chok chok
BUT...
BUT THE PEOPLE WHO DIED AREN'T GONNA FORGIVE ALL THE STUFF YOU DID.
THAT'S WHY, LIKE...
I'LL BEAR...
...YOUR SINS WITH YOU.

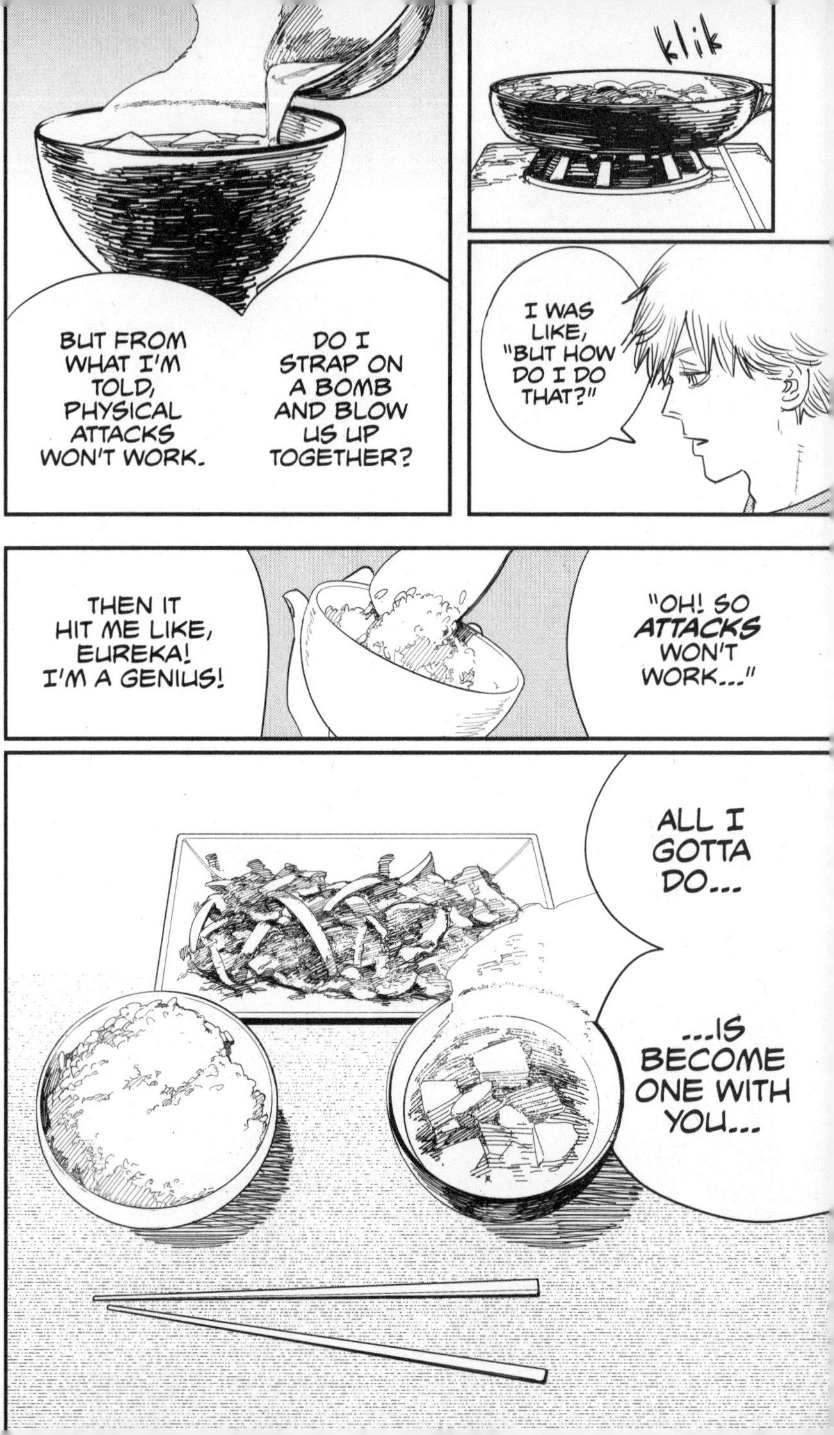
klik
I WAS LIKE, "BUT HOW DO I DO THAT?"
DO I STRAP ON A BOMB AND BLOW US UP TOGETHER?
BUT FROM WHAT I'M TOLD, PHYSICAL ATTACKS WON'T WORK.
"OH! SO *ATTACKS* WON'T WORK..."
THEN IT HIT ME LIKE, EUREKA! I'M A GENIUS!
ALL I GOTTA DO...
...IS BECOME ONE WITH YOU...

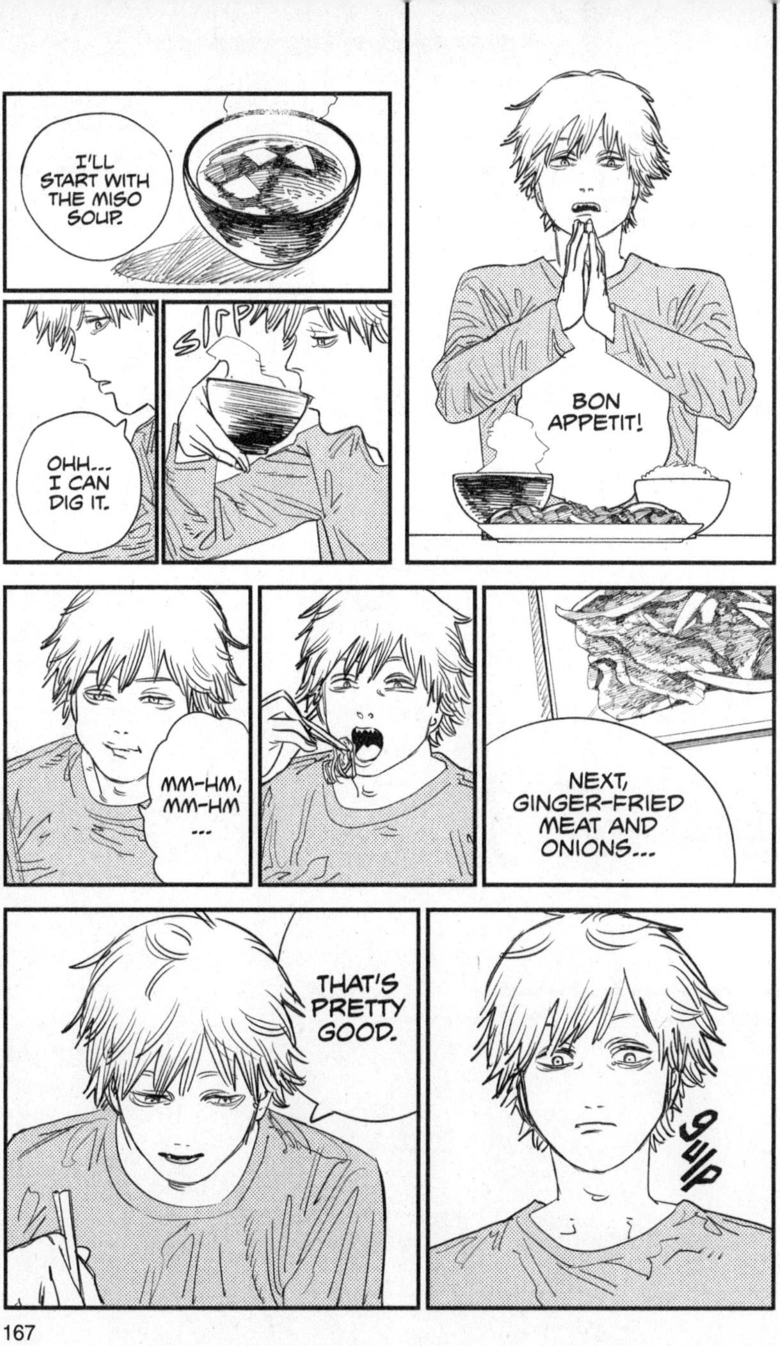
BON APPETIT!
I'LL START WITH THE MISO SOUP.
SLRP
OHH... I CAN DIG IT.
NEXT, GINGER-FRIED MEAT AND ONIONS...
MM-HM, MM-HM ...
THAT'S PRETTY GOOD.
GULP

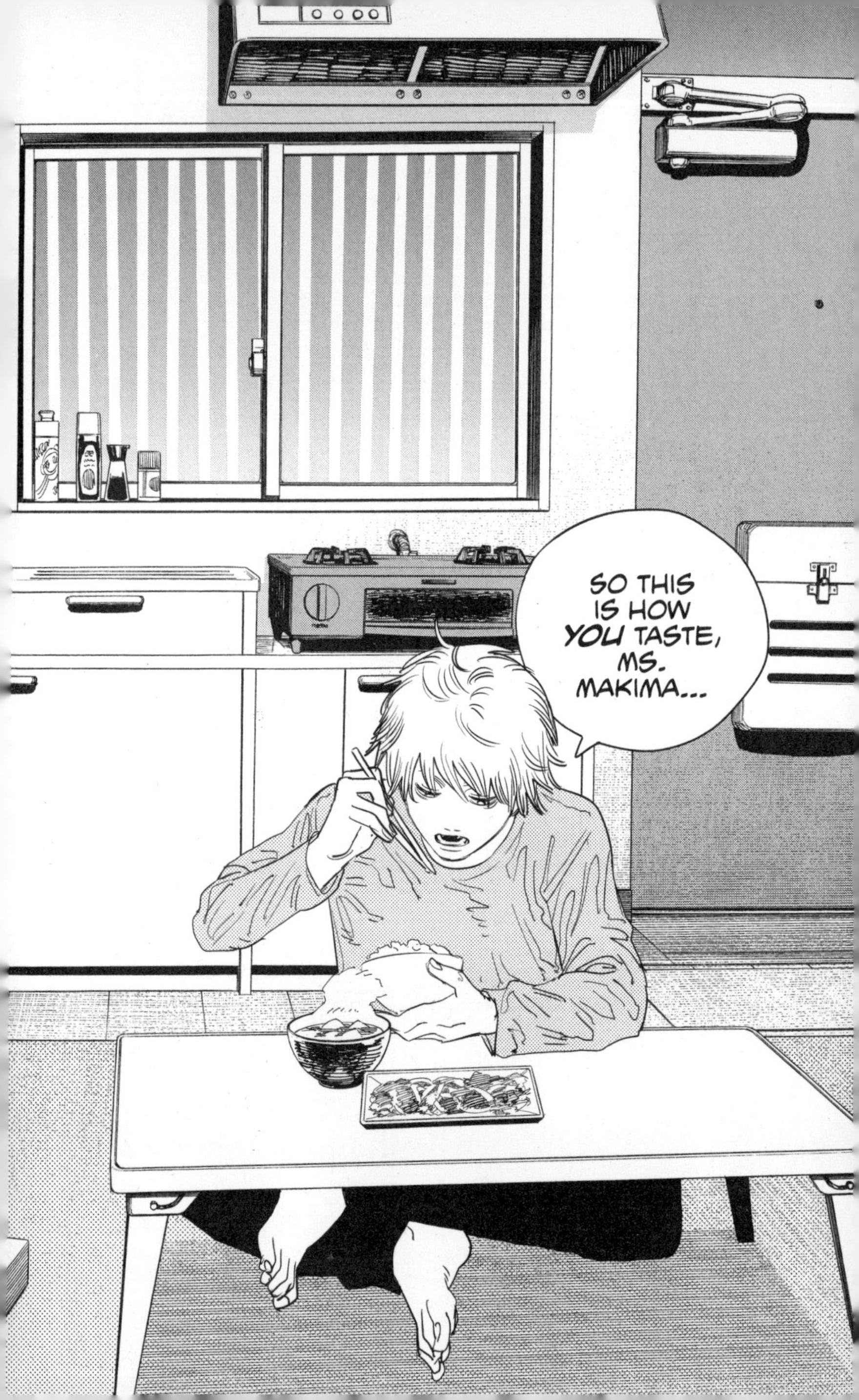
SO THIS IS HOW YOU TASTE, MS. MAKIMA...

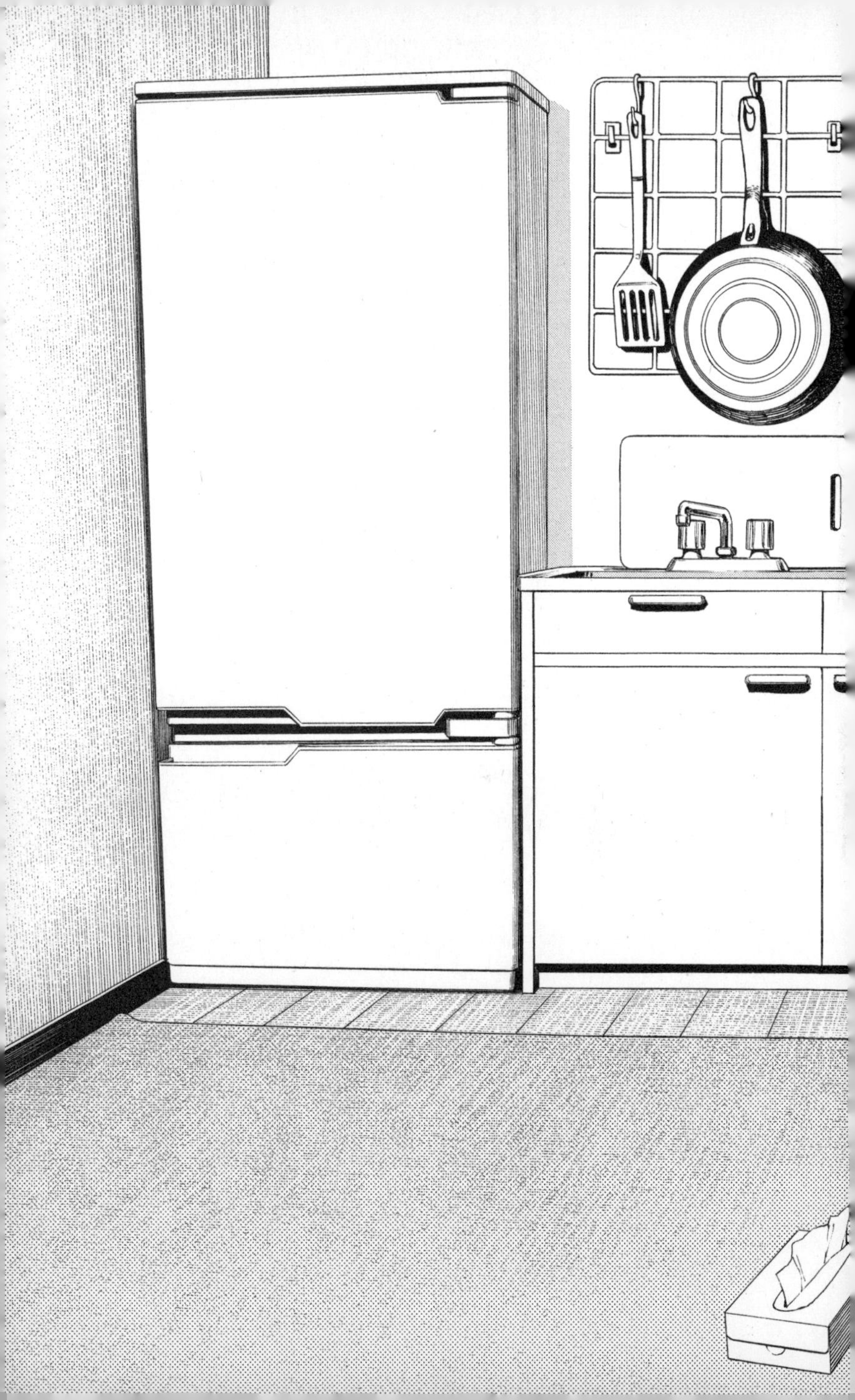

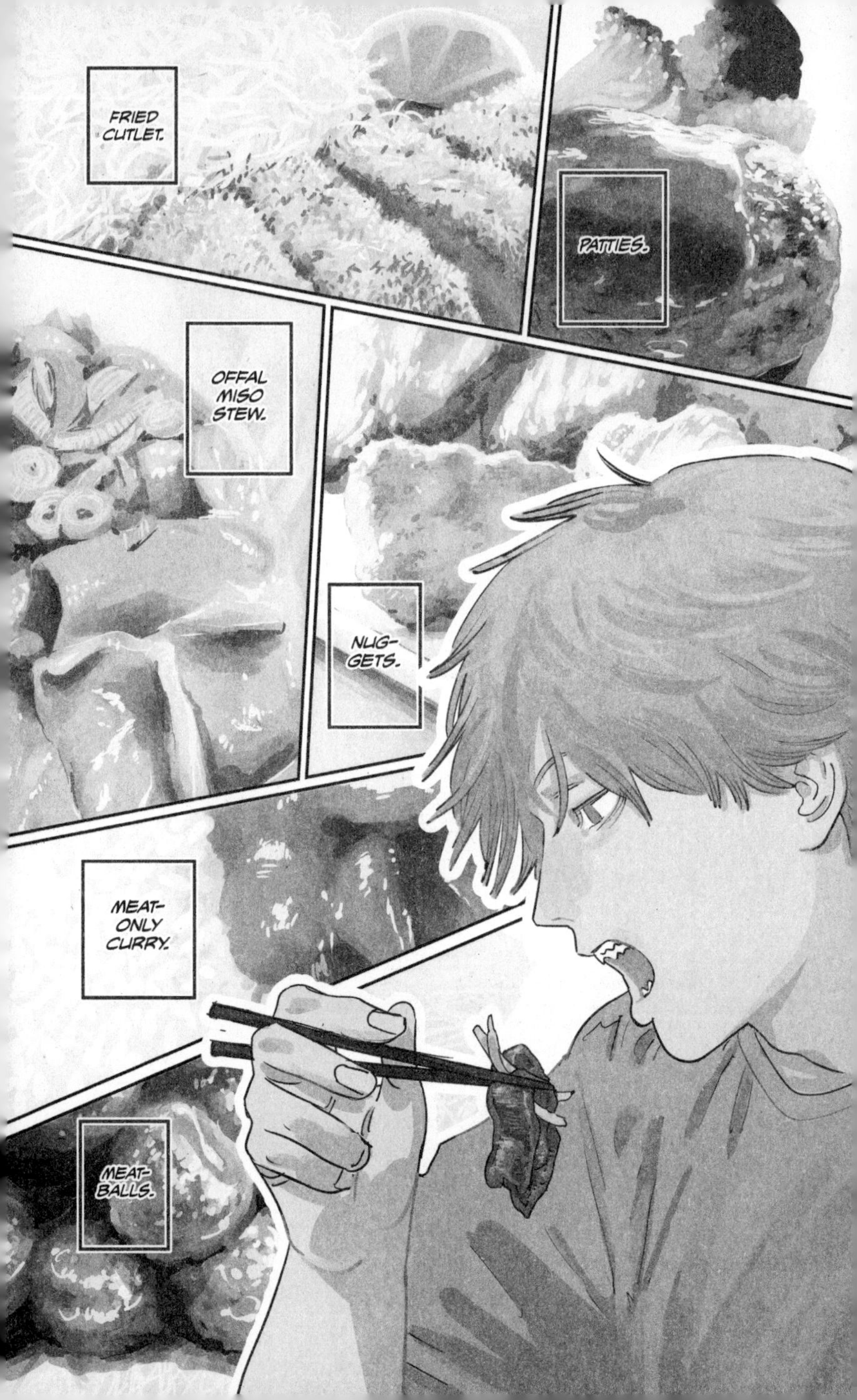
PATTIES.
FRIED CUTLET.
NUG-GETS.
OFFAL MISO STEW.
MEAT-ONLY CURRY.
MEAT-BALLS.

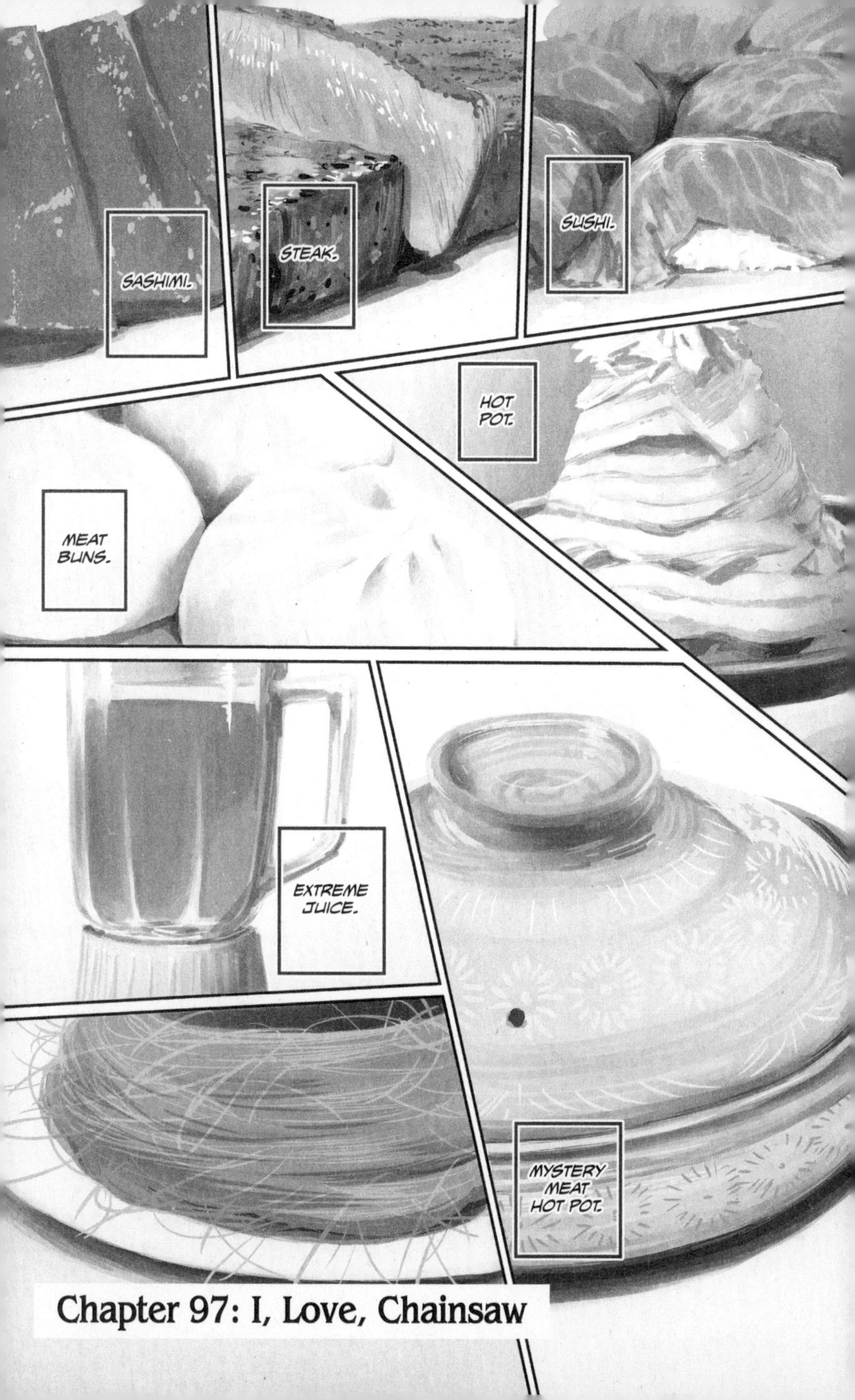
SUSHI.
STEAK.
SASHIMI.
HOT POT.
MEAT BUNS.
MYSTERY MEAT HOT POT.
EXTREME JUICE.

Chapter 97: I, Love, Chainsaw

Chain saw man

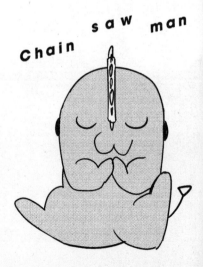

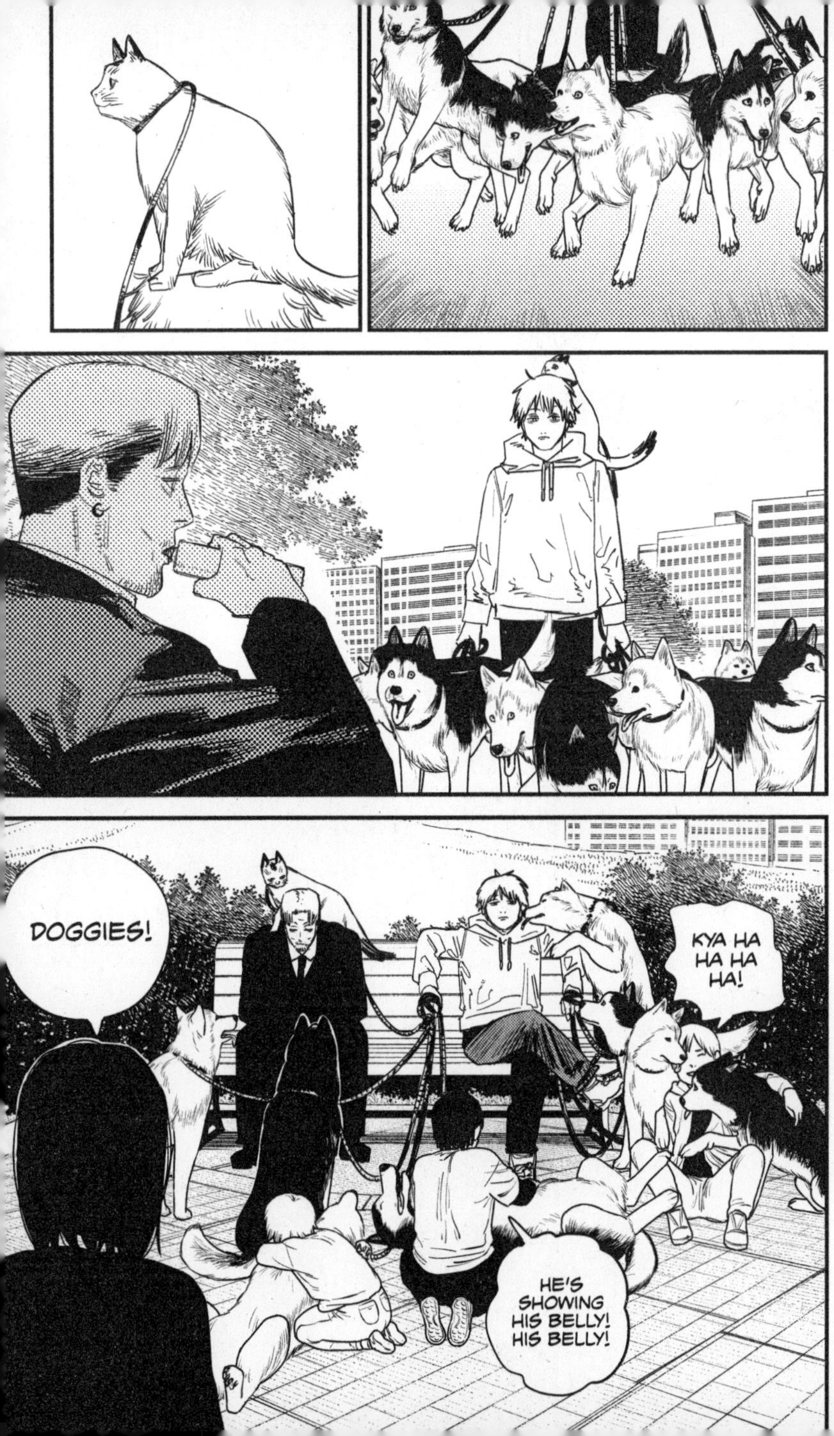
KYA HA HA HA HA!
DOGGIES!
HE'S SHOWING HIS BELLY! HIS BELLY!

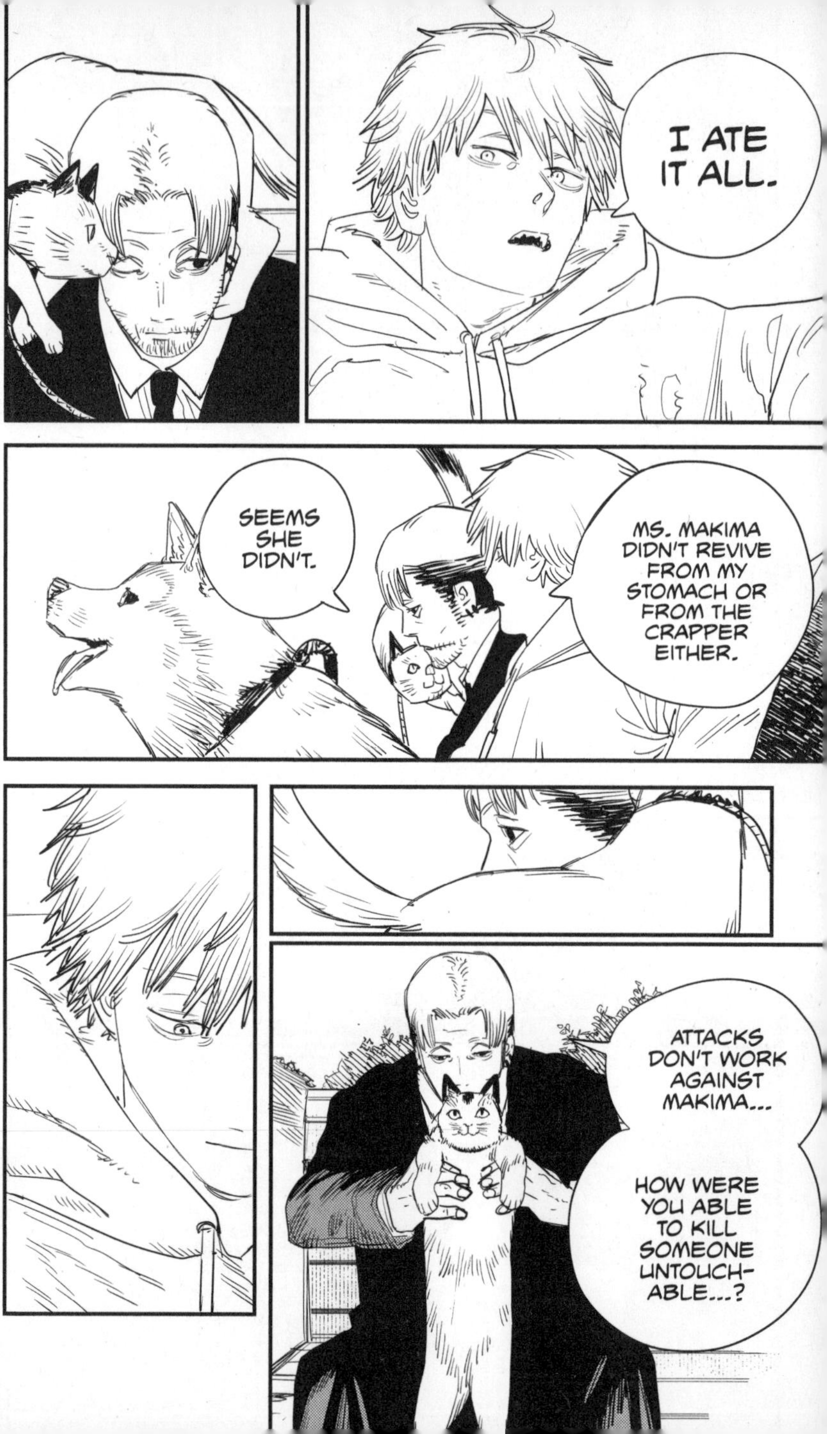
I ATE IT ALL.
MS. MAKIMA DIDN'T REVIVE FROM MY STOMACH OR FROM THE CRAPPER EITHER.
SEEMS SHE DIDN'T.
ATTACKS DON'T WORK AGAINST MAKIMA...
HOW WERE YOU ABLE TO KILL SOMEONE UNTOUCH-ABLE...?

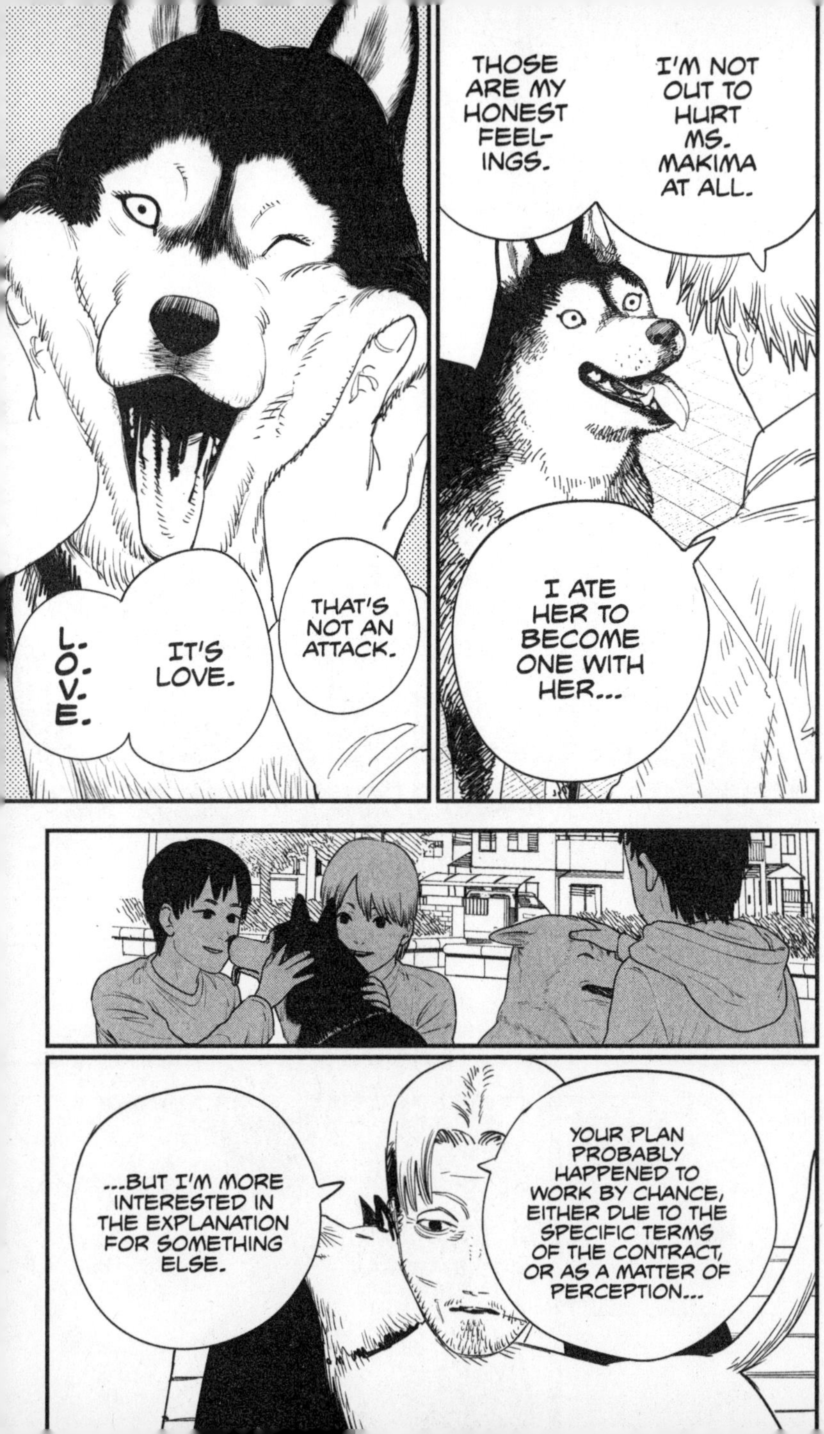
I'M NOT OUT TO HURT MS. MAKIMA AT ALL.
THOSE ARE MY HONEST FEEL-INGS.
I ATE HER TO BECOME ONE WITH HER...
THAT'S NOT AN ATTACK.
IT'S LOVE.
L.O.V.E.
YOUR PLAN PROBABLY HAPPENED TO WORK BY CHANCE, EITHER DUE TO THE SPECIFIC TERMS OF THE CONTRACT, OR AS A MATTER OF PERCEPTION...
...BUT I'M MORE INTERESTED IN THE EXPLANATION FOR SOMETHING ELSE.

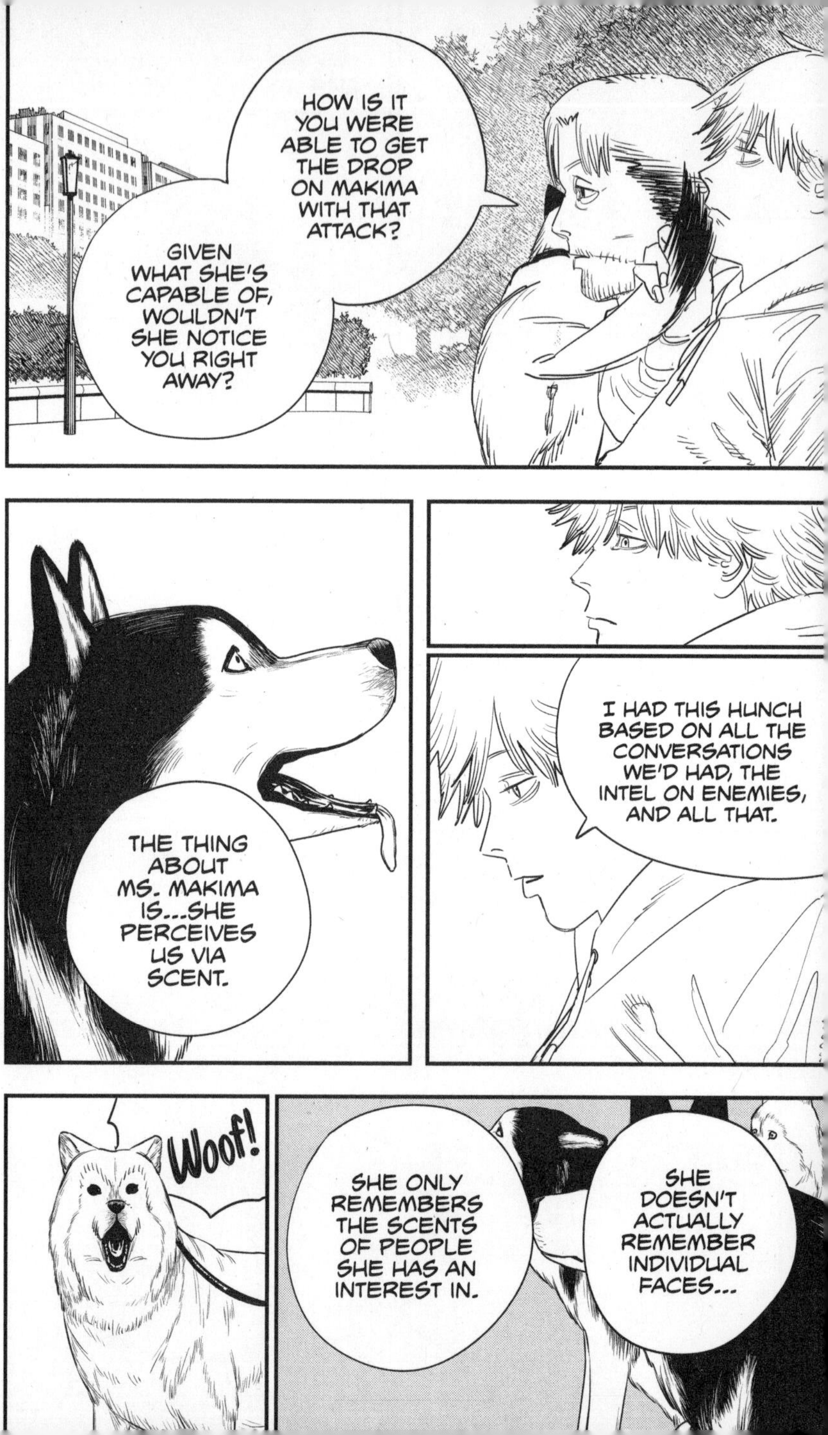
HOW IS IT YOU WERE ABLE TO GET THE DROP ON MAKIMA WITH THAT ATTACK?
GIVEN WHAT SHE'S CAPABLE OF, WOULDN'T SHE NOTICE YOU RIGHT AWAY?
I HAD THIS HUNCH BASED ON ALL THE CONVERSATIONS WE'D HAD, THE INTEL ON ENEMIES, AND ALL THAT.
THE THING ABOUT MS. MAKIMA IS...SHE PERCEIVES US VIA SCENT.
SHE DOESN'T ACTUALLY REMEMBER INDIVIDUAL FACES...
SHE ONLY REMEMBERS THE SCENTS OF PEOPLE SHE HAS AN INTEREST IN.
Woof!

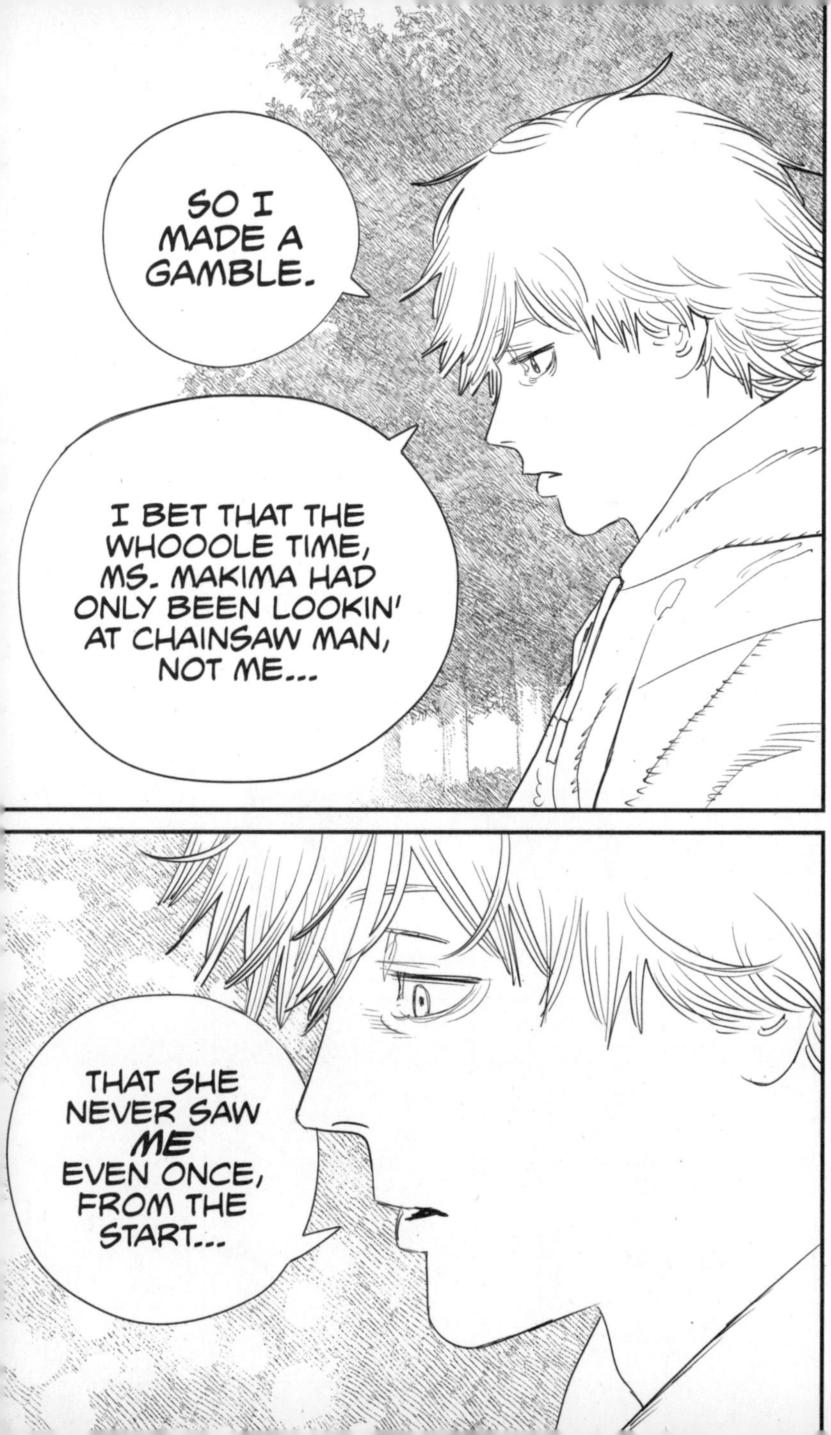
SO I MADE A GAMBLE.
I BET THAT THE WHOOOLE TIME, MS. MAKIMA HAD ONLY BEEN LOOKIN' AT CHAINSAW MAN, NOT ME...
THAT SHE NEVER SAW ME EVEN ONCE, FROM THE START...

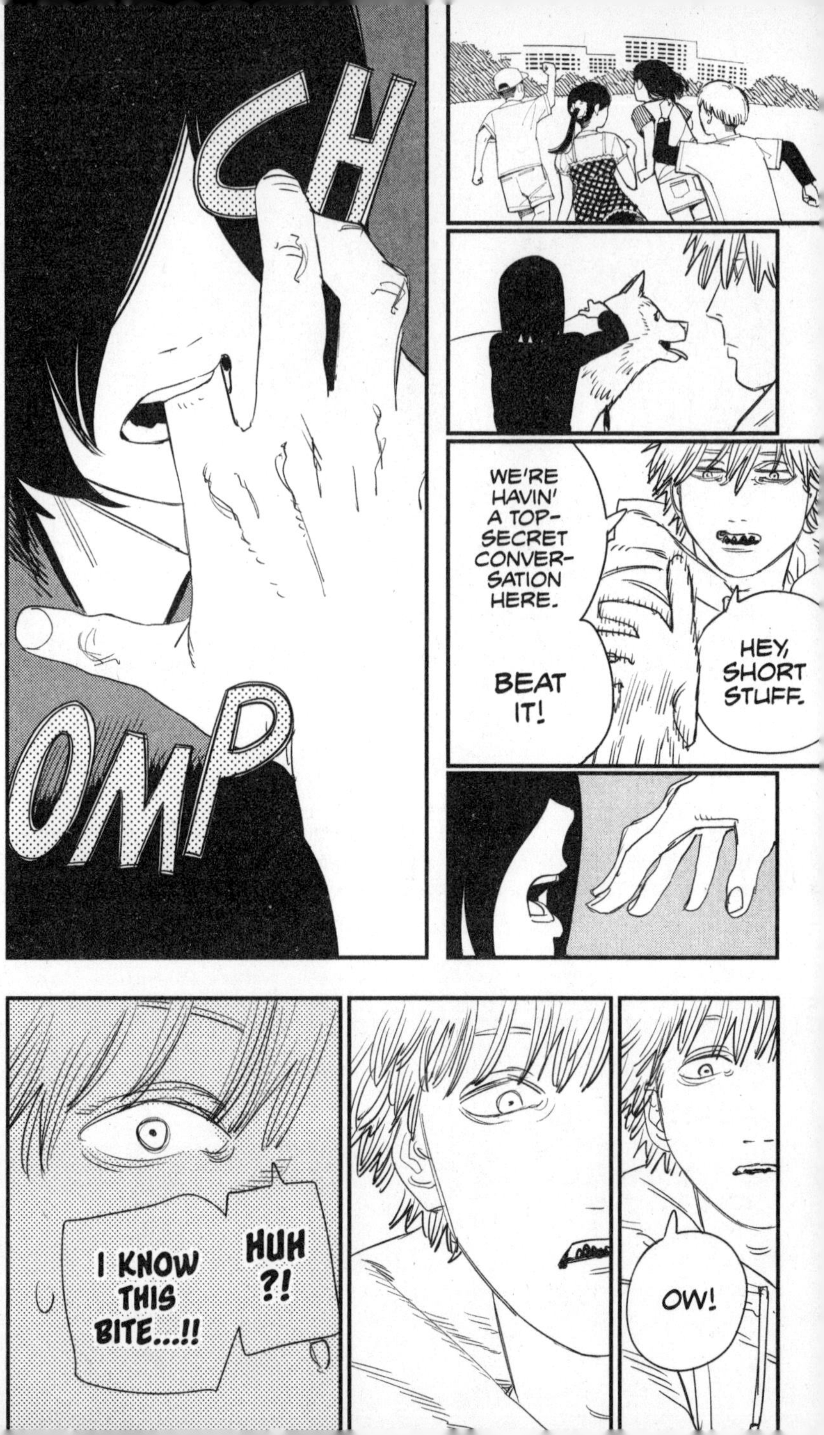
HEY, SHORT STUFF.
WE'RE HAVIN' A TOP-SECRET CONVERSATION HERE.
BEAT IT!
CH
OMP
OW!
HUH ?!
I KNOW THIS BITE...!!

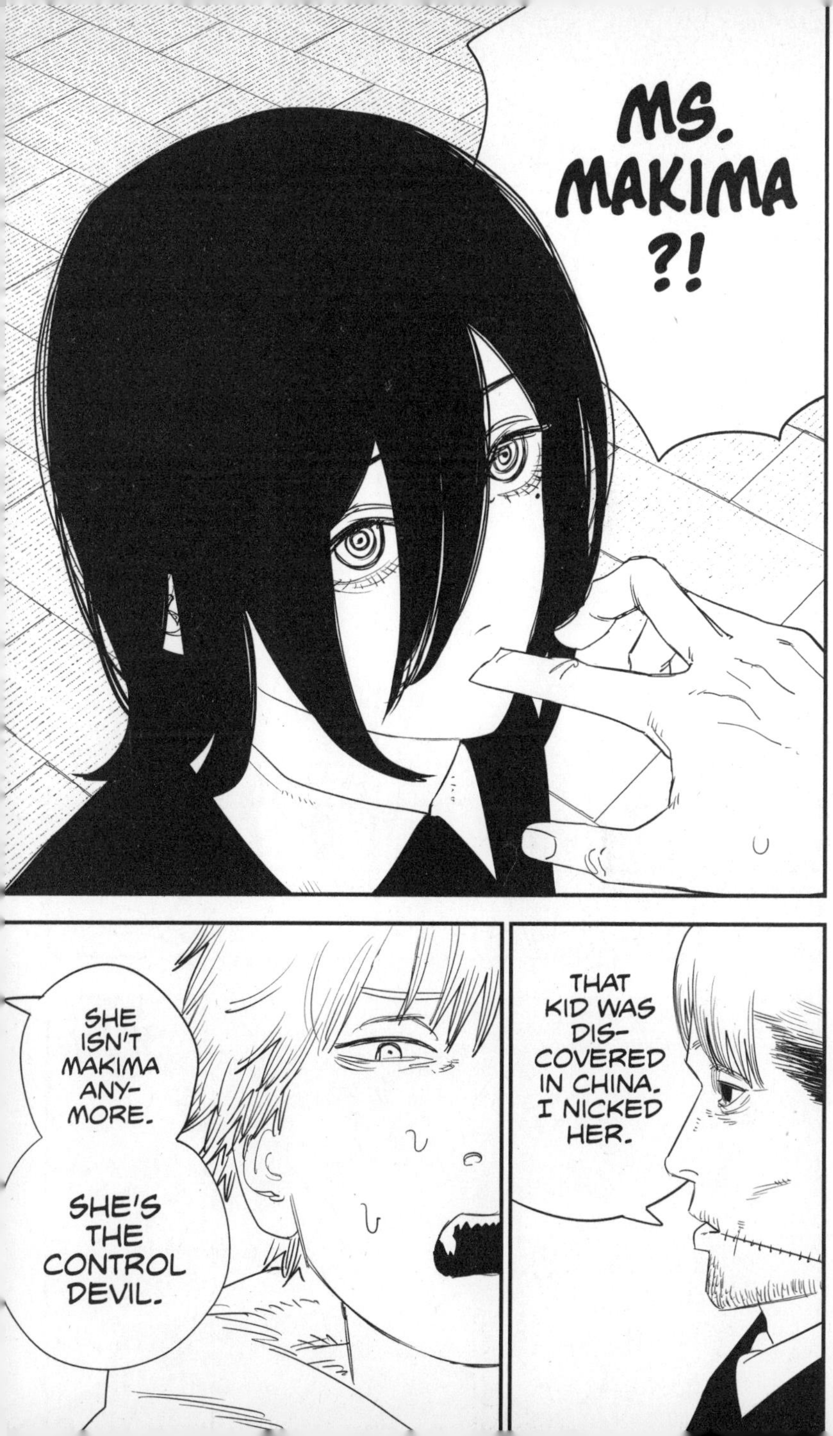
MS. MAKIMA ?!
THAT KID WAS DIS-COVERED IN CHINA. I NICKED HER.
SHE ISN'T MAKIMA ANY-MORE.
SHE'S THE CONTROL DEVIL.

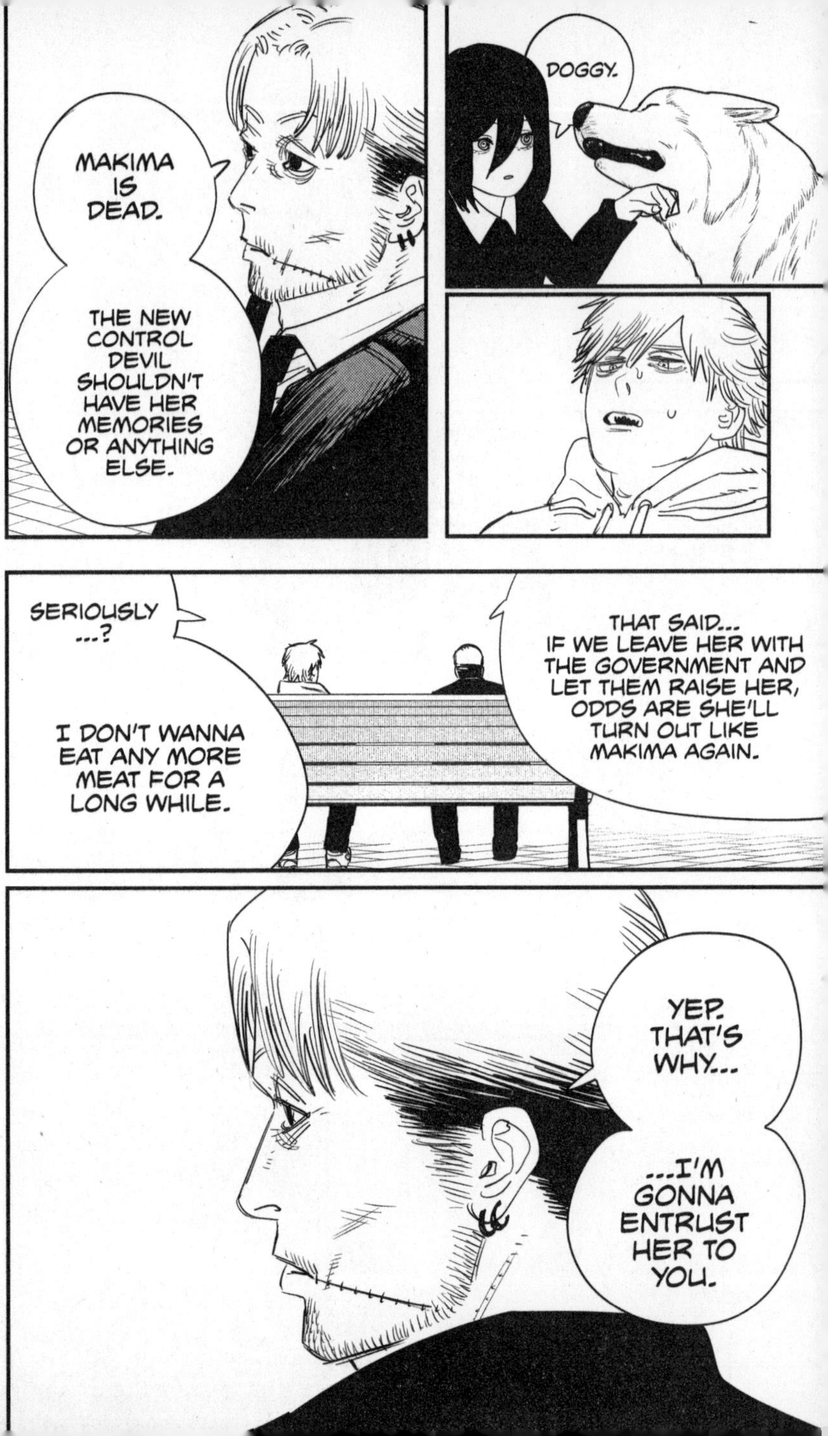
DOGGY.
MAKIMA IS DEAD.
THE NEW CONTROL DEVIL SHOULDN'T HAVE HER MEMORIES OR ANYTHING ELSE.
THAT SAID... IF WE LEAVE HER WITH THE GOVERNMENT AND LET THEM RAISE HER, ODDS ARE SHE'LL TURN OUT LIKE MAKIMA AGAIN.
SERIOUSLY ...?
I DON'T WANNA EAT ANY MORE MEAT FOR A LONG WHILE.
YEP. THAT'S WHY...
...I'M GONNA ENTRUST HER TO YOU.

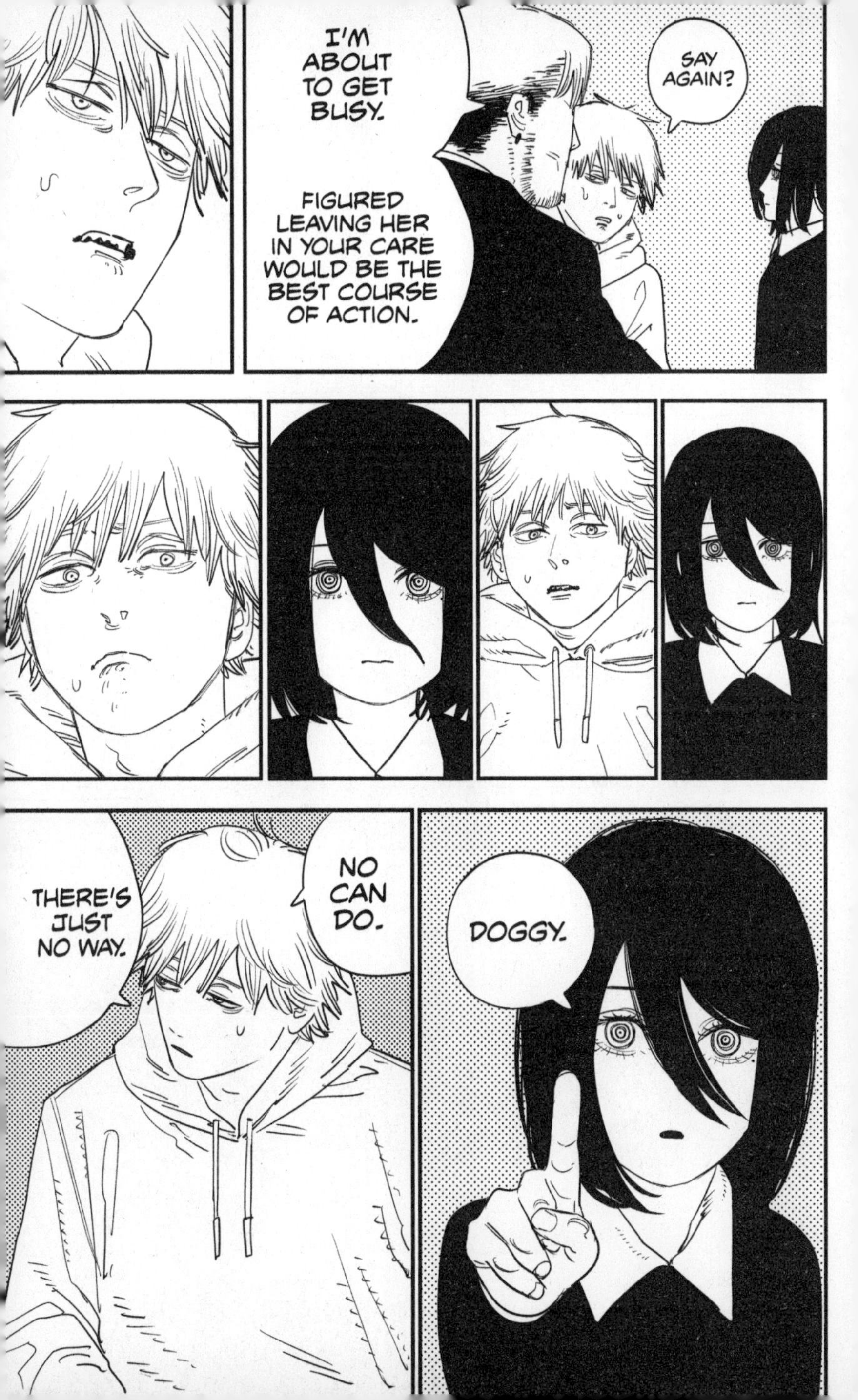
SAY AGAIN?
I'M ABOUT TO GET BUSY.
FIGURED LEAVING HER IN YOUR CARE WOULD BE THE BEST COURSE OF ACTION.
DOGGY.
NO CAN DO.
THERE'S JUST NO WAY.

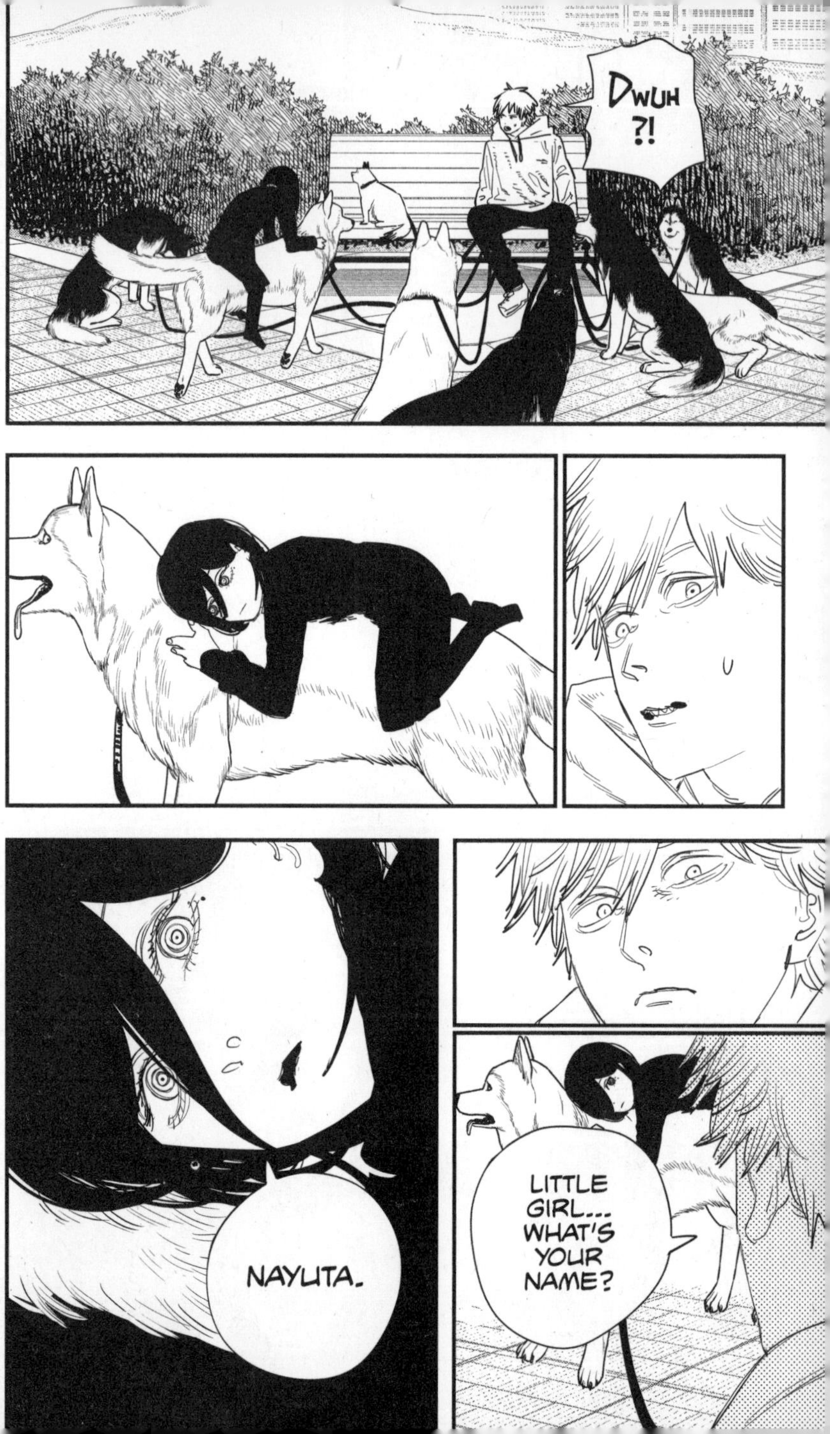
DWUH ?!
LITTLE GIRL... WHAT'S YOUR NAME?
NAYUTA.

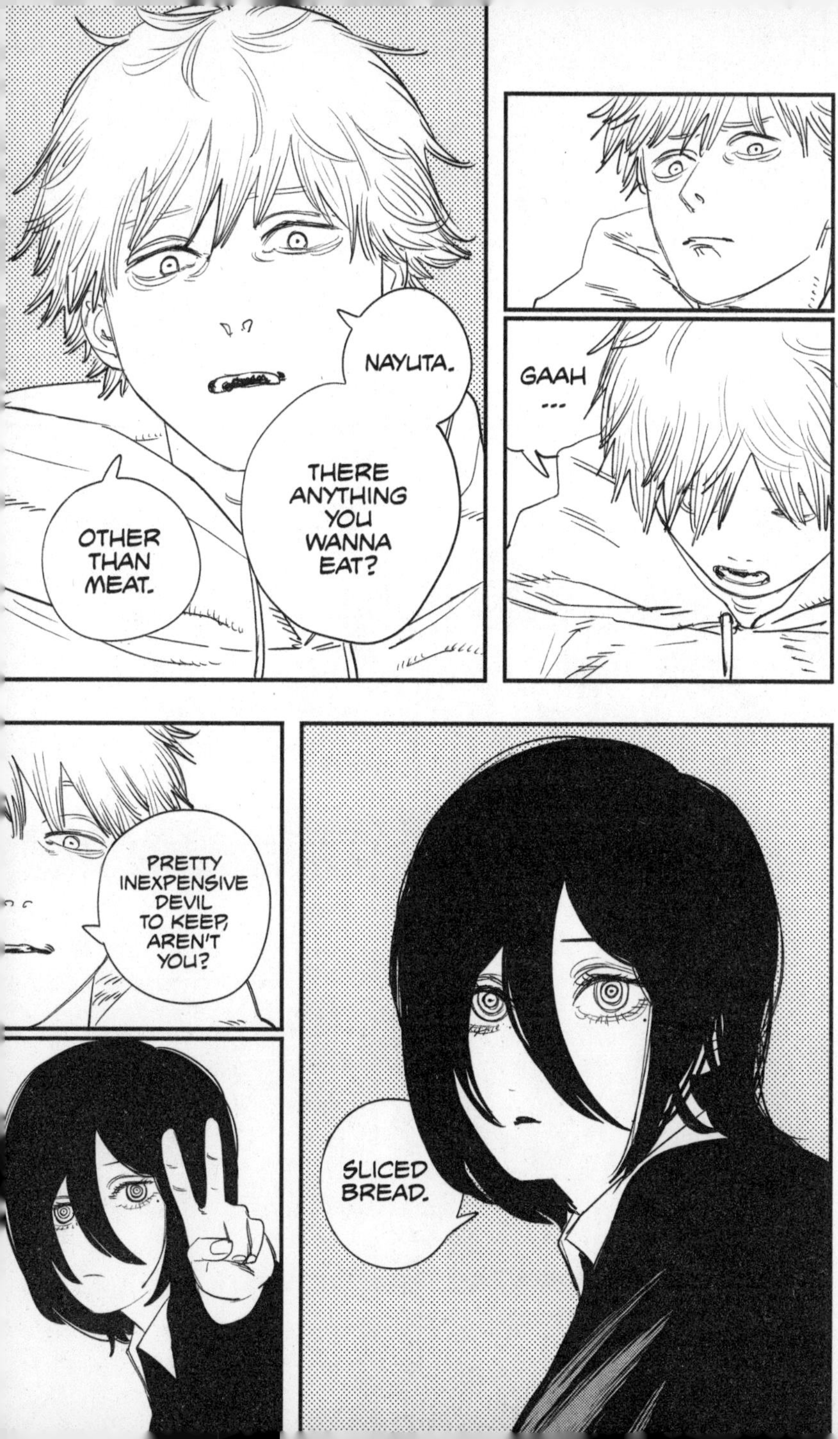
GAAH ...
NAYUTA.
THERE ANYTHING YOU WANNA EAT?
OTHER THAN MEAT.
SLICED BREAD.
PRETTY INEXPENSIVE DEVIL TO KEEP, AREN'T YOU?

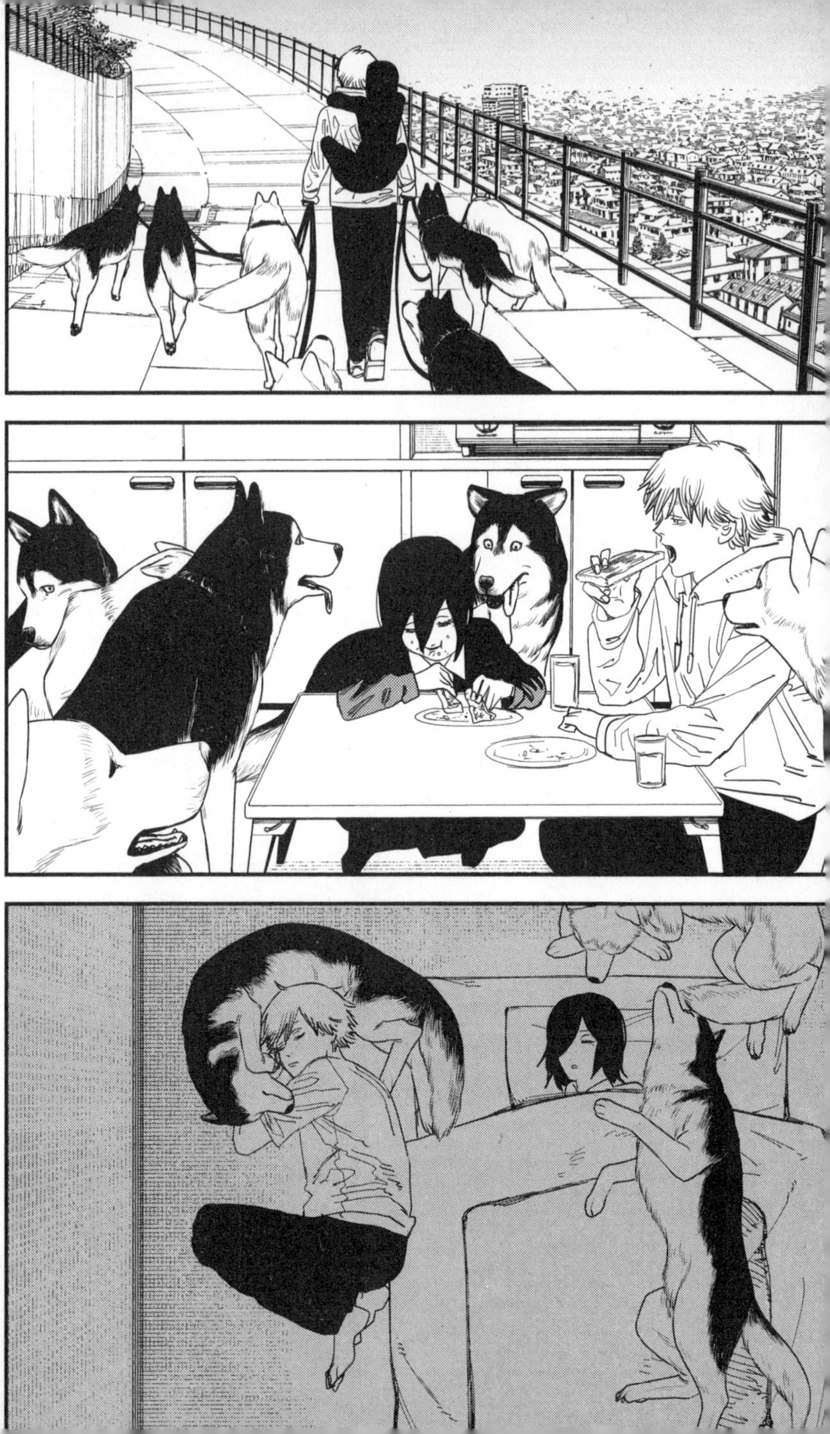

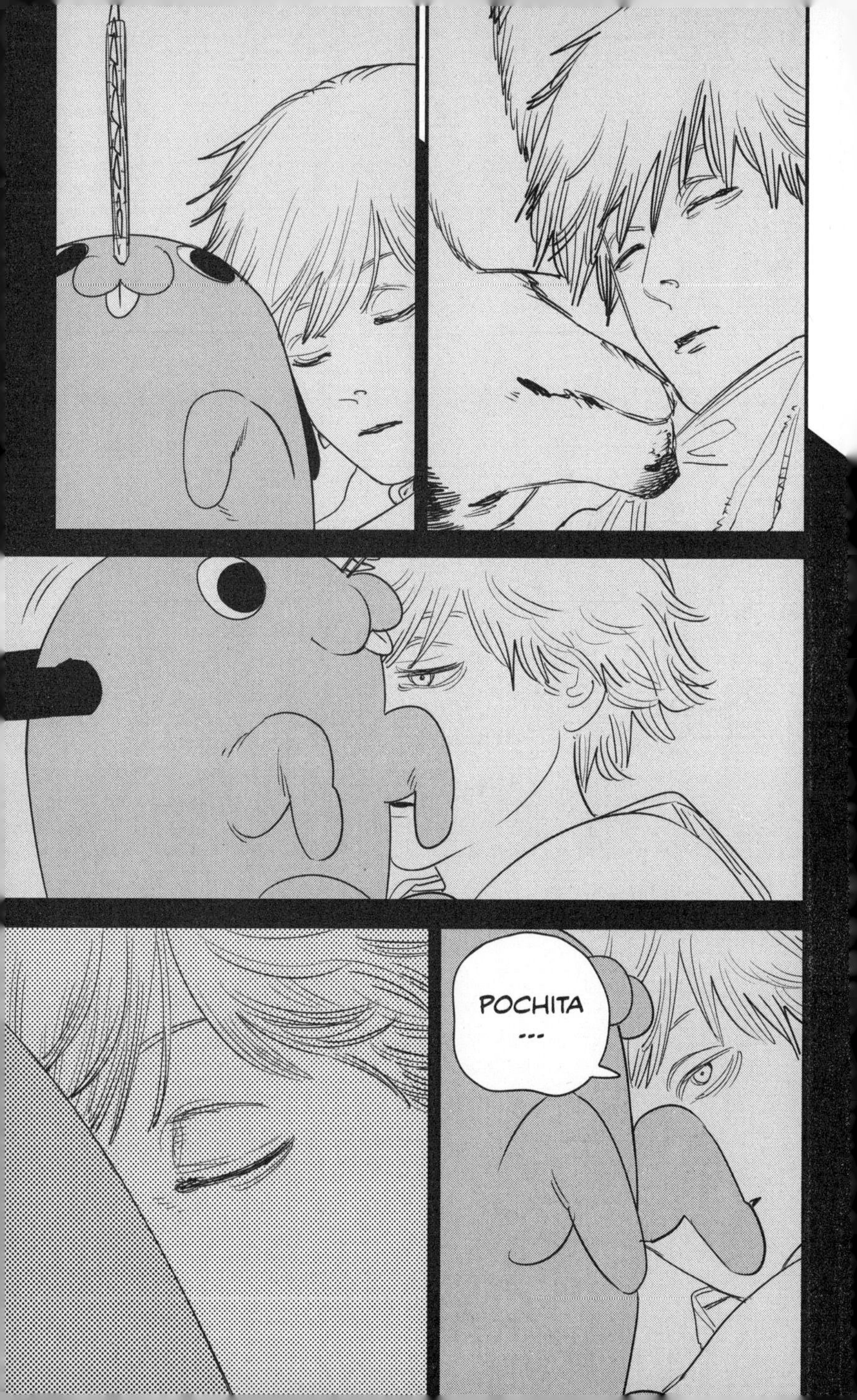
POCHITA
...

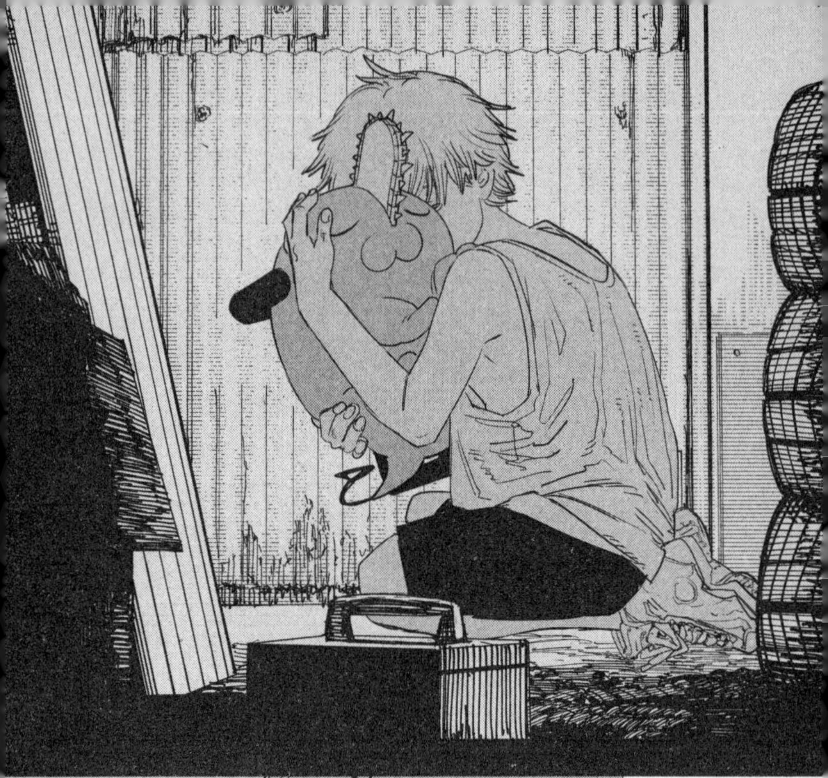

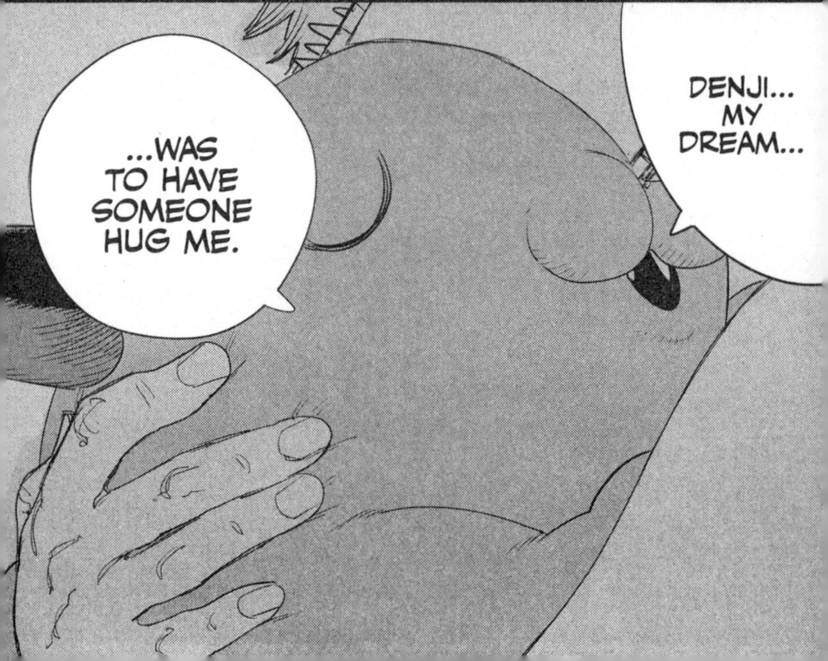
DENJI... MY DREAM...
...WAS TO HAVE SOMEONE HUG ME.

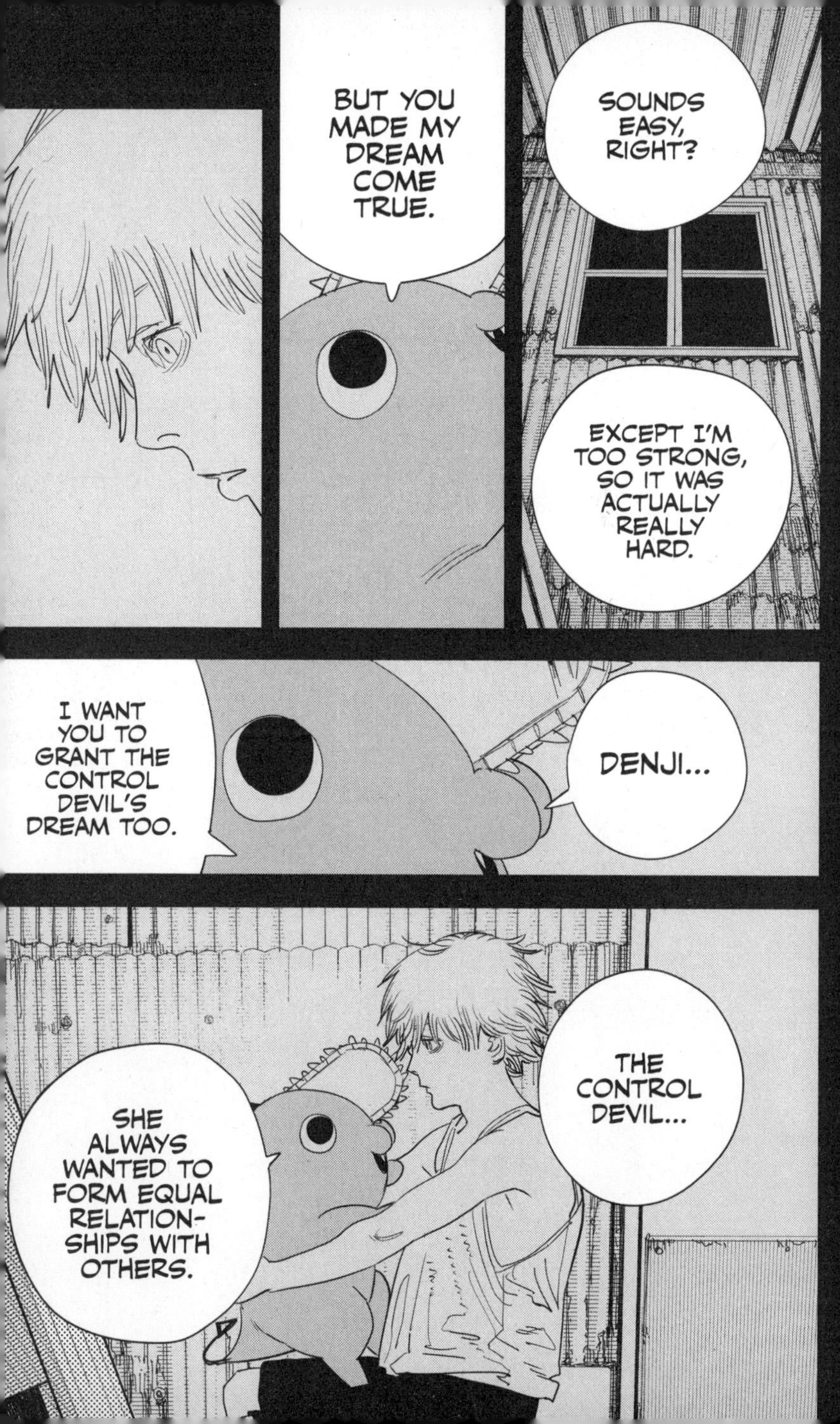
SOUNDS EASY, RIGHT?
EXCEPT I'M TOO STRONG, SO IT WAS ACTUALLY REALLY HARD.
BUT YOU MADE MY DREAM COME TRUE.
DENJI...
I WANT YOU TO GRANT THE CONTROL DEVIL'S DREAM TOO.
THE CONTROL DEVIL...
SHE ALWAYS WANTED TO FORM EQUAL RELATIONSHIPS WITH OTHERS.

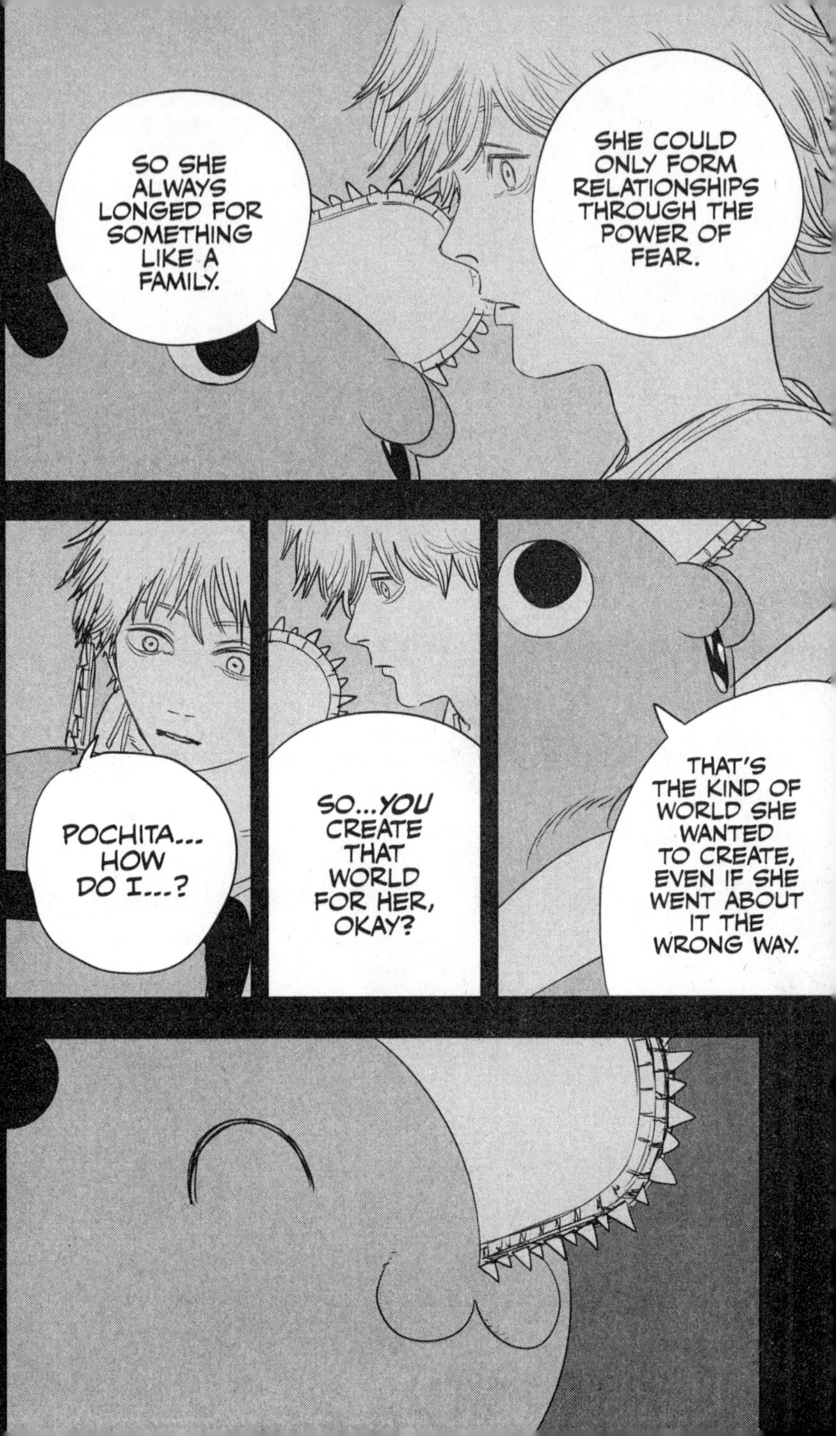
SHE COULD ONLY FORM RELATIONSHIPS THROUGH THE POWER OF FEAR.
SO SHE ALWAYS LONGED FOR SOMETHING LIKE A FAMILY.
THAT'S THE KIND OF WORLD SHE WANTED TO CREATE, EVEN IF SHE WENT ABOUT IT THE WRONG WAY.
SO...*YOU* CREATE THAT WORLD FOR HER, OKAY?
POCHITA... HOW DO I...?

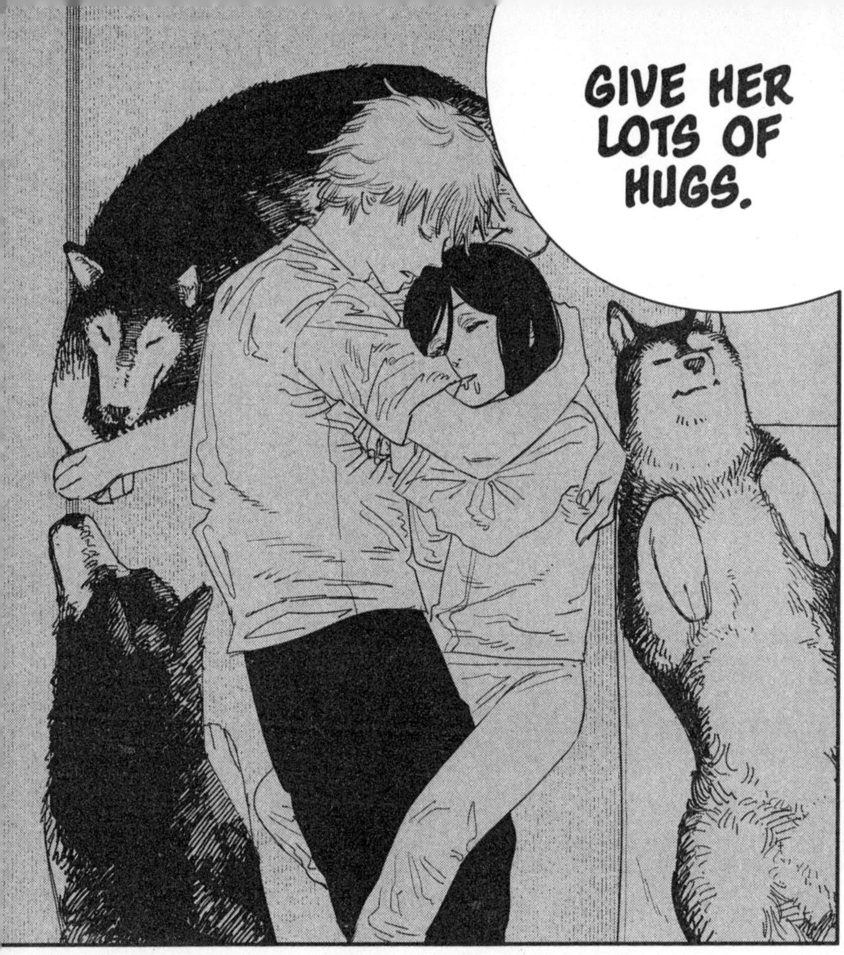
GIVE HER LOTS OF HUGS.
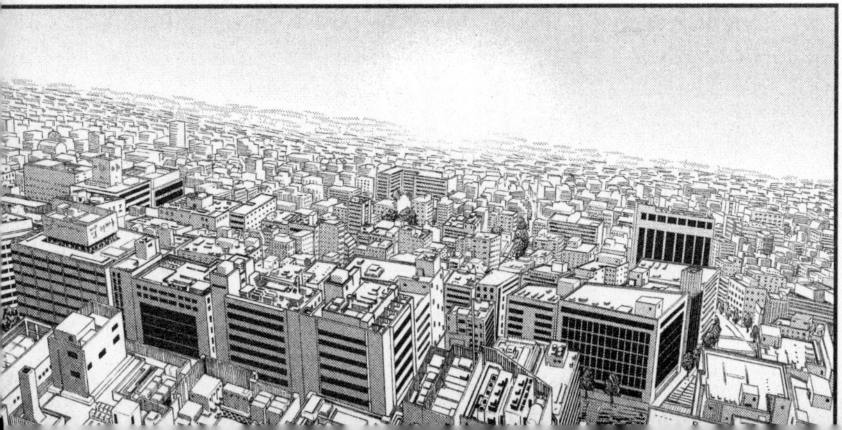

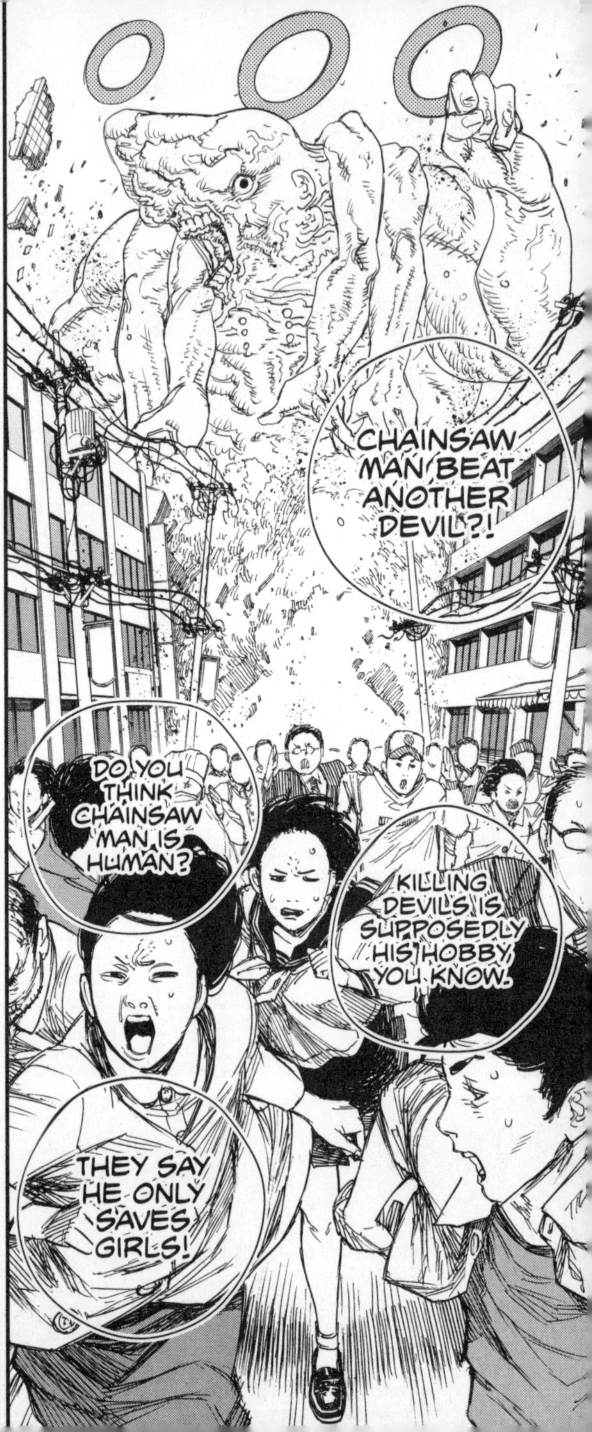
CHAINSAW MAN BEAT ANOTHER DEVIL?!
DO YOU THINK CHAINSAW MAN IS HUMAN?
KILLING DEVILS IS SUPPOSEDLY HIS HOBBY, YOU KNOW.
THEY SAY HE ONLY SAVES GIRLS!

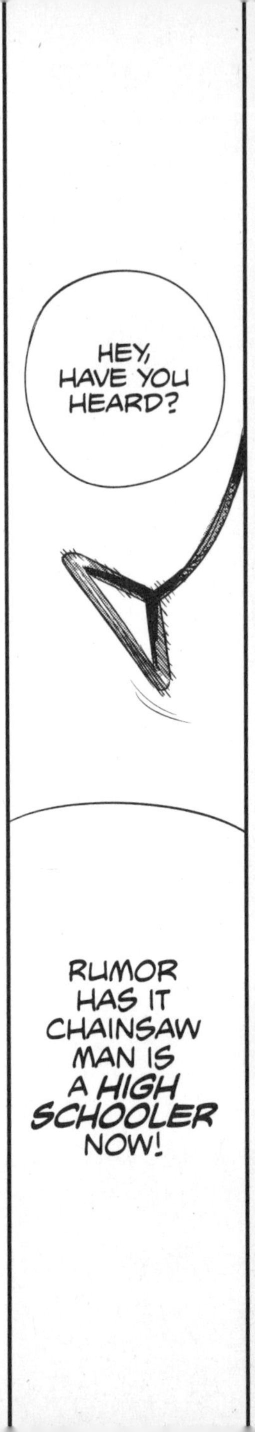
HEY, HAVE YOU HEARD?
RUMOR HAS IT CHAINSAW MAN IS A *HIGH SCHOOLER* NOW!

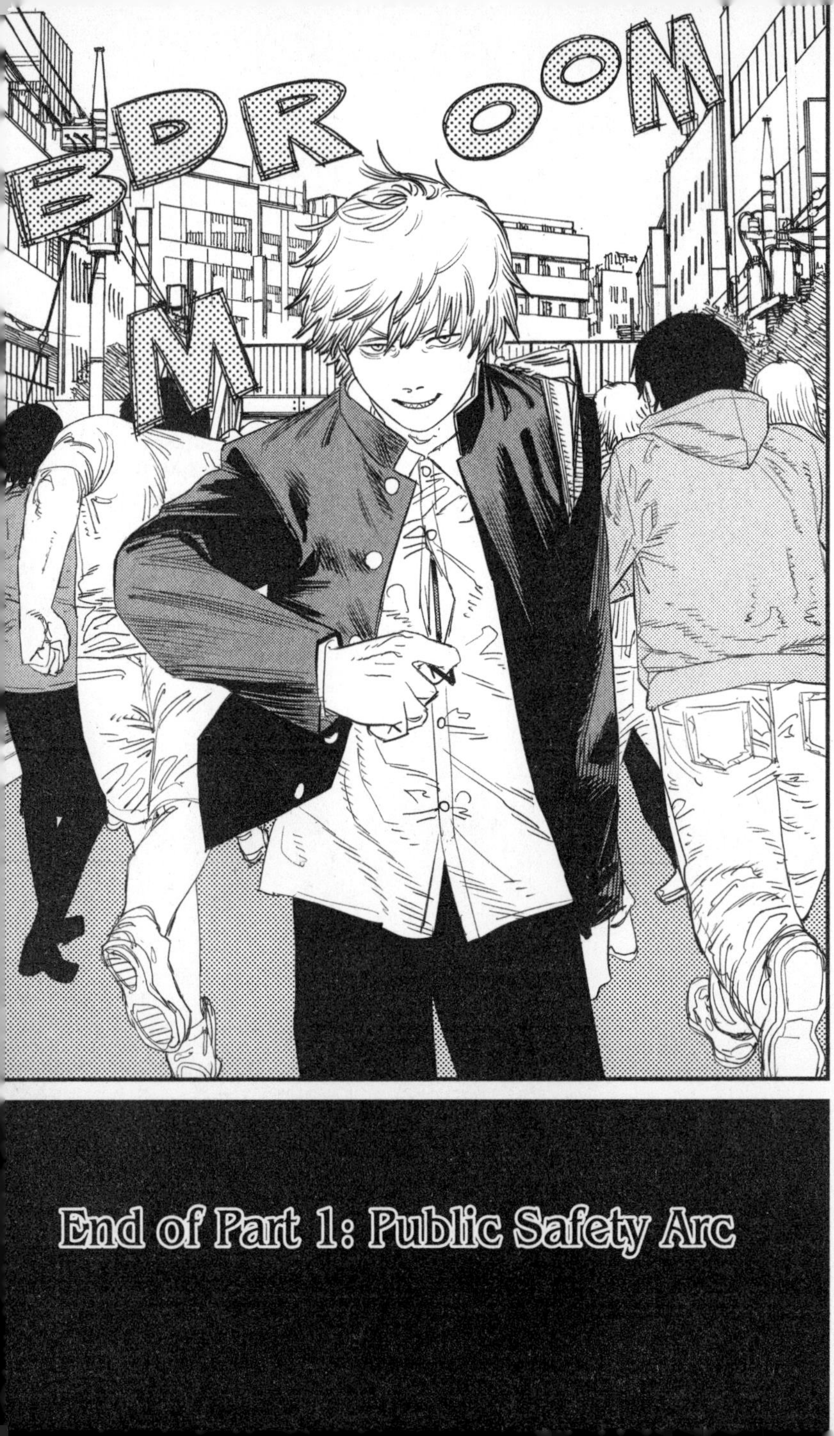
BDROOMM

End of Part 1: Public Safety Arc

YOU'RE READING THE WRONG WAY!

CHAINSAW MAN

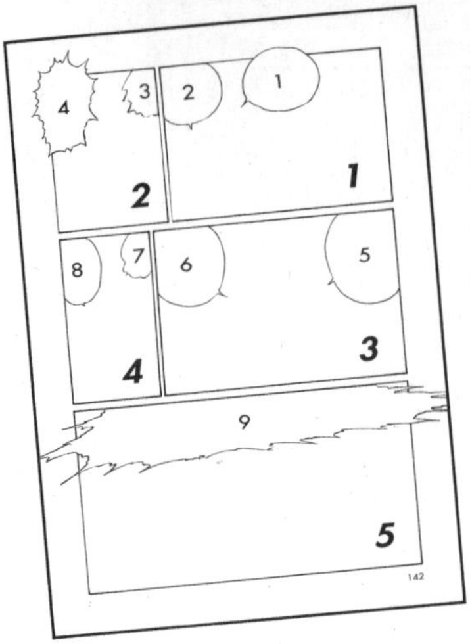

1
2
3
4
1
2
5
6
7
8
3
4
9
5
142

Chainsaw Man reads from right to left, starting in the upper-right corner. Japanese is read from right to left, meaning that action, sound effects, and word-balloon order are completely reversed from English order.

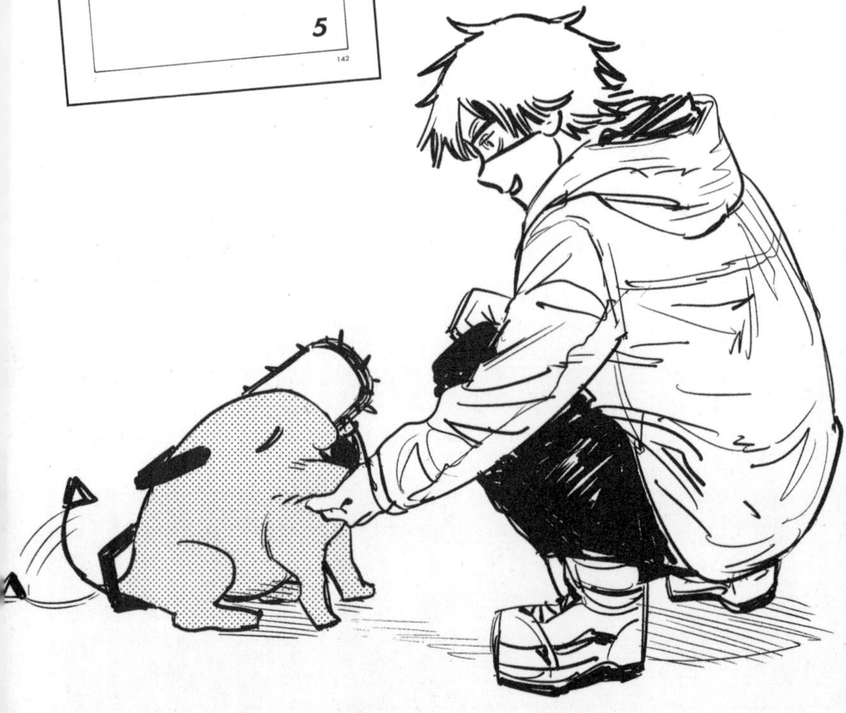